TOZER SPEAKS

*128 Compelling and Authoritative Teachings
of A.W. Tozer*

Volume Two

Tozer Speaks

128 Compelling and Authoritative Teachings of A.W. Tozer

VOLUME TWO

Compiled by Gerald B. Smith

WingSpread Publishers
Camp Hill, Pennsylvania

WingSpread Publishers
Camp Hill, Pennsylvania
www.wingspreadpublishers.com

A division of Zur Ltd.

Tozer Speaks, Volume Two
ISBN: 978-1-60066-271-3
LOC Control Number: 2010921880
© 1994 by Zur Ltd.

Previously published by Christian Publications, Inc.
First Christian Publications Edition 1994
First WingSpread Publishers Edition 2010

14   13   12   11   10   5   4   3   2   1

Scripture taken from
The Holy Bible: King James Version.

Cover Design by Viscul Media Design, Inc.

Tozer Speaks previously published as *The Tozer Pulpit* in two volumes.

*Book 5 previously published as The Tozer Pulpit, Volume 5 and as
I Call It Heresy!*

*Book 6 previously published as The Tozer Pulpit, Volume 6 and as
Who Put Jesus on the Cross?*

*Book 7 previously published as The Tozer Pulpit, Volume 7 and as
Tragedy in the Church*

*Book 8 previously published as The Tozer Pulpit, Volume 8 and as
Echoes from Eden*

Book 5

*Twelve Sermons in
Peter's First Epistle*

Contents

Preface

Dr. Keith M. Bailey, the Home Secretary of The Christian and Missionary Alliance, once gave this reference to the prophetic nature of the ministry of Dr. A. W. Tozer in his lifetime:

"Some aspects of the gift of prophecy—those relating to the giving of the Holy Scriptures—apparently ceased when the scriptural canon was completed.

"The gift of prophecy itself, however, has not died out. The gift of prophecy is still needed in our midst because it is the anointed ability to speak to the present need of men's hearts.

"It is possible to trace prophecy throughout the Old and New Testaments as a major thrust designed to speak to the contemporary human need—God's anointed message for the need of the hour.

"I think A. W. Tozer was a prophet. He could see far beyond most men in his generation. He was able to discern and analyze that which was decaying the church at its heart. In the prophetic sense, he was courageous in speaking to that truth with anointed ability and power.

"The more I study revival the more I am convinced that the gift of prophecy must be exercised among us if there is to be a real and lasting revival in the church. We need anointed men who are not afraid to speak to the need of the church because revival is the renewal of the people of God first of all."

We think this analysis of the contemporary prophetic gift is a proper setting for the twelve Tozer sermons in First Peter presented in this book. The sermons were among those preached by Dr. Tozer during his long pastorate in Chicago, Illinois.

The Publisher

The Apostolic Voice: The Wonder of Inspiration!

". . . The word of God, which liveth and abideth for ever . . . And this is the word which by the gospel is preached unto you." 1 Peter 1:23, 25

THERE ARE CHRISTIANS AMONG us today who seem to feel that their spiritual lives would have been greatly helped if they could have had voice-to-voice and person-to-person counsel from our Lord or from the Apostle Peter or Paul.

I know it is fair to say that if one of the apostles or any of the great early fathers of the church could return to this world from their yesteryear, there would not be room to contain the crowds that would rush in.

If it were known that St. Augustine or Chrysostom or Francis of Assisi or Knox or Luther or any of the great who have lived were to be present to speak, we would all give our closest attention and listen as though we were hearing indeed a very word from God.

Under the circumstances, we cannot hope to hear from men of God who centuries ago completed their ministries and went to be with the Lord. The voices of the great saints and mighty warriors of yesterday can no longer be heard in this twentieth century.

However, there is good news for those who are anxious to hear a word from the Lord! If we have a mind to listen, we may still "hear" the voice of an apostle for we are dealing with the words written by the man, Peter. He was indeed a great saint, even though we may not consider him the greatest of the apostles. I think it is safe to say that he was the second of the apostles, Paul alone, perhaps, having a higher place than the man, Peter.

So, as we look into his message, Peter will be speaking to us, even though it is through an "interpreter."

Often our missionaries have told us of difficult times they have had with interpreters. The expression of the missionary may go in one way and come out with a different sense to the hearer, and I think when we expound the scriptures, we are often guilty of being imperfect interpreters. I shall do the best I can to catch the spirit of the man, Peter, and to determine what God is trying to say to us and to reduce the interference to a minimum.

Now, I suppose more people would like me if I were to declare that I preach the Bible and nothing but the Bible. I attempt to do that, but honesty compels me to say that the best I can do is to preach the Bible as I understand it. I trust that through your prayers and the Spirit of Christ my understanding may be right. If you pray and if I yield and trust, perhaps what we get from First Peter will indeed be approximately what Peter would say if he were here in person. We will stay as close as we can to the Word of the Living God.

The man Peter had a reputation for being first because he was a most impetuous man. He was either the first or among the very first in almost everything that took place and that touched him while he was alive.

For this reason, I suppose that Peter would have made a wonderful American! He usually opened his mouth and talked before he thought and that is a characteristic of many of us. He rushed to do what he had to do—and that is also characteristic of us.

From the record of the Gospels, it appears that Peter may have been the first, or at least among the very first, to become a disciple of John the Baptist. He was among the first disciples who turned to Jesus when John the Baptist pointed and said, "Behold the Lamb of God that taketh away the sins of the world."

Peter was the first apostle called by our Lord to follow Him. I believe that Peter was the first convert for he was the first man to say, "Thou art the Son of the Living God,"

Peter was among the very first to see our Lord after He had risen from the dead. There are those who insist that Peter was the first, believing that the Lord Jesus appeared to no one else until after a meeting with His beloved friend, Peter.

Also, remember that Peter was the first of the New Testament preachers. It is quite in keeping with the temperament of this man that when the Holy Spirit had come at Pentecost and there was opportunity for someone to stand and speak the Truth, Peter should be the man to do it.

I think there is no profound theological reason back of this. I think it is a matter of temperament and disposition. When 120 persons are suddenly filled with the Holy Spirit and it falls to the lot of one of them to leap up and express the wonder of what has just happened, it would be normal for the man Peter to be the one. So, he got to his feet and poured out that great sermon recorded in the second chapter of the Book of Acts—the great sermon that converted 3,000 persons!

But Peter was a man, and in his early discipleship and ministry there were glaring contradictions and inconsistencies in his life. It is not possible for us to try to boast and say that this man, this second greatest of the apostles, never deviated one inch from the straight line from the moment of his conversion to the time of his death. I do believe in realism in religion and I do not think any good can come from hiding the bad and trying to reflect an unnatural righteousness which is not true to the whole character of the man.

Actually, I wish that every one of us could be like the angels or those strange creatures in the first chapter of Ezekiel, of whom it is said that when they went "they went every one straight forward."

I do not know what that means precisely, but I do know that it is an intriguing test—when they went they went straight forward. I wish that from the time I was converted at the age of 17 I had gone straight forward; but I did not and most of us have not. We zigzag on our way to heaven in place of flying a straight course. I am sorry about this. I don't excuse it, but I try to understand it!

Well, Peter was a bundle of contradictions and I take the position that it further glorifies the grace of God that He could take a weak and vacillating and inconsistent man like Peter and make Saint Peter out of him!

Read again all that the New Testament says about Peter and you will find glaring contradictions. In His very first meeting with Peter, Jesus said, "Thou art Simon the son of Jona: thou shalt be called Cephas, which is by interpretation, A stone." Jesus Himself in calling Peter gave him this new name meaning a rock, which is of course a solid and unshaking thing.

But this man—this "rock"—was so wavering that he denied his Lord! He clipped off a man's ear in an impetuous act to defend his Master, yet within a few hours denied that he had ever met Jesus. He was prone to rush into a situation, to act without thinking, and to apologize often. That was the rock—but a wavering rock—and that in itself is a contradiction!

I note also that Peter was not above rebuking his Lord and Master. He could walk up to Jesus and rebuke Him as though they were equals. But in the next moment, he might be down on his knees in a trembling reverence, crying, "Depart from me, Lord, for I am an unclean man!"

That was Peter—more daring than any of the apostles and often with more faith—but he had more daring than he had faith! Have you met any of God's children like that?

You remember that Peter was so daring that he rushed out of the boat and actually walked on the water, and yet he had such little faith that it would not support his daring. So he sank, and then had to be helped by the Lord to keep him from drowning!

Yes, this man Peter was the first one to confess his Lord and then the first one to deny Him.

He was the man that Jesus called "Blessed" and a little later called him Satan. "Blessed art thou, Simon Bar-Jona"; then, "Get thee behind me, Satan!"

I mention a few other contradictions about the man, Peter. He is said by a portion of the Christian church to be the vicar of Christ on earth, and yet Peter himself never seemed to have found out about it! He never referred to himself as the vicar or vice-regent of Christ; he called himself an apostle, one of the elders. That's all. The humblest elder in any Presbyterian church has a title as great as Peter ever claimed for himself, except that he said he was one of the apostles.

I could point out that Peter is supposed by many to have been the first of the popes and yet he was overshadowed by one of his fellow apostles, for without question, Paul overshadowed Peter.

The man Peter was a great man, but the man Paul was greater. It would seem to me that if God were to select a pope, the first one, He would have chosen Paul, the mightiest, the most intellectual of them all, rather than the wavering and inconsistent Peter.

I point out, too, that Peter fades out of the Book of Acts and as he does so, Paul moves in. By the time we come to the end of the Acts, Peter is not visible anywhere. Paul fills the horizon and when God would lay the foundations of His church, forming its doctrines deep and strong, He chose Paul and not Peter.

So, this is a simple and very brief sketch of the man, Peter. Many other things could be said about him, but he is able to speak to us again out of his New Testament letters for he was declared an apostle to the Jews as Paul was to the Gentiles.

The Jews had been scattered abroad and that is
the reason for this letter from Peter. They had been
dispersed into many nations and at the day of Pentecost, they had come back to Jerusalem, numbering
into the hundreds of thousands. Then when Peter
preached, they were converted in large numbers,
and returning to their own countries, carried the
message of the risen Saviour and the coming of the
Holy Spirit. Thus there were colonies of Christians
in all of the provinces of Rome and Peter felt that
he was to be pastor to that great number of Jewish
Christians scattered abroad. He accepted his apos-
tleship to the Jews most seriously and he wrote his
first pastoral letter to the Jewish converts to Christ
scattered throughout Roman Asia.

Actually, the circumstances in the Roman provinces that brought forth this letter from Peter were
very grievous indeed. The Roman emperors had
begun harsh persecution of the Christians. Jesus
had told them that they were to expect persecution
and now it was beginning to break over their heads
like billows over a sinking ship.

One of the men coming into great political
power was the emperor Nero, who is remembered
in history as the most incredibly wicked of all the
sons of Rome. His life and his acts and his habits
are among the most wretched and offensive in
all of history so no one can mention in public all
the crimes of which he was guilty. But he was the
Emperor—and Peter and the rest of the Christians
were under his control.

It is recorded of Nero that he set the city of Rome
on fire and then in his own tower played the harp
and sang Greek songs while Rome burned. But then

he became frightened, realizing that the Romans would turn on him if they knew he had set the fire, so he looked around for a scapegoat—and who could be easier to blame than the troublesome Christians?

These believers were vocal and they were in evidence everywhere. So, Nero turned on the Christians as Hitler turned on the Jews and he had them slain by the tens of thousands. Property was taken from them, they were thrown into jail, they were tortured in many ways and they were killed—all of this throughout the regions of Bithynia and Pontus and Cappadocia and Roman Asia.

Peter, the dear man of God, knew what was happening. He had seen some of it himself in the city of Jerusalem and he knew the fury of the persecution. Out of this knowledge came his letter of encouragement, a letter inspired by the Spirit of God as he waited on the Lord in long, amazing hours of prayer for his suffering Christian brothers and sisters.

I think it must be said of Peter that within himself he felt very keenly the loneliness of the "strangers" to whom he wrote. They were scattered, they were persecuted, they were in heaviness, they were isolated in this world for their Christian faith.

The Christian, the genuine Christian, realizes that he is indeed a lonely soul in the middle of a world which affords him no fellowship. I contend that if the Christian breaks down on occasion and lets himself go in tears, he ought not to feel that he is weak. It is a normal loneliness in the midst of a world that has disowned him. He has to be a lonely man!

Those to whom Peter wrote were strangers in many ways and first of all because they were Jews.

They were Jews scattered among the Romans and they never could accept and bow to the Roman ways. They learned the Greek tongue in the world of their day, but they never could learn the Roman ways. They were Jews, a people apart, even as they are today.

Besides that, they had become Christian believers so they were no longer merely Jews. Their sense of alienation from the world around them had increased and doubled. They were not only Jews—unlike the Gentiles around them—but they were Christians, unlike the Jews as well as unlike the Gentiles!

This is the reason that it is easily possible for a Christian believer to be the loneliest person in the world under a set of certain circumstances. This sense of not belonging is a part of our Christian heritage. That sense of belonging in another world and not belonging to this one steals into the Christian bosom and marks him off as being different from the people around him. Many of our hymns have been born out of that very loneliness, that sense of another and higher citizenship!

That is exactly the thing that keeps a Christian separated—knowing that his citizenship is not on earth at all but in heaven above, and that he looks for the Saviour to come. Who is there that can look more earnestly for the coming of the Lord Jesus than the one who feels that he is a lonely person in the middle of a lonely world?

Peter loved the Lord Jesus Christ and his letters to suffering believers clearly reveal that great and sweeping changes had come into his life. He had become stable, he had become solid, he had become the steady and dependable servant of Christ. Now he was able to see that suffering for Christ is one of the privileges of the Christian life and he prepared his brothers and sisters for the future with his counsel: "Beloved, think it not strange concerning the fiery trial which is to try you . . . but rejoice, inasmuch as ye are partakers of Christ's sufferings."

Fellow believers, it is the same kind of world in which we live in this twentieth century. We do well to let the Apostle Peter speak to us!

No matter who you are, no matter what your education, you can read Peter's First Epistle and understand it reasonably well and you can say to yourself, "The Holy Spirit is saying this to me!"

There isn't anything dated in the Book of God. When I go to my Bible, I find dates but no dating. I mean that I find the sense and the feeling that everything here belongs to me. There is nothing here that is obviously for another age, another time, another people.

Many other volumes and many other books of history contain the passionate outpourings of the minds of men on local situations but we soon find ourselves bored with them. Unless we are actually doing research we do not care that much about something dated, something belonging only to another age.

But when the Holy Spirit wrote the epistles, through Peter and Paul and the rest, He wrote them and addressed them to certain people and then made them so universally applicable that every Christian who reads them today in any part of the world, in any language or dialect, forgets that they were written to someone else and says, "This was addressed to me. The Holy Spirit had me in mind. This is not antiquated and dated. This is the living Truth for me—now! It is just as though God had just heard of my trouble and is speaking to me to help me and encourage me in the time of my distress!"

Brethren, this is why the Bible stays young always. This is why the Word of the Lord God is as fresh as every new sunrise, as sweet and graciously fresh as the dew on the grass the morning after the clear night—because it is God's Word to man!

This is the wonder of divine inspiration and the wonder of the Book of God!

An Evangelical Heresy: A Divided Christ!

"As obedient children, not fashioning yourselves according to the former lusts in your ignorance." 1 Peter 1:14

T HE SCRIPTURES DO NOT teach that the Person of Jesus Christ nor any of the important offices which God has given Him can be divided or ignored according to the whims of men.

Therefore, I must be frank in my feeling that a notable heresy has come into being throughout our evangelical Christian circles—the widely-accepted concept that we humans can choose to accept Christ only because we need Him as Saviour and that we have the right to postpone our obedience to Him as Lord as long as we want to!

This concept has sprung naturally from a misunderstanding of what the Bible actually says about Christian discipleship and obedience. It is now found in nearly all of our full gospel literature. I confess that I was among those who preached it before I began to pray earnestly, to study diligently and meditate with anguish over the whole matter.

I think the following is a fair statement of what I was taught in my early Christian experience and it certainly needs a lot of modifying and a great many qualifiers to save us from being in error:

"We are saved by accepting Christ as our Saviour;
We are sanctified by accepting Christ as our Lord;
We may do the first without doing the second!"

The truth is that salvation apart from obedience is unknown in the sacred scriptures. Peter makes it plain that we are "elect according to the fore-knowledge of God the Father, through sanctifica-tion of the Spirit unto obedience."

What a tragedy that in our day we often hear the gospel appeal made on this kind of basis:

"Come to Jesus! You do not have to obey anyone. You do not have to change anything. You do not have to give up anything, alter anything, surrender anything, give back anything—just come to Him and believe in Him as Saviour!"

So they come and believe in the Saviour. Later on, in a meeting or conference, they will hear another appeal:

"Now that you have received Him as Saviour, how would you like to take Him as Lord?"

The fact that we hear this everywhere does not make it right. To urge men and women to believe in a divided Christ is bad teaching for no one can receive half of Christ, or a third of Christ, or a quar-ter of the Person of Christ! We are not saved by believing in an office nor in a work.

I have heard well-meaning workers say, "Come and believe on the finished work." That work will not save you. The Bible does not tell us to believe in an office or a work, but to believe on the Lord Jesus

Christ Himself, the Person who has done that work and holds those offices.

Now, note again, Peter's emphasis on obedience among the scattered and persecuted Christians of his day.

It seems most important to me that Peter speaks of his fellow Christians as "obedient children." He was not giving them a command or an exhortation to be obedient. In effect, he said, "Assuming that you are believers, I therefore gather that you are also obedient. So now, as obedient children, do so and so."

Brethren, I would point out that obedience is taught throughout the entire Bible and that true obedience is one of the toughest requirements of the Christian life. Apart from obedience, there can be no salvation, for salvation without obedience is a self-contradictory impossibility.

The essence of sin is rebellion against divine authority.

God said to Adam and Eve, "Thou shalt not eat from this tree, and in the day that thou eatest thereof thou shalt surely die." Here was a divine requirement calling for obedience on the part of those who had the power of choice and will.

In spite of the strong prohibition, Adam and Eve stretched forth their hands and tasted of the fruit and thus they disobeyed and rebelled, bringing sin upon themselves.

Paul writes very plainly and directly in the Book of Romans about "one man's disobedience"—and this is a stern word by the Holy Spirit through the Apostle—by one man's disobedience came the downfall of the human race!

In John's Gospel, the Word is very plain and clear that sin is lawlessness, that sin is disobedience to the law of God. Paul's picture of sinners in Ephesians concludes that "the people of the world are the children of disobedience." Paul certainly means that disobedience characterizes them, conditions them, molds them. Disobedience has become a part of their nature.

All of this provides background for the great, continuing question before the human race: "Who is boss?" This breaks down into a series of three questions: "To whom do I belong?" "To whom do I owe allegiance?" and "Who has authority to require obedience of me?"

Now, I suppose of all the people in the world Americans have the most difficult time in giving obedience to anyone or anything. Americans are supposed to be sons of freedom. We ourselves were the outcropping of a revolt. We spawned a revolution, pouring the tea overboard in Boston harbor. We made speeches and said, "The sound of the clash of arms is carried on every wind that blows from the Boston Commons" and finally, "Give me liberty or give me death!"

That is in the American blood and when anyone says, "You owe obedience," we immediately bristle! In the natural sense, we do not take kindly to the prospect of yielding obedience to anyone.

In the same sense, the people of this world have a quick and ready answer to the questions: "To whom do I belong?" and "To whom do I owe obedience?"

Their answer is: "I belong to myself. No one has authority to require my obedience!"

Our generation makes a great deal out of this, and we give it the name of "individualism." On the basis of our individuality we claim the right of self-determination.

In an airplane, the pilot who sits at the controls determines where that plane is going. He must determine the destination.

Now, if God had made us humans to be mere machines we would not have the power of self-determination. But since He made us in His own image and made us to be moral creatures, He has given us that power of self-determination.

I would insist that we do not have the right of self-determination because God has given us only the power to choose evil. Seeing that God is a holy God and we are moral creatures having the power but not the right to choose evil, no man has any right to lie.

We have the power to lie but no man has any right to lie.

We have the power to steal—I could go out and get myself a better coat than the one I own. I could slip out through a side door and get away with the coat. I have that power but I do not have that right!

I have the power to use a knife, a razor or a gun to kill another person—but I do not have that right! I have only the power to do it.

Actually, we only have the right to be good— we never have the right to be bad because God is good. We only have the right to be holy; we never have the right to be unholy. If you are unholy you are using a right that is not yours. Adam and Eve had no moral right to eat of that tree of good and evil, but they took it and usurped the right that was not theirs.

The poet Tennyson must have thought about this for he wrote in his *In Memoriam*: "Our wills are ours, we know not how; our wills are ours to make them Thine!"

Oh, this mystery of man's free will is far too great for us! Tennyson said, "We know not how." But then he girds himself and continues, "Yes, our wills are ours to make them Thine." And that is the only right we have here to make our wills the wills of God, to make the will of God our will!

We must remember that God is Who He is and we are what we are. God is the Sovereign and we are the creatures. He is the Creator and therefore He has a right to command us with the obligation that we should obey. It is a happy obligation, I might say, for "His yoke is easy and His burden is light."

Now, this is where I raise the point again of our human insistence that Christ may sustain a divided relationship toward us. This is now so commonly preached that to oppose it or object to it means that you are sticking your neck out and you had best be prepared for what comes.

But how can we insist and teach that our Lord Jesus Christ can be our Saviour without being our Lord? How can we continue to teach that we can be saved without any thought of obedience to our Sovereign Lord?

I am satisfied that when a man believes on Jesus Christ he must believe on the whole Lord Jesus Christ—not making any reservation! I am satisfied that it is wrong to look upon Jesus as a kind of divine nurse to whom we can go when sin has made us sick, and after He has helped us, to say "Goodbye"—and go on our own way.

Suppose I slip into a hospital and tell the staff, I need a blood transfusion or perhaps an X-ray of my gall bladder. After they have ministered to me and given their services, do I just slip out of the hospital again with a cheery "Goodbye"—as though I owe them nothing and it was kind of them to help me in my time of need?

That may sound like a grotesque concept to you, but it does pretty well draw the picture of those who have been taught that they can use Jesus as a Saviour in their time of need without owning Him as Sovereign and Lord and without owing Him obedience and allegiance.

The Bible never in any way gives us such a concept of salvation. Nowhere are we ever led to believe that we can use Jesus as a Saviour and not own Him as our Lord. He is the Lord and as the Lord He saves us, because He has all of the offices of Saviour and Christ and High Priest and Wisdom and Righteousness and Sanctification and Redemption! He is all of these things and all of these are embodied in Him as Christ the Lord.

My brethren, we are not allowed to come to Jesus Christ as shrewd, clever operators saying, "We will take this and this, but we won't take that!" We do not come to Him as one who, buying furniture for his house, declares: "I will take this table but I don't want that chair"—dividing it up!

No, sir! It is either all of Christ or none of Christ!

I believe we need to preach again a whole Christ to the world—a Christ who does not need our apologies, a Christ who will not be divided, a Christ who will either be Lord of all or who will not be Lord at all!

I think it is important to agree that true salvation restores the right of a Creator-creature relationship because it acknowledges God's right to our fellowship and communion.

You see, in our time we have overemphasized the psychology of the sinner's condition. We spend much time describing the woe of the sinner, the grief of the sinner, and the great burden he carries. He does have all of these, but we have overemphasized them until we forget the principal fact—that the sinner is actually a rebel against properly-constituted authority!

That is what makes sin, sin. We are rebels. We are sons of disobedience. Sin is the breaking of the law and we are in rebellion and we are fugitives from the just laws of God while we are sinners.

By way of illustration, suppose a man escapes from prison. Certainly he will have grief. He is going to be in pain after bumping logs and stones and fences as he crawls and hides away in the dark. He is going to be hungry and cold and weary. His beard will grow long and he will be tired and cramped and cold—all of these will happen, but they are incidental to the fact that he is a fugitive from justice and a rebel against law.

So it is with sinners. Certainly they are heartbroken and they carry a heavy load. Certainly they labor and are heavy-laden. The Bible takes full account of these things; but they are incidental to the fact that the reason the sinner is what he is, is because he has rebelled against the laws of God and he is a fugitive from divine judgment.

It is that which constitutes the nature of sin; not the fact that he carries a heavy load of misery and sadness and guilt. These things constitute only the outcropping of the sinful nature, but the root of sin is rebellion against law, rebellion against God.

Does not the sinner say: "I belong to myself—I owe allegiance to no one unless I choose to give it!" That is the essence of sin.

But thankfully, salvation reverses that and restores the former relationship so that the first thing the returning sinner does is to confess: "Father, I have sinned against heaven and in Thy sight, and I am no more worthy to be called Thy son. Make me as one of Thy hired servants."

Thus, in repentance, we reverse that relationship and we fully submit to the Word of God and the will of God, as obedient children.

Now the happiness of all the moral creatures lies right here, brethren, in the giving of obedience to God. The Psalmist cried out in Psalm 103: "Bless the Lord, ye his angels, that excel in strength, that do his commandments, hearkening unto the voice of his word."

The angels in heaven find their complete freedom and highest happiness in obeying the commandments of God. They do not find it a tyranny—they find it a delight.

I have been looking again into the mysteries in the first chapter of Ezekiel and I don't understand it. There are creatures with four faces and four wings, strange beings doing strange things. They have wheels and still other wheels in the middle of the wheels. There is fire coming out of the north and there are creatures going straight ahead and some that lower their wings and wave them. Strange, beautiful beings and they are all having the time of their lives. Utterly, completely delighted with the Presence of God and that they could serve God!

Heaven is a place of surrender to the whole will of God and it is heaven because it is such a place.

On the other hand, hell is certainly the world of disobedience. Everything else that may be said about hell may be true, but this one thing is the essence—hell is the world of the rebel! Hell is the Alcatraz for the unconstituted rebels who refuse to surrender to the will of God.

I thank God that heaven is the world of God's obedient children. Whatever else we may say of its pearly gates, its golden streets and its jasper walls, heaven is heaven because it is the world of obedient children. Heaven is heaven because children of the Most High God find they are in their normal sphere as obedient moral beings.

Jesus said there are fire and worms in hell, but that is not the reason it is hell. You might endure worms and fire, but for a moral creature to know and realize that he is where he is because he is a rebel—that is the essence of hell and judgment. It is the eternal world of all the disobedient rebels who have said, "I owe God nothing!"

This is the time given us to decide. Each person makes his own decision as to the eternal world he is going to inhabit.

This is a serious matter of decision. You do not come to this decision as though it were a matter of being interviewed for a job or getting your diploma at a school.

We have no basis to believe that we can come casually and sprightly to the Lord Jesus and say, "I have come for some help, Lord Jesus. I understand that you are the Saviour so I am going to believe and be saved and then I am going to turn away and think about the other matters of lord-ship and allegiance and obedience at some time in the future."

I warn you—you will not get help from Him in that way for the Lord will not save those whom He cannot command!

He will not divide His offices. You cannot believe on a half-Christ. We take Him for what He is—the anointed Saviour and Lord who is King of kings and Lord of all lords! He would not be Who He is if He saved us and called us and chose us without the understanding that He can also guide and control our lives.

Brethren, I believe in the deeper Christian life and experience—oh yes! But I believe we are mistaken when we try to add the deeper life to an imperfect salvation, obtained imperfectly by an imperfect concept of the whole thing.

Under the working of the Spirit of God through such men as Finney and Wesley, no one would ever dare to rise in a meeting and say, "I am a Christian" if he had not surrendered his whole being to God and had taken Jesus Christ as his Lord as well as his Saviour, and had brought himself under obedience to the will of the Lord. It was only then that he could say, "I am saved!"

Today, we let them say they are saved no matter how imperfect and incomplete the transaction, with the proviso that the deeper Christian life can be tacked on at some time in the future.

Can it be that we really think that we do not owe Jesus Christ our obedience?

We have owed Him our obedience ever since the second we cried out to Him for salvation, and if we do not give Him that obedience, I have reason to wonder if we are really converted!

I see things and I hear of things that Christian people are doing and as I watch them operate within the profession of Christianity I do raise the question of whether they have been truly converted.

Brethren, I believe it is the result of faulty teaching to begin with. They thought of the Lord as a hospital and Jesus as chief of staff to fix up poor sinners that had gotten into trouble!

"Fix me up, Lord," they have insisted, "so that I can go on my own way!"

That is bad teaching, brethren. It is filled with self-deception. Let us look unto Jesus our Lord, high, holy, wearing the crowns, Lord of lords and King of all, having a perfect right to command full obedience from all of His saved people!

Just remember what the Bible says about the Person and the titles and the offices of Jesus:

"God hath made this same Jesus whom ye have crucified both Lord and Christ." Jesus means Saviour, Lord means Sovereign, Christ means Anointed One. The Apostle, therefore, did not preach Jesus as Saviour—he preached to them Jesus as Lord and Christ and Saviour, never dividing His person or offices.

Remember, too, that Paul wrote to the Roman Christians:

"What saith it? The word is nigh thee, even in thy mouth, and in thy heart: that is, the word of faith, which we preach; that if thou shalt confess with thy mouth the Lord Jesus, and shalt believe in thine heart that God hath raised him from the dead, thou shalt be saved."

The Apostle did not say that "Thou shalt confess with thy mouth the Saviour." He said, "Thou shalt confess with thy mouth the Lord Jesus, for with the heart man believeth unto righteousness; and with the mouth confession is made unto salvation; . . . for there is no difference between Jew and Greek: for the same Lord over all is rich unto all that call upon him. For whosoever shall call upon the name of the Lord shall be saved." (Romans 10:9-13)

Three times he calls Jesus Lord in these passages telling us how to be saved. He says that faith in the Lord Jesus plus confession of that faith to the world brings salvation to us!

God desires that we be honest with Him above everything else. Search the scriptures, read the New Testament, and if you see that I have given a germ of truth, then I urge you to do something about it. If you have been led to believe imperfectly in a divided Saviour, be glad that there is still time for you to do something about it!

A Blessed Reality: Begotten Again!

". . . the God and Father of our Lord Jesus Christ which . . . hath begotten us again . . ." 1 Peter 1:3

A PROFESSING CHRISTIAN WHO FINDS it necessary to keep on apologizing to this present world has missed the whole point of the New Testament revelation of salvation through our Lord Jesus Christ!

The Apostle Peter says that "God has begotten us again unto a living hope." And this constitutes a continuing miracle which should have put the Christian church on the offensive forever!

We have no cause to apologize to the world if we have been born again, changed and transformed through the miracle of supernatural grace and thus endued with the only living and eternal hope which has ever come into this sad and hopeless world!

Why don't we have the courage that belongs to our sound Christian faith? I cannot understand all of this ignoble apologizing and the whipped-dog attitude of so many professing Christians!

I cannot keep from mentioning the kind of confidence and enthusiasm and fanaticism which the faithful communist holds in his devil-inspired doctrine, and I remind you—communists never apologize!

But many Christians spend a lot of time and energy in making excuses, because they have never broken through into a real offensive for God by the unlimited power of the Holy Spirit! The world has nothing that we want—for we are believers in a faith that is as well authenticated as any solid fact of life. The truths we believe and the links in the chain of evidence are clear and rational. I contend that the church has a right to rejoice and that this is no time in the world's history for Christian believers to settle for a defensive holding action!

Brethren, let's not forget that the new birth is a miracle—a major miracle! It is a vital and unique work of God in the human nature. Peter in describing it relates it to the miracle of Jesus Christ rising from the dead, ". . . God, which hath begotten us again unto a lively hope by the resurrection of Jesus Christ from the dead."

So, there is a divine principle here—the fact that a man truly born again is a man who has experienced regenesis, supernatural regenesis. Just as God generated the heavens and the earth in the beginning, He generates again in the breast of the believing man!

Just as surely as God's calling the world out of nothing was a major miracle, the work of God in making a believing Christian out of a sinner is a major miracle as well.

In the light of what God is willing to do and wants to do, consider how we try to "get them in" in modern Christianity.

We get them in any way we can. Then we try to work on them—to adjust them and to reform them.

I may be misunderstood when I say this, but we even have two works of grace because the first was so apologetically meaningless that we try to have two.

I do not speak against the second work of grace; but I am pleading for the work that ought to be done in a man's heart when he first meets God. What I am asking is this: Why should we be forced to invent some second or third or fourth experience somewhere along the line to obtain what we should have received the first time we met God?

I believe in the anointing of the Holy Spirit after regeneration—but I also believe that we ought not to downgrade the new birth in order to find a place for the anointing of the Holy Spirit.

I have read much and studied long the lives and ministries of many of the old saints of God in past generations. I am inclined to believe that many of them were better Christians when they were just newly-regenerated than the run of the so-called "deeper life" people whom I meet today.

I think the difference is in the emphasis of the major miracle which we ought to expect in genuine Christian conversion. Those old-timers would not have believed if a major miracle had not taken place. They would never have been willing to accept a pale and apologetic kind of believing on the Son of God. They insisted on a miracle taking place within the human breast. They knew what Peter meant when he said that the Lord God has begotten us unto a living hope—and they accepted the principle of a miracle wrought in a human being through divine grace.

In reading the Old Testament, we are reminded again and again of the possibility of this miracle of cleansing and transformation.

"Create within me a clean heart, O God, and renew a right spirit within me"—there you have at least the hint of a miracle within the human being. The Old Testament men of God never told us that they had reasoned themselves into a position of faith and power—but that something had happened within their beings that could not be naturally and fully explained!

In Old Testament times, God plainly said: "This shall be the covenant that I will make with the house of Israel; After those days, saith the Lord, I will put my law in their inward parts, and write it in their hearts; and will be their God, and they shall be my people."

Again in Ezekiel, God said: "And I will give them one heart, and I will put a new spirit within you; and I will take the stony heart out of their flesh, and will give them an heart of flesh: that they may walk in my statutes, and keep my ordinances, and do them: and they shall be my people, and I will be their God."

I think you would have to call that a strong hint of regenesis and moral re-birth.

But come along into the New Testament and you will find that it is no longer veiled—the supernatural miracle of the new birth is boldly and openly proclaimed.

The Apostle John writes that our Saviour said that if we tried to come to Him and had not been born anew, we could not enter the Kingdom of God.

John also plainly reports that "as many as received him, to them gave he power to become the sons of God . . . which were born, not of blood, nor of the will of the flesh, nor of the will of man, but of God."

The Apostle Paul told the Corinthian church that "if any man be in Christ, he is a new creature: old things are passed away; behold, all things are become new."

Can you think of any way to make a statement stronger than that?

Peter describes the miracle in his day as "being born again . . . by the word of God, which liveth and abideth for ever."

In his epistle, James wrote that it was "of his own will begat he us . . . that we should be a kind of first-fruits of his creatures."

Throughout the New Testament it is made as plain as it can ever be made that God expected to perform a miracle of His transforming grace within the human life of every person willing to come to Him in faith.

If we believe the New Testament we must surely believe that the new birth is a major miracle, as truly a miracle of God as was the first creation, for the new birth is actually the creating of another man in the heart where another man had been.

I believe this is the kind of genuine Christian conversion that we are talking about—the putting of a new man in the old man's place, so that we are born "anew."

This is the point at which I insist that the new birth was provided in the love and grace and wisdom of God in order to draw a sharp line between those who acquire Christianity by any other method and those who have experienced regenesis.

This is a good place for me to comment that some professing Christians are still trying to find natural and reasonable explanations for that which God has said He would do miraculously by His Spirit.

Let me warn you that if you are a Christian believer and you have found a psychologist who can explain to you exactly what happened to you in the matter of your faith, you have been unfrocked! At the very moment that a man's experience in Christ can be broken down and explained by the psychologists, we have just another church member on our hands—and not a believing Christian!

That is my frank opinion for I am thoroughly convinced that the miraculous element in the genuine Christian experience can never be explained by means of psychological examination. The honest psychologist can only stand off respectfully and say, "Behold the works of the Lord." He never can explain it!

I don't mind telling you that it is my earnest faith that all that is worthwhile in Christianity is a miracle! Actually, I can get along nicely without the outward dressings of Christianity—the trappings and the exterior paraphernalia. I can get along without them because at the heart of our faith are the miracles that throb and beat within the revealed message of God and within the beings of those who truly believe—and that's about all there is to the Christian faith!

As far as I am concerned, I believe that supernatural grace has been the teaching and the experience of the Christian church from Pentecost to the present hour!

Now, to be genuinely born again is the miracle of becoming a partaker of the divine nature. It is more than just a religious expression; more than the hyphenated adjective we often hear, such as "He's a born-again man."

Some evangelicals are slow to admit it, but I know that this important matter of the new birth has fallen into cold hands, along with many other important Bible teachings. I don't have to tell you that in many Christian churches you will feel as though you are in a mortuary instead of the church of the Living God.

Christians who have been miraculously begotten again ought to be rejoicing in their deliverance from the tomb of spiritual death. Instead, we often feel as though we are in the presence of a corpse just brought in from the street. Sad indeed that the words "born again" have become words that seem to mean precious little because the emphasis of supernatural grace has dwindled away, even in some fundamentalist circles.

The new birth is still a miracle of God—it is not a matter of the mind, not just a mental thing. It is my judgment that there are many who talk about being born again on the basis of their mental assent to Christian principles. I think there are many who have received Christ mentally who have never discovered the supernatural quality of the grace of God or of the acts of God.

God fully expects the church of Jesus Christ to prove itself a miraculous group in the very midst of a hostile world. Christians of necessity must be in contact with the world but in being and spirit ought to be separated from the world—and as such, we should be the most amazing people in the world.

However, we have watered down the miracle of divine grace to a point where you actually must find a name on the record books to know whether an individual is a Christian or not.

Brethren, there is a difference! There is also a sad and terrible day of judgment yet to come, a day of revelation and shock for those who have depended upon a mental assent to Christianity instead of the miracle of the new birth!

It is only through the illumination of the new birth that we humans come to a full understanding of the word *hope* as Peter has used it in his epistles.

I like to think of *hope* as being one of the great words that Christ gave us even though it was used in the Old Testament and is actually used 140 times in the Bible.

But haven't you noticed in the New Testament that Jesus Christ made no effort to coin new words, novel words? He used words that are well-known, but He invariably charged these words with a new and wonderful meaning. That is why we find ourselves looking back to His expressions and then saying, "Jesus gave us that word!"

In that sense and understanding, we may well say that hope is a word which has taken on a new and deeper meaning for us because the Saviour took it into His mouth. Loving Him and obeying Him, we suddenly discover that hope is really the direction taken by the whole Bible. Hope is the music of the whole Bible, the heartbeat, the pulse and the atmosphere of the whole Bible.

Hope means a desirable expectation, a pleasurable anticipation. As men know this word, it often blows up in our faces and often cruelly disappoints us as human beings. Hope that is only human will throw us down and wound us just as pleasurable anticipation often turns to discouragement or sorrow.

But Peter assures us that the Christian hope is alive, that the Christian is begotten again—born again—unto a living hope. This English word for *lively* or *living* is the strongest word in the Bible for life, and is the word used of God Himself when it says He is the Living God.

So, in this way, God takes a Christian hope and touches it with Himself and imparts His own meaning of life to the hope of the believer!

There is a great lesson here for any Christian believer who has settled down into the present earthly situation and is becoming satisfied with the many good things he can now afford and is able to enjoy.

It is safe to say that the pleasurable anticipation of the better things to come has almost died out in the church of Christ. It is a great temptation to take the shallow view that we do not need any heaven promised for tomorrow because we are so well situated here and now.

This is the emphasis of our day: "We don't need to hope—we have it now!"

But the modern emphasis is wretched and it is wrong. When we do talk about the future we talk about eschatology instead of heaven. When I find any Christian who can live and work and serve here and snuggle down into the world like your hand fits into an old and familiar glove, I worry about him. I must wonder if he has ever truly been born again.

Brethren, we are still living in a wicked and adulterous generation and I must confess that the Christians I meet who really amount to something for the Saviour are very much out of key and out of tune with their generation.

You may not agree with me, but I must believe that when God works a miracle within the human breast, heaven becomes the Christian's home immediately, and he is drawn to it as the bird in the springtime is drawn to fly north to its summer homeland.

The trusting Christian has a homeland, too; but the fact that we are not anticipating it and not looking forward to it with any pleasure is a most telling and serious sign that something is wrong with our spiritual life!

I recall a recent poll in which it was reported that 82 per cent of the American people expressed a belief in God and the expectation of going to heaven. Personally, I do not like to deal in percentages, but from what I know personally of American men and women I should like boldly and bluntly to say that I will guess that about three-fourths of that 82 per cent are indulging an invalid hope.

It is sad, but it must be said that the earthly hope of men and women without God and without Christ and without faith is a vain hope. Certainly there is a great company of people all around us needing the reminder that if they are going to go to heaven they had better begin to live like it now and if they expect to die like a Christian they had better live like a Christian now.

The hope held by the worldling is vague and it is held in vain because of unbelief. It is unbelief that prevents our minds from soaring into the celestial city and walking by faith with God along the golden streets. It is unbelief that keeps us narrowly tied down here, looking eagerly and anxiously to the newspaper ads to find out who is coming to preach because we feel like we need to have our spirit cheered up.

Anyone who needs to be chucked under the chin all the time to keep him happy and satisfied is in bad shape spiritually. He can ignore the fact that the Bible urges us to go on unto perfection for he is of that part of the church that cannot be satisfied without a visit from the latest gospel peddler, who promises cowbells, a musical hand-saw and a lot of other novelties!

Brethren, we have been born of God and our Christian hope is a valid hope! No emptiness, no vanity, no dreams that cannot come true. Your expectation should rise and you should challenge God and begin to dream high dreams of faith and spiritual attainment and expect God to meet them. You cannot out-hope God and you cannot out-expect God. Remember that all of your hopes are finite, but all of God's ability is infinite!

Now, brethren, what is it that makes our Christian hope a living hope and gives it reality and substance for the future?

The answer is clear and plain—the resurrection of our Lord Jesus Christ is God's gracious guarantee of our blessed future.

I dare to say this to you, my friends—your Christian hope is just as good as Jesus Christ. Your anticipation for the future lives or dies with Jesus. If He is who He said He was, you can spread your wings and soar. If He is not, you will fall to the ground like a lump of lead.

Jesus Christ is our hope and God has raised Him from the dead and since Jesus overcame the grave, Christians dare to die.

Centuries ago unbelieving men thought they could stamp out the Christian gospel by parading those transformed, born-again followers of Jesus to the places of their violent torture and executions. Soon the unfeeling executioners began to feel something in the presence of joyful victory over death and they passed along this word: "Behold how these Christians die!"

I contend that they were able to die well because they had lived well and I think that the man who has not lived well will have a tough time getting in.

In our day, that statement will shock some of our "nickel-in-the-slot" theologians—those who insist that salvation is like putting a nickel in the slot of faith. Just pull down the lever and take eternal life which you cannot lose—and walk away!

The resurrection of Jesus Christ is our guarantee and a Christian dares to die if he has lived right and has a hope that is living and has been born of the Spirit and is walking with God!

CHAPTER 4

A Searching Question: Mercy or Justice?

"Blessed be the God and Father of our Lord Jesus Christ, which according to his abundant mercy . . ." 1 Peter 1:3

THERE ARE MANY IN our day who seem to hold to an idea that God deals with some people in mercy and with others in justice.

However, the Bible really leaves no room for doubt about this matter—it is plain that God deals with all men in mercy and that every benefit God bestows is according to mercy!

If God had not dealt with us all in mercy, we would have perished before we could have had time to be converted. I like to think of it in this way—we float on the vast, limitless sea of divine mercy for it is the mercy of God that sustains the worst sinner.

If we have life, it is according to the mercy of God. If we have protection, it is according to the mercy of God. If we have food and sustenance, it is of God's mercy. If we have providence to guide us, it is surely in the mercy of God.

David once cried out to the Lord, "Have mercy upon me and hear my prayer!"

Was he just using words for the sound of words? No, of course not, for mercy surely enters into the hearing of prayer. David's cry is a sound, clear, logical statement of theological fact. Mercy must enter into the holiest act that any man can ever perform and it is a constant mercy on the part of God.

The fact that I am sane instead of committed to an institution is an act of mercy on God's part. The fact that I am free and not in prison is due to the mercy of God. The fact that I am alive and not dead is God's mercy over me—and the same for you!

It is true for all men, Jew or Gentile or Mohammedan, whether they believe it or not. We ought to thank God for some knowledge and some comprehension of this great sea—the mercy of God!

Early in his first epistle the Apostle Peter blessed God, the Father of our Lord Jesus Christ, because of His abundant mercy towards those who believe and are begotten again.

Now, before we look at that adjective *abundant*, I want to point out that when Peter broke forth into that doxology he was not simply having himself a "spiritual time." He was not just simply letting himself go as it was said of the little old lady at camp meeting.

The Spirit-led life is a clear, logical and rational life. There were particularly sound theological reasons for Peter saying, "Blessed be the Lord!" He blessed God because He has begotten us again and because it was through His abundant mercy that He did it and through it all that we might have a living hope, not a dead one!

I point out that the Spirit-led Christian life is not according to whim or impulse and yet there are Christians who feel that you cannot be spiritual without being capricious and that the more impulsive you are the more spiritual you are.

Years ago there was a popular healing evangelist who boasted that he was too busy running around to plan anything very well. So he just sort of stumbled into the meetings and muddled through them. As a result, he was advertised as a "man of lightning changes." No one ever knew whether the service would open with a hymn, with the offering, or with the sermon.

Personally, I am not so sure about "men of lightning changes." It may be a matter of temperament, or it could be a cover-up for laziness and poor planning and lack of thought. My feeling is that men who depend upon capricious action and impulsive whims usually are not much good in the church of Christ and they wouldn't be any good if they worked for Ford or General Motors, either.

Why do I say that? Because I want to emphasize the manner in which the apostles were Spirit-led. They were not known as men of rash and impulsive moods, constantly changing decisions and judgments. Led by the Spirit of God, they wanted always to do what God wanted them to do. As a result, the things that God wanted them to do always seemed to fit perfectly into the total scheme of redemption and the whole will of God in the New Testament!

This allows me to say that Peter was of little use to God until he got the victory over being whimsical and temperamental and impulsive. While he was still temperamental, scolding the Lord of Glory for this or that, he was of very little use to the Lord. He was almost a total loss.

But when Peter was filled with the Holy Spirit and received a divine vision and began to suffer for Jesus' sake, he got leveled down and became the great apostle, second only to Paul in the New Testament. But God had to take those lightning changes out of Peter and stabilize him in the harness where he would work effectively and fruitfully for the Lord.

So, there is a clear answer for those who feel that if they are not acting queer, they are not spiritual and if an action isn't capricious, it cannot be of the Holy Spirit. The answer is this—we always find a clear, logical link between everything the apostles said in the New Testament and their reasons for saying it! That's true, always!

It should be that way in our Christian churches, too. We are not to be victims of caprice, the weather, the state of our health or whether or not we just happen to feel like praying.

We need to assemble ourselves together as believers whether the weather is good or bad. We have to pray and draw nigh unto the Lord whether we feel like it or not. Reading Peter's letter to those early Christians, we realize that they were living for Jesus regardless of circumstances or their mood.

Actually, there are very few Christians among us who can testify that their spiritual moods are always at a high, sustained level.

A Christian brother will say to me in private: "Brother Tozer, I believe I am a Spirit-filled man. My all is on the altar as far as I know. But I need advice and help about my weakness—I don't always have the same degree of feeling and spirituality. Sometimes I am up and sometimes I am down! What can I do about it?"

I am forced to reply in frankness: "I wish you could tell me because I do not know the answer! I do not know of any truly-honest Christian that can get up and say, 'I live at a consistently high level! I fly at an altitude of 30,000 feet all the way!'"

If any of you can honestly say that you have never ceased from that high level in your Christian experience, you are blessed and I honor you!

Brethren, we are not plugging for the necessity of an up-and-down Christian experience. I mean to say that we are men and women who are to live according to the high logic of spiritual truth, not according to our feelings and moods.

Some of the old fathers in the faith talked about a frame—they would put an entry in their diary:"Was of a very happy frame this morning." Perhaps later there was an entry: "Was of a very low frame this morning. Felt very depressed."Nothing had changed except their "frame." We say it a little differently, for we say "frame of mind." The song writer was actually saying: "I dare not trust the sweetest frame of mind, but wholly lean on Jesus' name!"

So you see, brethren, you and I live for God according to a holy, high spiritual logic and not according to shifting and changing frames of mind or moods. Amen!

Some people would not want me to put it like that; they would call it a very unspiritual doctrine.

"You have got to be blessed all the time," they say. Happy, happy, happy!

But if they would just quit fibbing and tell the truth, they would admit that there are days when they are not as "happy, happy"as they were the day before. The great remedy for us all is to remember the abundant mercy of God, read God's Word and pray, sing a song and take the means of grace and we will find ourselves satisfied in the Lord, as we ought to be!

So, all that He is doing for us is according to His mercy, His abundant mercy.

This word *abundant* comes from a Greek word which means very large, very great, the largest number. It means much and it means many—it can mean all of these things. "According to His largest number, His very large, very great, many mercies, God has begotten us again."

The word *abundant* is not really sufficient because everything God has is unlimited. Because He is the Infinite God, everything about Him is infinite which means that it has no boundary in any direction. I know that is hard for us to comprehend.

I remember preaching an entire sermon on "The Infinitude of God" and I recall that only one man ever spoke to me about it and told me that he had gotten the point of my sermon. So far as I know, everyone else just wrote that one off. But this concept is something that we must recognize even if it hurts our heads. We must come to this knowledge that God is infinite, unlimited, boundless, with no sign post anywhere in the universe saying "This is the end."

We do not need any enlarging adjectives when we speak of God, or of His love or mercy. God Almighty fills the universe and overfills it because it is His character—infinite and unlimited!

We do not need to say God's great love, although we do say it.

When we say God's mercy we do not need to say God's abundant mercy, although we do say it. The reason we say it is to cheer and elevate our own thoughts of God—not to infer that there is any degree in the mercy of God.

Actually, when we use the expression, "The mercy of God," we are referring to that which is so vast that the word *vast* does not begin to describe it, for we are talking about that which has no limits anywhere, that which has its center anywhere and its circumference nowhere.

Our adjectives can be useful only when we talk about earthly things—when we refer to the great love of a man for his family or we talk about little faith or great faith or more faith or much faith.

We talk about wealth and we speak of a man who has considerable wealth. Another man may represent very great wealth and a person who has really made it is a man of fabulous wealth. So we can go up and down the scale from considerable to fabulous because men have ways of measuring what they hold in material things.

But then we come to God—and there can be no such measuring point, no such evaluation. When we speak of the riches of God we must include all the riches there are. God is not less rich or more rich—He is rich—He holds all things in His being!

So it is with mercy. God is not less merciful or more merciful—He is full of mercy, for whatever God is, He is in the fullness of unlimited grace.

So, the word *abundant* is not used here for God— it is put in here for us! It is used to elevate our minds to the consideration of the unlimited vastness of the mercy of God.

Brethren, this all boils down to a simple statement: "God's mercies are equal to God Himself."

For that reason alone all comparisons are futile. If you want to know how merciful God is, discover how great He is and you will know!

I recall a true story told us by Rev. D. C. Kopp, missionary to Africa, on one of his furloughs from the Congo. He described the office of deacon in the national church and told of a fine stalwart Christian brother who had the job of disciplining the converts.

One young convert was proving to be a source of real trouble in the church because he was inclined to break the rules and do the things that a Christian brother should not do.

After he had been disciplined many times, this concerned deacon called in the erring brother once more and told him frankly:

"Now, brother, you have been failing us and disappointing us and disgracing your Christian calling and it is about enough! When we started dealing with you we had a bottle of forgiveness, but I am here to tell you that that bottle is just about empty! We are just about through with you!"

The missionary got a chuckle out of that incident for he thought it was a quaint and picturesque way to let the brother know that he was no longer passing inspection. But, on the other hand, it is far from being a demonstration of God's dealing with us for the bottle of God's forgiveness has neither top nor bottom!

God has never yet said to a man, "The bottle of my mercy is just about empty!"

Let us be thankful that God's mercy does not run out of a bottle. God's mercy is God acting the way He acts towards people—therefore, we can say it is abundant mercy.

Now, when does a person really become aware of this great sea of the mercy of God?

When by faith we come across the threshold into the kingdom of God we recognize and identify it and God's mercy becomes as sweet and blessed as though it were all brand new. It is through His abundant mercy that we are begotten again, but it is that same broad stream from God that kept and preserved the sinner, even through 50 or 60 years of presumption and rebellion.

My father was 60 years old when he bowed before Jesus Christ and was born again. That was a near-lifetime of 60 years through which he had sinned and lied and cursed. But when he gave his heart to the Lord Jesus Christ and was converted, the mercy of God that saved him and took him to heaven was no greater than the mercy of God that had kept him and endured him for 60 years.

There is an old story that fits perfectly here about the Jewish rabbi centuries ago who consented to take a weary traveler into his house for a night's rest.

After they had eaten together, the rabbi said, "You are a very old man, are you not?"

"Yes," the traveler replied, "I am almost a century old."

As they talked, the rabbi brought up the matter of religion and asked the visitor about his faith and about his relation to God.

"Oh, I do not believe in God," the aged man replied. "I am an atheist."

The rabbi was infuriated. He arose and opened the door and ordered the man from his house.

"I cannot keep an atheist in my house overnight," he reasoned.

The weary old man said nothing but hobbled to the door and stepped out into the darkness. The rabbi again sat down by his candle and Old Testament, when it seemed he heard a voice saying, "Son, why did you turn that old man out?"

"I turned him out because he is an atheist and I cannot endure him overnight!"

But then the voice of God said, "Son, I have endured him for almost 100 years—don't you think you could endure him for one night?"

The rabbi leaped from his chair, rushed into the darkness and, overtaking the older man, brought him back into the house and then treated him like a long-lost brother.

It was the mercy of God that had endured the atheist for nearly 100 years. It was the mercy of God that endured my father as a sinner for 60 years. The mercy of God endured me through the first 17 years of my life and has brought me through all of the years since. The Bible plainly declares that God deals with all of us in mercy and that He never violates mercy, for David testified that, "The Lord is good to all: and his tender mercies are over all his works!"

Any idea people may have that God works according to one facet of His nature one day and according to another facet the next day is all wrong. I repeat again—God never violates any facet of His nature in dealing with men.

When God sent Judas Iscariot to hell He did not violate mercy and when God forgave Peter it was not in violation of justice. Everything that God does is with the full protection of all of His infinite attributes. That is why a sinner may live to be 100 years old and sin against God every moment of his life and still be a partaker of the mercy of God. He still floats on that sea of mercy and it is because of the mercy of God that he is not consumed.

However, brethren, we know there will be a day when the sinner will pass from this realm where God's mercy supports him. He will hear a voice saying, "Depart from me, you that work iniquity, for I never knew you!" Hell will be the justly-apportioned abode of those who refuse redeeming mercy even though there has been a providential mercy at work on their behalf throughout their lives.

We Christians should realize, also, that we do not come through the door of mercy and then expect to live apart from that door. We are in the very room of mercy and the sanctuary is a sanctuary of mercy. We must not become self-righteous and imagine we are living such wonderful lives that God blesses us because we are good. That is not so!

God blesses us because of His abundant mercy, the mercy which He has bestowed upon us, and not because of any of our goodness. I do not believe that heaven itself will ever permit us to forget that we are recipients of the goodness of God and for that reason I do not believe that you and I will ever be permitted to forget Calvary.

Another thing in this regard is that although God wants His people to be holy as He is holy, He does not deal with us according to the degree of our holiness but according to the abundance of His mercy. Honesty requires us to admit this.

We do believe in justice and we do believe in judgment. We believe the only reason mercy triumphs over judgment is that God, by a divine, omniscient act of redemption, fixed it so man could escape justice and live in the sea of mercy. The justified man, the man who believes in Jesus Christ, born anew and now a redeemed child of God, lives in that mercy always.

The unjust man, however—the unrepentant sinner—lives in it now in a lesser degree, but the time will come when he will face the judgment of God. Though he had been kept by the mercy of God from death, from insanity, from disease, he can violate that mercy, turn his back on it and walk into judgment. Then it is too late!

Let us pray with humility and repentance for we stand in the mercy of God. I heard of a man who had learned the Ten Commandments so when he prayed he said, "Now, God, I admit I have broken Number One and Number Three and Number Four and Number Seven, but remember, Father, I have kept Number Two and Number Five and Number Six and Number Ten!"

How unutterably foolish—that as men we should appeal to God and try to dicker with Him and portion out our goodness like a storekeeper! What an example we have set for us by the life and faith of the old Puritan saint, Thomas Hooker, as his death approached.

Those around his bedside said, "Brother Hooker, you are going to receive your reward."

"No, no!" he breathed. "I go to receive mercy!"

What an example for us, because Brother Hooker rated very high in the ranks of holy men in the Body of Christ, yet he did not leave this life looking for a reward but still looking for the mercy of God!

Brethren, may I just say that if you have been looking at yourself—look away to the Lord of abundant mercy. Fixing yourself over and trying to straighten yourself out will not be sufficient—you must come as you are!

Paul Rader once told about the artist who had an idea for a powerful painting, depicting the plight of a tramp, a human derelict off the street.

He went to the Skid Row district and found just the subject he had in mind—a man who was dirty, disheveled, rundown at the heels, in rags, and completely at home among the disreputable elements of the city.

"I will pay you a fee if you will come to my studio tomorrow morning," the artist told him.

The bum's face brightened and his eyes took on a new light and he said, "You mean you want to put me in a picture?"

"Yes, I want to paint you into a picture and I will give you fifty dollars right now," the artist said. "Just show up at my house tomorrow morning and I will tell you what to do."

But when the artist's doorbell rang the next morning, the painter hardly recognized the man who stood there. He had been shaved, he had on a white shirt and his pants had a reasonable facsimile of a press.

"I didn't want to come to your fine place looking like a bum, so I spent the money getting myself cleaned up and fixed up," the man said with pride.

"But I cannot use you now for the painting I had in mind," the artist told him. "I thought you would come just as you were."

Jesus told about two men who went up into the temple to pray.

One said, "God, here I am. I am all fixed up—every hair is in place."

The other said, "Oh God, I just crawled in off Skid Row. Have mercy upon me!" God forgave the Skid Row bum, but sent the other man away, hardened and unrepentant and unforgiven!

We come to Him just as we are but in humble repentance, for when the human spirit comes to God feeling that it is better and more acceptable than others, it automatically shuts itself away from God's presence. But when the human spirit comes to God knowing that anything it receives will be of mercy, then repentance has done its proper work! God promises to forgive and bless that man and take him into His heart and teach him that all of God's kindnesses are due to His mercy. What more can a sinner ask?

An Everyday Exhortation: Be Ye Holy!

". . . as he which hath called you is holy, so be ye holy in all manner of conversation; because it is written, Be ye holy; for I am holy." 1 Peter 1:15, 16

Y OU CANNOT STUDY THE Bible diligently and earnestly without being struck by an obvious fact—the whole matter of personal holiness is highly important to God!

Neither do you have to give long study to the attitudes of modern Christian believers to discern that by and large we consider the expression of true Christian holiness to be just a matter of personal option: "I have looked it over and considered it, but I don't buy it!"

I have always liked the word *exhort* better than *command* so I remind you that Peter has given every Christian a forceful exhortation to holiness of life and conversation. He clearly bases this exhortation on two great facts—first, the character of God, and second, the command of God.

His argument comes out so simply that we sophisticates stumble over it—God's children ought to be holy because God Himself is holy! We so easily overlook the fact that Peter was an apostle and he is here confronting us with the force of an apostolic

injunction, completely in line with the Old Testament truth concerning the person and character of
God and also in line with what the Lord Jesus had
taught and revealed to His disciples and followers.

Personally, I am of the opinion that we who claim
to be apostolic Christians do not have the privilege of ignoring such apostolic injunctions. I do
not mean that a pastor can forbid or that a church
can compel. I only mean that morally we dare not
ignore this commandment, "Be ye holy."

Because it is an apostolic word, we must face up
to the fact that we will have to deal with it in some
way, and not ignore it—as some Christians do.

Certainly no one has provided us with an option
in this matter. Who has ever given us the right or
the privilege to look into the Bible and say, "I am
willing to consider this matter and if I like it, I will
buy it"—using the language of the day.

There is something basically wrong with our
Christianity and our spirituality if we can carelessly
presume that if we do not like a Biblical doctrine
and choose not to "buy" it, there is no harm done.

Commandments which we have received from
our Lord or from the apostles cannot be overlooked
or ignored by earnest and committed Christians.
God has never instructed us that we should weigh
His desires for us and His commandments to us in
the balances of our own judgment and then decide
what we want to do about them.

A professing Christian may say, "I have found a
place of real Christian freedom; these things just
don't apply to me."

Of course you can walk out on it! God has given
every one of us the power to make our own choices.

I am not saying that we are forced to bow our necks to this yoke and we do not have to apply it to ourselves. It is true that if we do not like it, we can turn our backs on it.

The record in the New Testament is plain on this point—many people followed Jesus for a while and then walked away from Him.

Once Jesus said to His disciples: "Except ye eat my body, my flesh, and drink my blood, there is no life in you." Many looked at one another and then walked away from Him.

Jesus turned to those remaining and said, "Will you also go away?"

Peter gave the answer which is still my answer today: "Lord, if we wanted to go away, where would we go? Thou alone hast the words of eternal life."

Those were wise words, indeed, words born of love and devotion.

So, we are not forced to obey in the Christian life, but we are forced to make a choice at many points in our spiritual maturity.

We have that power within us to reject God's instructions—but where else shall we go? If we refuse His words, which way will we turn? If we turn away from the authority of God's Word, to whose authority do we yield? Our mistake is that we generally turn to some other human—a man with breath in his nostrils.

I am old-fashioned about the Word of God and its authority. I am committed to believe that if we ignore it or consider this commandment optional, we jeopardize our souls and earn for ourselves severe judgment to come.

Now, brethren, I have said that the matter of holiness is highly important to God. I have personally counted in an exhaustive concordance and found that the word *holiness* occurs 650 times in the Bible. I have not counted words with a similar meaning in English, such as *sanctify* and *sanctified*, so the count would jump nearer to a thousand if we counted these other words with the same meaning.

This word *holy* is used to describe the character of angels, the nature of heaven and the character of God. It is written that angels are holy and those angels who gaze down upon the scenes of mankind are called the watchers and holy ones.

It is said that heaven is a holy place where no unclean thing can enter in. God Himself is described by the adjective *holy*—Holy Ghost, Holy Lord and Holy Lord God Almighty. These words are used of God throughout the Bible, showing that the highest adjective that can be ascribed to God, the highest attribute that can be ascribed to God is that of holiness, and, in a relative sense, even the angels in heaven partake of the holiness of God.

We note in the Bible, too, that the absence of holiness is given as a reason for not seeing God. I am aware of some of the grotesque interpretations which have been given to the text, "Without holiness no man shall see the Lord." My position is this: I will not throw out this Bible text just because some people have misused it to support their own patented theory about holiness. This text does have a meaning and it ought to disturb us until we have discovered what it means and how we may meet its conditions.

What does this word *holiness* really mean? Is it a negative kind of piety from which so many people have shied away?

No, of course not! Holiness in the Bible means moral wholeness—a positive quality which actually includes kindness, mercy, purity, moral blamelessness and godliness. It is always to be thought of in a positive, white intensity of degree.

Whenever it is written that God is holy it means that God is kind, merciful, pure and blameless in a white, holy intensity of degree. When used of men, it does not mean absolute holiness as it does of God, but it is still the positive intensity of the degree of holiness—and not negative.

This is why true Bible holiness is positive—a holy man can be trusted. A holy man can be tested. People who try to live by a negative standard of piety, a formula that has been copyrighted by other humans, will find that their piety does not stand up in times of difficult testing.

Genuine holiness can be put into the place of testing without fear. Whenever there is a breakdown of holiness, that is proof there never was any real degree of holiness in the first place.

Personally, I truly have been affected in my heart by reading the testimonies and commentaries of humble men of God whom I consider to be among the great souls of Christian church history.

I have learned from them that the word and idea of holiness as originally used in the Hebrew did not have first of all the moral connotation. It did not mean that God first of all was pure, for that was taken for granted!

The original root of the word *holy* was of something beyond, something strange and mysterious and awe-inspiring. When we consider the holiness of God we talk about something heavenly, full of awe, mysterious and fear-inspiring. Now, this is supreme when it relates to God, but it is also marked in men of God and deepens as men become more like God.

It is a sense of awareness of the other world, a mysterious quality and difference that has come to rest upon some men—that is a holiness. Now, if a man should have that sense and not be morally right, then I would say that he is experiencing a counterfeit of the devil.

Whenever Satan has reason to fear a truth very gravely, he produces a counterfeit. He will try to put that truth in such a bad light that the very persons who are most eager to obey it are frightened away from it. Satan is very sly and very experienced in the forming of parodies of truth which he fears the most, and then pawns his parody off as the real thing and soon frightens away the serious-minded saints.

I regret to say that some who have called themselves by a kind of copyrighted name of holiness have allowed the doctrine to harden into a formula which has become a hindrance to repentance, for this doctrine has been invoked to cover up frivolity and covetousness, pride and worldliness.

I have seen the results. Serious, honest persons have turned away from the whole idea of holiness because of those who have claimed it and then lived selfish and conceited lives.

But, brethren, we are still under the holy authority of the apostolic command. Men of God have reminded us in the Word that God does ask us and expect us to be holy men and women of God, because we are the children of God, who is holy. The doctrine of holiness may have been badly and often wounded—but the provision of God by His pure and gentle and loving Spirit is still the positive answer for those who hunger and thirst for the life and spirit well-pleasing to God.

When a good man with this special quality and mysterious Presence is morally right and walking in all the holy ways of God and carries upon himself without even knowing it the fragrance of a kingdom that is supreme above the kingdoms of this world, I am ready to accept that as being of God and from God!

By way of illustration, remember that Moses possessed these marks and qualities when he came down from the mount. He had been there with God 40 days and 40 nights—and when he came back everyone could tell where he had been. The lightning still played over his countenance, the glory of the Presence remained. This strange something which men cannot pin down or identify was there.

I lament that this mysterious quality of holy Presence has all but forsaken the earth in our day. Theologians long ago referred to it as the numinous, meaning that overplus of something that is more than righteous, but is righteous in a fearful, awe-inspiring, wondrous, heavenly sense. It is as though it is marked with a brightness, glowing with a mysterious fire.

I have commented that this latter quality has all but forsaken the earth and I think the reason is very obvious. We are men who have reduced God to our own terms. In the context of the Christian church, we are now told to "gossip" the gospel and "sell" Jesus to people!

We still talk about righteousness, but we are lacking in that bright quality, that numinous which is beyond description.

This mysterious fire was in the bush as you will remember from the Old Testament. A small fire does not frighten people unless it spreads and gets out of control. We are not afraid of fire in that sense, yet we read how Moses, kneeling beside a bush where a small fire burned, hid his face for he was afraid! He had met that mysterious quality. He was full of awe in that manifested Presence.

Later, alone in the mountain and at the sounding of a trumpet, Moses shook, and said, "I am fearfully afraid, and quake."

We are drawn again and again to that Shekinah that was over Israel for it sums up wonderfully this holiness of God's Presence. There was the overhanging cloud by day, plainly visible. It was a mysterious cloud not made of water vapor, not casting a shadow anywhere, mysterious.

As the light of day would begin to fade, that cloud began to turn incandescent and when the darkness had settled, it shone brightly like one vast light hanging over Israel.

Every tent in that diamond-shaped encampment was fully lighted by the strange Shekinah that hung over it. No man had built that fire. No one added any fuel—no one stoked or controlled it. It was God bringing Himself within the confines of the human eye and shining down in His Presence over Israel.

I can imagine a mother taking her little child by the hand to walk through the encampment.

I am sure she would kneel down and whisper to that little fellow: "I want to show you something wonderful. Look! Look at that!"

Probably the response would be: "What is it, Mama?"

Then she would reply in a hushed voice: "That is God—God is there! Our leader Moses saw that fire in the bush. Later, he saw that fire in the mountain. Since we left Egypt that fire of God has followed us and hovered over us all through these years."

"But how do you know it is God, Mama?"

"Because of the Presence in that fire, the mysterious Presence from another world."

This Shekinah, this Presence, had no particular connotation of morality for Israel—that was all taken for granted. It did hold the connotation and meaning of reverence and awe, the solemn and inspiring, different and wonderful and glorious—all of that was there as it was also in the temple.

Then it came down again at Pentecost—that same fire sitting upon each of them—and it rested upon them with an invisible visibility. If there had been cameras, I do not think those tongues of fire could have been photographed—but they were there. It was the sense of being in or surrounded by this holy element, and so strong was it that in Jerusalem when the Christians gathered on Solomon's porch, the people stood off from them as wolves will stand away from a bright camp fire. They looked on, but the Bible says "they durst not join themselves to them."

Why? Were they held back by any prohibition or restriction?

No one had been warned not to come near these praying people, humble and harmless, clean and undefiled. But the crowd could not come. They could not rush in and trample the place down. They stood away from Solomon's porch because they had sensed a holy quality, a mysterious and holy Presence within this company of believers.

Later, when Paul wrote to the Corinthian Christians to explain the mysterious fullness of the Holy Spirit of God, he said: "Some of you, when you meet together and you hear and obey God, know there is such a sense of God's presence that the unbelievers fall on their faces and then go out and report that God is with you indeed."

Now, that kind of Presence emanates from God as all holiness emanates from God.

If we are what we ought to be in Christ and by His Spirit, if the whole sum of our lives beginning with the inner life is becoming more Godlike and Christlike, I believe something of that divine and mysterious quality and Presence will be upon us.

I have met a few of God's saints who appeared to have this holy brightness upon them, but they did not know it because of their humility and gentleness of spirit. I do not hesitate to confess that my fellowship with them has meant more to me than all of the teaching I have ever received. I do stand deeply indebted to every Bible teacher I have had through the years, but they did little but instruct my head. The brethren I have known who had this strange and mysterious quality and awareness of God's Person and Presence instructed my heart.

Do we understand what a gracious thing it is to be able to say of a man, a brother in the Lord, "He is truly a man of God"? He doesn't have to tell us that, but he lives quietly and confidently day by day with the sense of this mysterious, awe-inspiring Presence that comes down on some people and means more than all the glib tongues in the world!

Actually, I am afraid of all the glib tongues. I am afraid of the man who can always flip open his Bible and answer every question—he knows too much! I am afraid of the man who has thought it all out and has a dozen epigrams he can quote, the answers which he has thought up over the years to settle everything spiritual. Brethren, I'm afraid of it!

There is a silence that can be more eloquent than all human speech. Sometimes there is a confusion of face and bowing of the head that speaks more divine truth than the most eloquent preacher can impart.

So, Peter reminds us that it is the Lord who has said: "Be ye holy as I am holy, and because I am holy."

First, bring your life into line morally so that God can make it holy; then bring your spiritual life into line that God may settle upon you with the Holy Ghost—with that quality of the Wonderful and the Mysterious and the Divine.

You do not cultivate it and you do not even know it, but it is there and it is this quality of humility invaded by the Presence of God which the church of our day lacks. Oh, that we might yearn for the knowledge and Presence of God in our lives from moment to moment, so that without human cultivation and without toilsome seeking there would come upon us this enduement that gives meaning to our witness! It is a sweet and radiant fragrance and I suggest that in some of our churches it may be strongly sensed and felt.

Now that I have said that, I had better stop and predict that some will ask me, "You don't go by your feelings, do you, Mr. Tozer?"

Well, I do not dismiss the matter of feeling and you can quote me on that if it is worth it!

Feeling is an organ of knowledge and I do not hesitate to say so. Feeling is an organ of knowledge.

To develop this, will you define the word *love* for me?

I don't believe you can actually define love—you can describe it but you cannot define it. A person or a group of people or a race which has never heard of the word *love* can never come to an understanding of what love is even if they could memorize the definitions in all of the world's dictionaries.

But just consider what happens to any simple, freckle-faced boy with his big ears and his red hair awry when he first falls in love and the feeling of it comes into every part of his being. All at once he knows more about love than all of the dictionaries put together!

This is what I am saying—love can only be understood by the feeling of it. The same is true with the warmth of the sun. Tell a man who has; no feeling that it is a warm day and he will never understand what you mean. But take a normal man who is out in the warm sun and he will soon know it is warm. You can know more about the sun by feeling than you can by description.

So there are qualities in God that can never be explained to the intellect and can only be known by the heart, the innermost being. That is why I say that I do believe in feeling. I believe in what the old writers called religious affection—and we have so little of it because we have not laid the groundwork for it. The groundwork is repentance and obedience and separation and holy living!

I am confident that whenever this groundwork is laid, there will come to us this sense of the otherworldly Presence of God and it will become wonderfully, wonderfully real.

I have at times heard an expression in our prayers, "Oh, God, draw feelingly near!"

I don't think that is too far off—in spite of those who can only draw back and sit in judgment.

"Oh, God, come feelingly near!" God drew feelingly near to Moses in the bush and on the mount. He came feelingly near to the church at Pentecost and He came feelingly near to that Corinthian church when the unbelievers went away awestruck to report that "God is really in their midst!"

I am willing to confess in humility that we need this in our day.

A Divine Inheritance:
God's Beneficiary!

"To an inheritance incorruptible, and undefiled, and that fadeth not away." 1 Peter 1:4

I'M A RICH MAN—GOD Himself has named me His beneficiary!

I came to the conclusion long ago that a Christian who places a proper value upon the true riches of eternity will have little inclination to fret and worry about being remembered here in some relative's last will and testament.

Peter deals with this matter of the reality of the divine benefits, describing our future inheritance with the words "incorruptible and undefiled."

He indicates that those persecuted and downtrodden strangers in the early church were believers in Jesus Christ, elect and begotten. The electing and the begetting were means leading into a hope and an inheritance, but they were not the end.

We would all be better Christians and wiser students if we would remember this—God rarely uses periods. There is rarely a full stop in His dealings with us—it is more likely to be with the effect of a colon or a semi-colon. In most instances, what God does becomes a means toward something else that He is planning to do.

Therefore, when God elects a man it does not mean that the man can sit down at his ease and announce, "I have arrived," because the election is only unto a begetting. Can any man who is begotten of the Spirit and has become a Christian believer presume to say, "I have arrived! Put a period there and write *finis* across my experiences"?

No, of course not. God begets us into His provision and that which is still before us is always bigger than that which is behind us. This is certainly true of His provision for us in the divine inheritance.

Now, I think we ought to get the facts straight. Peter was not merely using a figure of speech when he insisted that the begotten one, the true Christian believer, is actually the beneficiary of God. This is not a figure. It is not just a poetic phrase and neither is it an isolated reference. It is openly taught from Genesis to Revelation that the true believer stands to benefit from an inheritance. God being who He is, His beneficences and His benefits are infinite and limitless.

I believe that God always touches with infinity everything that He does and this leads to the thought that the inheritance we receive must be equal to the God who gives it. Being God, He does not deal in things which are merely finite. Therefore, the inheritance that the child of God receives is limitless and infinite.

What a contrast to our small gifts and legacies and benefits on this earth!

I recall that my father used to drive along the way and point to some great farm area and comment: "I hope before I die that I can buy that and leave it to you." But he didn't leave very much. I signed a quit-claim to one little piece of property and hurried it back airmail special.

We do benefit from our parents, however. They give us certain physical and mental inheritances. But they cannot give us what they do not have and it is always limited on this earth. Even the world's richest man can only leave what he has—nothing more. Somewhere, the millions give out and every estate has a boundary.

But, God being who He is, the inheritance we receive from Him is limitless—it is all of the universe!

That is the reason why no hymn writer has ever been able to state the facts, all of the facts, about God's eternal provision for His children. They can only sketch it. It is rather like gathering sea shells on the shores of the vast ocean that stretches away with island upon island, continent upon continent, all belonging to God and to His people in redemption. It all comes from Him!

We humans should remember that when our high flights of imagination have taken wings upward we can be sure that we have never quite reached as high as His provision, because our imagination will always falter, run out of energy and fall weakly to the ground. In contrast, there is no limit to the infinite benefactions of God Almighty to His redeemed ones.

Brethren, the Christian believer stands to receive riches for all parts of his being.

We are physical and mental and moral and spiritual—and I suppose we may say social. We are all of these.

Some Christians do not like the word *social* because they think it means going to church and eating out of a box, like a church social. But we are social in our being. We do have relationships—with the neighbors, in our precinct, to our state, our country and, in a larger way, to the whole world.

I have always thought that Bernard of Cluny, writing about 1140 A.D., knew what he was talking about when he said:

"I know not, Oh, I know not
What social joys are there;
What radiancy of glory,
What joy beyond compare."

He says there are social joys in heaven and I think it is perfectly true.

But man also has a spiritual life and a moral life, a mental life and a physical life. He may also have hidden facets of his life that are not thus classified for we are more than mental or physical beings. We are more than moral, although morality ought to touch all the rest of our being.

And, we are more than spiritual beings, although if we were not spiritual beings, we would not be much better than the beasts.

The point I make is this: we stand to receive infinite benefits from God in all parts of our nature. I refer, of course, to Christian believers, the promises having been made to the redeemed. The sinner, the alien from God, has no moral right even to get old, to say nothing of dying, because the older he gets, the nearer he moves toward the grave and judgment and hell.

But the redeemed and believing child of God can afford to get sick and to get old. He even has

a right to die—for God has made provision for a
new body and for the mental life, the moral life
and the spiritual life—a provision which is actually unsearchable.

I like that word *unsearchable*. It is a good word.
I am reminded that Clarence Darrow thought he
was inferring something nasty when he insisted
that Christians always say "It is a mystery" when
there is some aspect of Christian faith or truth that
defies description.

I have never accepted it as a nasty remark. I take
it in a friendly way because the Christian does run
into mystery almost everywhere he looks. The difference between the believer and the worldling
is that the world is always running into mystery
and calling it science or some such thing, while we
are frank to admit that we don't know what it is. I
admit that I do not know the full implications of
the word *unsearchable*.

We get a hint when we talk about the unsearchable riches of Christ—riches that cannot be counted
or measured, riches that cannot be fully searched
out. These are riches that have so many glorious
ramifications and endless qualities that their value
cannot be comprehended.

They are the unsearchable riches of Christ and
because God is the Living God and the Christian
stands in the relationship of child of God, he has
the promise of the divine inheritance—the riches
which cannot be fully searched out.

Now, God's benefactions are dispensed in
three ways and if you will really consider these,
you will be helped when you think and pray and
read your Bible!

First, I believe God is busy giving us direct, present benefactions.

There are some things which God gives directly in this present age while we are still on our feet, still alive, still conscious, still in this vale of tears and laughter.

For instance, He gives forgiveness. He is pleased to bestow forgiveness upon His believing children.

He gives eternal life. This is not an inheritance to be received at some time in the future; our life in Him is a present bestowment. It is now a present gift which we have—"hath eternal life." The forgiven sinner has this life the moment he believes.

God also gives us sonship: "Beloved, now are we the sons of God." In this relationship there are many other gifts we receive from God—and if we do not possess them it is because we are not God's children by faith.

Perhaps I should also speak of countless other gifts. We ask God to help us, to meet some need, to do something for us, and the Lord mercifully does it. I consider these the little and the trifling things, yet we make a great deal of them. But they are really the passing things compared to the great present benefactions of forgiveness, reinstatement in favor with God, sonship and eternal life.

Then, God has a second way of dispensing His blessings and that is by giving them as a reward for loving and faithful service in His name. The Bible portrays this truth—that some of the riches of God may come in the nature of a reward.

We are aware that all things belong to God, all riches and all blessings, and even though we talk about earning a reward, that is not really a proper expression. There isn't any sense in which we humans can earn God's benefactions.

Actually, as loving and faithful children of God, we are meeting a condition whereby God can bestow blessing as a reward for meeting that condition. That's about all there is to it.

He has said, "Blessed are you because you have been faithful in a few things—I will therefore make you ruler over others." He has spoken of His rewards with the admonition: "Be thou faithful unto death and I will give you a crown of life." These are things that God will bestow as the result of faithful and loyal service and they are future rewards, not yet to be received.

The third manner of God's bestowment is by way of inheritance. The blessings and riches of our divine inheritance are also to be realized in the future. These are not riches that will come to us for anything that is worthy or superior in ourselves, but because of our relationship in faith to the One who is the fount of every blessing.

In this inheritance the riches come from One who possesses and owns all to another whom. He delights to honor and who can establish his rightful claim. This is a principle that we know well in our probate courts—this is why we have recorded wills and bequests. These must all go through the probate court process and those who are named in the wills must establish their identification and rights to the inheritance through relationship.

Now, I repeat—an inheritance has not actually been earned. A boy may be very much of a wastrel and an ingrate and still prove his right to an inheritance because his father delighted to honor him and, because he was his son, made him his sole heir. The will is written and witnessed and on record so when the father dies it is only a matter of going before the proper authorities and proving identity and relationship as the rightful son. It is the right resulting from a relationship—not necessarily the right of goodness. So, there is an inheritance that belongs to the children of God by virtue of the fact that they are truly children of God.

But here I want you to note how many earthly things are upside down in contrast to that of the heavenly.

Among men, a legacy is received at the time of the death of the one who gives the legacy, the testator. But in the things of God, the legacy comes upon the death of the legatee, that is, the person who inherits.

That all sounds confused enough without my confusing it more, but I will try to put it in the form of another illustration.

Suppose a man has a son, an only son. He executes his will making his son the sole heir and giving him everything in the estate. But as long as the father lives that will does not become operative for the son as heir.

But, one day the father is stricken and dies.

After the proper period of mourning, the son goes before the probate authorities and proves that he is the one who is to receive the inheritance. He comes into possession of the inherited estate because his father had died and the will has become operative on behalf of the son.

In the Kingdom of God, it is exactly opposite— just the other way around!

The Father promises and provides an inheritance to His children, but this inheritance is not to be validated by the death of God, but actually upon the death of the child of God or at the coming of Christ, which adds up to the same thing in terms of the inheritance.

Paul knew about the inheritance and he expected it. He wrote about the fact that believers are co-heirs with Christ. He declares that we will realize this in its full implications when we see Christ face to face in a future time. I have said that only a Christian has the right and can afford to die. But if we believers were as spiritual as we ought to be, we might be looking forward to death with a great deal more pleasure and anticipation than we do!

I say that if we are truly believers in the second advent of the Saviour, we will be anticipating that second advent. Common sense and the perspective of history, the testimony of the saints, reason and the Bible all agree with one voice that He may come before you die.

Nevertheless, "it is appointed unto man once to die"—and the Christian knows that he may die before the Lord comes. If he dies, he is better off, for Paul said, "It is far better that I go to be with the Lord."

The difference between a believer living on this earth or being promoted into the presence of Christ is the difference between "good" and "far better," according to Paul.

Now, in conclusion, the Christian's future is still before him. I will give you time to smile at that, because it sounds like a self-evident bromide if ever one was uttered. But I assure you that it is not a self-evident banality; it is rather a proof that we ought to ponder soberly the fact that many Christians already have their future behind them. Their glory is behind them. The only future they have is their past. They are always lingering around the cold ashes of yesterday's burned-out campfire. Their testimonies indicate it, their outlook and their uplook reveal it and their downcast look betrays it! Above all, their backward look indicates it. I always get an uneasy feeling when I find myself with people who have nothing to discuss but the glories of the days that are past.

Yes, the Christian's future is before him. The whole direction of the Christian's look should be forward, Paul was an example for us in this regard for in his soul and spirit he was always looking forward. In his writings we find that he looked back only very briefly and I take it as we read that it is perfectly proper to occasionally steal a quick, happy backward look to see where we have been and to remind ourselves of the grace and goodness of God to us and to our fellow believers.

There is a small word from the Latin—*spect*—which has different forms and it means to see or to look. In our English, that little word has two prefixes which can be used. They are *retro*, meaning backwards; and *pro*, meaning forward.

Do you know that the richness of your Christian life, your usefulness and your fruitfulness, depend upon which prefix you attach to that word? You are bound to be looking somewhere! Even if you are blind, you are looking somewhere for your soul has to dwell either on the past or on the future. Your soul is facing in some direction as a Christian

and the Bible advises us to look steadfastly unto
Jesus, the Author and Finisher of our faith.

We are either retrospective or prospective in
our outlook and our whole future depends in great
measure upon which way we look. In that, I mean
our future here on earth and perhaps even our
future in the world to come.

We ought not to emphasize the "retrospective."
Let us speak of the past only when we have to. Paul
wrote, "Forgetting the things that are behind . . . I
press forward!" There were only a few times when
he had to do it, but he stood and pointed back and
told of his conversion—and that's legitimate!

But it is my advice that we ought not to get locked
into that position of looking back. Why should you
get a sore neck from looking back over your own
shoulder?

Personally, I have found that God will take care
of that fellow behind me, even if I can feel him
breathing on my neck.

Prospect is the word for you and me. Look forward! Look ahead! Live with faith and expectation
because the Christian's future is more glorious
than his past!

One moment of the Christian's tomorrow will be
more wonderful than all the glories of his yesterdays. Methuselah lived 969 years on earth and yet
if he died and went to be with God, and I think he
did, one single hour in the presence of God was
more wonderful to him than any part of his 969
years on this earth!

So, Christians, let us look forward! Look forward
with expectation and hope because we are begotten again unto an inheritance and that inheritance

comes from God our Father and is ours by virtue of our relationship to Him in faith.

Yes, we do have the benefits of present gifts and there are things which will be considered rewards; but the inheritance is ours because we are children of God!

That means that we have every reason to cheer up, believing and hoping, and looking forward to that day of God. For the most eloquent tongue or the most exquisite poetry can never adequately paint for us the glories that we will possess eternally by inheritance, by virtue of our sonship to God and our gracious relationship to Christ, our Saviour!

CHAPTER
7

Our Eternal Treasure: Reserved in Heaven!

". . . an inheritance . . . that fadeth not away, reserved in heaven for you." 1 Peter 1:4

THE CORROSIVE ACTION OF unbelief in our day has worn down the Christian hope of heaven until there seems to be very little joy and expectation concerning the eternal inheritance which God has promised.

I think we have a right to be startled by the thought that very few people really believe in heaven any more. Oh, we may hear a hillbilly with a guitar singing about heaven in a way that would make an intelligent man turn away from the thought of such a heaven. But, for the most part, we do not think about heaven very often and we talk about it even less!

Two men in our human history have had great influence upon modern man's general thinking in regard to heaven and the universe. I refer to Copernicus and Einstein.

Before Copernicus, men were geocentric in their thinking. They considered the earth to be everything and the center of everything. This was largely man's concept—"God made the earth and put it here and everything revolves around it. It is solid and fixed. God has nailed it down and established the foundations and there is nothing that can change that."

But along came Copernicus and, willing to risk his life as an heretic, proved that the earth does not stand still and it is not nailed down. As an astronomer he insisted that the sun, not the earth, is the center of the universe and the sun only seems to stand in the earth's motion. The sun, in fact, moves in a wider orbit, a faster and all but limitless orbit out yonder through the vast, vast space.

So, that knowledge filtered down from the scientists in to the colleges and then into the high schools and from the grade schools on to the street. Everyone knows it and accepts it now, with this common question resulting: "What about this heaven idea?"

There was a day when heaven was right "up there" and the stars were its peepholes. You could look up and see a bit of the light of the glory that was never on land or sea.

But now, the idea that heaven is actually a place is something to laugh about, for men have allowed new ideas and information about the universe to act like a corrosive in wearing down their belief in heaven.

The second man to whom I refer was Einstein who came along with his theories and statements of relativity. He not only took out the earth but he took out the sun and the stars and everything, insisting that nothing is actually fixed or established anywhere. It was his theory that nothing is standing still—everything is in motion. Everything exists only in relation to something else. There is not one thing against which you can measure

something else and conclude, "That's it!" This can
go on *ad infinitum*, world without end, and there is
nothing absolutely fixed, according to Einstein.

I do not know about you, but I get to a certain
point with the theories of scholarship where I am
inclined to say: "Oh, rest my long-divided heart,
fixed on this blissful center, rest!"

There is a place where neither Copernicus nor
Einstein troubleth and I am able to rest in the wisdom and love of God, who made all of these whirling
planets and the worlds which are within the worlds!

Personally, I do not see why the idea of relativity or the motions of the heavenly bodies should
destroy or erode the Christian's faith in heaven as
a place. If God could create an earth and put a race
on it, why could He not create another home and
put a redeemed race on it?

Perhaps it can be attributed to my small mind
and untroubled intellect, but I do not have the
problem that some people have in giving God
that much credit—that if He could make the earth
a race of humans, He could surely make another
place and call it heaven and put on it a race that has
been redeemed. This is very simple for me!

So, Copernicus and Einstein can lie down with
their follies and they won't bother me at all. But I
do realize they have taken away the idea and reality of heaven from many people.

Some are saying, "Heaven is just another dimension, let's not try to figure it out." Still others say
that heaven is a state of mind having to do entirely
with life here upon the earth.

All of our human reasoning which does not take
the Word of God into account is simply the artful

dodging of unbelief. I still believe that the God who made the earth and put people here can make heaven to be the habitation of His redeemed people. Do you?

Perhaps in our churches we have not adequately taught the qualities of the divine inheritance which awaits the children of God. Let us look now at three words used by Peter to describe the qualities of our heavenly inheritance and note that they are precisely the qualities which distinguish our inheritance from any earthly thing.

These are the words he uses: *incorruptible, undefiled*, and *unfading*. These are the inherent qualities of our heavenly legacy. They are part of it and they describe it. They do not define it, but they are the qualities that belong to our heavenly inheritance through Christ Jesus our Lord.

I think we must come to this point in our faith concerning God's great future plans for His children: to believe that the things of God and heaven are not simply an upward projection of our imagination of the very best that we have or can know or can imagine in this world. Actually, they are contrary to the things of earth because of their heavenly qualities—incorruptible, undefiled and unfading!

Now, I want to ask you what any man can possess in this world that has about it the quality of incorruptibility.

According to the meaning in the Greek language, our word *incorruptible* expresses the quality of undecaying in essence and endless in years. That which cannot be corrupted is undecaying in essence and, I suppose, only secondarily endless in years.

I ask you if there is anything on this earth that can properly and accurately be described as incorruptible, that does not decay in its essence and is endless in its sphere?

Our Lord Jesus said, "Lay not up for yourselves treasures upon earth, where moth and rust corrupt, and thieves break through and steal." Now, those were not the words of a cynic. Neither were they the words of a defeatist.

I know that we Christians are often charged with being defeatists. Psychologists will tell you that the black man in the south sings so beautifully about heaven and the golden streets because he has owned only a little wooden shack. Therefore, in his mind he is trying to create for himself what his master possessed in the slave days, and that is his idea of heaven.

Similarly, they tell us now that heaven is the dream of those who are defeated and unhappy—a dream of a happy, happy land where no one needs to wipe away a tear.

Well, that would explain everything except for the small matter that it is not true. Our Lord Jesus Christ was not a defeatist. He did not suffer as they said Abraham suffered. Because Lincoln pitied people, the experts surmise that he suffered from a "glandular deficiency."

Our Lord Jesus Christ had no such deficiency and He was not a defeatist. On the other hand, He certainly was not a silly optimist. Neither did He have any of the gloomy, heavy-hearted pessimism that has characterized a great many of this world's thinkers.

Jesus saw everything clearly and in a true light!

If there ever existed in the wide world a man who earned the right to be called a realist, Jesus Christ was that man.

It was all real to Him. He never shaded one edge of anything to bring something else into relief. He saw everything exactly as it was and described it and spoke of it exactly as it was.

Jesus Christ was the world's most perfect realist because He Himself was Truth!

Therefore, He was neither dreaming of some heaven that He had never seen, nor was He projecting His imagination upward away from the grief and miseries of this world to some lovely heaven, some mansion which was being prepared.

He spoke of things as they were and as they will be found to be. He spoke of all of man's treasures and warned that moth and rust will corrupt. He said corruption is an earthly reality and it is futile for a man to put his trust in the vanity of the corruptible things which he may possess.

Oh, what a cheat the devil is! What a deceiver and what a confidence man he is!

I think of the cheating devil when I think of the sly confidence men who have sold the Brooklyn bridge to poor people, grinning as they have taken their last dollar, leaving them to find out too late that the Brooklyn bridge was never on the market.

The devil is a liar, I say, and a deceiver. He is busy leading people to spend the best years of their lives laying up treasures for themselves, which even before they die will begin to rust and rot and decay.

Incorruptible is a word that cannot be applied to any earthly thing. There is nothing that *we* can know down here that is undecaying in its essence and endless in its years. But there is an inheritance which Jesus Christ the realist, Jesus Christ the heavenly one, came to give to His believing saints.

All of this leads on to the resurrection. This word *incorruptible* used to describe a quality of our inheritance is the very same word describing the state of the dead who are to rise up at the coming of Jesus Christ.

In one of our great Christian anthems, the singers declare with great feeling: "The dead shall be raised incorruptible!" That is exactly the same word describing the glorified human body that Peter used to describe the heavenly inheritance of the saints.

It cannot decay. It cannot be corrupted.

As a human being, I must think of what Job said in the Old Testament about the human prospect. Weary, sick and tired, Job said that he knew that the skin worms would devour his body. In spite of the fact that I like to spend my time thinking along more pleasant lines, I am well aware that the forces and elements that will devour our bodies in the grave are already at work in our physical bodies.

But God Himself has promised that there will be a day when those worms will be no more. God will shake them loose and He will say: "Let him alone. Let him alone forever!" The Bible says that the children of God will be raised with incorruptible bodies.

Incorruptible—without decay and endless in years! That is why I have said that this quality describing our heavenly inheritance is precisely the quality that distinguishes it from all earthly things.

For the second quality of our inheritance, Peter uses the word *undefiled*.

The question we must ask ourselves immediately is this: What earthly treasure do any of us possess that is safe from defilement?

The Bible has very few kind things to say about money and earthly possessions and it is most frank in its expressions against the heaping up of treasures.

The Bible mentions lucre, describing money and profit and earthly gain, and then drops in a startling and descriptive adjective to make it "filthy lucre."

The Apostle Paul, who was not a defeatist and was not compelled to rationalize his poverty, had given up a prominent position to become a follower of Jesus Christ. He wrote that the love of money is a root from which evil springs. He did not single out money itself, but he spoke of an attitude and condition of a man's heart that could put his greed and selfishness and love of money above everything else. We should note, too, that Paul did not insist that all evil springs from the love of money, but said that love of money is one of the roots from which evil springs.

Now, money and every other thing that we have in this world are defiled and have been defiled. A saint of God may own and possess certain things, but they rarely come to him without having been defiled.

You may have a ten-dollar bill folded in your wallet which you intend to give to the missionary cause. There is always a possibility that those dollars were once a part of a wad paid to someone to commit a murder. Or, it could easily have been part of a purse of money handed out in a gambling den or a scandalous brothel.

It has always seemed to me that the very smell of the currency we pass around indicates where it has been. It smells like itself—as though it could tell its own story of crime and violence and immorality!

Brethren, we keep ourselves clean in the midst of human defilement because we know the cleansing power of the blood of Christ, our Saviour! It is not morally wrong for us to have money for our needs, but we ought to guard our own spirits against defilement by virtue of the washing of the blood of Christ.

There is an element of defilement upon everything in this lost world. The very lot upon which your house now stands once belonged to an Indian tribe, and history is very plain in recounting the sad story. We white men came and without any payment in kind kicked the Indians out to the western sea. We put them on little lice-infested reservations and tossed them a pittance from year to year, trying to salve our consciences!

On the other hand, historians and anthropologists also tell us that the Indians we abused and chased out had in a previous time invaded the land and taken it from a race that preceded them.

It is the same situation around the world. Go to the map of Europe and you will see how men have argued and fought for their borders, those flexible and changing borders.

Long ago I threw up my hands in confusion and said, "I will never be able to decide which nation owns what land over there." If we go back far enough in history, we will find those who have the land got it by invasion, by massacre, by murder. Then they had squatters' rights, forgetting how they seized it with the only payment being the blood of the people that owned it.

So, almost everything we touch in this life is defiled. Injustice and oppression run through everything. You know what I think about the devil-possessed origins of communism and its godless partisans who criticize our faith and our ideals and our way of life. But it is the human defilement on every hand which gives the communist his one lone weapon—because what he says about us is not all lies.

I am pained by the injustices in our society. I drive by the gleaming mansions and the stately lake-shore hotels—and what do I think about?

I think about the poor, tired old women with their soap and buckets and mops. Weary, often-defeated and disenchanted people—thankful for a small wage for a night's dreary work!

Drive down the coast of Florida and notice those graceful yachts floating at anchor. It is our natural inclination to think: "It must be fantastic to be in that bracket!"

But if you knew how much of iniquity there was wrought into one of those graceful things, you would never desire it for yourself!

Emerson once said to a young man with political aspirations: "Young man, you want to be president? You want to go to the White House? Ah, if you only knew how much of his manhood that man had to sell out to get there, you wouldn't want it. If you only knew how he must obey those who stand erect behind the throne and tell him what to do, you wouldn't want it!"

I do not make this as political comment. No matter which party is in office or what man is in office, it is true that everything is defiled all over the world.

Why? Because everything flows out of the human being and the human being is defiled. You cannot draw pure water from a defiled fountain. You cannot pluck sweet figs from a thorn tree. You cannot pick sweet grapes from a wild vine and you certainly cannot get edible chicken eggs from a buzzard.

Likewise, you cannot get pure treasures from impure hearts!

Before we leave this subject, I must make this observation: I do not go along with those who hold that every businessman is a crook. I want to say that I know there are men in public life who would scornfully turn their back on anything that is not honest and fair. I believe, particularly in the Christian faith, that it is possible to live a clean and upright life.

My point is this: because of humanity's lost and defiled condition, money and influence and power generally bear the taint and touch of defilement upon them. This is in contrast to the believer's divine inheritance, pure and unsoiled.

So, we trace our inheritance back to its source. Because it flowed out of the pure, undefiled heart of Jesus Christ, it is as undefiled as He is, and He is the one who is described as holy and harmless and undefiled, separate from sinners.

The third quality of our eternal inheritance is that it fadeth not away. It is unfading!

Now, I refer you to your knowledge of this present world once again. Do you know of anything in this present world that can be described as unfading in quality or value?

In all of our larger cities, you can drive down certain streets and avenues and find clusters of old brownstone mansions. When they were built, they were the pride of the wealthy and the elite. They were a mark of social standing and of the so-called "blue bloods."

But the years have passed and the splendor of those mansions has faded away. In many places they are now shabby and in need of repair, often housing a dozen or more families of low income status.

The social royalty of a few generations ago has passed away. Though their names were in the Who's Who they didn't happen to know what's what! In their lifetime they would not have dreamed that those mansions would deteriorate, lose their value and, in effect, fade away.

That is the way it is with the things of this life.

A young man marries his bride today in her blushing womanhood. She is beautiful to behold. But a few years pass and she notices this human process that we call fading.

So, she scrambles off to the beauty parlor and the cosmetics counter and probably even to the pharmacist in the drug store; she feels she has to do something to prop up her fading beauty.

Also, I know lots of men who may not be concerned about their looks but they are supporting the druggists and the medicine houses because of an ulcer or a rheumatic pain; they realize their physical health is fading!

Old letters fade as do old books and other old things. Sometimes they can be restored for a price, but in another generation or two they will have to be restored again and each restoration means a fading.

The Bible plainly and clearly tells us that we are like the flower of the field that fadeth. Today it is and tomorrow it is cut down and is withered and gone.

I don't mind telling you that I am vitally interested in this inheritance which is reserved in heaven for us! As far as I am concerned, it is just as real as my right hand. I am satisfied with Peter's description of our future inheritance and his promise that we are kept by the power of God through faith unto that inheritance.

"Kept by the power of God through faith unto an inheritance . . ."

Why does Peter speak of us in this way? Why didn't he speak of the inheritance itself as being kept?

No, he speaks of our inheritance and then plainly says, "We are kept by the power of God."

I think I have the answer.

It would be unthinkable if our inheritance was incorruptible and then we corrupted, wouldn't it?

It would be unthinkable if our inheritance was unfading and we ourselves faded.

It would be unthinkable if our treasure outlasted us and God found Himself in the embarrassing position of preparing unfading treasure for a people He could not keep to enjoy it!

Is God going to be caught in such an emotional tangle? Is God going to allow Himself to preserve an inheritance for a people whom He cannot preserve?

Never, never! Not while the world stands, for we are kept by the power of God through faith unto an inheritance reserved in heaven for us.

So, I am leaning back very strongly on the keeping power of God!

Now, finally, if you are being kept by the power of God, what kind of indications of that plan and of that power are being reflected in your daily life?

Peter has made it plain in this same passage: we are elect, begotten, obedient and believing!

That is the entire answer.

Elect—that is God's business and it was His business before we knew anything about it!

Begotten—that is God's business as we believe in His Son!

Obedient and believing—we who are kept by the power of God through faith unto an inheritance.

So there we are, friends—and as Christians, we are not only rich but nobly rich! Rich with riches which need no apology. Riches which have no taint of having come to us through defiled hands!

I wonder when we will begin to behave and to live on the level of our riches instead of acting like poverty-stricken creatures trying to crawl under a leaf so we will not be seen.

Let's let the world know how rich we really are! Let's tell it—we are being kept by the power of God unto an inheritance reserved in heaven for us!

That's the fulltime business of the child of God!

A Spiritual Uniform: Clothed with Humility!

". . . be clothed with humility: for God resisteth the proud, and giveth grace to the humble." 1 Peter 5:5

THE APOSTLE PETER, ADVISING Christian believers to be clothed with humility in all of their relationships with one another, actually infers that genuine Christian humility should be their identifying uniform from day to day!

In the custom of that distant culture, men dressed according to their status and place in society.

In our own day, we also are accustomed to identifying many public servants by the kind of uniform they wear. If we suddenly need help or assistance, even in a strange city, we look around quickly to find a helpful man in the policeman's uniform.

We have no fear of the mailman who daily steps on our property. His grey uniform tells us that he is a servant of our government and that he has a responsibility for helpful public service.

So, the Holy Spirit through the apostle cites the necessity for members of the Body of Christ to be subject to one another in the bonds of love, mercy and grace. This honest posture of submission and humility becomes our uniform, and adornment really, indicating that we are the redeemed and obedient disciples of Jesus Christ and that we belong to Him!

Peter's request is not strange when we remember that it was Jesus Christ our Lord who dressed himself in humility and then took that difficult course down, down, down—to the death on the cross!

It is a scriptural and divine example that we have in the person of Jesus, "who, being in the form of God, thought it not robbery to be equal with God: but made himself of no reputation, and took upon him the form of a servant, and was made in the likeness of men: and being found in fashion as a man, he humbled himself, and became obedient unto death, even the death of the cross. Wherefore God also hath highly exalted him, and given him a name which is above every name."

I think it is most important for believers to acknowledge the fact that because Christ Jesus came to the world clothed in humility, He will always be found among those who are clothed with humility. He will be found among the humble people. This is a lesson that not all of us have learned.

I want to refer here to a rather striking passage in the Song of Solomon which I think throws practical light upon the desire of the heavenly Bridegroom to be in fellowship with those dear to him in places of humble service.

I am using this Old Testament story as a good and forceful illustration even though someone may insist that it does not stand up under the rigorous criticism of the Bible scholar and expositor. Frankly I do not know how anyone is going to soundly expound the Song of Solomon—we are more likely to get every man's idea of what it means!

The illustration is in chapter five and the bride is telling of her distress because her beloved had called her during the evening to go with him and she was slow to respond. He called to her saying that his head was covered with the dew and his locks with the drops of the night, for he had been gathering lilies and myrrh and caring for his sheep.

In a kind of summary, she recalls that she was garbed beautifully for the night chamber but not in the attire which would allow her to respond quickly to his call, for he wanted her to join him in his humility and service among the sheep and in the duties of the gardens and fields.

Then she confesses: "I opened to my beloved; but my beloved had withdrawn himself, and was gone. . . . I sought him, but I could not find him; I called him, but he gave me no answer."

By the time she was willing to put on the proper garment to join him in his humble duties, he was gone.

Now, the scriptures are conclusive in teaching that God is always on the side of the humble man and Peter is in full agreement with the statement that God resists the proud and gives grace to the humble.

Perhaps human beings are generally of the opinion that they will find Jesus Christ wherever they are; but I think there is such a thing as finding Christ wherever He is—and that will be in the place of humility, always!

God resists the man who is proud—and stubborn!

I believe God has to consider the attitude of the proud man as being resistance to Him. It is not very often—perhaps once in a hundred years—that a person will actually raise his face to God and exclaim: "God, I resist you, I defy you!"

There is no general pattern of that kind of defiance among men. We are much more likely to oppose God by resisting the side He is on and resisting His ways.

But the scriptures plainly teach that when a proud and stubborn man resists God, he may expect to find that God is resisting him.

The man who sets his jaw and takes action against a Christian, even though he may be right in point of fact, nevertheless will find God in resistance to him because he is wrong in spirit and attitude.

I think God looks beyond the situation to the spirit and attitude. I think He is more concerned with how we react to abuse and mistreatment than to the fact that we have been abused by someone.

Some of us have had experiences of being "told off" most eloquently by people with a very descriptive flow of language; but the eloquence is lost comletely insofar as God is concerned. If you are His child taking some abuse or persecution for His sake, His great concern is the attitude that you will show in return.

Will you reveal a stubborn spirit intent upon revenge? If you resist the Spirit of God asking you to demonstrate the love and grace of Jesus Christ, your Saviour, you can be sure of one thing: God will resist you!

Now, that doesn't mean that God is going to switch and take the side of the other man who has abused you. It just means that God will have to resist you because He will always resist the stubborn man.

Even if you have the facts on your side, God will know whether you are wrong in your spirit. When God resists a man for his pride, it is not likely that He will send immediate and dramatic judgment. God probably will not signal His resistance to the stubborn man by a judgment that will come in the public place.

Rarely does God send His judgment dramatically. I have wondered if we might learn our lessons of humility and obedience more quickly if God were to resist a man as one soldier to another, with the clash of sword and the letting of blood?

But it does not work that way. When God resists a man for the sins of his spirit and attitude, a slow, inward spiritual degeneration will take place as a signal of the judgment that has come. A slow hardening that comes from unwillingness to yield will result in cynicism. The Christian joy will disappear and there will be no more fruits of the Spirit. That man will sour as a jar of fruit sours—and it is not an exaggeration to say that the man who has earned the resistance of God will continue to sour bitterly in his own juice.

God does resist the proud and I think the significant factor is this: the man may not have been wrong in point of fact, but he failed the test in his spirit!

It is significant, too, that the scripture assures us that the same God who must resist the proud always stands ready to give grace to the humble.

The Bible advises men and women to humble themselves under the mighty hand of God. It is my opinion that if our humility had to show itself only under the hand of God, it would be a relatively easy gesture.

If the Lord should say to me, "I am coming and will stand at the front of the church and I will expect you to come and kneel before me and humble yourself," it would be an easy thing for me to do because I know that no one will ever lose face in kneeling humbly before God Himself.

Any man would feel just as proud as ever even though kneeling before the eternal Majesty on high. But God knows our hearts and He doesn't allow us to fulfill His demands for humility with a mere gesture.

God may use people whom you think are not worthy to shine your shoes and in a given situation He will expect you to humble yourself meekly and take from them whatever it is they are pouring on you. In that spirit of meekness you would be humbling yourself under the mighty hand of God!

Think of the example of our Saviour, cruelly beaten and cut with the lash. That whip was not wielded by an archangel but by the hands of a pagan Roman soldier. The abuse that was heaped on Jesus did not come from any multitude of the heavenly host—but from wicked, blasphemous and dirty-tongued men who were not worthy to clean the dust from the soles of His sandals.

Jesus willingly humbled Himself under the hand of men and so He humbled Himself under the hand of God.

Christians have often asked: "Must I humble myself and meekly accept every situation in life?"

I think this is the answer: As Christians, we must never violate morals or truth in humility.

If in humbling ourselves we compromise the truth, we must never do it. If it means a compromise of morality, we must never do it.

I am confident that no man is ever called of God to degrade himself, either morally or in truth. But we do have a calling from God to humble ourselves under His mighty hand—and let the other party do the rock-throwing!

In this call to His people for true humility, God adds the promise that He will exalt us in due time! "Due time." I think that means a time that is proper to all of the circumstances. It will be the time that God knows is best suited to perfect us and a time that will bring honor to God and the most good to men. That is "due time."

It may be that in God's will He will expect us to wait a long time before He can honor us or exalt us. He may let us labor in humility and subjection for a long period because it is not yet His time—due time.

Brethren, God knows what is best for each of us in His desire to make us the kind of saints that will glorify and honor Him in all things!

Many of us have harmed our own children in such ways as these: teaching them to drive our cars before they were old enough; giving them too much money before they knew its value; giving them too much freedom before they knew the meaning of responsibility and maturity.

These things come out of our misdirected kindnesses, but they will harm the child. To reward a man for things he has not earned and does not deserve will surely harm the man.

Likewise, for God to come too quickly to the defense, before the saint has gone through the fire, will harm the saint.

We are faced here with Bible truth and not with the fiction of men.

A modern book of fiction would have had Daniel well protected. As he was about to be placed in the lions' den, a voice out of the sky would have spoken and every lion would have dropped dead.

But what actually happened?

God allowed Daniel's enemies to put him in the den of lions and he slept there with the lions until morning because God's "due time" for Daniel was in the morning, not the night before!

I would also like to see how the modern fiction writers would handle the story of the three Hebrew children in the fiery furnace. They could make a whole book out of that!

They would be forced to some climactic, human trick to put out that fire just before the three young men were to be tossed into the furnace—but that would be putting out the fire too soon!

For God to have His own way and to be glorified in due time, those saints had to go into the fire and stay there throughout the night—due time was in the morning.

God has said He will exalt you in due time, but remember, He is referring to His time and not yours!

Some of you are actually in a fiery furnace right now. You are in a special kind of spiritual testing. The pastor may not know it and others may not know it, but you have been praying and asking the Lord: "Why don't you get me out of this?"

In God's plan it is not yet "due time." When you have come through the fire, God will get you out and there will not be any smell of smoke on your garment and you will not have been harmed.

The only harm that can come will be from your insistence that God must get you out sooner than He plans.

The Lord has promised to exalt you in due time and He has always kept His promises to His people.

As children of God, we can always afford to wait. A saint of God does not have to be concerned about time when he is in the will of God.

It is the sinner who has no time. He has to hurry or he will go to hell, but the Christian has an eternity of blessedness before him.

So, if you are in a furnace, don't try to come out too soon! Wait it out in the will of God and He will exalt you in due time—time proper to the circumstances. It will be a time properly designed to glorify God and to bless your own spirit!

One of our great weaknesses as Christian men and women is our continued insistence upon getting vindicated before the trial is over. God has said that He wants to try us and test us and when the trial is over, He Himself will bring in the verdict: "Tested—and found worthy!"

I only pray that we all may know how to conduct ourselves as trusting children of God during this period in which we await His return. Paul wrote that. Jesus first came to earth in the fulness of time—it was God's time for Him to come that He might die for our sins.

Peter wrote that God will exalt us in "due time," speaking of the fact that Jesus will again return to earth in God's time. God's plan for us in these days is to be subject one to another in humility in preparation for the return of His Son to be exalted with His saints!

The True Adorning: Husbands and Wives!

"Likewise, ye wives, be in subjection to your own husbands . . . Husbands, dwell with them according to knowledge, giving honour unto the wife . . . whose adorning . . . the ornament of a meek and quiet spirit." 1 Peter 3:1-7

WE HAVE COME TO a sorry time in history when public speakers—including many preachers—see fit to deal with problems between men and women, husbands and wives, as a kind of humor calling for a bushel of laughs.

Throughout man's existence, the biological positions of the two sexes have remained unchanged, but the psychological attitudes and the social relations have been altered radically from time to time.

In recent years there has been a positive and radical revolution with respect to the relationships of the sexes and I think its origins can largely be traced in the United States. It is an impossibility for me to analyze here the impetus and the details of this movement which has been widely acclaimed as seeking "liberation" for women of the world.

What I do want to say about the relationships of husbands and wives will boil down to this: for the Christian of either sex, there is only one rule to follow and that is, "What does the Bible say?"

Christians are first of all children of God, and as children of God we are committed to the Word of God. We are committed to a Man and a Book, the man being the Lord Jesus Christ and the book, of course, the Holy Scriptures.

When we have discovered what the Bible has to say with finality about any subject and have determined what pleases the Man in the glory, there is no room left for argument.

In this epistle, Peter makes a plain statement that Christian wives ought to be in subjection to their own husbands, enforcing what the Bible seems to teach in other places—that the man as head of the race is head of the home.

Go back to Genesis and you will find that God made Adam from the dust of the ground and blew the breath of life into his nostrils. Then, because it was not good for him to be alone, God made the woman from a part of the man—and the woman must understand and accept that.

But, quickly and on the other hand, it must be said that there is absolutely no scriptural authority, neither precept nor biblical example, to allow any husband to behave as a brutal lord, ruling his home with an iron hand.

Read again the story of Abraham and Sarah and you will note the noble leadership of the man Abraham. He never ruled with an iron hand!

Go on to poor Jacob with all of his domestic difficulties. There was always a graciousness and a kindness within his family circle!

You can continue through Old Testament history and although it was a bit in the shadows compared with the New Testament, still and nevertheless, there was never any brutal masculine domination in the families with whom God was dealing.

In your serious study of the Bible as the Word of God, you will have to agree that the Bible seems to teach that the husband and wife should supplement one another. In other words, it seems to be the will of God that husband and wife together may become what neither one could be apart and alone!

Certainly the Bible picture is plain in denying the husband any right to be a dominating despot delighting in hard-handed dealings with his wife and family.

On the other hand, neither is a dominating and rebellious wife ever recognized nor approved in the scriptures!

An overwhelming and mischievous wife is; the product of sin and unbelief and such a role has no place whatsoever in the will of God for the Christian family.

Actually, I think we may interpret the scriptures as teaching that God never intended there should be a continuing rivalry and competition between husbands and wives. Rather, it teaches the ideals of understanding and cooperation.

There is to be the understanding that two people have entered into a covenant by their choice and by force of circumstance, living in the same home and situation. The understanding should include the fact that the husband, according to the scripture and the will of God, is the head of the race and the home, but that he should function wisely, according to Peter's gentle admonition: "Ye husbands, dwell with them according to knowledge."

Peter is advising the husband to use his head and the common sense he has been given: ". . . giving honour unto the wife, as unto the weaker vessel, and as being heirs together of the grace of life."

In other words, husband and wife are children of God together, equal heirs of the grace of life.

If we will remember this fact prayerfully, I think we will become aware that it is at this point that chivalry was born! I am speaking of Christian chivalry, as we understand it.

The world in which we live and the society of which we are a part have often sought to lampoon and satirize the concept of woman as the weaker vessel. There have been thousands of jokes, and cartoonists have had a field day with their drawings of the buxom woman leading the meek, little lamb-of-a-man down the street.

But we remember that the scriptures say that the man and the woman are heirs together of the grace of life. Husband and wife, if both are Christians, are Christian heirs together! They are united in their strongest bond—they are one in Jesus Christ, their Saviour!

Now, Peter makes a very strong comment in this passage for the benefit of husbands.

"Husbands, your prayers will be hindered if you do not give honour unto the wife, as unto the weaker vessel . . ."

I suppose there are many Christian husbands whose prayers are not being answered and they can think up lots of reasons. But the fact is that thoughtless husbands are simply big, overbearing clods when it comes to consideration of their wives.

If the husband would get himself straightened out in his own mind and spirit and live with his wife according to knowledge, and treat her with the chivalry that belongs to her as the weaker vessel, remembering that she is actually his sister in Christ, his prayers would be answered in spite of the devil and all of the other reasons that he gives.

A husband's spiritual problems do not lie in the Kremlin nor in the Vatican but in the heart of the man himself—in his attitude and inability to resist the temptation to grumble and growl and dominate!

There is no place for that kind of male rulership in any Christian home. What the Bible calls for is proper and kindly recognition of the true relationships of understanding and love, and the acceptance of a spirit of cooperation between the husband and wife.

Peter also seeks to give us a plain answer in this passage concerning the life and conduct of a Christian wife who has an unbelieving and scornful husband.

We dare not deal with this only as a problem out of ancient history. In all of our congregations, we do face the question of the Christian wife: "How do I adjust my Christian life so that I can be obedient to the scriptures while I am living with a man who hates God and showers me with grumbling and abuse when I insist that I am going to God's house?"

First, we must admit that there is the kind of woman who talks about praying for her husband, but she will never live to see him converted because she refuses the scriptural position that God has given her, and more bluntly, because her husband has never seen any spiritual characteristics in her life that he would want for himself!

Peter could hardly give Christian wives any plainer counsel: "Be in subjection to your own husbands; that, if any obey not the word, they also may without the word be won by the conversation of the wives; while they behold your chaste conversation coupled with fear."

The scriptural advice is to this effect: that the quiet, cooperative Christian wife is a powerful instrument for good in the home, and without too many words, is still an evangelist hard to resist. Peter strongly infers that the man, seemingly rejecting her doctrine and laughing at her faith, is badly smitten deep in his own conscience by her meek and quiet spirit and her chaste conversation coupled with godly fear.

In summary, we have mentioned two extremes—the harsh husband whose prayers are not answered, and the wife whose life does not show consistent godliness and patience in adversity.

I thank God that in between those two positions there are great throngs of good, decent people trying to do the best they can for God in their life situations, overlooking the obvious irritations and together experiencing the grace of God!

I thank God indeed for that great number of believing men and women who get along together in Christ's bonds and with the help of the Spirit of God succeed in establishing a consistent example to their families, their neighbors and their friends!

I am aware that at about this point some of you are wondering if I will ignore the rest of Peter's admonition to the Christian women of his day.

There is a problem in this passage, but I may die tomorrow and I would not want to die knowing that only a day before I had been too cowardly and timid to deal with a text of scripture!

Here it is, in Peter's counsel to the wives:

"Whose adorning let it not be that outward adorning of plaiting the hair, and of wearing of gold, or of putting on of apparel; but let it be the hidden man of the heart."

First, notice the manner which Peter lifts the entire questions up and beyond the plane where there is division between the sexes and puts the matter on a spiritual plane where there is no division and where it is the hidden being of the heart and the spirit that really matters.

Second, what does the Bible really teach here about the outward adorning of the person?

It says that the woman is not to seek to be attractive by outward adorning and dress. Does it expressly forbid the plaiting of the hair, the wearing of gold and the putting on of apparel? This is a question often asked.

Let's say "yes" and then go on from there and see where we stand.

When I was a boy they used to call plaiting of the hair "braiding." Every little girl had a pigtail that came to her hips. The longer the pigtail the prouder the girl!

My sister used to wear braided hair and that's what it means—exactly what plaited hair once meant in England.

Does the Bible say, then, that a woman must not be adorned with braided hair?

If we say, "Yes, that's what it means"—that rules out the braiding of your hair.

The advice continues: "Let it not be the wearing of gold."

Does that mean that gold can never be worn in any way by a Christian woman?

We will agree for the moment and say that gold is out!

"Nor the putting on of apparel."

Now, wait a minute! We are in trouble with our reasoning here, because this certainly does not mean that the woman is not to put on any apparel.

If it doesn't mean a strict ban on fixing the hair or wearing of gold or putting on of apparel, what does it mean?

It means the true attractiveness of the person is not outward but inward! Therefore, the Christian woman should remember that she cannot buy true attractiveness—that radiance which really shines forth in beauty is of the heart and spirit and not of the body!

That is what Peter meant and anything else by way of exclusion or structure is of narrow, private interpretation and will lead into an unloving fanaticism!

There is not one line of expression here that would lead us to believe that Peter was laying down the law that it is wrong for a woman to braid her hair. The women know they have to do something with it!

Nor is there anything in the scripture that teaches that the use of gold is forbidden in proper ways. God in creation made gold and strung it all around. It is pretty to look at and it is an element in itself. If we have any of it and can afford it, there is nothing in the scripture that says "Don't wear it" any more than it says, "Don't wear apparel!"

So, the teaching is plain: don't let your apparel be your true attractiveness. Don't try to substitute gold or jewelry for the true beauty of the being!

I am sure that we would not be mistaken to presume that Peter had a reason for writing this, for history bears out the fact that there were customs and fads and styles in those days, too.

I suppose it was the vogue and the thing to do—make the braided hair a kind of work of art, with great displays of gold and jewelry and fine apparel among the worldly and unsaved women of that pagan time.

Perhaps Peter sounds a trifle sour to some when he writes and says, "You Christian women are a different kind of person than you were before you knew the Lord. As Christians you should be more interested in character and inward spiritual life than in your clothing and adornment."

Having said this about the true inward attractiveness of the person, it must also be said that no Christian woman should ever sink into slovenly habits of dress and appearance. How can it be possible for any Christian woman, carrying her big Bible and teacher's quarterly, to become known as a proverbial "dowd"?

She cannot impress me with her professed spirituality. I can only shrug and think about her unkempt dress: "Did she go to the old bureau in the attic and pull out the old rag or did she sleep in it?"

I can be very positive about this—I don't believe that true spirituality can afford to leave that kind of slovenly impression. There is no place in the heart of Jesus Christ nor in that of the tender, artistic Holy Ghost for dowdiness nor dirt nor inconsistency!

I remember the account of the old Quaker brother who had to make a call at the home of one of the Christian sisters in his city.

They greeted one another in the traditional dignified manner of the Quakers and then had a brief conversation about the things of God.

As he was about to leave, she said, "Brother, would you care to pray with me before you go?"

He said, "No," and she said, "Why?"

He answered, "Your house is dirty and God never told me to get down on my knees in a dirty house. Clean up your house and I will come back and pray."

Perhaps she had been too busy praying to keep the house clean, but I believe an orderly and well-kept house would have helped her Christian testimony, and perhaps she could have prayed better, as well.

Now, there has to be some sort of outward adorning and I would summarize it in four familiar words: *clean, neat, modest, appropriate.*

None can say that they do not understand the word *clean.* However poor we may be, we may still be clean. Nearly everyone has enough water available for basic cleanliness.

Why can't we all be neat in our daily contacts? I do not think anyone ever needs to look as though he had gone through a cyclone and had no time since to get "accumulated."

In our day, some folks seem to think the word *modest* is a comical word. You can laugh it off if you want to, but it is one of the words that we will face in that great day of coming judgment.

In our Christian lives, we should know the strength of the word *appropriate*. I think every Christian woman should dress appropriately, properly and suitably to her circumstances and to her income. A Christian woman who tries to give out tracts dressed in loud, flashy apparel or in dirty and disheveled garb will be a poor advertisement for the gospel she is trying to proclaim publicly!

I realize that some women excuse their manner of dress in public by the fact that they have so little money to spend for clothing.

I contend that a woman still doesn't have to be grotesque in her garb even though she must wrestle with the problems of small income.

You know that I ride the public busses occasionally and for the small price of the fare it is a wonderful place to observe human nature.

When I see some of the inappropriate and grotesque things worn by women boarding the busses I have wondered why others in the family did not protest: "Please, Mama, don't go out like that! People will think you have escaped.

I think there is a great contradiction apparent among us. Many women are working so hard in all kinds of jobs that they are making themselves old in the effort to get money enough to buy the clothes and cosmetics that are supposed to make them look young.

As far as I am concerned, it does not reflect any credit on the common sense or spirituality of any woman who knowingly goes beyond her financial bracket to decorate herself for the sake of appearance!

Finally, I think that a Christian woman must be careful about the kind of person she sets up as a model of character and example in daily life. It is a sad thing to have our minds occupied with the wrong kind of people.

I don't think English history books will ever report that Suzanna Wesley was one of the best-dressed women of her day or that she ever received a medal for social activity. But she was the mother of Charles and John Wesley, those princes of Christian song and theology. She taught her own family, and her spiritual life and example have placed her name high in God's hall of fame for all eternity.

So, if you want to take models to follow day by day, please do not take the artificial, globe-trotting females who are intent only upon themselves, their careers and their publicity. Rather, take Sara, the princess who gave her love and obedience to Abraham; or Suzanna Wesley or Florence Nightingale, Clara Barton or Mary Fuller.

There are so many good examples and it is a serious matter, for the judgment shall declare every person's faith and work and influence!

I have not been trying here just to fill the role of a feminine counselor, but to remind you that the Apostle Peter, a great man of God, said it all a long time ago! True adorning is the lasting beauty that is within. It is the glowing but hidden being of the heart, more radiant than all of the jewels that one can buy!

God help us all, men and women of whatever marital, social or domestic status, that we may do the will of God and thus win our crown!

CHAPTER 10

A Word for Reason: Emotions in Control!

"Wherefore gird up the loins of your mind, be sober, and hope to the end for the grace that is to be brought unto you at the revelation of Jesus Christ." 1 Peter 1:13

W E ARE IN THE good company of the apostles when we seek to put in a word for reason in the expression of our Christian life and character.

Peter and the other New Testament preachers were fervent in their exhortations to Christian believers that they should always exhibit the loftiest kind of spirituality regardless of the human circumstances.

Why did Peter, then, add a practical dimension of caution that the child of God should "gird up the loins of his mind," and be sober-minded in the daily expression of his Christian worship and witness?

It is my interpretation that the Apostle was cautioning the believers that their human emotions were not to be allowed to get out of control. I think he was pleading for the kind of spirituality that comes with the filling of the Holy Spirit and is marked by our walking in heavenly places in Christ Jesus, and certainly is not degraded by dethronement of the sentinel we call reason!

The spirit of the prophet is always subject to the prophet. When the Spirit of God moves into a man's heart, He will make that man generous but He will never make a fool out of him. He will make the man happy but He will never make him silly. He may make him sad with the woe and the weight of the world's grief but He will never let him become a gloomy cynic. The Holy Spirit will make him warmhearted and responsive but He will never cause him to do things of which he will be ashamed later.

Peter was not promoting or predicting a cold and lifeless and formal spirituality in the Christian church when he advised believers to gird up the loins of their minds and be sober.

He was saying to the early Christians as he hopes to say to us now: "Brethren, if ever there was an hour when we needed to be serious about our Christian faith, this is the hour! We need to be sober men—and spiritual men!"

No Christian church ought to be a mere tombstone, even though the tombstone is probably the most sober of all things. A tombstone will just continue to sit throughout the years, showing no change whether in cold or wind or show or heat, in peacetime or in war, no matter what the developments in history.

The tombstone just sits there, always in the same orthodox position, faithfully reminding the passing visitor that Mr. John M. Jones 1861-1932, lies there. That's the story and witness of the tombstone!

I admit that there are some Christian churches like that. In order to keep sober and formal and quiet, they are contented to stay dead! But that is not the kind of church that Peter would have chosen and neither is it the kind of congregation with which we want to be identified.

Peter had some basis of concern for writing to Christian believers with this expression of caution and the Holy Spirit has seen fit to pass it along to us. I think we see in this the Bible method.

The Bible, like everything else God has made, has method in it. I can see His method in the fact that this Bible verse begins with the connecting word, "Wherefore." It looks back at something that has been said and forward to something that is to be done.

The biblical method is to lay down strong foundations of truth and these foundations of truth are declarations of God. Principally, they are declarations of what God is doing or has done, or both.

Then, after this foundation has been laid, it is the Holy Spirit's method and desire to show that this revealed truth constitutes a moral obligation.

It is at this point that I am in controversy with some elements of leadership in our Christian churches today. It is my considered opinion that one of the greatest weaknesses in the modern church is the willingness to lay down foundations of truth without ever backing them up with moral application!

The great American evangelist, Charles Finney, went so far as to declare bluntly that it is sinful to teach the Bible without moral application. He asked what good is accomplished merely to study a course in the Bible to find out what it says, if there is to be no obligation to do anything as a result of what has been learned?

There can be a right and a wrong emphasis in conducting Bible classes. I am convinced that some Bible classes are nothing more than a means whereby men become even more settled in their religious prejudices.

Only when we have moral application are we in the Bible method!

When we give ourselves seriously to Bible study, we discover the Holy Spirit's method.

"This is what God did, and this is what God did. Therefore, this is what you ought to do!" That is always the Bible way.

You will not find a single book of the Bible that does not have godly exhortation. There is not a single Bible portion that God wants us to study just to get a cranium full of knowledge or learning.

The Bible always presents the truth and then makes the application: "Now, if this is true, you ought to do something about it!" That is the meaning of moral application of spiritual truth.

In the case before us, Peter had just recited some of the great and gracious things God has done:

"Blessed be the God and Father of our Lord Jesus Christ, which according to his abundant mercy hath begotten us again unto a living hope by the resurrection of Jesus Christ from the dead, to an inheritance unfading."

"Wherefore," he continues, "because of these things I have just told you, gird up the loins of your mind, be sober, and hope . . ."

Girding up the loins is a biblical figure of speech. Peter did not have to explain it because everyone knew what he meant by the analogy. It had to do with their manner of dress.

People wore a kind of tunic in those days, a Mother Hubbard style of garb, we might say. Some of these garments were simply like a blanket with a hole cut in the middle and then strung down over the body. In a sense, this flowing garb was always in the way, whether the person was working or walking.

The tunic was always in the way so it was handled in this manner: if the person was very poor, he simply took a piece of dry leather and cut it in such a way that it could be tied around the waist and pulled into a loop. In this fashion, the person was girded.

With that belt or girdle tied and holding the garment close to the body, a person could run or walk or travel or climb or work and the garment did not hinder either hands or feet.

There is a good New Testament illustration that we all remember. John the Baptist came to his ministry wearing a cumbersome tunic made of camel's hair. He was a man of great activity, but he was a poor man. We are told that he girded his garment with a leather girdle. The rich and the affluent were able to use more expensive woven belts and girdles, but they accomplished the same thing—freedom of feet and hands for necessary walking and activity in everyday life.

Peter tells the Christian believers that they are to gird up the loins of their minds.

I trust no one holds the idea that our minds are not a part of our inner life.

Let us deal with this principle first insofar as it relates to the natural man, unconverted persons, the sons and daughters of Adam and Eve.

In general, the natural man born into this world and growing up in it, regardless of his rank or station, education or possessions, will be by his very nature indifferent and careless and disorganized within his inner life.

The popular and accepted manner of life is followed by the average man, not because he thinks that is all there is, but because he really doesn't think about it at all.

Even a sinner, if he really gives himself to serious thoughts, will rebel against the tyranny of the popular and accepted ways. There have been many unconverted men throughout history who rebelled against the ways and the manners of the day in which they lived. I admire independence of spirit in men, for it takes a serious-thinking man to stand up and refuse to bow and bend; but the average man will not give himself to this kind of stern thinking.

The average man has only petty things to think about: Is there enough time left on that meter? Who will win the World Series? How much profit will I make on this deal?

He does not give himself to thought about those things that touch character, that seek to touch his inner life. He keeps everything on the shallow surface of his life—that's the sinner I am talking about.

The sinner is careless and disorganized and indifferent, except for the area where he has to tighten up his belt. He may be an expert in some field—mathematics, science, industry or business—and in his field he is forced to do some careful thinking, but it does not reach over into moral thinking. It is not the kind of thinking that will touch his inner life or his conduct.

The average man's life is all ungirded and ragged and at loose ends while he is carefully thinking and applying himself in his own prescribed field. He has never learned to think through to the truth and then make the necessary personal application to his own needs, his own standards, his own person.

Peter insists that it is the converted, born-again men and women who are to gird up the loins; of their minds.

I do not believe we do Peter any injustice to infer that he expected this to be one of the first things we will do after we are converted to Jesus Christ—to gird up our minds and become sensitive to eternal values!

There were two aspects of girding up the loins in the Old Testament figure of speech. First was the preparation for working and toiling without hindrance, and second was readiness for sudden departure and travel. Both Peter and Paul use this phrase in urging spiritual preparation and readiness in writing to New Testament Christians.

It is only after we yield to Jesus Christ and begin to follow Him that we become concerned about the laxity and thoughtlessness of our daily lives. We begin to grieve about the way we have been living and we become convicted that there should continue to be aimlessness and futility and carelessness in our Christian walk.

I have been forced to admit that one of the things hardest for me to understand and try to reconcile is the complete aimlessness of so many Christians' lives.

They certainly are not shooting directly at anything, so if they should hit it, they would not know it, anyhow! Many of their lives are at loose ends. They are not girded up!

Probably the worst part of this situation among us is the fact that so many of our Christian brothers and sisters have unusual gifts and talents and capacities—yet they have not exercised this discipline of girding up the mind and spiritual potential in order to make the necessary progress in the Christian life.

Why should a pastor have to confess total failure from year to year? Why should he have to go from one church to another, starting something, trying something—only to admit failure again?

I don't think he has ever really girded himself. He has abilities but they are not disciplined. He has a fine mind but it is not girded up. He is like a man with a treasured Stradivarius violin that has never been put in tune. He has never taken time to sit down and tune that priceless instrument, therefore he gets no melody and harmony from it.

All Christians must be sober and thoughtful at this point of carelessness and looseness. Twenty years from now, what assessment will be made of our Christian lives, our maturity and spiritual growth and progress? Will someone say of us: "He's the same old man—a little thicker, a little balder, a little heavier—but he has made no progress in his inner spiritual life. He failed to grow and mature because he never learned the discipline of girding up."

I fully believe that it was Peter's expectation that laxity and carelessness and aimlessness would all be repudiated and forsaken by the serious-minded Christian believer.

What does this say to the average Christian who refuses to think about these factors because they will touch his moral and spiritual life?

I am thinking here of the average Christian as I have known him. He is willing to make a gesture of brief meditation, but only enough to ease his conscience, and then he reverts back to his aimless life. In spiritual matters, he is actually tossed around like a cork on the waves, a puppet of circumstances.

He does not know what it means to navigate a straight course for God, like a ship on her way to the harbor.

We have been schooled theologically to excuse this kind of Christian life on the basis of weakness and frailty, and we tell ourselves that it is not really sinful. Personally, I think there must be some kind of limit to the time that believers can continue their selfish and aimless habits of life without bordering on sin!

Actually, I think that we can get so prodigal with our talents and so careless with our time and so aimless with our activities that we will be faced with the fact of sin in our lives—for we know what we should do and what we should be, but we would rather excuse our failures!

The Book of Proverbs tells us about the man who lies on his bed, turning like a door on its hinges, while the weeds grow up in his garden, choking and killing his crop. Then, when harvest has come, he has nothing and is reduced to begging for help.

Now, staying in bed when he should be cultivating his garden may not be overly sinful—but I think there is no argument but what a wilfully lazy man is a sinful man.

It follows then, in my estimation, that a person who is intellectually lazy is a sinful person. God had a reason for giving us our heads with intellectual capacity for thinking and reasoning and considering. But what a great company of humans there are who refuse to use their heads and many of these are Christians, we must confess.

Many a preacher would like to challenge the intellectual and thinking capacity of his congregation, but he has been warned about preaching over the people's heads.

I ask, "What are people's heads for? God Almighty gave them those heads and I think they ought to use them!"

As a preacher, I deny that any of the truths of God which I teach and expound are over the heads of the people. I deny it!

My preaching may go right through their heads if there is nothing in there to stop it, but I do not preach truths which are too much for them to comprehend. We ought to begin using our heads. Brother, you ought to take that head of yours, oil it and rub the rust off and begin to use it as God has always expected you would. God expects you to understand and have a grasp of His truth because you need it from day to day.

I have been reading in the works of the saintly Nicholas Herman, better known to us as Brother Lawrence. He recommends that Christian believers should nourish their hearts on high and noble thoughts of God. The question revolves around our daily use of our minds and thought life—sensational magazines and soap operas and doubtful stories will forever keep us from nourishing our hearts on noble thoughts of God!

The Holy Spirit knows us well and enforces the exhortation to gird up our minds, to pull up our spiritual standards, to eliminate carelessness in word and thought and deed, and in activities and interest!

Now, let us think of what Peter must have had in mind when he added the words, "be sober," to the discipline of right thinking.

Sobriety is that human attitude of mind when calm reason is in control. The mind is balanced and cool and the feelings are subject to reason and this statement is proof enough for me that the Holy Spirit will never urge believers into any kind of spiritual experience that violates and dethrones reason.

All of us are aware of instances where men and women have taken part in unreasonable and unseemly acts and then excused them on the grounds that they were moved by the Spirit.

Frankly, I must doubt that! I doubt that the Holy Ghost ever moves to dethrone reason in any man's mind.

In regard to my own personal and spiritual life, I must testify that the highest, loftiest and most God-beholding moments in my own experience have been so calm that I could write about them, so peaceful that I could tell about them and analyze them.

I do believe that the human reason, blessed and warmed and shining with the love of God, must always be in control.

Think of the completely opposite picture, that of drunkenness. If you walk past the corner bar, you are likely to find a fellow staggering out of the bar, drunken to the point that reason has actually been dethroned and human judgment is completely impaired.

Someone a long time ago called liquor "a liquid damnation" and wrote about the man who opens his mouth and drinks down something that makes "his brains go out." Actually, the emotions get completely out of control—that's what happens to a drunk man.

Out of control—and the first sign is that he gets too happy and talkative. Then he gets affectionate and generally with people whom he did not even know until an hour earlier.

Then he will probably get sad, and because his emotions are out of control, he wants to tell the bartender and everyone who will listen about the wife who doesn't understand him and the family that doesn't appreciate him.

That's what liquor does for many unthinking, weak and careless people in our day; it robs them of all control of their emotions and judgment. Most of them are sorry and embarrassed and ashamed the morning after; but they refuse to thoughtfully gird up their minds, so weakness becomes a pattern.

The Apostle Paul stands with Peter in this serious-minded approach to the use of our faculties under the guidance and blessing of the Holy Spirit. He wrote to the Ephesian church with a caution to be wise in the understanding of the will of the Lord and advises them:

"And be not drunk with wine, wherein is excess; but be filled with the Spirit;

"Speaking to yourselves in psalms and hymns and spiritual songs, singing and making melody in your heart to the Lord;

"Giving thanks always for all things unto God and the Father in the name of our Lord Jesus Christ."

Peter and Paul thus join in urging us to practice and display the loftiest fruits of the Spirit of God with the Spirit Himself in control of our emotions and our affections, our worship and our praise.

Yes, brethren, the Spirit will make the believing child of God generous but He will never make him foolish! He will make him happy but He will never make him silly! The Spirit will warm the inner life of the Christian's being but He will never lead him to do the things that would cause him to hang his head in shame afterward.

I say "Thank God" for the kind of enduring joy which comes to the believer whose emotional life is in the keeping of the Spirit. I stand with the dear child of God whose reason is sanctified and who refuses to be swept from his mooring in the Word of God either by the latest popular vogue in religious fad or the ascendence of the most recent sensational personality in gospel circles.

The child of God will not be swept away by fear nor feeling nor love of anything earthly; he is sailing by the stars!

The illustration is about the young sailor who was pressed into service at the helm of the ship.

"You see that bright star?" he was asked. "Just keep that star a little off your port bow and you will stay right on course."

But when the ship's officer returned, the sailor had the ship far off course.

"Why didn't you keep your course by that star?" he was asked.

"Oh, I passed that star miles back," he responded.

Well, he had lost his star, and some of God's people in our churches are showing a lot of impatience with our determination, by the grace of God, to navigate with His star out there ahead of us.

I confess that we do not have as much popularity and acclaim and we do not preach to the largest crowds and there never seems to be excess money floating around, but we are looking with hope to the future. In the long run, it will be something very precious to know that when men's minds were all at loose ends and going to pieces, we were able to gird up the loins of our minds by the help of our Lord Jesus Christ!

We are not Christian dreamers engaging in idle and wishful thinking. We know who we are and to whom we belong and we know where we are going. Ours is a forward look in hope and expectation and we are surely among those whom Paul describes in writing to the Thessalonian church:

"Therefore, let us not sleep as do others; but let us watch and be sober. For they that sleep sleep in the night; and they that be drunken are drunken in the night.

"But let us, who are of the day, be sober, putting on the breastplate of faith and love; and for an helmet, the hope of salvation.

"For God hath not appointed us to wrath, but to obtain salvation by our Lord Jesus Christ."

Amen! We are looking forward to it because God Himself has said it by His Spirit, and He cannot lie!

A Happy Contradiction: Rejoicing in Trials!

"... ye greatly rejoice, though ... ye are in heaviness through manifold temptations." 1 Peter 1:6

I HAVE ALWAYS FELT COMPASSION for Christian men and women who seem to major in pessimism, looking on the dark and gloomy side and never able to do anything with life's problems but grumble about them!

I meet them often, and when I do I wonder: "Can these people be reading the same Bible that I have been reading?"

The Apostle Peter wrote to the tempted, suffering and persecuted believers in his own day and noted with thanksgiving that they could rejoice because they counted God's promises and provision greater than their trials. They looked for a future state of things which would be much better than any current situation on this earth.

Now, I know that in any church setting it is possible to find Christians who are intent upon a wrong emphasis in either of two directions.

First, there are always those who are taken up entirely with the emphasis of the sweet bye and bye.

They are contented with getting by on a spiritual appeal of "Come now—and wait for the feast!"

In spiritual matters, they are much like the little boy whose mother says, "Johnnie, here is a piece of bread and butter. We will not be eating for another hour, you know."

Johnnie probably has a ravenous appetite, but in this instance he is forced to piece out his hunger until the dinner is finally ready.

Some Christians seem satisfied to go along without even a slice—but on a bare crumb! They are putting all of their emphasis on the feast to come in the sweet bye and bye.

But, on the other hand, there are those who make the mistake of putting all of the emphasis upon the "sweet now and now," therefore thinking very little about the world to come.

I am sure this brings the question: "What, then, is the proper emphasis?"

The right thing to do is to put the emphasis where God puts it—and I think that is the emphasis that there are some things you can have now and some things you cannot have now!

I insist that the Lord expects His people to be thorough and sincere students of the Bible so that we will not be guilty of surrendering anything that is promised for us now or demanding anything presently that is promised as a later benefit. There would be a lot less tension among believers and much less nervous pressure and misunderstanding if we would study our Bibles with that thought in mind!

Actually, there is no promise of any such thing as absolute perfection now. Perfection is a relative thing now and God has not really completed a thing with us, as yet.

Absolute perfection is for the time when the sons of God shall be revealed and completeness awaits the time when we shall look upon the Son and become grownup sons, indeed. Peter said that the persecuted and suffering Christians of his day looked for a state of things immeasureably better than that which they knew, and that state of things would be perfect and complete!

Oh, what great changes there will be when we come to that time of perfect completeness and complete perfection!

The very earth itself and all of nature surrounding us will reveal the blessings of God's perfection in that coming time.

The Apostle Paul, speaking as the man of God, tries to tell us how the realm of nature will be changed, in the Epistle to the Romans:

> "Not that I count these present sufferings as the measure of that glory that is to be revealed in us.
> "The creation is full of expectancy, that is, because it is waiting for the sons of God to be made known.
> "Created nature has been condemned to frustration not for some deliberate fault of its own, but for the sake of him who so condemned it; namely, that nature in its turn will be set free from the tyranny of corruption to share in the glorious freedom of God's sons.
>
> "The whole nature as we know groans in a common travail of all of life.
>
> "Not only do we see that, but we ourselves do the same. We ourselves, although we have already begun to reap our spiritual harvest, yet groan in

our hearts waiting for that adoption which is the
ransoming of our bodies from their slavery."

Paul is trying to make it plain to us that mankind
is so related to the earth that when the Lord comes
in triumph to glorify mankind, He will also glorify
the earth and nature. He insists that the earth and
nature will share in the glorification with the sons
of God who were once sons of Adam but are now
children of the King.

This old earth, as we know it, did go down in a
collapse with the sons of Adam when we all went
down together. Floods and typhoons and earthquakes, tornadoes and tidal waves are all the result
of the distorted state of fallen nature. Sickness and
insanity and all of our weaknesses and frailties in
the flesh can be traced to this fallen state of affairs
for we are still very much a part of the earth and
of nature.

Man and his home—this earth—are very much
alike and so God will redeem the earth by redeeming people. In the hour that He comes to glorify
redeemed mankind, He will also allow that glorification to overflow and spread throughout the earth!

That means, also, that great changes in human
society will be wrought in that day of completeness
and perfection.

We could read for hours in the Old Testament,
noting the quotations which look forward to that
day in which the earth will be full of the knowledge
of the Lord, illustrated by the manner in which we
know the waters cover the sea.

There will be a kind of human society which we
have not yet known. There will no longer be great

problems between management and labor and between landlords and tenants because "no man will build and another inhabit."

There will be no need for rent ceilings and price controls. There will be no need for people to live in rat-infested tenements because everything will belong to God and everyone will possess his own land and live in his own house.

There will be no problem concerning labor and toil because one will not plant and another reap, but every man will reap what he plants! God will take care of that for the earth will be full of the knowledge of the Lord.

The believing children of God should have an optimistic outlook about God's future plans for this earth and human society, based upon the realities expressed in the prophetic scriptures. We cannot accept man's own horrible predictions of destruction, which range from this earth falling into the sun to destruction by a runaway comet sweeping the earth to a dreadful fate.

As Christians and students of the Word of God, we believe that this earth is yet to be the home of a redeemed people and a changed society that will recognize His Lordship.

Also, for Christian believers, it is a more personal note to learn from the Bible that the great day of perfection and rejoicing will bring great changes, affecting our bodies, our minds and souls.

The Apostle John clearly spoke to Christian believers when he wrote:

"Beloved, now are we the sons of God, and it doth not yet appear what we shall be: but we know that, when he shall appear, we shall be like him; for we shall see him as he is."

Then the Apostle Paul, in spite of the imperfections of language, gave the Corinthian Christians the divinely-inspired description of the great changes to be wrought in bodies of the believing children of God in that great day of revelation and transformation:

"Perhaps someone will ask, How can the dead rise up? Or they will say, What kind of body will they be wearing when they appear?"

At this point, Paul was not quite as patient with questions as he might have been. He answered:

"Poor fool! When thou sowest seed in the ground, it must die before it can be brought to life and what thou sowest is not the full body that it is one day to be. It is only bare grain, of wheat it may be, or some other crop.

"It is for God to embody it according to His will. Each grain in the body that belongs to it. "Nature is not all one. Men have one nature, the beasts another, the birds another. The fish is another, so too there are bodies that belong on earth and bodies that belong to heaven. And heavenly bodies have one kind of beauty, earthly bodies another. "The sun has its own beauty, the moon has hers and the stars have theirs. One star differs from another star in its beauty.

"So it is with the resurrection of the dead. What is sown corruptible rises incorruptible. What is sown unhonored, rises in glory. What is sown in riches is raised in power.

"What is sown in natural body rises a spiritual body. If there is a natural body, there must be a spiritual body, too. Mankind begins with Adam who became as the scripture tells us, a living soul, but mankind is fulfilled in the Adam who has become a life-giving spirit, that is, Christ.

"It was not the principle of spiritual life that came first. Natural life came first, then spiritual life. The man who came first came from earth fashioned of dust. The man who came afterwards came from heaven and his fashion is heavenly. The nature of that earth-born man is shared by his earthly sons, and the nature of the heaven-born man by his heavenly sons. So it remains for us who once bore the stamp of the earth to bear this stamp of the heavenly."

These are among the reasons that believing Christians, whether in the apostolic time or in our own, may be expected to have an optimistic and cheerful outlook, waiting for this salvation which shall be revealed in the last time and engaged in great rejoicing as they wait!

This note of rejoicing is very clear throughout the entire Bible and in the New Testament it rings forth like a silver bell.

The life of the normal, believing child of God can never become a life of gloom and pessimism. In every age we will have some people whose concept of Christianity is a kind of gloomy resignation to the inevitable. But it is the Holy Spirit who has promised the ability for the Christian to rejoice in God's promises day by day.

Of course, the Christian believer is serious minded and he can weep with those who weep. But he is alert and optimistic and has a cheerful hope because he is looking for that changed state of affairs which is so far beyond anything that this world has to offer.

Peter states it as a paradox: the obedient Christian greatly rejoices even in the midst of great heaviness, trials and suffering. God's people know that things here are not all they ought to be, but they are not spending any time in worrying about it. They are too busy rejoicing in the gracious prospect of all that will take place when God fulfills all of His promises to His redeemed children!

This leads us directly into a summary of the glorious contradictions which make the life of the Christian such a puzzle to the worldling. We must admit that the true Christian is a rather strange person in the eyes of the unbeliever.

I use the adjective *true* in regard to the Christian not only to point out the necessity for the new birth but to indicate, also, the Christian who is living according to his new birth. I speak here of a transformed life pleasing to God, for if you want to be a Christian, you must agree to a very much different life. The life of obedience to Jesus Christ means living moment by moment in the Spirit of God and it will be so different from your former life that you will often be considered strange. In fact, the life in the Spirit is such a different life that some of your former associates will probably discuss the question of whether or not you are mentally disturbed. The true Christian may seem a strange person indeed to those who make their observations only from the point of view of this present world which is alienated from God and His gracious plan of salvation.

Consider now these glorious contradictions and you will no longer wonder why the true believer in Jesus Christ is such an amazement to this world.

The Christian is dead and yet he lives forever. He died to himself and yet he lives in Christ.

The reason he lives is because of the death of another.

The Christian saves his own life by losing it and he is in danger of losing it by trying to save it.

It is an interesting thing that when he wants to get up, the Christian always starts down, for God's way up is always down, even though that is contrary to common sense. It is also contrary to the finest wisdom on the earth, because the foolish things of God are wiser than anything on this earth.

You may also note about the true Christian that when he wants to sin, he always surrenders. Instead of standing and slugging it out, he surrenders to a third party and wins without firing a shot or receiving a bruise. He surrenders to God and so wins over everyone else!

Another strange thing about him is that he is strongest when he is weakest and weakest when he is strongest. It is God's principle in his life that his strength lies in his weakness for when he gets up thinking that he is strong he is always weak. However, when he gets down on his knees thinking he is weak, he is always strong!

Again, he may be poor—and if he is a real Christian, he usually is—and yet he will always make others rich. Paul was a poor man in prison, but he

immeasurably enriched the entire Christian world.
John Bunyan was a poor man in Bedford jail, but he
gave us *Pilgrim's Progress.*

You can go on down the scale throughout history
and you will find that a rich Christian was generally
poor and the poor Christian made everyone rich.

This man who is a true Christian is at his highest
when he feels the lowest and he is lowest when he
feels the highest. He is in the least danger when
he is fearful and trusting God, and in most danger
when he feels the most self-confident.

He is most sinless when he feels the most sinful and
he is the most sinful when he feels the most sinless.

Yes, he is a strange fellow, this Christian! He has
the most when he is giving away the most and he
has less when he is keeping most. That is contrary
to the common sense of this world and that is why
we are considered a peculiar group of people—but
they don't know us!

When they try to figure it out, they cannot get
the true picture.

A man will say, "Well, I am willing to believe and
to go to church at Christmas and on Mother's Day,
but I cannot understand this strange fanatic who
seems to have the most when he is giving the most!"

He has never discerned God's principle of blessing the nine-tenths which the Christian has for
himself so that it is actually more than the ten-
tenths without any provision for God or His causes.

Here's a strange thing about the Christian
believer. He sometimes is doing the most when he
is not doing anything at all. Sometimes to get the
most done, God calls him to the side and says, "Sit
down there." Sometimes he goes the fastest when

he is standing still for in faith he may hear the whisper: "Stand still and see the salvation of the Lord!"

One of the important principles in the Christian's daily life is this: he is saved now and is ready to declare it with shining face and yet he expects to be saved later! He is continually looking for a salvation ready to be revealed in the last time.

We must look at this for someone is sure to say, "Make up your mind! Is he saved now or is he anticipating salvation?"

I don't have to make up my mind; I already know the answer!

Of course he is saved now; but he is also looking to be saved. He has life now, but he is also looking for the perfection to be revealed in the future plan of God. Now, you will not be able to explain that to your neighbor; he will just underscore the fact that it is part of your strange religious fanaticism. He does not understand that you are a true Christian!

Neither will the world ever understand our insistence that the Christian born on this earth is actually a citizen of another country which he has not yet visited. He is born on earth and yet he knows by faith that he is a citizen of heaven.

The Bible tells us plainly that while we are walking on this earth we are seated in the heavenly places in Christ Jesus our Lord—and that doesn't refer to the midweek prayer service! It means that by faith and by spiritual position in Christ we are seated in the heavenly places.

The believer knows that in himself he is nothing, but even while he is humbly telling the Lord that he is nothing, he knows very well that he is the apple of God's eye!

Some of our critics say: "You Christians talk about yourself and your relation to God as if you were God's very best."

I have a good answer to that, too! The very Christian who believes that he is the apple of God's eye is the same unselfish Christian who is giving sacrificially of his money, sending his sons and daughters or going himself to preach the gospel to the least and the last of the peoples of the earth!

Finally, the good Christian is in love with one he has never seen, and although he fears and reveres God, he is not afraid of God at all!

Many of the philosophers and poets phrased it all wrong when they tried to advise everyone on earth not to be afraid of God for He is a good fellow and all will be well!

The true Christian fears God with a trembling reverence and yet he is not afraid of God at all. He draws nigh to God with full assurance of faith and victory and yet at the same time is trembling with holy awe and fear.

To fear and yet draw near—this is the attitude of faith and love and yet the holy contradiction classifies him as a fanatic, too!

Today, as in all the centuries, true Christians are an enigma to the world, a thorn in the flesh of Adam, a puzzle to angels, the delight of God and a habitation of the Holy Spirit.

Our fellowship ought to take in all of the true children of God, regardless of who and where and what, if they are washed in the blood, born of the Spirit, walking with God the Father, begotten unto a living hope through the resurrection of Jesus Christ and rejoicing in the salvation to be revealed!

A Biblical Certainty: Christ's Second Coming!

". . . might be found unto praise and honour and glory at the appearing of Jesus Christ." 1 Peter 1:7

ARE YOU READY FOR the appearing of Jesus Christ or are you among those who are merely curious about His coming?

Let me warn you that many preachers and Bible teachers will answer to God some day for encouraging curious speculations about the return of Christ and failing to stress the necessity for "loving His appearing"!

The Bible does not approve of this modern curiosity that plays with the scriptures and which seeks only to impress credulous and gullible audiences with the "amazing" prophetic knowledge possessed by the brother who is preaching or teaching!

I cannot think of even one lonely passage in the New Testament which speaks of Christ's revelation, manifestation, appearing or coming that is not directly linked with moral conduct, faith and spiritual holiness.

The appearing of the Lord Jesus on this earth once more is not an event upon which we may curiously speculate—and when we do only that we sin. The prophetic teacher who engages in speculation to excite the curiosity of his hearers without providing them with a moral application is sinning even as he preaches.

There have been enough foolish formulas advanced about the return of Christ by those who were simply curious to cause many believers to give the matter no further thought or concern. But Peter said to expect "the appearing of Jesus Christ." Paul said there is a crown of righteousness laid up in glory for all those who love His appearing. John spoke of his hope of seeing Jesus and bluntly wrote: "Every man that hath this hope in him purifies himself, even as he is pure."

Peter linked the testing of our faith with the coming of the Lord when he wrote of ". . . the trial of your faith, being much more precious than of gold that perisheth, though it be tried with fire, might be found unto praise and honour and glory at the appearing of Jesus Christ."

Think of the *appearing* of Christ for here is a word which embodies an idea—an idea of such importance to Christian theology and Christian living that we dare not allow it to pass unregarded.

This word occurs frequently in the King James version of the Bible in reference to Jesus, and has various forms—such as *appear, appeared, appearing.* The original word from which our English was translated has about seven different forms in the Greek.

But in this usage, we are concerned only with the word *appearing* in its prophetic use. Unquestionably, that is how Peter used it in this passage. Among those seven forms in the Greek there are three particular words which all told may have these meanings: "manifest; shine upon; show;

become visible; a disclosure; a coming; a manifestation; a revelation."

I point this out because Peter also wrote that the Christians should "gird up the loins of their mind and be sober and hope to the end for the grace that is to be brought at the revelation of Jesus Christ."

Some of you might like to ask the translators a question, but they are all dead! The question might well be, "Why was the similar form of the original word translated in one case as the *appearing* and in the other as the *revelation* of Jesus Christ?"

There may have been some very fine shade of meaning which they felt must be expressed by one word and not the other, but we may take it as truth that the words are used interchangeably in the Bible.

We do not have to belabor this point, and actually some people are in trouble in the scriptures because they try too hard! The Lord never expected us to have to try so hard and to push on to the end of setting up a formula or a doctrinal exposition on the shades of meanings and forms of a single word.

Some of the cults do this. There are prophetic cults whose entire prophetic idea and scheme rest upon the words *appearing* or *revelation* or *manifestation* or *disclosure*. Their leaders write page after page and book after book upon the difference between one shade of meaning and another.

I can only say that I have learned this, having been around for a while—if that cult is forced to belabor a word in order to make a point, check it off and give it no more thought!

If that cult that is obviously a cult with no standing in the historic stream of Christianity and no standing in the long corridor of approved Christian truth tries to build on one word's shade of meanings, you can just shrug it off.

Why do I say that?

Because the Bible is the easiest book in the world to understand—one of the easiest for the spiritual mind but one of the hardest for the carnal mind! I will pay no mind to those who find it necessary to strain at a shade of meaning in order to prove they are right, particularly when that position can be shown to be contrary to all the belief of Christians back to the days of the apostles.

So that is why I say it is very easy to try too hard when we come to the reading and explanation of the scriptures. You can actually try too hard at almost anything, including baseball.

A certain baseball team, for instance, at the opening of the season tries so hard to win that the players get up-tight, become jittery and jumpy, and they make many errors.

After they find out that they do not really have a chance at the championship, they become relaxed and suddenly they are playing very good baseball. They didn't change any of the men around; they just relaxed and quit pressing so hard!

I think this matter of pushing and trying too hard may also be of concern to the young preacher getting up before his first audience. His muscles tighten, his throat gets dry, he may not remember his main points—(and I have been there myself)— pushing; like everything, trying too hard!

But we will never mature in the Kingdom of God by pushing and pressing because the Kingdom of God is not taken that way. Rather, you trust the Lord and watch Him do it!

The same thing is true concerning interpretation of the Bible. If we insist upon those fine shades of definitions, we may just be trying too hard and we may end up with the wrong point of view!

Perhaps we can illustrate it. Suppose a Chicago man visits his family in Des Moines and after getting back home, writes a number of letters in which he mentions the trip to Iowa.

In one letter he writes, "I visited Des Moines last week."

In a second, he says, "I went to Des Moines last week," and in a third, "I motored to Des Moines last week." In still another, he mentions, "I saw my brother in Des Moines last week."

He seals all of the letters, mails them, and thinks no more of it.

But what would happen if a group of interpreters were turned loose on those five letters after a thousand years, particularly if they were interpreters pushing too hard, insisting that there are no synonyms in the Bible and that the Kingdom of God and Kingdom of Heaven are never used synonymously?

They would make their notes and insist that the writer must have had something special in his mind when he wrote, "I went to Des Moines," and "I motored to Des Moines." Therefore, he must have made at least two trips or he would have said the same thing each time! And then, he must have had some reason for saying in one letter that he visited in Des Moines, which must mean that he stayed longer that time than when he merely saw his brother!

Actually, he was only there once, but in writing, he knew the English language well enough to be able to say it in four different ways.

So, when we come to Peter's use of this word *appearing*—just relax, for that is what it means! If a different form or word is used in another place and the same thing is being stated in a different way, it simply shows that the Holy Ghost has never been in a rut—even if interpreters are! The Spirit of God never has had to resort to cliches even though preachers often seem to specialize in them!

The appearing of Jesus Christ may mean His manifestation. It may mean a shining forth, a showing, a disclosure. Yes, it may mean His coming, the revelation of Jesus Christ!

The question that must actually be answered for most people is: "Where will this appearing or coming or disclosure or revelation take place?"

Those to whom Peter wrote concerning the appearing of Christ were Christian men and women on this earth. There is no way that this can possibly be spiritualized—the scene cannot be transferred to heaven.

Peter was writing to Christians on this earth, to the saints scattered abroad by trial and persecution. He was encouraging them to endure affliction and to trust God in their sufferings, so their faith may be found of more worth than gold at the appearing of Jesus Christ!

Common sense will tell us that this appearing could only be on the earth because he was writing to people on this earth. He was not writing to angels in any heavenly sphere. He was not saying it to Gabriel but to people living on this earth.

Now, Peter also spoke of this as an event to happen in the future, that is, the future from the time in which Peter wrote 19 centuries ago. Writing in the year 65 A.D., Peter placed the appearing of Christ some time in the future after 65 A.D.

We are sure, then, that Peter was not referring to the appearance of Jesus at the Jordan river when John baptized Him, for that had already taken place 30 years before.

Jesus had also appeared in Jerusalem, walking among the people, talking to the Pharisees and elders, the rabbis and the common people, but that had also taken place 30 years before. He had suddenly appeared in the temple, just when times were good and people were coming from everywhere with money to have it exchanged in order to buy cattle or doves for sacrifice. Using only a rope, He drove the cattle and the money changers from the temple. He appeared on the Mount of Transfiguration and after His resurrection appeared to the disciples. He had made many appearances. He was there in bodily manifestation, and He did things that could be identified. He was there as a man among men. But Peter said, "He is yet to appear" for the other appearances were all 30 years in the past.

Peter was saying: "I want you to get ready in order that the trial of your faith, your afflictions, your obedience, your cross-bearing may mean honor and glory at the appearing of Jesus Christ"—the appearing in the future!

There is no reputable testimony anywhere that Jesus Christ has appeared since the events when He appeared to put away sin through the sacrifice of Himself.

Actually we haven't found anyone that says Christ appeared to him in person, except some poor fanatic who usually dies later in the mental institution.

Many new cults have arisen; men have walked through the streets saying, "I am Christ." The psychiatrists have written reams and reams of case histories of men who insisted that they were Jesus Christ.

But our Lord Jesus Christ has not yet appeared the second time, for if He had, it would have been consistent with the meaning of the word as it was commonly used in the New Testament. He would have to appear as He appeared in the temple, as He appeared by the Jordan or on the Mount of Transfiguration. It would have to be as He once appeared to His disciples after the resurrection—in visible, human manifestation, having dimension so He could be identified by the human eye and ear and touch.

If the word *appearing* is going to mean what it universally means, the appearing of Jesus Christ has to be very much the same as His appearing on the earth the first time, nearly 2,000 years ago.

When He came the first time, He walked among men. He took babies in His arms. He healed the sick and the afflicted and the lame. He blessed people, ate with them and walked among them, and the scriptures tell us that when He appears again He will appear in the same manner. He will be a man again, though a glorified man! He will be a man who can be identified, the same Jesus as He went away.

We must also speak here of the testimonies of Christian saints through the years—if Christ being known to us in spiritual life and understanding and experience.

There is a certain sense in which everyone who has a pure heart "looks upon" God.

There are bound to be those who will say, "Jesus is so real to me that I have seen Him!"

I know what you mean and I thank God for it—that God has illuminated the eyes of your spiritual understanding—and you have seen Him in that sense. "Blessed are the pure in heart, for they shall see God."

I believe that it is entirely possible for eyes of our faith, the understanding of our spirit, to be so illuminated that we can gaze upon our Lord—perhaps veiled, perhaps not as clearly as in that day to come, but the eyes of our heart see Him!

So, Christ does appear to people in that context. He appears when we pray and we can sense His presence. But that is not what Peter meant in respect to his second appearing upon the earth. Peter's language of that event calls for a shining forth, a revelation, a sudden coming, a visible appearance!

Peter meant the same kind of appearance that the newspapers noted in the appearance of the president of the United States in Chicago. He meant the same kind of appearance which the newspapers noted when the young sergeant appeared suddenly to the delight of his family after having been away for more than two years. There has not been any appearance of Jesus like that since He appeared to put away sins by the sacrifice of Himself!

We can sum this up and say that there is to be an appearance—in person, on earth, according to Peter—to believing persons later than Peter's time. That appearing has not yet occurred and Peter's words are still valid.

We may, therefore, expect Jesus Christ again to appear on earth to living persons as He first appeared.

My brethren, I believe that that is the gist of the Bible teaching on the second coming—we may expect an appearing! In Peter's day the Lord had not yet returned, but they were expecting Him. Peter said He would appear.

When our Lord had not yet come in the flesh, some were expecting Him. They said, "He will appear," for God had told the woman and the serpent, and Abraham and all the prophets, that Jesus Christ would appear to put away sin by the sacrifice of Himself!

Then one day He appeared!

He was not an apparition. He was not a ghost. It was not what some of the old madames with their spooky costumes would call a materialization. No one ever said that Jesus Christ would materialize, it was the prophecy that He would appear and that is quite different!

The Bible never talks about materialization. According to the promise of His return, Jesus Christ is not going to materialize, He is going to appear! You can throw out the word *materialize;* it is a weird word stolen and employed by the spiritists and devil cults. To materialize, a ghost today would have to put on fleshly garments and still walk among us tomorrow. To become material when you are not material, that is to materialize!

There continues to be a lot of curiosity about such matters, and I find that the curiosity that once killed the famous cat has hurt a lot of Christians. There is a certain "eeriness" about them—not spirituality. Eeriness!! There are Christians who seem to be ghost-conscious and they can move right into the middle of a supernatural thing and feel right at home—right at home with the mediums, the funny wizards and telepathists and all the rest.

Personally, I don't feel at home with them at all. I cannot feel at home in the realm of the eery and the uncanny.

The Bible calls it peeping and muttering. I do not accept the peepers and mutterers and I will never feel at home among them! I recognize, however, that there is a certain type of mentality that does, and when such a person gets converted, if he does not ask God to sanctify his mind, he will carry this thing right into the church!

In cases where this has happened, their theology consists of a lot of theological peeping and muttering.

Let me mention in this regard my dear old grandmother, who did not know much about the Bible, but spent quite a bit of time with her dream book.

Her dream book was dog-eared and thumb-marked because Grandma would not drink her coffee in the morning until she had consulted the dream book to check up on her dreams.

I know there are people who do not dream very much, but Grandma was a dreamer. She must have had some dreams every night, because she would always open that book when she got up in the morning.

Her dream book had an alphabetical index, and for illustration, we will start at *A* for Apple. If she had dreamed about apples, the book would tell her what it signified. *B* for Beets, *C* for your Country, and so on down the line to *Z* for Zebra. She had a glossary that told her what she might expect on the basis of what she had dreamed.

May I comment to you that that is a dreadful way to live!

No wonder Grandma was a hustler, for she must have been miserable and worried most of the time, thinking about the meaning of her dreams and the results prophesied in that book!

Actually, Grandma was a sharp little woman and she taught me nearly everything I learned until I was about 15 years old. But this dream book thing was one of her eccentricities.

I don't know whether she got it out of a similar book, but Grandma had a real thing in her mind about barking dogs.

More than once she told me that if a dog barked under our window, someone would die, sure enough!

At this point in my life I can only comment that if I had died every time a dog barked under my window, I would have been the best customer the undertakers of this country had ever seen! It seems that dogs delight in barking under my window and mosquitoes delight to come into my room, and if there is a fly in the parsonage it will head directly for me!

I have some kind of magnetic attraction for such things and if it had meant something in the realm of the peepers and mutterers, I would have been in a strait jacket and padded cell a long time ago.

I know these curious tenets do not mean a thing and I thank God for a simple, skeptical mind that has kept me from going through my time on earth worrying about such things.

Being of this disposition, I have my own feelings about the prophetic teacher who begins to unroll his chart to impress people with his ideas and theories! When he starts that, I begin to look for the exit because he is trying too hard.

He is pushing too hard, like the man who is trying to understand the Sistine Madonna by getting a microscope and examining the toe of the Virgin. You cannot understand or appreciate the beauty of the Sistine Madonna by examining a microscopic portion of it; you have got to get back and give it geography!

It is the same when you come to the scriptures—you can be led into a blind alley by curiosity about some minor point of emphasis and fail to see the great, broad outlines of truth concerning the spiritual impact which the hope of His coming should have in our daily living!

The Word of God was never given just to make us curious about our Lord's return to earth, but to strengthen us in faith and spiritual holiness and moral conduct!

When Paul wrote to Timothy in his second letter, we find some of the dearest and most gracious words of the entire Bible:

"I charge thee therefore before God, and the Lord Jesus Christ, who shall judge the quick and the dead at his appearing . . . preach the word; be instant in season, out of season; reprove, rebuke, exhort with all longsuffering and doctrine. For the time will come when they will not endure sound doctrine."

Here the apostle cautions that our Lord Jesus Christ will judge the quick and the dead at His appearing, and then he links that appearing and judgment with the earnest exhortation that Timothy must preach the Word, being instant in season and out of season.

A bit later, Paul writes more about events to happen when Jesus Christ appears.

He wrote: "I have fought a good fight, I have finished my course, I have kept the faith: Henceforth there is laid up for me a crown of righteousness, which the Lord, the righteous judge, shall give me at that day: and not to me only, but unto all them also that love his appearing."

It is plainly stated, brethren: those who love the appearing of Jesus Christ are those who shall also receive a crown.

There are some who would like to open this up: "Doesn't it really mean anyone who believes in the pre-millennial position will receive the crown of righteousness?"

I say no! It means that those who are found loving the appearing of Jesus will receive the crown of righteousness! It is questionable to my mind whether some who hold a pre-millennial position and can argue for it can be included with those whose spirit of humility and consecration and hunger for God is quietly discernible in their love and expectation of the soon coming of their Saviour!

I fear that we have gone to seed on this whole matter of His return. Why is it that such a small proportion of Christian ministers ever feel the necessity to preach a sermon on the truth of His second coming? Why should pastors depend in this matter upon those who travel around the country with their colored charts and their object lessons and their curious interpretations of Bible prophecy?

Should we not dare to believe what the Apostle John wrote, that "we shall be like him because we shall see him as he is"?

Beloved, we are the sons of God now, for our faith is in the Son of God, Jesus Christ! We believe in Him and we rest upon Him, and yet it doth not yet appear what we shall be; but we know that when He shall appear, when He shall be disclosed, we shall be like Him, for we shall see Him as He is!

Then, John says bluntly and clearly: "Every man that hath this hope in him purifies himself, even as he is pure." Everybody! Everyone, he says! He singularizes it. Everyone that hath this hope in him purifies himself as He is pure!

Those who are expecting the Lord Jesus Christ to come and who look for that coming moment by moment and who long for that coming will be busy purifying themselves. They will not be indulging in curious speculations—they will be in preparation, purifying themselves!

It may be helpful to use an illustration here.

A wedding is about to take place and the bride is getting dressed. Her mother is nervous and there are other relatives and helpers who are trying to make sure that the bride is dressed just right!

Why all this helpful interest and concern?

Well, the bride and those around her know that she is about to go out to meet the groom, and everything must be perfectly in order. She even walks cautiously so that nothing gets out of place in dress and veil. She is preparing, for she awaits in loving anticipation and expectation the meeting with this man at the altar.

Now John says, through the Holy Ghost, that he that hath this hope in him purifies and prepares himself. How? Even as He is pure!

The bride wants to be dressed worthy of the bridegroom, and so it is with the groom, as well!

Should not the church of Jesus Christ be dressed worthy of her bridegroom, even as He is dressed? Pure—even as He is pure?

We are assured that the appearing of Jesus Christ will take place. It will take place in His time. There are many who believe that it can take place soon—that there is not anything which must yet be done in this earth to make possible His coming.

It will be the greatest event in the history of the world, barring His first coming and the events of His death and resurrection.

We may well say that the next greatest event in the history of the world will be "the appearing of Jesus Christ: whom having not seen, we love; in whom, though now we see him not, yet believing, we rejoice with joy unspeakable and full of glory!"

The world will not know it, but he that hath this hope in him will know it for he has, purified himself even as Christ is pure!

Book 6

*Twelve Messages on
Well-Known and
Favorite Bible Texts*

Contents

Preface

Those who were friends and associates of Dr. A. W. Tozer during his lifetime knew of his very strong convictions against any kind of false profession or "phony" attitudes in the Christian life and ministry.

The reader of these sermons will note in several chapters the manner in which Dr. Tozer was willing to bare his own soul in affirmation of Christian honesty, candor and transparency among ministers and laymen alike.

In the chapter, "What Is It Costing You to Be a Christian?", Dr. Tozer asked his congregation to pray for him and the integrity of his ministry:

> "Pray that I will not just come to a wearied end—
> an exhausted, tired, old preacher, interested only
> in hunting a place to roost. Pray that I will let my
> Christian standards cost me something right down
> to the last gasp!"

He never lost that insistent spirit on behalf of genuineness and truth. Just a few weeks before his unexpected death in 1963, Dr. Tozer was asked by an official of the National Association of Evangelicals to address the annual convention of the NAE in Buffalo, New York.

Because he had not been a proponent of Christian and Missionary Alliance membership in the NAE, Dr. Tozer asked frankly: "Do you think I have something to contribute to your meeting—or are you just trying to 'butter' me up?"

Assured of the integrity of the invitation, Dr. Tozer consented and gave a memorable address on Christian commitment to the NAE convention delegates. It was his last public address and presentation of the claims of Christ outside of his own pulpit prior to his death in May 1963.

The Publisher

Are There Shortcuts to the Beauty of Holiness?

"Awake, O north wind; and come, thou south; blow upon my garden, that the spices thereof may flow out. Let my beloved come into his garden, and eat his pleasant fruits." Song of Solomon 4:16

I WOULD LIKE TO BE able to ask every Christian in the world this question: "Are you really interested in God's producing in you the beautiful fruits and fragrances of the Holy Ghost?"

For every affirmative answer, I would quickly recommend:

Then look to your own willingness to be regular in the habits of a holy life—for flowers and fruit do not grow in thin air! They grow and come up out of a root and "the root of the righteous yieldeth fruit."

For every beautiful garden that you see, whose fragrance comes out to welcome you, has its roots down into the hard earth. The beautiful flowers and blooms will grow and appear and flourish only when there are deep roots and strong stalks. If you take the roots away, the blossom and flower will endure perhaps one day. The sun will scorch them and they will be gone.

Now, we Christians, for the most part, reserve most of our interest for the fruit and the spice and the beauty of the garden. Most of us go to church, I think, for the same simple reason that a child climbs into its mother's arms after a long day at play, with many falls and bumps and frights and disappointments. The child wants consolation.

It appears that most people go to church for consolation. In fact, we have now fallen upon times when religion is mostly for consolation. We are now in the grip of the cult of peace—peace of mind, peace of heart, peace of soul, and we want to relax and have the great God Almighty pat our heads and comfort us. This has become religion.

This, along with one other item: the threat that if you don't be good the nuclear bomb will wipe out your modern civilization!

These seem to be the only two motives that remain in the wide world for religion. If you are not good, they warn, civilization will fall apart and the bomb will get us all, and if you do not come to the Lord, you will never have peace!

So, between fear and the desire to be patted and chucked under the chin and cuddled, the professing Christian staggers along his way.

My brethren, there is something better than this, something that has roots.

According to my Bible, there should be a people of God—they do not all have to belong to one church—but there should be a people called out by the Lord God and subjected to a spiritual experience given by God. Then they are to learn to walk in the way of the Truth and the way of the scriptures, producing the righteous fruit of the child of God whatever world conditions may be.

They know that those who destroy the body are not important—only those who destroy the soul. You can disintegrate a man, a saint of God, with a bomb and he is in heaven immediately with his Lord. The enemies of God have slain many Christians and sent them off quickly to be with God. They cast their bodies aside as unclean things, but the souls of those men and women were immediately with the Lord.

Then there is the matter of constant consolation and peace—the promise of always feeling relaxed and at rest and enjoying ourselves inwardly.

This, I say, has been held up as being quite the proper goal to be sought in the evil hour in which we live. We forget that our Lord was a man of sorrow and acquainted with grief. We forget the arrows of grief and pain which went through the heart of Jesus' mother, Mary. We forget that all of the apostles except John died a martyr's death. We forget that there were 13 million Christians slain during the first two generations of the Christian era. We forget that they languished in prison, that they were starved, were thrown over cliffs, were fed to the lions, were drowned, that they were sewn in sacks and thrown into the ocean.

Yes, we want to forget that most of God's wonderful people in the early days of the church did not have peace of mind. They did not seek it. They knew that a soldier does not go to the battlefield to relax— he goes to fight. They accepted their position on earth as soldiers in the army of God, fighting along with the Lord Jesus Christ in the terrible war against iniquity and sin. It was not a war against people but against sin and iniquity and the devil!

There was much distress, many heartaches, painful bruises, flowing tears, much loss and many deaths.

But there is something better than being comfortable, and the followers of Christ ought to find it out—the poor, soft, overstuffed Christians of our time ought to find it out! There is something better than being comfortable!

We Protestants have forgotten altogether that there is such a thing as discipline and suffering. We live within an economy that enables us to have plenty. We live under a political system that enables us to believe anything we want or nothing at all and still not be in trouble with the law. The result is that we have concocted a religion of sweet wine which we drink eagerly in the hope that we can walk around in a state of pleasant intoxication.

Now is that what God really wants to do for men and women?

No. God wants to bring us the fruit of the Spirit—love, joy, peace, longsuffering, gentleness, goodness, faith, meekness and temperance. The apostle Paul made it very plain in his language to the Ephesians that God wants to do something within every one of us that will cause us to love everybody, letting all bitterness and wrath and clamour and evil speaking be put away from among us, assuring that we will be kind to one another, tenderhearted, forgiving one another, even as God has, for Christ's sake, forgiven us.

That is what God wants to do: to bring out the likeness of Christ in the heart and life of the redeemed man. That is the purpose of God—not to make him happy, although in that condition he is likely to be happy. Not to make his civilization safe, although if there are enough people like that in the world, civilization has a better chance to survive.

So, this is our difficulty, brethren. We try to arrive at the fruits of Christianity by a shortcut. Of course, everybody wants peace and joy and love, goodness and gentleness and faithfulness. Everybody wants to be known as being spiritual, close to God, and walking in the Truth.

So, this is the answer. Every flower and every fruit has a stalk and every stalk has a root, and long before there is any bloom there must be a careful tending of the root and the stalk. This is where the misunderstanding lies—we think that we get the flower and the fragrance and the fruit by some kind of magic, instead of by cultivation.

There is something better than being comfortable and lazy and relaxed, and Paul is good authority for it: "Be ye therefore followers of God, as dear children; and walk in love, as Christ also hath loved us, and hath given himself for us an offering and a sacrifice to God for a sweetsmelling savour." This is the likeness of Christ in the human heart and life—and our neighbors are waiting to see Him in our lives!

Now, I want to be practical and down-to-earth, and mention a few of the things which I consider to be necessary roots of true Christian living, out of which the fruits and the flowers of deep spirituality appear.

I am thinking first of such necessary spiritual roots as loyalty and faithfulness to God and to His church, the body of Christ on this earth.

Many people boast of their loyalty to their own denomination, but I refer to something greater and more basic than that. I refer to a loyal and prayerful identification with the very cause and truth of

Jesus Christ as Lord to the point that we are willing to sacrifice for it. Most Christian churches are already showing signs of a great breakdown in loyalty in these modern times. Every church must have its few who are completely loyal to the implications of Jesus Christ actually being Saviour and Lord and are willing to suffer, if need be, for their love and faith.

Loyalty is surely interwoven with faithfulness, and we do well to remember that Jesus promised His disciples that God would reward us for our faithfulness. In a parable of the kingdom of heaven, Jesus taught that the master, upon his return from the far country, said to his faithful servants, "Well done . . . enter thou into the joy of thy lord."

I know that faithfulness is not a very dramatic subject and there are many among us in the Christian faith who would like to do something with more dash and more flair than just being faithful. Even in our Christian circles, publicity is considered a great and necessary thing, so we are prone to want to do something that will be recognized, and perhaps get our picture in the paper. Thank God for the loyal and faithful Christians who have only one recognition in mind, and that is to hear their Lord say in that Great Day: "Well done . . . enter into the joy of thy Lord."

It is a plain truth that goodness and faithfulness are at the root of much of the consistent fruit-bearing among the witnessing children of God!

In God's Word, the Lord has always placed a great premium on the necessity of faithfulness in those who love Him and serve Him.

Noah was faithful in his day. If old Noah had been a baseball fan or had taken an early retirement or had placed some other interest in his life above God's work, there would have been no ark, no seed preserved and no human race.

Abraham was faithful in his day. If, in his wanderings, Abraham had struck uranium or gold and had given up the idea of going down to Palestine and establishing a people there from whom Jesus Christ would come, what would have happened to God's great plan? If Abraham had turned aside and built himself a little city, making himself mayor and living on the fat of the land, where would we be today?

Moses was faithful in his day. The scriptures leave no doubt about the faithful spirit and ministrations of Moses as God's man for his day and time—"Choosing rather to suffer affliction with the people of God, than to enjoy the pleasures of sin for a season; esteeming the reproach of Christ greater riches than the treasures in Egypt: for he had respect unto the recompence of the reward."

What do we need to say about the faithfulness of our Saviour, Jesus Christ? The world threatened Him all around. The devil was there with his lies and his temptations, offering Jesus the world if He would not go to the cross. But Christ was faithful to His Father and to us. Should we not be faithful to Him? Faithfulness is a wonderful, productive root and out of it comes much fruit.

When we look to our spiritual roots, we dare not dismiss the emphasis of the Word of God on plain, downright honesty and God-ordained goodness in our daily lives.

Honesty that can be trusted and respected is a very fragrant flower in the life of the Christian. Honesty has never yet grown in a vacuum—it is a blossom and a fragrance that grows and develops with spiritual care and nurture. There is a great deal of carelessness about the truth even among Christian believers. Some are surely guilty of stretching the truth about certain things even when they give their Christian testimony. Preachers and evangelists have been known to have exaggerated the numbers and the results of their Christian assemblies.

We joke about such things and forgive the brethren on the basis that their exaggeration was really "evangelistically speaking." But on behalf of God-honoring honesty in our daily lives, it needs to be said that any lie is of its father, the devil, whether it is told in a church service or anywhere else.

God's work does not need pious lies to support it. Rather we ought to follow the spirit of the old saying, "Tell the truth and shame the devil!" In our Christian fellowship, we should be known for being perfectly frank and wholly honest, for honesty has a good root that will also produce other sterling Christian virtues.

Do you know that one of the things that marked the lives of the original Quakers was their honest handling of the truth? They would not lie and they would not stretch the truth. They would not steal and they would not use flattering words. Someone in history wrote about the lives of the Quakers and commented that they "astonished the Christian world by insisting upon acting like Christians." In England they were often kicked around and some languished in jail because they insisted on honoring only God and refused to bow down to people who did not deserve it. In the midst of professing Christians who generally acted like the world, the honest, God-honoring Quakers were considered queer because they sought to live as Christians should.

Many people in our day seem to dream of becoming great while there are far too few who spend any time in concern about being good. The Bible tells us about many good men and few of them would be considered great men. One of them was Jabez, a good man in the Old Testament who is mentioned in only three verses. Saul and Ahab came to places of leadership, and while they were considered great and important men of their times, they were not good men.

The Bible makes it plain to us that our Lord always placed the emphasis upon goodness, rather than upon greatness. Inherently, man does not have a good nature, and that is why Jesus Christ came to this earth and wrought the plan of salvation that makes bad men good. Christ died to wipe away our past sins, to give us new birth, to write our names in the Book of Life, to introduce us to the Father in eternal life.

When we say that Christ died to make us good, we are not being liberal in theology—we are being scriptural. What more can you say about any man than the tribute that he was a good man and full of the Holy Ghost?

Now, let me return to the root of this whole matter—are we Christians willing to be regular in the habits of a holy life, thus learning from the

Holy Spirit how to be dependable and faithful, unselfish and Christlike?

The crops in the fields are regular, and the birds and the animals have a regularity of life. We see it in the rising and the setting of the sun, and in the regularity of the phases of the moon.

The Old Testament revelation itself was built around regularity. It is said of the old man of God that he went into the temple of God in the order of his course and everything in the temple was laid out in order.

God has ordained, as well, that order and regularity may be of immense value to the Christian life.

You should learn to be regular in your prayer life, in your giving to God and His work, and in your church attendance.

But there are too many in the church who say, "I believe in Christ and I have had a spiritual experience and I have the right doctrine"—and then after that go to pieces and become whimsical, and pray according to impulse and give according to the way they feel at the moment, attend church when the weather is good, and do what they do with whimsical irregularity. No wonder they do not carry the sweet fragrance of the Spirit when they come to worship.

It is because people have neglected the root, and the flowers have died. The root of regularity has been forgotten, with the result that when the root is gone, the flowers die shortly thereafter.

But I can hear someone protest, saying, "I wanted to get into the Christian life, the spiritual faith, in order that I might be freed from necessity and from a law of having to do things regularly."

Well, you have missed it, my brother! You might as well close your Bible and walk out because you are in the wrong church and the wrong pew and the wrong dispensation! God would have His people learn regular holy habits and follow them right along day by day.

He doesn't ask us to become slaves to habits, but He does insist that our holy habits of life should become servants of His grace and glory.

Now, of course, this kind of order and regularity in our Christian lives must be tied in with the reality of dependability.

Nature again is the great example of dependability. If you plant corn, you will reap corn. Plant barley and you get barley, not wheat or corn. Set a hen on hens' eggs and you will get chickens, not guinea hens. So with everything after its kind.

Everything is dependable in nature—except man, and even in human society there is a certain amount of dependability.

If your car fails you a few times, you get rid of it, for you need a dependable car. You women know that your refrigerator and freezer must foe dependable or the food will spoil unknown to you.

Our monetary system must be dependable, or there would be chaos. What would happen if the dollar was worth a dollar in Chicago, but worth only 75 cents in Milwaukee, 32 cents in St. Louis and in Detroit they wouldn't take it at all?

So, in society we have to know dependability, with the mail and with the milkman and with the schools. You have to be able to trust somebody. The sad thing about it in our human society is that people, as a rule, are trusted and dependable because they get something out of it.

The milkman doesn't come around every morning just because he is a nice fellow; he comes because he is getting paid for it. The mailman doesn't deliver the mail just because he is interested in you and hopes you get a card from Aunt Mabel; he's paid for doing it. The people who make your car build dependability into it because they want you to buy another one, which you won't do if it proves undependable.

How sad to think that it is only at the altar of God that men and women can't be depended upon. Why is it that it is so difficult to find people *in* the sanctuary who can be depended upon?

The root of dependability is dead in most churches, except for a faithful few, and these few have to take abuse from the unfaithful, undependable ones. The faithful few can always be depended upon and are always in evidence, so they are criticized for wanting to run the show.

Now, I want to ask you a question, and it is not something new and original. Think about your religious life, your holy habits, your church attendance, your giving to the Lord's work, your pattern of dependability during the past 12 months.

Now, be honest with yourselves, and ask an answer of your own heart: "If everyone in this church had been exactly as dependable as I am, where would our church be today?"

That's a question we ought to ask on our knees with tears and with sorrow, praying that God will help us to be dependable. When you are asked to do something, even if it is something simple, do it. It seems that so many of us only want to do the dramatic things—no one wants to be known as being dependable.

If you are waiting until you can do something with a flourish and a flair, something big and grand in the church of God, the chances are that you never will, and if you do, it will simply be a flash in the pan, a rainbow without any meaning, having no final stability!

Why doesn't anyone want to be dependable in the work of Christ?

Brethren, remember that sweet flowers are beautiful to look at and very fragrant to smell, but someone has to be out there on his knees in the dirt, long before there are any blossoms—fertilizing and digging, and going back and doing it again, watching the weather and watering when it gets too dry, and looking after that root.

One of the roots of the Christian life is dependability, and you cannot have spirituality without dependability any more than you can have a begonia without a begonia stalk.

Now, this is probably the place to consider punctuality in the work of God, also.

Isn't it strange that the very fault that would wreck a business, sink a ship, ruin a railroad, is tolerated at the very altar of God?

Why is it that in the church of God so few are concerned about lack of punctuality? The carelessness they show about the work of God would wreck a business or upset the economy, or if done in our bodies would ruin our health.

Now, punctuality is a beautiful thing, but Sunday school teachers don't realize it. Many a

Sunday school superintendent has found his hair turning gray because of his worries about getting teachers who will be on time on Sunday morning. Everything we do for God should be done with beautiful precision.

We have a sacred duty. In church and Sunday school, we have in our hands the teaching of immortal souls. We have character to mold and souls to win and the work of God to do.

I have been around a long time and I am convinced that generally people are not spiritual at all if they are not punctual. If they are so lacking in self-discipline and so selfish and so inconsiderate of others and their time that they will not be punctual in the service of God and His church, they are fooling nobody! I repeat it again—if you are not punctual, you are not spiritual!

Everyone can be excused for the emergencies of life—there are accidents that will at times keep any of us from meeting our appointments. But I am trying to show my concern about those who practice the art of not being punctual until it has become a habit in their life.

There isn't anyone important enough to justify that kind of behavior, and anybody that is not punctual, habitually, is guilty of deception and falsehood. He says he will be there—then he fails to appear!

Punctuality is a beautiful thing. You can't have a rose without a rose bush, and punctuality is the bush on which the rose grows!

So, love and faith, joy and peace may bloom in the heart of the Christian. Beautiful is the Christian character and the sweet smile of the holy man or woman, but that holy life is not by accident nor by coddling. Rather it comes by the bearing of strong burdens, by putting the yoke on his own neck and saying, "For Christ's sake, who bore the cross for me, I will take this self-imposed yoke."

Therefore, let us settle for being good, spiritual people—and let those be great who can! Let us seek first that we might be good, remembering that goodness grows from the roots of obedience, prayer, Bible reading, and surrender. Amen!

Why Do Men Refuse
the Streams of Mercy?

". . . this people refuseth the waters of Shiloah that go softly . . ." Isaiah 8:6

THERE ARE, IN THE Bible, many references where God has used the precious, reviving and life-sustaining qualities of streams of water to give us a true and adequate figure of the gracious, life-giving salvation which He offers all mankind.

He has promised, "I will give you streams of living water."

You will find these scriptural allusions to water and refreshment and cleansing and fruit-bearing in figures of speech, in God's gracious invitations, some spoken in poetic terms.

In the very last chapter of the Bible—in Revelation—God tells us that the Spirit and the bride: say "Come," adding that whosoever will may come and "take of the water of life freely."

The historical reference in this text in Isaiah is to the quietly-flowing waters of Shiloah, a stream sometimes wrongly called Siloam.

Shiloah is said to have been the only perennial stream in the city of Jerusalem, the only one that did not dry up seasonally. It seems to me that it is exquisitely named. God Himself must have named it, because this Shiloah means tranquility and rest. The waters of Shiloah are the waters of tranquility, the peaceful waters that go softly.

The Bible repeats important things often and it is certainly repetitive in making plain that water is one of man's necessary and most valuable assets. It is old and familiar truth that three-fourths of the world's surface is covered with water and that the composition of the human body is 70 per cent water. There is a large water content in our food, as well. Without water there could be no births, no growth, no digestion, no cleansing, no plants, no animals, no atmosphere. Take away water from the face of the earth and this globe we now call our familiar earth would be little more than a parched and ghastly death's head flying endlessly and meaninglessly through space.

But, even above and beyond the scientific interest is the dependence of every farmer and every gardener upon the availability of water.

I recall that when I was a boy I thought the heavy snowfall which covered the fields would smother and freeze the winter wheat and rye, but my father would actually express his thanks, to no one in particular, for the heavy snow cover on the fields. He knew that a good spring crop depended largely upon the heavy snow that kept the ground warm and that the slow melting of the snow in the early spring provided the right kind of moisture.

In some areas of our country, the productivity of the arid land is completely dependent upon the availability of water for irrigation. Farmers everywhere know that they will experience futility and emptiness if there is no water. The crops and fruits and vegetables will never come to fruition without the necessary supply of water. The man tending his herds of animals is in the same situation—for unless he has a place for his cattle to water he cannot use the grazing grounds.

The traveler, too, knows what it would mean to go into the desert without a supply of water and without a guide. It means to invite death. The simplest way to commit suicide, although not the most painless, would be to walk out across the Sahara or any of the other great deserts of the world without a guide and without sufficient water.

Oh, the precious nature of water—as precious as our blood, of which it is a large part. If there is no water, as in the case of fatal necessity on the desert, there will be a certain and speechless death. This is a strange fact—no one dies crying for water. As he nears death, the poor victim has such swollen tongue and dryness of mouth and cracking of lips that it is impossible to form any words. So, without water, it is not just death but a speechless death—a death that cannot even cry!

When the Lord keeps referring in the scriptures to the precious and necessary streams of living water, He is trying to bring attention and emphasis to the great spiritual needs of the inner man. He is continually hopeful that men and women will heed His truth and admonitions, learning that if streams of water are so vitally important to the well-being and health and welfare of the outer and physical man, how much more should a person be responsive to God's offer of the streams of spiritual life for the immortal part of his being, the soul?

Actually, we find a great preoccupation today with man's physical needs throughout the world. I suppose there never has been a time in the history of the world when there was more interest in the human body than there is today. You can flip open any magazine or periodical and you will find many articles and a great deal of advice about caring for your body, but only occasionally will you find any help for your soul or spirit.

Actually, many people are getting rich, cashing in on our great love for our physical bodies. I must confess that when I read about the many ways in which the human body is groomed and fed and pampered I think about the publicity for Julius the First, a young Angus bull featured in the livestock shows.

You may not believe it, but the owners or handlers of Julius the First brush his teeth every day. They curl the hair on his forehead just like a young fellow brushing himself before he takes off to see his girl. Julius is just an Angus bull, but they brush him and groom him and watch his weight in the hope that he will win the top prizes in the show ring.

What a picture of our humanity! Men and women are brushed and groomed and massaged, intent upon diets and vitamins, completely preoccupied with the outer man, the physical body. The irony of it all is expressed in the fact that in the livestock auction, Julius the First will bring a price of about $16,000—and you know you could not begin to get anything like that for your human body, even in youth, with strength and energy and beauty at their maximum!

Oh, it is the inner man that really matters, for the outward man must perish and go back to the elements from which it was taken, but the inner man lives on and on after the physical body drops away in death.

That body of yours, to which you give so much thought and care, is only the outer tabernacle. The apostle Paul told us about the importance of the inner man and he said he was willing to let the outer man die a little at a time in order that the inner man might be renewed. Throughout the Bible, God emphasizes the value and worth of the inner man, although certainly not to the exclusion of His concern for our physical bodies. We do well to remember the scriptural balance, for the Bible does say that "the Lord is for the body." Certainly, we are putting the emphasis in the wrong place if we become too physical in our outlook, insisting that the most important concern is for the body.

Well, we know for certain that God is much more concerned with the inner man than with man's outer tabernacle, so He gives us water—the sweet waters, the soft-flowing waters of Shiloah. These are streams of tranquility and peace and He gives them to the inner man.

What a gracious truth—that there is an inner and spiritual man!

Jacob once said, "I go down to Sheol, mourning for my son." Yet, when Jacob died and was buried, they could tell you where his body was. Jacob did not say, "My body will go down." When he said, "I will go down," he was referring to the inner man, that part of him that was the soul, the real Jacob.

On the cross Jesus cried out, "Father, into Thy hands I commit my spirit." They laid His body in the grave and it was there three days, but His inner man, the spirit, was committed unto the Father.

Judas, it is said, went unto his own place—yet we know what happened to his body. It was buried in a field, but Judas himself went unto his own place. There was a Judas, an inner man apart from the body. There was a Jacob apart from the body. There was a Jesus apart from the body.

Abraham's body had been lying in the cave of Machpelah with the dust of centuries upon it when the rich man, Dives, lifted up the eyes of the inner man after his own death and discerned the beggar, Lazarus, resting on Abraham's bosom. It was the real Abraham he discerned—the immortal inner man—there in paradise and it was the real Lazarus who had gone to be with Abraham.

Brothers and sisters, there is a real sense in which we will never know each other until we shuck off this old earthly tabernacle of deception. There is a sense in which our bodies actually veil us from one another. We are uncertain. We shake a hand and look at a face. The influence of that hand or face is a physical thing—and the real you, the inner man, is deeper than that, and beyond and past all of that.

What did it actually mean for mankind when Jesus Christ came into our world?

No one should think for even one second that He came just to bring a state of peace between nations, or that He came merely to give prosperity so we would all have richer food to eat, softer beds in which to sleep and finer homes in which to live!

God's Word leaves no doubt about it—Jesus came in order that our spirits might prosper! He came that our inner man, the eternal and undying part of us, might prosper! He died to open a fountain of such gracious nature that to partake and drink means a spiritual transformation, never to hunger and thirst again for temporal and passing things.

Now, what is this water, this softly-flowing stream of peace and tranquility and rest? God wants us to be sure—either we know or we do not know!

If this is not a reality, it is simply poetry with which I am regaling you to earn my living.

I ask you: can you not put aside all of the poetry and figure and metaphor and get through to something basic and solid and real, where you can say, "Thank God there is mercy and forgiveness and cleansing and eternal life for the guilty soul, the inner man who has sinned!"?

I heard the voice of Jesus say,
Behold, I freely give
The living waters; thirsty one
Stoop down and drink and live!

I came to Jesus, and I drank
Of that life-giving stream,
My thirst was quenched, my soul revived,
And now I live in Him!

There it is—there is the mercy of God! Man's great difficulty is that we have religion without guilt, and religion without guilt just tries to make God a big "pal" of man. But religion without guilt is a religion that cannot escape hell for it deceives and finally destroys all who are a part of it.

Religion without any consciousness of guilt is a false religion. If I come to Jesus Christ without any confession of guilt, simply to gain some benefit, I still have woe upon me, as did the Pharisees before me! But if my guilt drives me to Jesus, then I have my guilt taken from me and I find mercy. Oh, the mercy of God! We sing about the mercy of God, and I hope we know what we are singing about: "O depths of mercy, can it be, that gate is left ajar for me."

The good mercy of God—that is the water to a thirsty man—the man whose conscious guilt and sin are causing him pain and anguish.

That thirsty man can come to the Lord Jesus and drink of the waters of Shiloah—the waters of mercy!

My brother, you will never have inward peace until you have acknowledged your guilt. This is something you cannot dodge and evade, because you have a conscience and your conscience will never let you rest until you get rid of the guilt!

Guilt must be dealt with and taken away! Oh, you can be smoothed over and given a little theological massage, patted on the head and told that it is all right, but that treatment will not take away guilt and condemnation. Sins that you thought were) absolved by religion will always come back to haunt you.

Only the Redeemer and Saviour, Jesus Christ, can forgive and pardon and free from guilt—and the sins He has forgiven will never come back to haunt you as a child of God—never while the world stands! He forgives and forgets, burying your old load of guilt so that it no longer exists. God has promised, "I will not remember thy guilt." Since God is able to remember everything, the only way to figure this is that God beats that guilt and condemnation back out of being so it does not even exist any more! The sin that God pardons is no longer an entity—it is gone forever!

Christians have often talked about the "covering" of our sins and I know it is a common phrase. I have used it myself, but it is a figure of speech—for sin is not covered. The sinner must be cleansed. Let me explain. In the Old Testament, sin was covered as they waited for the Lamb to come and die on the cross! But in the New Testament sinners could look back on the finished work already done by Christ, blood already spilled. Sins are not covered now. They are cleansed and forgiven! That is why the believing Christian can have inward peace and joy.

There it is—the water of grace, the flow of mercy to the sinner, poverty stricken and spiritually bankrupt. The grace of our Lord Jesus Christ flows like the waters of Shiloah—the quiet waters that are so readily available.

Did you know that sheep cannot drink from noisy, running water? A sheep's nostrils are so close to his mouth that if he starts to drink and the water is moving, he will choke and could perhaps drown. It is necessary for the shepherd to dam the stream until a quiet pool is formed, and the moving water becomes still. Then the animal can put his muzzle into the water and drink without choking and gasping for air. When David wrote about our Lord being our shepherd, he said, "He leadeth me beside the still water."

The grace of God is like the still, quiet pool of water. The water flows softly! Oh, Grace of God, how you have been wounded in the house of your friends! Grace of God, how you have been made into a fetish before which modern men bow in worship. The sweet grace of God—how it has been used to hide what people really are. The grace of God has been preached in ways that have damned men instead of saved them. Yet it is still full and free—the grace of God!

If God could not extend us His mercy and grace, and treated us exactly as we deserved, there would be only one course for Him to follow. God would have to turn an angered face to us in life and He would have to turn His back to us in death. That would happen to the best human beings that ever lived, if we should receive only what we deserve.

But, oh, the grace of God! God through the plan of salvation in Jesus Christ will go beyond our merits, beyond that which we deserve. Even if our sins have been like a mountain, it is the grace of God that assures our forgiveness. There is cleansing for the defiled, gracious and satisfying cleansing—a beautiful element in Christianity as revealed by the Lord Himself, and not just abstract theology.

I saw a magazine cover which pictured four men. It was an unusual picture for it showed the youngest man preaching his first sermon, for he had just come out of prison where he had received Christ—a redeemed, converted, transformed follower of Jesus, now determined to tell others the good news. With him was the pastor of the church in which the young man was preaching, the lawyer who had been the prosecutor in his trial, and the judge who had sentenced him to prison. Many judges and lawyers will admit that when most criminals are returned to a happy and useful life it is because they have purgation in the blood of the Lamb, the power of Christ to change a man, to cleanse from defilement, to transform his life and character.

This is a beautiful thing—that a former car thief can stand with a big grin on his face and hold an open Bible in his hand, and witness to the power of the Christian gospel.

Men will ask: How can it be? Because the blood of Jesus Christ cleanses from all sin. Because there is a fiery purgation in the Christian message that can take any sinful man and make him clean and make him good, for Christ's sake!

Knowing the power of this gospel, I am willing to put myself on record that I would rather be preached to by a converted car thief than be lulled to death by the educated gentlemen who have reduced Christianity to nothing more than a psychology of comfort. Even their church ads woo men and women with the appeal, "Come to church and be comforted."

Brothers and sisters in Christ's church, you do not want consolation and comfort—you want to know the facts, you want to know where you stand before God Almighty!

In recent days I have had two persons come to me personally to tell me that my preaching has been cutting them to pieces, making them miserable and desirous of something better God has for them in their lives.

I think that is a beautiful thing and I thank God that I am worthy of that. People should not come to Christ and to His church with the expectation that all spiritual problems are consummated in comfort and consolation. If that is all people want in their church going, they will find a large number of preachers waiting to rock them to sleep with the consolation, "Bye, bye now, and here's your bottle!"

What do we know about today? Any of us can have a sudden heart attack and be called from this life. How will it be with our souls and where will we go—those are the things we want to know for sure. Following Christ, we want to know how we can go on to be holy and live holy and be right with God, turning our backs on sin and living in the Spirit!

Men are always faced with choices and decisions as the loving and eternal God deals with them, now in mercy and in patience.

I must confess as a pastor and minister that I have had to say "Goodbye" to people in some instances when they have said: "We cannot worship here. You are too strict. Your standards are too strict for this day and age. Your message is too strict!"

My only apology is that I am still not as strict as the Bible is. I have to confess that I am still not up to the standard of the scriptures. I am trying, but I am not that strict.

But, occasionally, we have to say farewell to someone who says they have to find a different kind of church, an easy-going church, a church that majors in relaxation.

What did Jesus say to us? He said that unless we are ready to turn from everything and follow Him with devotion, we are not yet ready to be His disciples, and unless we are ready to die for Him, we are not ready to live for Him. The whistle is going to blow for us one of these days and then we will have to appear and tell God how we carried on His work, how we conducted ourselves in the light of what Jesus said.

So we cannot afford to let down our Christian standards just to hold the interest of people who want to go to hell and still belong to a church. We have had carnal and fleshly and self-loving people who wanted to come in and control young people's groups and liberate us from our spiritual life and standards and "strictness."

I would like to know why people of that kind of disposition want to go to church. I know what I would do if I were determined just to eat, drink and be merry—I would never want to show up among people who are devoted to Jesus Christ and to His saving gospel. If I were of that mind and disposition and found myself at church, I would at least go to the furnace room and stay there until church was over!

I thank God for Christian men and women who want to know the facts and the truth as it has come from God. Thank God, they are not just looking for someone to give them a relaxing religious massage! These are the facts—the blood of Jesus Christ cleanses. There is a purging element in Christianity. Then there is the Holy Spirit, the blessed Spirit of God who brings us the peace and tranquility of the waters of Shiloah.

The living God invites us to this stream, the only perennial stream in the world, the only stream that never runs dry, the only stream that never overflows and destroys.

Yet, the prophet Isaiah went on to record the fact that he could not understand how the people of Israel could refuse the soft-flowing waters sent by the Lord.

The prophet voiced his incredulity and amazement: "How can it be? Israel refuses the soft waters of Shiloah sent by the Lord; the healing, tranquilizing stream that brings peace to the heart and conscience. They refuse it and turn to men like themselves instead."

Isaiah then warned that those who refuse the still and peaceful streams from God have only one thing to anticipate—the overflowing torrents of judgment. He said, "If ye choose to turn away from the soft waters of Shiloah, the Lord God bringeth upon you the waters of the river, strong and many, and he shall come over all his channels, and go over all his banks."

I do not think we are overly-serious in our approach. I do not think we have made extreme statements, statements that need modification, in light of New Testament truth given by our Lord Jesus Christ. I do not think we are as severe as God would have us be in the facing of coming judgment, for it was Jesus Himself who told the Jews in His day, "The Father . . . hath committed all judgment unto the Son."

Who Put Jesus on the Cross?

"He was wounded for our transgressions, he was bruised for our iniquities: the chastisement of our peace was upon him; and with his stripes we are healed." Isaiah 53:5

THERE IS A STRANGE conspiracy of silence in the world today—even in religious circles—about man's responsibility for sin, the reality of judgment, and about an outraged God and the necessity for a crucified Saviour.

On the other hand, there is an open and powerful movement swirling throughout the world designed to give people peace of mind in relieving them of any historical responsibility for the trial and crucifixion of Jesus Christ. The problem with modern decrees and pronouncements in the name of brotherhood and tolerance is their basic misconception of Christian theology.

A great shadow lies upon every man and every woman—the fact that our Lord was bruised and wounded and crucified for the entire human race. This is the basic human responsibility that men are trying to push off and evade.

Let us not eloquently blame Judas nor Pilate. Let us not curl our lips at Judas and accuse, "He sold Him for money!"

Let us pity Pilate, the weak-willed, because he did not have courage enough to stand for the innocency of the man whom he declared had done no wrong.

Let us not curse the Jews for delivering Jesus to be crucified. Let us not single out the Romans in blaming them for putting Jesus on the cross.

Oh, they were guilty, certainly! But they were our accomplices in crime. They and we put Him on the cross, not they alone. That rising malice and anger that burns so hotly in your breast today put Him there. That basic dishonesty that comes to light in your being when you knowingly cheat and chisel on your income tax return—that put Him on the cross. The evil, the hatred, the suspicion, the jealousy, the lying tongue, the carnality, the fleshly love of pleasure—all of these in natural man joined in putting Him on the cross.

We may as well admit it. Every one of us in Adam's race had a share in putting Him on the cross!

I have often wondered how any professing Christian man or woman could approach the communion table and participate in the memorial of our Lord's death without feeling and sensing the pain and the shame of the inward confession: "I, too, am among those who helped put Him on the cross!"

I remind you that it is characteristic of the natural man to keep himself so busy with unimportant trifles that he is able to avoid the settling of the most important matters relating to life and existence.

Men and women will gather anywhere and everywhere to talk about and discuss every subject from the latest fashions on up to Plato and philosophy—up and down the scale. They talk about the necessity for peace. They may talk about the church and how it can be a bulwark against communism. None of these things are embarrassing subjects.

But the conversation all stops and the taboo of silence becomes effective when anyone dares to suggest that there are spiritual subjects of vital importance to our souls that ought to be discussed and considered. There seems to be an unwritten rule in polite society that if any religious subjects are to be discussed, it must be within the framework of theory—"never let it get personal!"

All the while, there is really only one thing that is of vital and lasting importance—the fact that our Lord Jesus Christ "was wounded for our transgressions; he was bruised for our iniquities; the chastisement of our peace was upon him; and with his stripes we are healed."

There are two very strong and terrible words here—*transgressions* and *iniquities.*

A transgression is a breaking away, a revolt from just authority. In all of the moral universe, only man and the fallen angels have rebelled and violated the authority of God, and men are still in flagrant rebellion against that authority.

There is no expression in the English language which can convey the full weight and force of terror inherent in the words *transgression* and *iniquity*. But in man's fall and transgression against the created order and authority of God we recognize perversion and twistedness and deformity and crookedness and rebellion. These are all there, and, undeniably, they reflect the reason and the necessity for the death of Jesus Christ on the cross.

The word *iniquity* is not a good word—and God knows how we hate it! But the consequences of iniquity cannot be escaped.

The prophet reminds us clearly that the Saviour was bruised for "our iniquities."

We deny it and say, "No!" but the fingerprints of all mankind are plain evidence against us. The authorities have no trouble finding and apprehending the awkward burglar who leaves his fingerprints on tables and doorknobs, for they have his record. So, the fingerprints of man are found in every dark cellar and in every alley and in every dimly-lighted evil place throughout the world—every man's fingerprints are recorded and God knows man from man. It is impossible to escape our guilt and place our moral responsibilities upon someone else. It is a highly personal matter—"our iniquities."

For our iniquities and our transgressions He was bruised and wounded. I do not even like to tell you of the implications of His wounding. It really means that He was profaned and broken, stained and defiled. He was Jesus Christ when men took Him into their evil hands. Soon He was humiliated and profaned. They plucked out His beard. He was stained with His own blood, defiled with earth's grime. Yet He accused no one and He cursed no one. He was Jesus Christ, the wounded one.

Israel's great burden and amazing blunder was her judgment that this wounded one on the hillside beyond Jerusalem was being punished for His own sin.

The prophet foresaw this historic error in judgment, and he himself was a Jew, saying: "We thought He was smitten of God. We thought that God was punishing Him for His own iniquity for we did not know then that God was punishing Him for our transgressions and our iniquities."

He was profaned for our sakes. He who is the second person of the Godhead was not only wounded for us, but He was profaned by ignorant and unworthy men.

Isaiah reported that "the chastisement of our peace was upon him."

How few there are who realize that it is this peace—the health and prosperity and welfare and safety of the individual—which restores us to God. A chastisement fell upon Him so that we as individual humans could experience peace with God if we so desired. But the chastisement was upon Him. Rebuke, discipline and correction—these are found in chastisement. He was beaten and scourged in public by the decree of the Romans. They lashed Him in public view as they later lashed Paul. They whipped and punished Him in full view of the jeering public, and His bruised and bleeding and swollen person was the answer to the peace of the world and to the peace of the human heart. He was chastised for our peace; the blows fell upon Him.

I do not suppose there is any more humiliating punishment ever devised by mankind than that of whipping and flogging grown men in public view. Many men who have been put in a jail have become a kind of hero in the eye of the public. Heavy fines have been assessed against various offenders of the law, but it is not unusual for such an offender to boast and brag about his escape. But when a bad man is taken out before a laughing, jeering crowd, stripped to the waist and soundly whipped like a child—a bad child—he loses face and has no boasting left. He will probably never be the bold, bad man he was before. That kind of whipping and chastisement breaks the spirit and humiliates. The chagrin is worse than the lash that falls on the back.

I speak for myself as a forgiven and justified sinner, and I think I speak for a great host of forgiven and born-again men and women, when I say that in our repentance we sensed just a fraction and just a token of the wounding and chastisement which fell upon Jesus Christ as He stood in our place and in our behalf. A truly penitent man who has realized the enormity of his sin and rebellion against God senses a violent revulsion against himself—he does not feel that he can actually dare to ask God to let him off. But peace has been established, for the blows have fallen on Jesus Christ—publicly humiliated and disgraced as a common thief, wounded and bruised and bleeding under the lash for sins He did not commit; for rebellions in which He had no part; for iniquity in the human stream that was an outrage to a loving God and Creator.

Isaiah sums up his message of a substitutionary atonement with the good news that "with his stripes we are healed."

The meaning of these "stripes" in the original language is not a pleasant description. It means to be actually hurt and injured until the entire body is black and blue as one great bruise. Mankind has always used this kind of bodily laceration as a punitive measure. Society has always insisted upon the right to punish a man for his own wrongdoing. The punishment is generally suited to the nature of the crime. It is a kind of revenge—society taking vengeance against the person who dared flout the rules.

But the suffering of Jesus Christ was not punitive. It was not for Himself and not for punishment of anything that He Himself had done.

The suffering of Jesus was corrective. He was willing to suffer in order that He might correct us and perfect us, so that His suffering might not begin and end in suffering, but that it might begin in suffering and end in healing.

Brethren, that is the glory of the cross! That is the glory of the kind of sacrifice that was for so long in the heart of God! That is the glory of the kind of atonement that allows a repentant sinner to come into peaceful and gracious fellowship with his God and Creator! It began in His suffering and it ended in our healing. It began in His wounds and ended in our purification. It began in His bruises and ended in our cleansing.

What is our repentance? I discover that repentance is mainly remorse for the share we had in the revolt that wounded Jesus Christ, our Lord. Further, I have discovered that truly repentant men never quite get over it, for repentance is not a state of mind and spirit that takes its leave as soon as God has given forgiveness and as soon as cleansing is realized.

That painful and acute conviction that accompanies repentance may well subside and a sense of peace and cleansing come, but even the holiest of justified men will think back over his part in the wounding and the chastisement of the Lamb of God. A sense of shock will still come over him.

A sense of wonder will remain—wonder that the Lamb that was wounded should turn His wounds into the cleansing and forgiveness of one who wounded Him.

This brings to mind a gracious moving in many of our evangelical church circles—a willingness to move toward the spiritual purity of heart taught and exemplified so well by John Wesley in a time of spiritual dryness.

In spite of the fact that the word *sanctification* is a good Bible word, we have experienced a period in which evangelical churches hardly dared breathe the word because of the fear of being classified among the "holy rollers."

Not only is the good word *sanctification* coming back, but I am hopeful that what the word stands for in the heart and mind of God is coming back, too. The believing Christian, the child of God, should have a holy longing and desire for the pure heart and clean hands that are a delight to his Lord. It was for this that Jesus Christ allowed Himself to be humiliated, maltreated, lacerated. He was bruised, wounded and chastised so that the people of God could be a cleansed and spiritual people—in order that our minds might be pure and our thoughts pure. This provision all began in His suffering and ends in our cleansing. It began with His open, bleeding wounds and ends in peaceful hearts and calm and joyful demeanor in His people.

Every humble and devoted believer in Jesus Christ must have his own periods of wonder and amazement at this mystery of godliness—the willingness of the Son of Man to take our place in judgment and in punishment. If the amazement has all gone out of it, something is wrong, and you need to have the stony ground broken up again!

I often remind you that Paul, one of the holiest men who ever lived, was not ashamed of his times of remembrance and wonder over the grace and kindness of God. He knew that God did not hold his old sins against him forever. Knowing the account was all settled, Paul's happy heart assured him again and again that all was well. At the same time, Paul could only shake his head in amazement, and confess: "I am unworthy to be called, but by His grace, I am a new creation in Jesus Christ!"

I make this point about the faith and assurance and rejoicing of Paul in order to say that if that humble sense of perpetual penance ever leaves our justified being, we are on the way to backsliding.

Charles Finney, one of the greatest of all of God's men throughout the years, testified that in the midst of his labors and endeavors in bringing men to Christ, he would at times sense a coldness in his own heart.

Finney did not excuse it. In his writings he told of having to turn from all of his activities, seeking God's face and Spirit anew in fasting and prayer.

"I plowed up until I struck fire and met God," he wrote. What a helpful and blessed formula for the concerned children of God in every generation!

Those who compose the Body of Christ, His church, must be inwardly aware of two basic facts if we are to be joyfully effective for our Lord.

We must have the positive knowledge that we are clean through His wounds, with God's peace realized through His stripes. This is how God assures us that we may be all right inside. In this spiritual condition, we will treasure the purity of His cleansing and we will not excuse any evil or wrongdoing.

Also, we must keep upon us a joyful and compelling sense of gratitude for the bruised and wounded One, our Lord Jesus Christ. Oh, what a mystery of redemption—that the bruises of One healed the bruises of many; that the wounds of One healed the wounds of millions; that the stripes of One healed the stripes of many.

The wounds and bruises that should have fallen upon us fell upon Him, and we are saved for His sake!

Many years ago, an historic group of Presbyterians were awed by the wonder and the mystery of Christ's having come in the flesh to give Himself as an offering for every man's sin.

Those humble Christians said to one another: "Let us walk softly and search our hearts and wait on God and seek His face throughout the next three months. Then we will come to the communion table with our hearts prepared—lest the table of our Lord should become a common and careless thing."

God still seeks humble, cleansed and trusting hearts through which to reveal His divine power and grace and life. A professional botanist from the university can describe the acacia bush of the desert better than Moses could ever do—but God is still looking for the humble souls who are not satisfied until God speaks with the divine fire in the bush.

A research scientist could be employed to stand and tell us more about the elements and properties found in bread and wine than the apostles ever knew. But this is our danger: we may have lost the light and warmth of the Presence of God, and we may have only bread and wine. The fire will have gone from the bush, and the glory will not be in our act of communion and fellowship.

It is not so important that we know all of the history and all of the scientific facts, but it is vastly important that we desire and know and cherish the Presence of the Living God, who has given Jesus Christ to be the propitiation for our sins; and not for ours only, but also for the sins of the whole world.

How Can a Moral Man Ever Find Saving Truth?

"Jesus said unto him, If thou wilt be perfect, go and sell that thou hast, and give to the poor, and thou shalt have treasure in heaven: and come and follow me.

"But when the young man heard that saying, he went away sorrowful: for he had great possessions."
Matthew 19:21-22

I HAVE NEVER FELT THAT it was my ministry to personally expose or defrock those whose religious views happen to fall far short of the New Testament demands of Jesus Christ, but I do believe there is one man in the New Testament record whose "debunking" has been delayed almost 2,000 years.

I refer, of course, to that person who has become so well known to Bible students and to Christian audiences as "the rich young ruler" who came to Jesus to talk about the terms of eternal life.

Christian congregations throughout the years have heard a countless number of sermons in which this young religious leader has been portrayed as a Sir Galahad of his time—"whose strength was as the strength often because his heart was pure."

Personally, I have found it strangely amazing to look back into the records of scholars and preachers and find that great ranks of religious people down the years have misunderstood the manner in which Jesus dealt with this inquirer.

Almost everyone has gone over to the side of this young man in accepting his word as valid testimony when he said: "The commandments? All of these I have kept from my youth up!"

"I have kept them," he said. So there is a great chorus of moral applause and for centuries that nameless man has been preached and praised as a paragon of morality and a sincere seeker after truth.

There are several things for us to review as we consider this incident in the earthly life of our Lord. Perhaps the most common misunderstanding about the "rich young ruler" is the presumption of many that he was a political or government leader, but the gospel records indicate that he was a religious leader among the Jews, probably in one of the synagogues. The word *ruler* should not indicate to us a man with crown and scepter and a robe—it simply means that the man was a chairman, a president, a leader of a local worshipping group.

Another thing to notice is that even though he was recognized among those in religious circles, he was still trying to satisfy the uncertainties of his own inner life. I mention this because it makes it appear that things have not changed a great deal in 2,000 years. Personally, I have never before had a year in which so many persons of high place and status in church circles have sought me out for counsel regarding their own spiritual condition and problems. The point I make is this: these are not beginners in the faith. They are not unbelievers. Some are highly placed in our own evangelical circles.

What can be wrong when religious leaders are uncertain and shaken and miserable? I say that they have been brought into the Christian faith without any confrontation with total commitment to Jesus Christ as Lord, without any instruction that Christian victory means complete abandonment of our self and person to Jesus Christ!

Now, this review of the gospel record: This young Jewish leader came to Jesus, asking, "Good master, what good thing shall I do, that I may have eternal life?"

Jesus answered, "Why do you call me good? There is only one who is truly good and that is God; but if you will enter into life, keep the commandments."

Then, looking into Jesus' face, he asked: "Which commandments? Are you teaching some commandments that I do not know about?"

The answer Jesus gave him was direct: "No, I am talking about the regular commandments with which you are familiar as a religious Jew. God's commands: Thou shalt do no murder, thou shalt not commit adultery—you know them all."

It was then that the young man, looking into the face of Jesus Christ, said: "All of these things I have kept from my youth—what lack I yet?"

Jesus then gave him the opportunity for spiritual decision—the opportunity of self-renunciation, the privilege of putting spiritual things above material things, the complete abandonment of himself as a follower and disciple of Jesus, God's Son, and messianic provision for lost men.

There follows one of the sad and depressing statements of the New Testament record: "But when the young man heard that saying, he went away sorrowful, for he had great possessions."

Let us notice a great truth here—a religious life and religious practice have never provided the eternal assurance for which the heart longs. This young man was in religious leadership and yet he came to Jesus to discuss the void in his own being. He wanted something more than a conclusion drawn from a text. He was undoubtedly groping for the knowledge in his own heart that he had entered into a state of eternal benediction—we refer to it now as the assurance of eternal life.

His question to Jesus was: "What good thing must I do?"

Remember that our Lord Jesus Christ had never studied the books, but He was a master in dealing with people. He was a master psychologist, which means simply that He knew the ways of men and how their minds work. That is the basis of true psychology, anyway.

Jesus heard what this young man said and immediately was able to appraise him. Jesus knew that he was a religious leader. Jesus knew that he read the Hebrew scriptures and that he lifted his hands to God and led the people in their ancient prayers. Yet Jesus knew that he was not satisfied, that he was still miserable because of the aching lack within his own being.

In dealing with him, Jesus took him where he found him, and for the sake of the argument, He accepted him at his own estimate.

"You have come to talk to me, and you lay this matter of your relationship to God and eternal life on the foundation of doing good things to obtain life," Jesus reminded him.

"Just how good would that good thing have to be?" Jesus continued. "You do know there is only one good and that is God, and if you are going to do something good enough to move God to give you the gift of eternal life, how good must your action be?

"Seeing there is only one good, and you do not believe I am God, for you called me good master and good teacher, all in the same breath, what could you do that would be good enough? How are you going to be good enough if there is only one good and that is God? To win anything from God on the devil's terms, you would have to do something good enough for God to accept.

"So, young man, if you insist on buying your way in, I have the answer: Keep the commandments. That is the way you will have to do it."

The reply to Jesus was, "All of these I have kept from my youth up."

Now, we will all agree that without doubt this young man had kept certain of the commandments from his youth. I doubt that he had ever murdered anyone. He had probably never committed adultery. I suppose it had never been necessary for him to steal. Probably he had honored his father and mother, for the Jews did this, as a rule.

This young man has been praised so often in sermons because he was what we call "a moral man." Let me tell you what a moral man really is: he is good enough to deceive himself and bad enough to damn himself!

This young man did not realize the danger of being a moral man. He was self-deceived—and because his goodness prevented him from knowing his badness, he turned his back on God and walked away.

It is plain in every age that many men and women deceive themselves by accepting the idea that any kind of religion is all right, any kind of religion will do.

Is any kind of old mustard plaster all right in dealing with cancer in the body?

Is any kind of food all right for the health and growth of a tiny baby?

Is any kind of old beat-up airplane all right for transporting men and women through the skies, several miles above the earth?

No, my friends. Sometimes, having anything is worse than having nothing. Frankly, I would much rather have no religion at all than to have just enough to deceive me.

This was the downfall of this rich young ruler. He had just enough religion to delude himself and deceive himself. He was just good enough to make himself think that he was all right, to answer that he had kept God's laws.

I am going to ask you to decide whether he had—or not.

The Bible says, "Thou shalt have no other gods before me."

I believe that Jew and Catholic and Protestant all would agree that whatever comes before God is god to them, and that whatever shuts out God and stands between the soul and God is an idol, a god.

This young man knew very well the command that God must have first place in our lives. Yet, he was very rich and when our Lord put to him on his own terms the question of selling everything and giving it away, making God first in his life and becoming a disciple, he turned his back on it.

He turned his back on God because he had another god that he loved, although he would not admit it. He was able to lead the people in worship and in prayer and in the songs of Zion, but unknown to them, he had a god, an idol, tucked away. When the chips were down, he chose the god of gold instead of the God of his fathers.

I say that the rich young ruler was not a keeper of the law. He shattered and smashed the first one like a glass on the pavement. When the God of his fathers instructed, "Sell everything and follow me," he turned his back and walked away.

Again, our Lord summed up all of the commandments in His words: "Thou shalt love the Lord thy God with all thy heart."

When this young man came face to face with the vital question of his love for God or his love of wealth, he went away because he had great possessions. So, he broke and shattered this summation of all of the commandments of God.

Jesus also coupled with love of God the command that "thou shalt love thy neighbor as thyself."

Even as this young man talked with Jesus, the poor and the beggars and the crippled and the starving were all around them. Old men and women in poverty, little children without enough food to eat, lepers trying to find roots and grasshoppers and snails in an effort to keep their emaciated and ailing bodies from falling apart.

Yet, knowing the reality of human need for countless thousands, this young man could stand in the temple and pray and lead out in song in an effort to glorify his God and Abraham, Isaac and Jacob. When Jesus suggested that, as a condition of following Him, he distribute his earthly goods, the young man flatly refused.

Surely, he did not exactly love his neighbor as himself. But in his own eyes he was a noble keeper of the law. He could stand and say to Jesus, "All of these I have kept." I do not believe he was lying— but he was terribly deceived.

The last commandment in the decalogue says to every man: "Thou shalt not covet."

This means a great many things, for the word *covet* in the rest of the Bible, in both the Old and New Testaments, clearly means wanting anything with inordinate desire.

The young man shattered that one wide open, even as Jesus talked with him: "Distribute thy goods, and come and follow me—like Peter and the rest. We may be known as poor, but we owe nothing. I owe nothing. Come and go with me—for there is a regeneration taking place."

But he refused. He was unable to leave his bank accounts and his properties. So, he was a covetous man. He was a lover of self instead of loving his neighbor. He was a lover of his own wealth rather than loving God with his innermost being. The living God was not first in his life and in his love— and so the commandments were broken.

There is an important teaching for each of us here.

It is entirely possible for us to imagine ourselves to be all right when we are not all right. It is entirely possible to jockey our souls around over the checkerboard of our conscience to make everything appear to be all right.

That's what this moral young man was doing as Jesus talked to him and instructed him. It is well to note that our Lord plainly faced him with the terms of eternal salvation: full acknowledgement of sin rather than a defensive attitude, complete trust in the person of Jesus Christ, and utter abandonment to His Lordship alone.

Actually, there have never been any other terms laid down for salvation anywhere or at any time. Men with their multitudes of petty gods are still like this young man—ready to declare their own goodness even while standing knee-deep in broken laws.

A man who truly comes to God in repentance and contrition of heart does not work up a defense on the basis that he has not broken every law and every commandment. If he is truly penitent in seeking pardon and forgiveness, he will be so overcome with the guilt of the commands that he has broken and the sins he is confessing that he will be down before the great God Almighty, trembling and crying out, "Oh, God, I am an unclean man and I have sinned against Thee!"

Remember, an outlaw is not a man who has broken all the laws of his country—he may actually have ignored and flouted and violated only a few. The bandit Jessie James may have broken only a couple of laws—those that say "You shall not kill" and "You shall not steal." But he was a notorious outlaw with a price on his head, even though there were thousands of other laws on the books which he had not violated.

Brethren, when I come before my God as an outlaw, returning home as the prodigal, returning from the pig pen, I will not be dickering and bargaining with God about the sins that I did not commit. I will not even be conscious of those—for the fact that I have broken any of God's laws or committed any sins will so overwhelm me that I will go before God as though I were the worst sinner in all the wide world.

The defensive attitude of "moral" men and women is one of the great problems confronting Christianity in our day. Many who are trying to be Christians are making the effort on the basis that they have not done some of the evil things which others have done. They are not willing to honestly look into their own hearts, for if they did, they would cry out in conviction for being the chief of all sinners.

Look at the record of the apostle Paul. He took an honest look at his own sinful nature, and the fact that he had committed any sin at all bit down so hard on him that it crushed him like an eggshell.

Paul could testify that as far as conscience was concerned, he had tried to honor it. As far as was humanly possible, as a member of one of the strictest sects, he had been concerned with keeping the laws of God. Actually, no one can go into the record and try to pin the awful, daily variety of gross and heinous sins on Paul, for, in most ways, he was a strong and noble and moral man. He did the best he could in his own unregenerate state before he met Jesus Christ. But out of his own crushed heart, after experiencing the transformation that Christ brings within, Paul confessed that he saw his own being as God had seen it: "I am chief of sinners. I have been the worst sinner in the world!"

Oh, the difference Jesus Christ makes in our attitudes!

Because Paul finally saw himself as the worst man in the world, God could make him one of the best men in the world and in history.

The rich young ruler never had this sense of his own sin and unworthiness. He dared to stand before Jesus Christ, of whom he was inquiring the way of eternal life, and defend himself.

"I am no heathen," he said. "I have kept God's laws."

Oh, how wrong he was. The very fact that he could remember that he had kept any of God's laws disqualified him instantly for eternal life. He trusted in his own moral defense rather than acknowledge his sin and his need.

Now, the matter of complete trust in the person of Christ.

No man has any hope for eternal salvation apart from trusting completely in Jesus Christ and His atonement for men. Simply stated, our Lord Jesus is the lifeboat and we must fully and truly be committed to trusting the lifeboat.

Again, our Lord and Saviour is the rope by which it is possible to escape from the burning building. There is no doubt about it—either we trust that rope or we perish.

He is the wonder drug or medication that heals all ills and sicknesses—and if we refuse it, we die.

He is the bridge from hell to heaven—and we take the bridge and cross over by His grace or we stay in hell.

These are simple illustrations, but they get to the point of the necessity of complete trust in Jesus Christ—absolute trust in Him!

I wonder how many people in our own day really trust Christ in that way. There are so many who want to trust Christ plus something else. They want to trust Christ and add their own morals. They want to trust Christ and add their own good works. They want to trust Christ and then point to the merits of their baptism or church membership or stewardship.

Let me tell you straight out that Jesus Christ will never stand at the right side of a plus sign. If you will insist upon adding some "plus" to your faith in Jesus Christ, He will walk away in His holy dignity. He will ever refuse to be considered the other part of a "plus" sign. If your trust is in the plus—something added—then you do not possess Jesus Christ at all.

The rich young ruler thought that he possessed all of the necessary plus signs. The truth was that he possessed nothing that really mattered.

Then, a man's salvation involves utter abandonment to Jesus Christ. Our Lord taught this fundamental truth throughout His earthly ministry, so it was not a new concept proposed for the rich young ruler. Jesus skillfully got that man into a place where He could clearly and plainly tell him this great fact of the spiritual life: "Do not keep anything in your life that is more important than God Himself; come and follow me in complete trust and abandonment!"

I wonder also how many Christians in our day have truly and completely abandoned themselves to Jesus Christ as their Lord. We are very busy telling people to *accept* Christ"—and that seems to be the only word we are using. We arrange a painless acceptance.

We are telling people that the easiest thing in the world is to *accept* Jesus Christ, and I wonder what has happened to our Christian theology which no longer contains any hint of what it should mean to be completely and utterly abandoned to Jesus Christ, our Lord and Saviour.

I think it is a good sign that we are having a restlessness and a dissatisfaction among professing Christians concerning their own spiritual state. I find that we are having to start all over with many of them because they have never been taught anything but "the acceptance of Christ." They need the plain statement of the terms of eternal salvation: acknowledgement of sin and complete trust in Christ and utter abandonment to Him and His Lordship.

At this point, the rich young ruler was not interested. These were terms that he had not anticipated and he could not accept them at all. So, we read in the scripture: "He, sorrowing, went away."

You see, like all men, he had a basic interest in eternal life, but there were other things that he wanted more! No doubt he had some urge to follow Christ as the Messiah, but there were other things he wanted more!

Let me point out here something I feel about this young man and many others like him who live around us today.

I do not believe that every person who is spiritually unbelieving and lost is morally careless. We all know men and women who care very deeply about life, about evil conditions and changing moral standards. Many of them work and teach and try to do the best they can—but they are still lost because they have never acknowledged God's terms for eternal salvation and they are not abandoned to Jesus Christ, our Lord.

It is not only the careless who perish. Those who are careful and busy about many good things will perish as well. The rich young ruler took the human way and perished, even though he cared enough to come to Jesus and ask the way of life in a reverent and tender question.

He was a religious man of his day—but he was a lost man. He was a sinner, a law-breaker, a rebel—and the Lord quickly brought the truth to the surface.

It is actually true that many people engage in earnest prayers on their road to perdition. In a way, they want God, but they don't want Him enough. They are interested in eternal life, but they are still more interested in other things. They know that they should follow Jesus in true faith, but other things keep them from that decision.

I hope that God can burn this frightful fact into our souls—the truth that men and women can be respectable and religious and prayerful and careful and eager and ask the right questions and talk about religion—and still be lost!

In our churches today, we feel that we have found a real treasure if we find someone who appears to be eagerly seeking the truth of God. Actually, we rarely find anyone who seems to be as eager as the rich young man who came to Jesus.

They don't seem to be coming to us in the churches. We have to go out after them—joke with them, talk with them about their sports, try to find some common ground, and then gingerly tell them that if they will receive Jesus they will have peace of mind, good grades in school and everything will be all right. Amen!

Now, that is a fair rundown on modern Christianity, and it explains why there are Christians who ask, "What's the matter with me, brother? What's the matter with me?"

They have not come into the kingdom of God through repentance and trust and abandonment. The result is exactly what we would expect in those who have been "leaked" into the kingdom of God, taken in between the cracks, crawling in through a side window. There is no inner witness. There is no assurance. There is no inward peace.

When we think we have found someone who is a seeker, we settle back and say, "That's wonderful! He will be all right—he is a seeker."

Here is the caution, brethren: if you could see all the seekers who are in hell today who were seekers while they were on earth, you would know that many have sought and found out what they had to do—and then refused to do it.

This rich young ruler was a seeker. The church today would have put his name down on a card and would have counted him among the statistics. But he walked away and turned his back on the offer and the appeal of Jesus Christ.

Every faithful pastor can tell you, with great sorrow and concern, the stories of young people and men and women who walked away from the church and straight Bible teaching and warm Christian fellowship to have their own way. When the old nature stirred, they turned their backs on God and walked away. They went into questionable marriages. They went into worldly alliances. They took jobs in which there was no chance to please and glorify God. They went back into the world.

Now, they did not walk out of the house of God because they did not want God—but because they found something they wanted more than God! God has given men and women the opportunity for free will and free choices—and some are determined to have what they want most.

The rich young ruler made his decision on the basis of what he wanted most in life. The last thing we know about him is the fact that he turned from Jesus and walked away. He was sorry about it and sorrowful, because he had great earthly possessions. But Jesus looked upon him as he walked away and Jesus was sorrowful, too.

Those who walk away from Christian fellowship, leaving the church and the choir, directly into the arms of sinners, do not actually leave with happiness and great joy. I have had some of them who came back to counsel and consult with me. I believe they are trying to get a pastoral excuse or rationalization for the manner in which they turned their backs on God.

I have committed sins in my day which I believe the blood of the everlasting covenant has cleansed and blotted away forever—but that kind of rationalization is not one of them. I can say that I have never told anyone, "It will be all right; don't worry about it," when it was not all right, in fact. There are many virtues as a minister that I do not have, but those who have turned their backs on God and wanted me to give them some excuse have found that they have never succeeded in softening me up.

People often come to me to find out where they have missed the secret of the victorious and joyful Christian life. Generally, I discover that they want to live in two worlds. They want to live a holy life like Dr. A. B. Simpson, but at the same time they want to be as worldly as the heathen. They aspire to the saintliness of the saintly McCheyne, but they are satisfied to be as worldly as the world—and it is impossible to have both!

I admit that there are parents who counsel me about the danger of losing the young people from our church life because I am faithful in preaching against this present world and the worldly system in which we live.

I can only say that I am concerned and I will stand and cry at the door when they decide to go, but I will not be guilty of deceiving them. I refuse to deceive and damn them by teaching that you can be a Christian and love this present world, for you cannot.

Yes, you can be a hypocrite and love the world.

You can be a deceived ruler in the religious system and love the world.

You can be a cheap, snobbish, modern Christian and love the world.

But you cannot be a genuine Bible Christian and love the world. It would grieve me to stand alone on this principle, but I will not lie to you about it.

The rich young ruler wanted God, but he turned back to his money and possessions. He was grieved within himself that he had to pay such a price—the true knowledge of eternal life—in order to keep the things he loved the most.

How about the men and women all around us who seem satisfied with their choice of this present world, having turned their backs on God? They are determined to have and to hold what they love the most, but they are actually grieved at the knowledge of what it has cost them to have their own way. They choose and take what they want, but they grieve for the God they have deserted.

We have many like the rich young ruler among us still. It is not enough to inquire about the power of the crucified life and the Spirit-filled life. It is not enough to want it—it must be desired and claimed above everything else. There must be an abandonment to Jesus Christ to realize it. The individual must want the fullness of Christ with such desire that he will turn his back on whatever else matters in his life and walk straight to the arms of Jesus!

So much for the case of the rich young ruler. His veil was taken away and he turned from Jesus Christ. He was still the hypocrite, still a covetous man, a money-lover, a breaker of the law. Above all, he was still a sinner, and Christless.

He had to pay a great price to keep what he loved most. Actually, he had to sell Jesus even as Judas Iscariot sold Him. Judas sold Him for 30 pieces of silver. We have no idea in terms of money and land and possessions what the rich young ruler paid in his refusal to follow Jesus.

I do not think I have been over-serious in this appraisal of what it means to become a true and devoted disciple of Jesus Christ. I do not think I have been as severe as the New Testament actually tells it. And I do not think I have said as much as

Jesus said when He laid down His terms of discipleship in the New Testament.

What about you? If you are a seeker after Jesus Christ in truth, He is saying to you: "It is not enough to inquire. Give up that which is the dearest thing you hold in life; and come, and follow me!"

CHAPTER
5

What Is It Costing
You to Be a Christian?

"And then shall appear the sign of the Son of man in heaven: and then shall all the tribes of the earth mourn, and they shall see the Son of man coming in the clouds of heaven with power and great glory." Matthew 24:30

I T IS VERY EASY in our day to discern a glaring inconsistency among many well-groomed and overfed evangelical Christians, who profess that they are looking for Christ's second coming and yet vigorously reject any suggestion that Christian faith and witness should be costing them something.

I have come to believe that when we discuss the prophetic scriptures and the promises of the Lord Jesus Christ that He will return, we must necessarily examine the kind of love we really have for Him in our hearts.

If we are soon going to look upon His blessed face, should we not be expecting that He will search out the true nature of the love and adoration which we profess?

The Bible makes it plain that the love of many shall wax cold in the terrible and trying period just before Jesus does return to earth. It is well, then, to face up to a searching question: "How ardent, how genuine, and how meaningful is your love for the Lord Jesus Christ?"

A second question follows in quick succession:

"What are you doing to prove your love for the Saviour? What is your faith and witness of Jesus Christ actually costing you in your daily life?"

I confess that a preacher cannot bring this kind of message to laymen without making a request for prayer on his own behalf. I do believe that we are living in those times that Jesus said would come when the love and concern of many would wax cold.

Will you pray for me as a minister of the gospel? I am not asking you to pray for the things people commonly pray for. Pray for me in light of the pressures of our times. Pray that I will not just come to a wearied end—an exhausted, tired, old preacher, interested only in hunting a place to roost. Pray that I will be willing to let my Christian experience and Christian standards cost me something right down to the last gasp!

It is impossible for us to dismiss the explicit teachings of our Lord Jesus concerning the end of this age and His return to earth. It is impossible to dismiss the emphasis of the entire Bible concerning God's plan for this earth and the consummation of all things. A large percentage of Bible truth is actually predictive in nature, telling us what will come to pass. Some of these passages are already fulfilled. Others remain to be fulfilled.

When the World Council of Churches held one of its most important international assemblies in Evanston, we were struck by the unusual significance of the theme, "Christ, the Hope of the World."

It turned out that many of the American and European leaders of the World Council were embarrassed when many of the representatives of overseas Christian groups interpreted the theme to mean that the hope of the world lies in the second return of Christ to our earth.

Actually, the leaders were embarrassed because they had been playing down any emphasis upon the prophetic scriptures for years, and because they denied all reality in relationship to a visible and specific return of Jesus Christ to this earth.

I can think of at least three reasons why the strenuous effort was made to contain the discussions and to keep the world delegations from coming out with a clear-cut statement on the second coming of Christ as the world's greatest hope.

First, there are many churchmen and church organizations which have their own ideas for society and for their own nations. Bible prophecy concerning the return of Christ does not fit in with those ideas at all.

Second, these men and their groups are well aware of the spiritual implications of Christ's prophecies, and to believe sincerely in His return would necessitate a willing separation from this world system and its ungodly practices.

Third is the immediate rejection of any kind of link with literal Bible prophecy because of those who have made themselves ridiculous by insisting upon their own wild speculations and by going far beyond the bounds of interpretation set in the scriptures themselves.

Some basic things should be very clear to all. Our Lord taught that He would come back to earth again. The chosen apostles taught that the Saviour would come back to earth to reign. For centuries the church fathers emphasized that Jesus would return to earth as the final and ultimate hope and consolation of the Christian church.

At the time of the ascension of Christ, the angelic message assured that "this same Jesus, which is taken up from you into heaven, shall so come in like manner as ye have seen him go into heaven."

Most of us have encountered the glib explanations of those who refuse any literal interpretation of the prophetic words.

Through the years, some have taught that the return of Christ was fulfilled in the destruction of Jerusalem. That is so ridiculous that I see no reason for attempting to refute it.

Others have been satisfied to believe that Christ's promise of returning to the earth has been fulfilled over and over again when Christians die. However, the scriptures plainly teach that in God's great plan for humans and for this earth, there would be only two advents—one, to die; and the other, to reign. If Christ were keeping His promise to return to earth every time a Christian dies, it would leave no basis for the clear instructions He gave concerning two climactic and significant advents to earth.

Well, it is evident that no one can study the implications of the prophetic scriptures without realizing that in our generation we are living in days which are not only grave and sobering, but are grand days, as well.

Grave and grand—dramatic days! Greater days than you and I realize. Solemn days in which we are to give heed to the prophetic scriptures.

Now, I do not say that any of us can stand and proclaim and predict the world developments as if by schedule. The Bible does not have a schedule like the local train—giving the name of every stop and the time it will arrive and the time it will leave.

For anyone to say that the scriptures can be interpreted in that way is to distort and misinterpret prophetic truth. The Bible is a book of great and grand outlook and scope, and it tells us of the future, but it tells us in great, sweeping strokes like an artist painting a picture across the sky. The size would be so tremendous that you would have to retreat to a point far away to sense it and take it in. There would be no place in that kind of painting for tiny details, with vast brush strokes that would start with one star and extend across to another.

So, we cannot predict for one another what may come tomorrow. Not even the angels know that— our tomorrow is in the knowledge only of our Father in heaven.

It is not only the little fellow, the common man, who is helpless to predict how things may fall in the future—the great leaders in world society are just as helpless.

Leaders and groups and nations often think they have something great and enduring and superior going for them in human society, and because we don't jump on the bandwagon and remark, instead, that "This, too, will pass away," we get a look of anger with the comment, "You are a cynical pessimist."

Let me say that it is very difficult to have any brains in this day in which we live and not get blamed for it. It is hard to have any insight and not be considered a cynic. It is hard to be realistic and not be classed with the pessimists.

But with most men and their methods and movements in society, a few months, at the most a few years, bring an entirely new perspective. People who disagreed with you and were engaged in flag-waving for someone's scheme or speech six months ago are probably looking back on that same thing and see it now just as you foresaw it.

It is a wonderfully exhilarating thing to be able to anticipate and foresee just a little bit—but it is also an ability that will bring you much criticism and hostility from those with lesser foresight and judgment.

Well, the great men of the earth are still only men. Think what they would be willing to give for a supernatural gift of foretelling events of the future! The world leaders must be great men in some respects; otherwise, we would be there and they would be here!

But, if I am not mistaken, it will be the great men of the earth who will be crying for the mountains to fall on them in the coming day of judgment, according to the book of Revelation.

Again, if I am not mistaken, there was not one man considered great in human leadership and ability that recognized the plan and Presence of God when He was incarnated in the womb of the Virgin. Not one great man recognized what God was doing. Then, when Jesus ministered, it was only the plain people who heard Him gladly.

I believe there is something inherent in human greatness and fame and recognition that works subtly against the quality of fine spiritual insight in the human mind. World leaders as a rule do not possess spiritual insight.

The leaders in most of the nations make a great deal of their desires and their campaigns for peace. There are few people anywhere in the world who are not interested in nations being able to live in peace and harmony. We could all wish that nations would beat their cannons and guns into implements of agriculture and peaceful production.

But such hopes for peace among nations are fleeting. The leaders who call for peace and tranquility have not done their homework in the study of the Bible and what it has to say about the future.

Even the so-called diplomats and statesmen have little knowledge and even less control over the day-to-day incidents that bring tension and violence among the nations. The story has been told of one of our own State Department officials saying to another as they arrived at the Washington offices in the morning, "Well, what is our long-range, unchanging foreign policy going to be today?"

We may smile at that, but it does illustrate the point that men and nations are completely uncertain about each new day's events. National strategy becomes sort of a game of expediency—we act or we react according to whatever another nation has done or said. In that sense, it is like a game of chess among the nations. You do not sit down and think the whole game of chess through ahead of time. You do what you are forced to do one move at a time according to the moves the other fellow makes.

I have only heard one prediction made by a world statesman in recent years that was absolutely foolproof, and that was a remark that the next war will be fought in the future!

Well, there are no certainties, but it is sobering to realize that this present world with its great store of bombs and weapons is a powder keg, indeed. It will take only greed or lust for power or thoughtlessness on the part of some careless man to toss the match that will set it all off again.

Where will the blame fall—on politics? on religion? on morals?

I think it is possible that these three elements of national life and world society are so intertwined that they cannot be separated.

After all, what most any nation is at its heart depends upon its religious heritage and background.

It follows that the moral life and standards of a nation will also follow the pattern of its religious instruction.

As for the ultimate politics of any given nation, you may be sure that governmental and political decisions will very likely follow the national pattern seen in the religious and moral teachings and standards.

All of these things are on the human and natural side of the growing suspicions and uncertainties among nations—and there is no prediction of man that can be counted upon as a certainty for tomorrow.

But our Lord Jesus Christ does have a certain word for us and the Bible does offer us a more sure word of prophecy.

The words of Jesus spoken to His disciples concerning the signs and evidences of His soon return at the end of the age have come down to us in the scripture record.

In this twenty-fourth chapter of Matthew's Gospel, we will note several characteristics in human society in the days just before His return.

Jesus told His followers to watch out for a growing pattern of messianic delusions.

"For many shall come in my name saying, I am Christ, and shall deceive many," Jesus warned.

He continued with the cautions that "Many false prophets shall rise and shall deceive many," and "There shall arise false Christs, and false prophets, and shall shew great signs and wonders; insomuch that, if it were possible, they shall deceive the very elect."

Now, Jesus was not saying that it would be a new kind of thing for false prophets and false Christs to appear in the end of the age, for history records that this type of fanatic and self-proclaimed prophet and redeemer has appeared quite often through the centuries. The emphasis that Jesus made was this: there will be a great number of false messiahs as though the end of the age and the perilous times that will exist will bring about an open season for this kind of false proclamation.

We may expect a greater concentration of these false prophets as the second appearing of Jesus Christ nears and the distress of nations becomes worse. These are some of the promises we will hear: "I am the Christ." "I have the answer." "I can bring peace to the world." "I can lead you into Utopia— the Promised Land." "Tomorrow the Millennium— Prosperity for all!"

A great many of these so-called "saviours" will be religious. Others are certain to be political in promise and program. Their numbers will increase as the world hastens into the vexing political, social and economic tangle of the end-time.

We note, also, that a part of the warning that Jesus gave His disciples had to do with war and violence and revolt, famines and pestilence. He said to them: "Ye shall hear of wars and rumours of wars: see that ye be not troubled: for all these things must come to pass, but the end is not yet. For nation shall rise against nation, and kingdom against kingdom: and there shall be famines, and pestilences, and earthquakes, in divers places."

In all of the teachings of Jesus concerning the conditions on earth prior to His return, there are indications of increasing dependence upon military power among the nations.

Some of us have lived long enough to see how the war and anti-war pendulum swings. Soon after World War I, there were strong anti-war movements among the people of many nations. Many preachers found it very fitting and convenient to take leading roles as pacifists and "ban-the-war" leaders.

As a result, the people of many church congregations were carried along with ministerial leaders who declared, "We outlaw war!" and who issued manifesto after manifesto to prove that mankind had learned its most important lesson with this result: "There will be no more war!"

As a result, a generation started growing up in the twenties believing that a great war could never break out again. So, we sold our unwanted scrap iron to Japan and they turned it into weapons and bombs and threw it back on us at Pearl Harbor. Almost the whole world was on fire like a tenement house and the blaze and destruction continued throughout the years of World War II. Then, the notorious A-bombs were dropped on the Japanese cities and the great war came to its costly, grisly end.

The United Nations came into being, and men and nations assured themselves once more: "Mankind has really learned his lesson this time—war must certainly be outlawed now. We will find a better way."

I ask only one question: who holds the power behind nearly every government in the world in our time?

I am sure you know the obvious answer: the military leaders!

I think back into the history of our own country. Our government is established upon the principle that the civilians—the people—will rule themselves and direct the destiny of the nation. It was long repugnant to Americans that so many nations were virtually armed camps, with generals and admirals and other military people in full control.

I suppose it is because of the kind of world in which we live, but little by little we have seen a shifting of governmental emphasis. Military men speak for the necessity of great military budgets, and generals and admirals are among those who point out the way that we must take as a nation. It is enough to make thinking men wonder if we are drifting back into the very situation in which Europe found itself before the great conflagration of World War II and the decimation that brought European nations to their knees.

Many find it easy to consider the warnings of Jesus with the casual response that war is in the nature of man, and I question whether there has ever been a time of even 365 consecutive days since the time of Christ when all the nations and all the tribes and all the divisions of mankind were actually at peace with one another.

Brethren, I do not think Jesus was cautioning us about the minor feuds and arguments between small tribal groups. Jesus could foreknow the complexities of international relations of the last days of this age; He knew full well the conditions among nations that could spawn a hellish World War III overnight.

Reading again in Matthew 24, you will find that Jesus forewarned His disciples: "And then shall many be offended, and shall betray one another, and shall hate one another."

Just think with me of all the totalitarian states and nations in today's world. What kind of control do these states have over the lives of the people, the citizens?

An important part of the totalitarian technique for control and regimentation of the people is the employment of disloyalty and hatred and betrayal within every family unit.

It is my opinion that if all of the families in Russia could have maintained complete loyalty and concern for one another within the family circles, communism would have died out in ten years. But the very basic party line is built upon so subverting the minds of the individuals that they are willing to surrender and betray their family ties as well as their former ties to church and knowledge of God.

How sad and how perverted that millions of boys and girls have been willing to betray and sell out their parents in order to get a higher mark and a higher status in the party!

As in the case of the sign of false prophets and messiahs, Jesus does not point out hatreds and betrayals as a new manifestation among humans. Jesus is making the emphasis that when this happens in the very last days before His return, it will be a great worldwide "season" for betrayal. The philosophy of treason and disloyalty is becoming an accepted and successful technique throughout the whole world.

Persecution is linked to this philosophy among modern man and Jesus said about the time of the beginning of sorrows, "Then shall they deliver you up to be afflicted, and shall kill you: and ye shall be hated of all nations for my name's sake."

I need not recite for you the well-known terror and horror which have marked the persecutions taking place in our world since Hitler came to the European scene and turned his hatred and fury against the Jews of the world. I do not have to document for you the persecutions, regimentations and strictures which have taken place in such modern nations as Spain, Argentina and Colombia. I do not have to tell you that persecution is one of the techniques of totalitarianism, both in church and state. Jesus seemed to be pointing to a "season" for an outbroken philosophy of persecution as one of the signs of His near return.

Speaking of the last days of this age, Jesus also instructed the disciples that "because iniquity shall abound, the love of many shall wax cold."

Jesus plainly connects the increasing of iniquity in the earth with a spiritual falling away and a coldness among the people of God.

Again, we return to the fact that Jesus was not speaking of normal times among men, but of a great, concentrated "season" for sin and lawlessness as well as a "season" for coldness and callousness among the professors of religion.

I believe that Jesus meant to shake us up!

I believe that He meant for us to consider seriously what it would mean and what it would cost to keep our lamps trimmed and burning brightly in a time of great lawlessness and apostasy.

Our Lord knew that in these times there would be those in our churches who are just highly-groomed showpieces of Christianity—middle class and well-to-do, satisfied with a religious life that costs them nothing.

Oh, yes, we do tithe! But the nine-tenths that we keep is still a hundred times more than our mothers and fathers used to have. It is right that we should tithe because it is God's work, but it does not really cost us anything—it does not bring us to the point of sacrificial giving. An old prophet of God long ago said something for us all: "Shall I offer God something that costs me nothing?"

Brethren, what has our Christian faith and witness cost us this week?

Oh, yes, you have been to church twice this week. But you would have been just as hot if you had stayed home—so it did not cost you anything. You met your friends and it was a pleasure to go to church—that did not cost you anything. You gave your tithe but you had something left to put in the bank. That did not cost you anything.

Is it not time that we face up to the fact that most of us do only those things for the Lord and for His church that we can do conveniently? If it is convenient, we will be there. If it is not convenient, we just say, "Sorry, Pastor! You will have to get someone else."

It is a generally accepted fact that most Protestant Christians serve the Lord at their own convenience. We say we believe in such things as prayer and fasting but we do not practice them unless it is convenient. Very few of us are willing to get up before daybreak as many Catholics do in order to be present in their daily services.

I am not saying that we ought to be Catholics, but I am saying that we have great throngs of professing Christians who are the slickest bunch alive in getting their religion for nothing!

We are very willing to let Jesus do all the suffering and all the sweating, all the bleeding and all the dying. It seems a great bargain to us that simply by faith we may take over all the results of His agony and death. We pat ourselves on the back for making such a good bargain, and then go galloping along to our own convenient affairs and habits.

Brethren, I realize that this message will not win any popularity prizes in the Christian ranks, but I must add this based on my observations on the current state of the church: Christianity to the average evangelical church member is simply an avenue to a good and pleasant time, with a little biblical devotional material thrown in for good measure!

It is time that we begin to search our hearts and ask ourselves: "What is my Christian faith costing

me? Am I offering to God something that has cost
me absolutely nothing in terms of blood or sweat
or tears?"

The members of many Christian churches dare
to brag about being part of a "missionary-minded
congregation," somehow failing to realize that it
is the same old story—let the missionaries go out
and suffer in the hard places. We say we are vitally
interested in missions—and that seems to be true
as long as it does not inconvenience us at home and
the missionaries are willing to go and endure the
hardships in the jungles overseas.

People in the Christian churches who put their
own convenience and their own comfort and their
own selfish interests ahead of the claims of the
gospel of Jesus Christ surely need to get down on
their knees with an open Bible—and if they are
honest as they search their own hearts, they will be
shocked at what they find!

Oh, brethren, have we forgotten that it was the
smug, affluent, middle-class crowd that delivered
Jesus to be killed when He came into our world the
first time?

The poor and the oppressed and the outcasts—
they heard Him gladly and they believed in Him.
But how many of the poor and oppressed of our
own day do we welcome into the ranks of our
church fellowship with open arms?

A despised publican with his unsavory name
and reputation believed in Him, and Jesus was
criticized for dining with him.

But the middle-class folks, largely religious
and proud and selfish, believed not and received
Him not.

Well, we cannot leave these words of Jesus in Matthew 24 without emphasizing His instructions that "this gospel of the kingdom shall be preached in all the world for a witness unto all nations; and then shall the end come."

There is no doubt that the outreach of Christian missionary activity is now greater and more extensive than at any other time in history. This should be a great rallying point for the believing children of God, and a source of strength and stability in this awful and unusual hour in which we live.

"The gospel of the kingdom shall be preached," Jesus said.

Now, let me ask you: what is a kingdom without a king? While men of this earth and the worldly kingdoms are in confusion and competition, concerned with persecutions, disloyalty and betrayal, God is in His holy temple and His throne is in heaven. In all of these situations of earth, God Almighty is trying us and testing us. He is trying the nations and the kings and the rulers of the nations.

Our Lord wants to hold us steady in these days and He asks us to look upward, for there is a kingdom, and there is a King sitting upon an eternal throne. God has promised that He will look after His people, and thus we are kept, and given His own spiritual calmness, even in the eye of the gathering storm.

Christian brethren, there will be multitudes in panic and distress because of world conditions before Christ returns as King of kings and Lord of lords. But there is a special provision for the believing Body of Christ, those who make up His church, for the angels of the Lord encamp around those who fear Him, and delivereth them. We do not yet have the heavenly understanding of all of God's promises, but there have been so many instances where true children of God in danger have been surrounded as by a wall of invisible fire that we dare to rest back on His deliverance.

I must confess that my soul delights in the words and prophecies of our Lord Jesus, because I sense that He was able to look down the long corridor of all of the years of history, viewing the future as with a telescope, and telling us with such detail that we can be sure that He knows all things. He Himself was God and He had lived all of our tomorrows when He walked in Galilee, because He is God eternal. I delight in the inward knowledge that Jesus Christ, the Son of God and our coming Lord, will be sufficient for every situation which is yet to come to pass. We will never panic along with this present world system as long as we are fortified with our knowledge of who Jesus Christ really is.

The Word of God is the foundation of our peace and rest. Even in these dangerous and dramatic hours, "God is our refuge and strength, a very present help in trouble. Therefore will not we fear though the earth be removed, and though the mountains be carried into the midst of the sea; though the waters thereof roar and be troubled, though the mountains shake with the swelling thereof.

"There is a river, the streams whereof shall make glad the city of God, the holy place of the tabernacles of the most High. God is in the midst of her; she shall not be moved: God shall help her, and that right early.

"The heathen raged, the kingdoms were moved: he uttered his voice, the earth melted. The Lord of hosts is with us; the God of Jacob is our refuge. Come, behold the works of the Lord, . . . he maketh wars to cease unto the end of the earth."

Notice that this is the kingly strength and dominion of our Lord—not the United Nations!

He breaketh the bow and cutteth the spear in sunder. Be still and know that He is God.

In other words, get alone with God and His Word every day. I recommend that you turn off the radio and the television and let your soul delight in the fellowship and the mercies of God.

Be still and know that He is God. He will be exalted among the nations. He will be exalted in the earth. The Lord of hosts is with us. Fear not, little flock—it is the Father's good pleasure to give you the kingdom.

And the gates of hell cannot prevail against it!

Do You Know about the Next Chapter after the Last?

". . . Fear not ye: for I know that ye seek Jesus, which was crucified. He is not here: for he is risen, as he said. Come, see the place where the Lord lay." Matthew 28:5-6.

THE ACCOUNT OF THE life of Jesus Christ is the only biography known to man that does not end with death and burial—the only record of a human life that joyfully hastens on to the next chapter after the last!

The book of Matthew is biography—literally, the writing of a life. It tells the story of the birth and life and death of a man, and by common consent, we would include the burial. Every man knows that when the last tattered remnants of his body are finally taken to the grave, the last chapter of his life will have been written. The writing of the life ends where the life ends and at the burial the word *finis* closes out the human manuscript. The word *more* is no longer a consideration.

In any common biography of man, if there is any notation after the burial, it is not true biography. It may be editorial comment, it may be a summary of the man's teachings, it may be eulogy—but it is not biography. The writing of the life ends where the life ends and this is a fact by the logic of sad necessity. It holds true in every land, among all people and in the midst of every culture.

Many of the moral philosophers of the past dared to dream about a hope for tomorrow but they could never cope with the finality of death. They had always to take into account that fact that when a man is dead and buried he talks no more, he writes no more, he paints no more, he travels no more. No matter how beloved he has been, he speaks no more to his friends. The man is gone and that is the end. So, we write a respectful *finis* after the last word of the biography and it is over.

The man is gone and with the passing of the man no other chapter is possible. The last chapter has been written.

It is against this factual background that we come to the biography of Jesus. In the book of Matthew, it is a short sketch but it is a biography and it follows the common pattern of all biography.

Matthew begins with the ancestors of Jesus, back to Abraham himself, and then traces His ancestry forward to Mary. After identifying the mother of Jesus, he tells about the birth of the child, of the wise men coming from the East to see Him. Quickly Matthew proceeds to the manhood of Jesus, to the baptism with the Spirit descending like a dove and resting upon Him and preparing Him for the temptations offered by Satan in the wilderness.

The chapters that follow describe the beginning of His public ministry. Matthew records the Sermon on the Mount and then goes on to tell of the

miracles of Jesus, the feeding of the 5,000, the rais-
ing of the dead, the stilling of the waves and the
calming of the winds. There is a clear picture of His
conflict with the hypocritical religious leaders of
His day and the slow decline of His popularity with
the people. It is a striking record of the pressures of
public hatred moving in to surround Jesus like the
gradual falling of darkness.

Then follows the account of the arrest of Jesus
by His detractors and the manner in which He was
turned over to the Romans to be crucified. It is in Matthew's twenty-seventh chapter that Jesus is taken out
to the hill and there, still wet with the bloody sweat of
the previous night's agony, is nailed to the cross.

We learn in some detail the story of the six sad
hours that followed and the humiliation of His
death, the bowing of His wearied head and the
words, "It is finished!" as He gave up His spirit—
and He was dead.

The human biography comes to an end. Friends
begged the body and tenderly placed it in a tomb
and the Roman soldiers were there to place the
official seal upon the grave in compliance with the
Roman law. Jesus was dead—the grave was closed
and sealed. His enemies were satisfied, moving on
to their other interests.

There ends the human biography. This Man
who had been proved to be of the seed of Abraham according to the flesh; this Man who had been
declared to be the Son of God and proved so to be
by His wonders and miracles and words; this Man
who had struggled and fought His way with kindness and gentleness and love through the ranks
of those who hated Him through three wonderful

and terrible years; this Man who in love had gone out to die for His enemies is now finished. Human biography ends in the twenty-seventh chapter.

Amazingly, we find another chapter and it is there because for the first time in human history, it became necessary to get out that pen again and add another chapter—authentic biography!

Matthew 28 is not annotation! It is not composed of footnotes or summary! It is not an editorial comment or human eulogy! It is an authentic chapter in the biography of a Man who had died one chapter before.

How can this be? This Man is talking and eating, walking and making a journey with His friends on the Emmaus road. He is sharing truths about the kingdom of God and of His own coming and telling men to go into all the world preaching the gospel and witnessing of eternal life.

How can this be? His enemies and the world system had sealed the grave and written *finis*. They had satisfied themselves as well as they could that they would hear no more from this Man who had challenged their sins and their selfishness.

This is a new chapter because Jesus Christ, the Son of God, upset all of the old patterns of human life and existence. Jesus Christ took life into the grave and brought life out of the grave again and He who had been dead now lives again! For that reason, and for the first and only time in human history, it was necessary for the evangelist to add the chapter that has no ending.

Jesus Christ is alive again! This is the great truth that suddenly brought frantic confusion to those who had counted upon the old, reliable logic of death. This Man was alive again—not simply memories of Him, not just quotations from His lovely teachings, not words of commendation sent in by friends—but authentic and continuing biography!

They saw Him. They heard Him. They touched Him. They knew He was there. He stood among them. He said, "Mary!" He called His friends by name and looked at Peter and cooked fish on the sandy shore and said, "Children, have you any meat? I have some breakfast for you!"

Yes, it is an entirely new chapter. There is now a certainty of victory over death—death that had taken every man and traced him with that lipless, toothy grin; death that had waited as he went from cradle to the grave and then had written "The End."

Now it is death and the grave that are shaken with confusion for Jesus Christ is alive, having made a fool of death, and that toothless grin is as hollow now as the skull itself. Thank God there is another chapter, for He is risen. He is no longer in the grave!

We who are men must quickly ask: "What does this mean to you and me?"

Thankfully, it means for the believing and trusting Christian that the iron reign of death is ended! For those who are Christ's people, it means that the logic of death no longer applies. For Christ's believing; children, it means that death is not the end—there is more to follow.

For an example of what it means, let's look at the experience of another man, the apostle Paul.

We have good biographical material here. Paul was born as other men and grew up through the maturing processes of life. He was educated at the feet of the finest teachers. He became a member of the Jewish Sanhedrin, which is equivalent to being a member of the Supreme Court in the United States. He stood high in his day as one of the orthodox Pharisees, the strictest sect among his people. But on the Damascus road he was suddenly and miraculously converted to believe and trust in the One whom he had hated. He was filled with the Holy Spirit, commissioned and sent forth to preach the gospel everywhere. He went from place to place preaching the Word, establishing churches, writing encouraging letters to the new churches.

Brought to trial one day, he was freed. On trial another day, again he was freed. Charged and tried again a third time, he was condemned.

It was then that Paul wrote a letter to a young friend, Timothy.

"The day of my departure is come and I am now ready to be offered," he wrote. He knew that death was near, so he wrote on: "I have fought a good fight"—past perfect tense!

"I have finished my course"—past perfect tense!

"My testimony has been given. I am a martyr and a witness. I have done all that I could for Jesus. The war is over and I will take off my uniform. I have completed God's plan for me on earth."

According to the logic of death, the next words should have been "The End," for within a few days, Paul knelt on the flagstones of a Roman prison and the executioner severed his head from his body with a sword.

He had written his last testimony, but he did not say, "This is the end of Paul." Instead, he had purposely added one of those conjunctive words that speaks of a yesterday and connects it to a tomorrow.

"I have finished my course; *henceforth* . . ."

Paul's judges and jailers and executioner would have said that Paul was in no position to talk about *henceforth*—which means from here on in! Using the old logic of death, they would have said that Paul was a man with no tomorrow. His head was off. His earthly course was finished.

The fact that death was near had not caused Paul to despair. He had grasped that pen again, tired and weary as he was, and wrote in faith: "Henceforth there is laid up for me a crown of righteousness, which the Lord, the righteous judge, shall give me at that day."

Now, if it were not for that word *henceforth*, I respectfully submit that Paul could be considered one of the great fools of all time.

Consider that he was a man who had highest status in the esteem of his own nation and countrymen. He was a man of great education, culture and judgment. The historians say he undoubtedly had some wealth. He testified that he had given up all of this, counting it but refuse, turning his back on his own people, stoned one day and beaten the next, thrown into jail and bound in stocks, beset with perils and dangers, facing the schemes of those who were trying to kill him, possessing only the garments he wore and having given up everything else for Jesus' sake. When the time came for this aging man to lose his head in the Roman prison, his use of the word *henceforth* indicated that he knew he had not been a fool, and his relationship to Jesus Christ and eternal life made the sufferings in the sea and the floggings in jail and the starvation and damp rottenness in the prison seem as nothing.

Paul was testifying: "All of these things were a part of the human biography, but I am going on to another and better and eternal chapter!" For Paul, it was the blessed experience of coming to the next chapter after the last!

Thus did Paul confuse his human biographers. He knew what he was doing, for he had written: "If men do not rise again from the dead, then we are of all men most miserable"—and that is still the truth!

The promise of the resurrection makes the difference for the man who is a believing Christian. If men are not to be raised from the dead, why not eat, drink and be merry, for tomorrow we die!

But the Christian stands with Paul in the knowledge that there is another chapter because Jesus Christ is alive. We stand in faith and expectation alongside the martyrs, even though we have not been called upon to share the extremes of their sufferings. These are the believing saints of God who staunchly insisted upon the reality of another chapter after the last. They were thrown to wild beasts and were torn limb from limb. Impaled on stakes, they were allowed to die in slow agony under the sun by day and the stars by night. They were sewed into sacks and thrown over the cliffs into the waves of the ocean beneath. They were starved to death in prisons; some were driven into the wilderness to slowly die of exposure and starvation. The tongues of some were cut out; arms and hands were severed. They were fastened to carts and dragged to death through the streets while the crowds screamed with applause.

Was it worth all that?

If there had been no eternal tomorrow for those martyrs, no crown awaiting in a better land, then those torn and charred and tortured bodies would have screamed to high heaven above and hell below that Christianity is a fraud—only a cruel, treacherous story. But another chapter is waiting!

While we live in this world, we see only a few chapters of what men call earthly biography. Church history tells us that Timothy, to whom Paul wrote that final letter of triumph, died while being dragged through the streets at the tail of a cart. If that had been all for Timothy, everyone could have said, "Poor Timothy! It is too bad that he did not have sense enough to let Christianity alone!"

But you can be assured that God said to Gabriel and to those who write the records of the martyrs above: "This is not the end—just write 'More to follow!'" The divine Editor yonder in the skies knows that this is not the end of Timothy. There will be a long gap and there will be nothing written about him for a time, but this is only an episode. Another chapter follows and that chapter will have no ending!

It is God Almighty who puts eternity in a man's breast and tomorrow in a man's heart and gives His people immortality, so what you see down here really is not much. But when the bird of immortality takes to the wing, she sails on and on, over the horizon and out into the everlasting tomorrows and never comes down and never dies.

Thank God for the gracious chapter still being written, the chapter titled "Immortality." It is the chapter of God's tomorrows. It is the chapter of the *henceforths* known only to the children of God.

There is another day yet to be for there is to be a day of resurrection. I know this because there was once a Man, a lonely Man. They put Him in the grave and they sealed Him in. But the third day He arose again from the dead according to the scriptures, and ascended to the right hand of God the Father Almighty.

Besides this, I dare say that if all the books in the world were blank and were being written in by a multitude of angels until they were filled, they still would not be able to record all of the glorious deeds and words of Jesus Christ since the day evil men thought they had laid Him in the grave forever.

I want to tell you what I believe about the resurrection. When the grave that held the body of Jesus was sealed, I believe Death sat grinning beside the Roman seal, thinking, "I've got another one!" But the Life that could not stay dead broke that seal as easily as we break the seal on a letter, and Jesus walked forth, alive!

I believe that so completely that I believe it all the time. This is not an Easter "thing" that I try to believe once a year. I believe it so fully and so completely that it is a part of my being, every moment of every day. I stand humbly in this faith with all of God's dear children who are convinced that God has promised another chapter after the last.

I think often of the earthly biography and ministries of dear old Dr. R. A. Jaffray, that great missionary pioneer and statesman in the Far East and in the Pacific islands. After many fruitful years of vision, sacrifice and compassion, pressing on into all of the most forbidding and unlikely places of earth with the gospel of Jesus Christ, the last chapter of his earthly life was spent languishing in a wartime concentration camp, prisoner of the Japanese. The man who occupied the next cot while they were housed in a virtual pig pen said of Dr. Jaffray: "I never saw such godliness in any man in my lifetime."

But now, starved and sick and exhausted, Dr. Jaffray curls up on that poor little prison cot, thousands of miles away from his nearest friends, and his human life ends. His biography says that he died. It does not say that that was the end, for Dr. Jaffray knew a gracious tomorrow in Jesus Christ and anticipated the chapter yet to come. All that he earned for himself by the grace of God will be his in the tomorrows and the complete life of Jaffray has not yet been written.

Brethren, you and I are the plain and ordinary Christians, but this shining hope relates to every one of us. We are not martyrs. We were not among the great reformers. We are not apostles.

We are the plain, everyday Christians in the family of God and there is a gracious word for us from the Saviour about our next chapter after the last. One by one we also break from the ranks and slip away.

There is nothing heroic about our passing, leaving families and friends, but then, death is never heroic and it is never kind. Death is never artistic, always much more likely to be crude and messy and humiliating.

The preacher who once stood with strength and keenness to preach the living Word of God to dying men is now in his bed, his cheeks hollow and his eyes staring, for death is slipping its chilly hand over that earthly tabernacle.

The singer whose gifts have been used to glorify God and to remind men and women of the beauty of heaven above is now hoarse, dry-lipped, whispering only a half-spoken word before death comes.

But, brethren, this is not the end. I thank God that I know that this is not all there is. My whole everlasting being, my entire personality—all that I have and all that I am are cast out on the promises of God that there is another chapter!

At the close of every obituary of His believing children, God adds the word *henceforth!* After every biography, God adds the word *henceforth!* There will be a tomorrow and this is a reason for Christian joy.

The Romans thought they had seen the last of Paul, but they were wrong. The Jews thought they had seen the last of Jesus, but they were wrong. The Japanese thought they had seen the last of Jaffray, but they were mistaken. Thank God, the Christians will be around again! This world gets rid of us, buries our bodies in the ground, charges for the trouble, and presumes that we are gone forever— but we are not! Perhaps a neighbor that hated you because you loved God will say when you die, "Well, that fellow is out of my hair. He was always giving me a tract or suggesting that I go to church. And he bored me stiff." Oh, he doesn't know that you will be around again! Yes, God's people will be around again. Paul will be back, Stephen will be back, and Timothy, who was dragged at the tail of that cart, will be back. Dr. Simpson will be back. Wesley will be back—no longer gray and weak, but in the bloom of his youth! In fact, the whole believing family of God in Christ. This is the eternal promise of God!

I recall that there was a good man of God by the name of Samuel Rutherford, whose witness shone like a star in dark England in days gone by. He was a poet, an author, and a great preacher—a man who loved Jesus probably better than any man of his times. His convictions were unpopular and he was in trouble because he refused to conform his preaching to the dictates of the state church. When he was an old man, the officials decided to try him as a criminal because he would not submit to the rules of the state church. The date of his trial was set, and he was notified by Parliament that he must appear for trial.

Rutherford knew that he was on his deathbed and so he wrote a letter in reply. He said, "Gentlemen, I have received your summons, but before I got yours, I received one from a higher source. Before the day of my trial, I will be over there where very few kings and great men ever come. Farewell!"

That was Samuel Rutherford, witnessing to all of England that an entire new chapter awaits the Christian when our Lord says, "Welcome home!"

And "the kingly King to His white throne, my presence does command, where glory, glory, glory dwellest in Emmanuel's land." Ah, yes, there is another chapter, friends. There is a tomorrow for the people of God because there was a tomorrow for Jesus Christ our Lord. "For if we believe that Jesus died and rose again, even so them also which sleep in Jesus will God bring with him. . . . For the Lord himself shall descend from heaven with a shout, with the voice of the archangel, and with the trump of God: and the dead in Christ shall rise first: Then we which are alive and remain shall be caught up together with them in the clouds, to meet the Lord in the air: and so shall we ever be with the Lord." Then he added rather climactically, ". . . comfort one another with these words."

Ah, what a comfort this is! It is a promise to every Christian that has bid goodbye to loved ones in Christ. You will see them again! They will be around. There is another chapter, and it will have no ending. The bird of immortality is on the wing. Thank God for our faith that begins with our sins and ends with our glorification!

What Is the Supreme Sin of a Profane Society?

"He was in the world, and the world was made by him, and the world knew him not." John 1:10

THE BIBLE TELLS US in a variety of ways of an ancient curse that lingers with us to this very hour—the willingness of human society to be completely absorbed in a godless world!

It is still the supreme sin of unregenerate man that, even though Jesus Christ has come into the world, he cannot feel His all-pervading Presence, he cannot see the true Light, and he cannot hear His Voice of love and entreaty!

We have become a "profane" society—absorbed and intent with nothing more than the material and physical aspects of this earthly life. Men and women glory in the fact that they are now able to live in unaccustomed luxury in expensive homes; that they can trade in shiny and costly automobiles on shinier and more costly automobiles every year; and that their tailored suits and silk and satin dresses represent an expenditure never before possible in a society of common working people.

This is the curse that lies upon modern man—he is insensible and blind and deaf in his eagerness to forget that there is a God, in his strange belief that materialism and humanism constitute the "good life."

My fellow man, do you not know that your great sin is this: the all-pervading and eternal Presence is here, and you cannot feel Him?

Are you not aware that there is a great and true Light which brightly shines—and you cannot see it?

Have you not heard within your being a tender Voice whispering of the eternal value of your soul—and yet you have said, "I have heard nothing"?

This is, in essence, the charge that John levels at human kind: Jesus Christ, the Word of God, was in the world, and the world failed to recognize Him.

Now, our word *world* in the English needs a bit of definition. In the Bible it has three distinct meanings, and two of them concern us in this passage in John's Gospel. *World* here means nature and mankind—both coming from the very same Greek word. They are used together without clear distinction, so that when the Bible says, "He was in the world, and the world knew him not," the two meanings are apparent. You must check the context to learn which meaning is which, because they come from a precise word in the original.

In the Bible, the word *world* comes from a root word meaning to tend and take care of and provide for. Then, it also means an orderly arrangement plus a decoration.

As far as I am concerned, everywhere I look in His world I see God and my soul is delighted. I look into a dry, old book that looks like a telephone directory gone mad—we call it a lexicon—and I find that in the New Testament the word *world* means "an orderly arranged system, highly decorative, which is tended, cared for, looked after and provided for." It is all there in that one word.

Anyone who knows God, even slightly, would expect God to make an orderly world because God Himself is the essence of order. God was never the author of disorder—whether it be in society, in the home, or in the mind or body of man.

I have noticed that some people let themselves go to seed in a number of ways, thinking it makes them more spiritual—but I disagree. I think it is proper to comb your hair, if you have any. I do not think it is a mark of deep inward spirituality for a man to forget that a soiled shirt is easily cleaned and that baggy trousers were originally meant to have an orderly crease in them. I am sure God is not grieved when His Christian children take a little time every day to present themselves in clean and orderly appearance.

Some of the saints of God also insist upon completely informal and spontaneous worship. I do not think our Lord is grieved by a service of worship in which we know what we are going to sing—because God is a God of order.

So the word *world* has this idea of order in it, and we can expect God to be orderly because it is necessary to His nature. The world is a mathematical world and the essence of mathematics is order—it has to be that way.

Those who have gone on to know God better will also expect that God would make a beautiful world and that is exactly what the Bible teaches. God has made an orderly and beautiful world, and He is looking after it, providing for it, and tending it.

I think this is a delightful thing—God can take an old, dry word which has been dead for hundreds of years and speak to the bones and they get up and stand and sing a solo. That is what God has done here with the word *world*.

You will think about this the next time you are asked to sing: "For the beauty of the earth, For the glory of the skies, / For the love which from our birth over and around us lies, / Lord of all, to Thee we raise This our hymn of grateful praise. / For the wonder of each hour Of the day and of the night, / Hill and vale, and tree and flower, Sun and moon, and stars of light, / Lord of all, to Thee we raise This our hymn of grateful praise."

Let me tell you that the man who wrote that was not simply having himself a poetical time. He was putting in harmonious language a truth—and that truth is that God made a world beautiful in its order.

At this point I anticipate a word of argument from Mr. Worldly Wiseman, the man who has more brains than he has heart, who thinks more than he prays, and who tries to understand and measure the unapproachable glory of God with his poor little peanut head.

He is likely to say, "Now, wait a minute. You are talking about God making the world so beautiful, but don't you know that *beauty* is a word only—a word we use to describe that which happens to please us? If a person likes the way something looks, he says it is beautiful. On the other hand, if we don't like the way something looks, we say it is ugly. So, nothing is beautiful or ugly in itself— it just depends upon whether we happen to like it or not!"

So, Mr. Worldly Wiseman tells us that this idea that God made a beautiful world is all wrong. He is of the opinion that such an idea is only the figment of an over-heated religious imagination.

Frankly, Mr. Worldly Wiseman does not frighten me by his learned criticism and I am not looking for a place to hide, because I think that he is the dumb one, after all.

Listen, brethren. God made us in His image and in His own likeness and there is a similarity between the minds of men and the mind of God, sin being excepted. Take sin out of the mind of man and the similarity to God is there because God made man in His image. I repeat—if the human race would only see that God made us in His image, we would stop wallowing in the gutter and try to behave like God ordained when He made us in His own image and likeness.

When He made us in His image, part of that was mental and aesthetic so that my mind is somewhat like God's mind as soon as I get sin out of it. There is no doubt that when God makes a thing beautiful and orderly, it pleases the mind of God.

I say that it is only a half-educated man who insists that *beauty* is only a word that we give to something that happens to please us. The simple fact is that God made things to please Himself and for His pleasure they are and were created. Why should we apologize because we have the God-given ability to like what God likes and to be pleased with that which pleases God?

Now, I think that God first makes things orderly for utility. Whenever He made something in this universe it was because He had a purpose for it.

I do not believe there is anything in the universe that just got here by accident. Everything in the universe has a meaning.

My father was philosophical about many things and I remember that he used to sit during the summertime and ponder why God made the mosquitoes. I still do not have the answer, but I am just a human being, and just because I do not have that answer, I am not going to accuse the Creator of making a cosmic blunder. I know the mosquito is not a blunder—he is just a pest. But God made him.

The same principle is true of a great many other things. I do not know why God does some things, but I am convinced that nothing is accidental in His universe. The fact that we do not know the reason behind some things is not basis enough for us to call them divine accidents.

If I am allowed to go into an operating room in a hospital, I find many strange and complex things all around me. I am completely ignorant as to what most of them are and how they are supposed to be used. But the surgeon knows—and all of those tools and instruments are not there by accident.

If I could step into the cab of one of the great, powerful diesel locomotives, I would be perplexed and confused trying to figure out why there are so many buttons and handles and bars. I could wreck the whole thing in a few minutes if I started pushing buttons and pressing bars. But the engineer knows—and he gets the proper results when he pushes the right buttons.

So, when God Almighty stepped into the cab of His locomotive, which we call the cosmos, He was at the controls and He has always pushed the right buttons. Just because there are things in the universe beyond my human explanation does not allow me to accuse God of making a lot of unnecessary truck to clutter up the universe. God made everything for some purpose.

I have mentioned utility in this regard. In the book of Genesis, we find that usefulness was God's first plan. God said, "Let there be light," and He saw that it was good and that it had a purpose. So He divided the light from the darkness, and called the light day and the darkness night.

God did the same thing with the waters and throughout those two chapters of Genesis there is a beautiful exercise in utility—God making an orderly world for a purpose, with everything having a reason for existence.

With God usefulness was first, and so it is with people.

Whenever a pioneering man has gone out to the undeveloped plains to get himself a homestead, a little plot of ground which is to become his home, he does not think about beauty but about utility and usefulness. He knows he must have a log house or some kind of safe dwelling before the blizzards come. You will still find many such plain, often ugly houses scattered throughout the West. It is a place to live, it is home, it is a place to rest when a man is tired. It may be primitive, but it fulfills its purpose.

In the second place, God added decoration. That is the expression that is actually in the Greek root. The word *decorative* is in it. First, He created for utility and purpose and then added decoration and beauty. There probably is a sense in which we could get along without the decoration, but it is a lot better to have it.

There is that which is in the mind of God that desires to be pleased—not only satisfied. Order and usefulness and purpose bring satisfaction, but God desired that there should be beauty in His work.

I think it would be a great thing if more human beings discovered the truth that it does not cost any more to have things pleasing and beautiful than it does to have them useful and ugly. We could start out right here in our own city. You start to drive out of the city in almost any direction and you soon wonder if there is anything beautiful left in the world. Smoke stacks and smell and the sprawling apparatus for making gasoline out of crude oil—ugly, ugly, ugly! But, of course, the utility is inherent in our factories and foundries and refineries. If it were not for that kind of utility, many of you could not have driven to church—useful but not beautiful.

Well, perhaps the day will come in the millennium when we will make things beautiful as well as useful. I still think it does not cost any more to add the beauty and the pleasure and the delight. It costs no more to raise a beautiful daughter than to raise a homely daughter, and a beautiful wife does not eat any more than a homely wife.

You choose two men and give each of them a pot of paint, and one of them will turn out a masterpiece to hang in a gallery, and the other will turn out a horrible insult to the human imagination. All of that with just the same amount of paint and just the same amount of time. One is an artist and the other is a dauber.

Give two architects a free hand, each with a carload of bricks, and one will come up with a monstrosity—like some church buildings I have seen—while the other will add a touch entirely pleasing and satisfying. The costs will be the same— it is just a question of beauty in arrangement.

God could have made a river to go roaring right down to the sea—a plain, straight, ugly-looking channel. It would have fed the fish and done its job. But I think God smiled and made it to meander around under trees and around hills, a stream that catches the blue of the sky and reflects it to those nearby. People are intrigued by the meandering stream and comment, "Isn't it beautiful?" And God says, "Thank you for seeing it. I made you to see it." God is able to make things useful and beautiful. That is what the word *world* means.

Now, you say, what is this—a lecture on art?

No, it is a theological talk on what the word *world* means in the Bible—the created world which is God Almighty's decorated order which He watches and tends.

The other use of this word *world* is that which means mankind—the organized world and society of men and women.

When God reports that Christ was in the world and the world neither recognized nor knew Him, He was not referring to the created clouds and hills and rocks and rivers. He was referring to human society, the world of mankind, and it was this organized world of man that knew Him not.

John testified that God's Word, His only begotten Son, became flesh and dwelt among us. What was He doing in our kind of world, in our kind of fallen society?

Before the incarnation, He was the all-permeating Word of God moving creatively in His universe. When

Jesus Christ became man, God incarnate in a human body, He did not cease to be the all-permeating Word of God. To this very day, the all-permeating Word still fills the universe and moves among us.

How few men there are who realize His presence, who realize that they have Him to deal with. He is still the Light of the world. It is He that lighteth every man that cometh into the world. After His ascension from Olivet's mountain, He still remains as the all-permeating, vitalizing, life-giving Word operative in the universe.

What is He doing in the universe?

The scriptures tell us that "by him were all things created, that are in heaven, and that are in earth, visible and invisible, whether they be thrones, or dominions, or principalities, or powers: all things were created by him, and for him: and he is before all things (in time), and by him all things consist (or hold together)." The all-permeating Word which is in the world is the adhesive quality of the universe. That is why we do not fall apart. He is, in a very true sense, the mortar and the magnetism that holds all things together.

That is why He is here, for this is not a dead planet that we inhabit. Sin is the only dead thing. This is a living world we inhabit and it is held together by the spiritual presence of the invisible Word. He was in the world and the world was made by Him.

The scriptures continue speaking of Him: "Who being the brightness of his (God's) glory, . . . and upholding all things by the word of his power, when he had by himself purged our sins, sat down on the right hand of the Majesty on high." He is upholding all things by the word of His power.

When a little child looks up into the starry sky at night there may be a natural and childish fear that the sky will fall down. The parents laugh and pat the child on the head and apologize that he is tired—but the child is not as dumb as we might think.

Why doesn't the sky fall down? Why is it that stars and planets do not go tearing apart and ripping off into chaos?

Because there is a Presence that makes all things consist—and it is the Presence of that One who upholdeth all things by the word of His power. This is basically a spiritual explanation, for this universe can only be explained by spiritual and eternal laws. This is why the scientists can never manage to get through to the root of all things and never will, for they deal only with the things that they can see and touch and taste and mix in the experimental test tubes.

The scientist does not know how to deal with this mysterious Presence and Force that holds all things together. He can mix elements and chemicals and note the reactions that take place and then write an article and say, "I did not see God in the formula." But the scientist is only able to come up with dependable and consistent formulas because of God's faithfulness and power in holding all things together.

The scientist announces that a certain star will be in a definite place in the universe after another 2,510 years and twenty minutes! Then he sits back from his computer and boasts, "I have run God out of His world! I can predict where the stars will be in the future."

Oh, what a foolish man! The stars would all grind themselves to powder unless God in His faithfulness continues to keep them in their courses and in their systems. He upholds all things by the word of His power.

Again, we read in the scriptures: "Lift up your eyes on high, and behold who hath created these things, that bringeth out their host by number: he calleth them all by names by the greatness of his might, for that he is strong in power; not one faileth."

We lose a good deal of the expression of this passage in our English translation, but it is still one of the most beautiful in the Bible. It is a companion piece to the twenty-third Psalm, dealing with the astronomical host instead of His care for human beings.

The man of God says, "Lift up your eyes on high, and behold who hath created all these things." He is referring to that great display of shining, bright, diamond things that look down upon the country and the city and reflect on the waters of the sea. These stars yonder—who has created these things that bring out their host by number?

Why do they bring out their host?

Because they are like sheep, and this is the figure of a shepherd bringing his sheep out by number and calling them all by name, counting them as they come out and naming every one, and leading them across the green grass of the meadows and beside the still waters.

So, the shepherd-minded poet, Isaiah, saw that the starry hosts above were like a flock of sheep and that God, the great Shepherd, called and they came sailing out through the inter-stellar space as He numbered them and said, "They are all here!" Then He called them by their names, throughout the boundless universe, and because He is strong in power, not one faileth!

I believe that this can be said to be the most majestic and elevated figure of speech in the entire Bible—with no possible exception. We still know so little about the far reaches of the universe, but the astronomers tell us that the very Milky Way is not a milky way at all—but simply an incredible profusion of stars, billions of light-years away, and yet all moving in their prescribed and orderly directions.

We delight in the fact that it was God who called them all out, who knows their numbers, and He calls them all by name as a shepherd calls his sheep. What a lofty, brain-stretching illustration of what God is doing in His universe, holding all things together in proper courses and orbits.

He is that kind of Creator and God—yet the world knew Him not. That is mankind. He is still in the world, but mankind scoffs in its ignorance of Him, almost completely unaware of His revelation that the Word can be known and honored and loved by the humble human heart.

Now, the Word in His Presence can be known by mankind of the world. I am not conferring salvation upon every man by this statement. I mean to say that an awareness and consciousness of the Presence of God has often been known among men.

May I put it like this?

In the early days of America, when our founding fathers were writing constitutions and drafting laws and making history, many of the men in high places were not believing Christians. As a nation, we have been dreamy-eyed about some of those old boys and have made them out to be Christians when they were not.

I recall that Benjamin Franklin, who often said that he was not a believing Christian, suggested prayer to Almighty God at a time when the young nation was being threatened. The leaders did pray and they got out of the tight place.

Now, Franklin was not a Christian, but he believed there was a God operative in the world and he did not deny the awareness of that Presence. Daniel Webster confessed that the profoundest thought he had ever entertained in this life was his "responsibility to a holy God."

Surely, our fathers were not all fundamental Christians and many were not born again, but most of them were men who held a reverent and profound belief in the Presence of God in His world. A modern generation considers them old-fashioned and laughs at them, but they drafted farsighted legislation and a world-renowned code of personal and national ethics and responsibilities that remain to this day.

Standing up for the awareness and consciousness of a Creator God did not save them, but it stamped them in character and manhood as apart from some of the poker-playing, whiskey-drinking rascals who have never given any thought to the idea of God and His Presence in our day. The Word is in the world and the world knows Him not—but it is possible to know.

A Moslem falls down on the ground five times a day in reverence to God in heaven—and a lot of people laugh at him. The Hindu measures himself painfully on the way to the Ganges river to bathe himself—and a lot of people comment, "How foolish can you get?"

But I would rather be a Moslem or a Hindu or a primitive tribesman living in a cootie-infested hut in Africa, kneeling before bones and feathers and mumbling some kind of home-made prayer, than to come into judgment as a self-sufficient American businessman who ruled God out of his life and out of his business and out of his home.

Many an unthinking, secular-minded American would reply: "I'm willing to take my chances!"

What foolish talk from a mortal man!

Men do not have the luxury of taking their chances—either they are saved or they are lost. Surely this is the great curse that lies upon mankind today—men are so wrapped up in their own godless world that they refuse the Light that shines, the Voice that speaks, and the Presence that pervades.

If you can stop this modern, self-sufficient man long enough to talk, he will assure you that preaching is for the down-and-out bum on Skid Row. He will assure you that he has never robbed a bank, that he is a good husband and a good citizen.

Citizenship is not the final issue with God. Morality and obeying the law are not the final issues with God. The Spirit of God tries to speak to this modern man of the great curse that lies upon his heart and life—he has become so absorbed with money and bank accounts and profit and loss and markets and loans and interest that any thought of God and salvation and eternity has been crowded out. There are dollar signs before his eyes and he would rather close another deal and make a neat profit than to make his way into the kingdom of God.

Many others in our human society are completely hooked on fame and notoriety and public attention. A well-known actress and singer recently told the press about her long career and the fame and fortune which have come to her, and she summed it all up in these words: "Fate made me what I am!"

After an entire life absorbed in a godless world and society, no better answer than some kind of esoteric, weird fate. She has lived only for the kind of fame and notice that men can give, and she would rather have her name on the marquee of a theater than to have it eternally inscribed in the Lamb's Book of Life. The Voice has been here with us, but she has never heeded it. The Light is here, but she has never seen it. The Presence is in our world, but she cannot feel it.

Money and profits, fame and fortune—and with millions of others it is a complete addiction to pleasure. Flesh contacts, nerve endings, sensuous delight, carnal joy—anything to take the seriousness out of living, anything to keep humans from sensing that there is a Presence, the Way, the Truth and the Light.

Brethren, do not charge me with acting like a mystic.

Instead, hear again these words of scripture: "In him was life; and the life was the light of men. And the light shineth in darkness; and the darkness comprehended it not." And "in the beginning was the Word," and the Word "was in the world."

Now, there is the Word—and He is the Voice and He is the Light.

And the Word "was in the world"—there is His Presence. This is not poetry. This is the truth of God. And because our generation does not recognize the Voice and does not perceive the Light and has no sense of the Presence, we have become a profane generation. We dote on things—secular things—until we mistakenly assume that there is nothing in the universe but material and physical values. The profane man has come to the conclusion that he alone is important in this universe— thus he becomes his own god.

It is sad but true that a great and eternal woe awaits the profane and completely secular man whose only religion is in the thought that he probably is not as bad as some other man. I think that there is an Old Testament portion in the book of Job that fits modern, profane man very well: "Woe is me, that I was ever born, that my mother ever conceived me. Let the stars of the twilight of that night be as darkness. Oh, that I might have been carried from my mother's knees to the grave, where the wicked cease from troubling and the toil-worn are dressed."

I am thinking actually of men who give lip service to the church and some mental assent to religion, but they have forgotten that they were created, that they have a responsibility to God, and they have ignored Jesus Christ—His Presence, His Voice, His Light.

Actually, you can be too bright and too educated and too sophisticated, and thus fail to hear and to heed God's entreaty. But you cannot be too simple!

I was an ignorant 17-year-old boy when I first heard preaching on the street, and I was moved to wander into a church where I heard a man quoting a text: "Come unto me, all ye that labour and are heavy laden, and I will give you rest. Take my yoke upon you, and learn of me; for I am meek and lowly in heart: and ye shall find rest unto your souls."

Actually, I was little better than a pagan, but with only that kind of skimpy biblical background,

I became greatly disturbed, for I began to feel and sense and acknowledge God's gracious Presence. I heard His Voice—ever so faintly. I discerned that there was a Light—ever so dimly.

I was still lost, but thank God, I was getting closer. The Lord Jesus knows that there are such among us today, of whom He says: "Ye are not far from the kingdom of God."

Once again, walking on the street, I stopped to hear a man preaching at a corner, and he said to those listening: "If you do not know how to pray, go home and get down and ask, 'God, have mercy on me, a sinner.'"

That is exactly what I did, and in spite of the dispensational teachers who tell me that I used the wrong text, I got into my Father's house. I got my feet under my Father's table. I got hold of a big spoon and I have been enjoying my Father's spiritual blessings ever since.

Actually, I have paid no attention to those brethren pounding on the window outside, shouting at me and beckoning to me, "Come on out of there, boy. You got in by the wrong door!"

Dispensations or not, God has promised to forgive and satisfy anyone who is hungry enough and concerned enough and anxious enough to cry out, "Lord, save me!"

When Peter was starting to sink under those waters of Galilee, he had no time to consult the margin of someone's Bible to find out how he should pray. He just prayed out of his heart and out of his desperation, "Lord, save me!" And his Lord answered.

Brethren, why don't we just let our hearts do the praying? If a man will just get his heart down on its knees, he will find that there is an awful lot that he does not need to know to receive Jesus Christ! He is here now. "The Word became flesh and dwelt among us." He went away in His human body, but He is still with us—the everlasting, all-permeating Word—still with us to save! He only waits for a childlike prayer from a humble and needy heart— "Oh, Lamb of God, I come, I come!"

Is It True that Man Lost His Franchise to the Earth?

"In my Father's house are many mansions: if it were not so, I would have told you. I go to prepare a place for you." John 14:2

WHEN THE FOLLOWERS OF Jesus Christ lose their interest in heaven they will no longer be happy Christians and when they are no longer happy Christians they cannot be a powerful force in a sad and sinful world. It may be said with certainty that Christians who have lost their enthusiasm about the Saviour's promises of heaven-to-come have also stopped being effective in Christian life and witness in this world.

I still must lean in the direction of the old camp meetings songs in which happy and effective Christians gloried in the promises of a heavenly home where there is no need of sun or moon because the Lamb is the light thereof! Those enthusiastic souls were much nearer the truth than today's dignified theologians who discourage us from being too pragmatic about the joyful prospects of our future home.

It is very clear in Bible revelation that God created all things to display His own glory and then ordained that man should be the supreme instrument through which He might display those glories. It was for that reason that man was made in God's own image and likeness—a description of man alone and a term never used concerning any other of God's creatures.

There is no doubt that man was created for this earth. For reasons known only to God, God chose the earth as man's sphere of activity. He made man of the dust of the ground and adapted our nature to earth's conditions.

Did you ever stop to thank God that you are adapted to the environment around you? You could not live on the moon. You could not live on any of the heavenly bodies, as far as we know, but you can live on this earth. God adapted our natures so we can live here even as He adapted the fish to the water and the birds to the air. So, He made the earth to be our home and our garden, our workshop and our bed.

But, as we know, the conditions of the earth which God made specifically for mankind were not those we know today. It is the same body geographically—but in its creation it was the Eden of perfect love, where God walked with men in peace and beauty. In the beauty of His living presence God created the heaven and the earth, and the downshining of God upon the earth made the very fields and meadows and arbors and grassy places glorious and heavenly.

Then came the fall of man.

No one should ever be able to argue and persuade us that the fall of man from his glory and perfection was not real. Many already challenge

our right to believe that man is a fallen creature—
but that is exactly what he is.

The fall of man set in motion a great moral shock.
It was a shock felt in the heart of God and in all of
earth's circumference and certainly in the whole
nature of man—body and soul and mind and spirit.

It is not too much to say that this disaster that we
describe as the fall of man was of a magnitude never
known before in all of the vast creation of God. It was
of greater magnitude than the fall of angels whom
the Bible says kept not their first estate but left their
proper habitation and because of this were hurled
down into everlasting darkness and judgment.

This is the magnitude of man's fall and man's
sin—man lost his God-given franchise to this earth,
and thus can remain here only for a brief time!

Bernard of Cluny wrote of man: "Brief life is
here thy portion"—but that was not God's plan
and desire for man in the beginning. God adapted
man to the earth and the earth to man when He
said, "Increase and multiply and replenish the
earth, and subdue it . . . it shall be thine . . . thou
shalt eat of every tree of the garden, and the herbs
of the field shall be thine for food."

Then man sinned and lost his franchise and it
was necessary for the Creator to say: "You can now
stay only for a little while." And during that little
while that he is staying here, he suffers the loss of
Eden with its paradise of peace and love, while the
earth itself suffers pollution. Sickness and disease
must be reckoned with, toil and sorrow, and mortality and death itself.

Someone is likely to challenge the listing of both
mortality and death as though the two are identical.

Actually, mortality is the sentence of death. Death is the carrying out of the sentence of mortality. They are not the same. Death is the final act—man's mortality lies in his knowledge that he can never escape!

In history there is the account of a famous political prisoner standing before his judge. Asked if he had anything to say before sentence was pronounced, the man said "No." The judge intoned, "I therefore pronounce that on a certain day you shall be hanged by the neck until death. I sentence you to die." It was then that the prisoner spoke: "Your honor, nature has sentenced you to die, as well." In dignity, he turned and walked away to his cell.

For mankind, the earth has become the symbol of death and mortality, of the loss of Eden with all of its joys and the loss of paradise of peace and the presence of God. That is why the earth does not have a good reputation with believing Christians. The more mature we become in spiritual life and in dedication to Christ, the less we desire the things of this earth. It has become plain to us that this earth, with its darkness and shadows, with its empty promises and disappointments, with its lies and deceptions, its pains and sorrows and griefs that cry out in the night, is a symbol of everything that is unlike God.

In the very face of this truth, the Christian still knows for certain that God has not forgotten him. Man who was made in the image of God has; not been forsaken—God promised a plan to restore that which had been made in His image.

Those angels that rebelled and did not keep their first estate have no redeemer, for they were not made in the image and likeness of God. Those strange, weird creatures we call demons were not made in His image. They have no redeemer. Lucifer, the son of the morning, who said, "I will be like God," has no redemption and salvation from his fall, for he was not created in God's image.

Only that creature whom he called "man" did God make in His own image and likeness. So, when man failed and sinned and fell, God said, "I will go down now."

God came down to visit us in the form of a man, for in Jesus Christ we have the incarnation, "God manifest in the flesh." God Himself came down to this earthly island of man's grief and assumed our loss and took upon Himself our demerits, and in so doing, redeemed us back unto Himself. Jesus Christ, the King of glory, the everlasting Son of the Father, in His victory over sin and death opened the kingdom of heaven to all believers!

That is what the Bible teaches. That is what the Christian church believes. It is the essence of the doctrines of the Christian church relating to atonement and salvation.

Beyond His death and resurrection and ascension, the present work of Jesus Christ is twofold. It is to be an advocate above—a risen Saviour with high priestly office at the throne of God; and the ministry of preparing a place for His people in the house of His Father and our Father, as well.

Now, it must be said that sin necessitates a separation of body and soul. While it is proper to say that man is made for the earth, it is actually necessary to say that man's body is made for the earth. It was his body that was taken from the dust of the ground, for man became a living soul when God breathed into his nostrils the breath of life. The image of God was not in the body of the man, but in the spirit that made him man. The body is simply the instrument through which the soul manifests itself down here—that is all.

It is out of this context, however, that we need the caution that the worth and value of our human body should not be played down.

God has seen fit to give us this amazingly delicate and adaptable and beautiful instrument—the human body. If there had been no sin, there would never have been even the remotest shadow of doubt concerning the beauty, the dignity and usefulness of the body.

We should not think it is humility to berate and cry down this body which God has given us. It serves us well, but it has no power in itself. It has no will of its own. The body cannot express affection or emotion. The human body has no thought processes. Our human thought processes lie within the soul, in the human mind, in the human spirit. But God has ordained that it is through the instrument of the body that our ability to think shines forth and expresses itself.

The apostle Paul gave us plain teaching in this regard when he said: "Let not sin therefore reign in your mortal body, that ye should obey it in the lusts thereof. Neither yield ye your members as instruments of unrighteousness unto sin: but yield yourselves unto God, as those that are alive from the dead, and your members as instruments of righteousness unto God. . . . But God be thanked, that ye were the servants of sin, but ye have obeyed from the heart that form of doctrine which was delivered you. Being then made free from sin, ye became the servants of righteousness. I speak after the manner of men because of the infirmity of your flesh: for as ye have yielded your members servants to uncleanness and to iniquity unto iniquity; even so now yield your members servants to righteousness unto holiness."

It is important that we realize the human body is simply an instrument, because there are those who have taught that Christ could not be God in the flesh because the body is evil and God would not thus come in contact with evil.

The false premise there is the belief that the human body is evil. There is no evil within inert matter. There is nothing evil in matter itself. Evil lies in the spirit. Evils of the heart, of the mind, of the soul, of the spirit—these have to do with man's sin, and the only reason the human body does evil is because the human spirit uses it to do evil.

For example, a gun lying in a drawer is a harmless thing and of itself has no power to injure or harm. When an angry man takes the gun in his hand he becomes the lord of that instrument. The instrument is said to inflict pain and death, but that is not really true. The motive and intent and the direction to harm is in the will and the emotion of the man and he uses the gun as an instrument.

Men have been known to use their hands to choke others to death in the high pitch of human anger and jealousy and lust. The hands kill—but yet the hands do not really kill. Take the direction of that distorted spirit away from these hands and they will lie inert until they rot.

No, sin does not lie in the human body. There is nothing in the human body that is bad. Sin lies in the will of the man and when the man wills to sin, he uses his body as a harmless, helpless instrument to do his evil purposes.

The fact that the body cannot act apart from the spirit of man is good truth and we cite it here as prelude to the fact that there are many mansions in our Father's house in heaven, in the New Jerusalem, in the city four-square.

I think Christians ought to know and understand God's reasoning and philosophy behind His eternal provision for His children. I am not happy with the attitude of some Christians who are little more than parrots concerning the truths of God.

Some people think it is spiritual just to accept all of the dogmas without any real thought or comprehension—"Yes, I believe it. The Bible says it and I believe it."

We are supposed to be mature and growing Christians, able to give an answer with comprehension concerning our faith. We are supposed to be more than parrots.

The parrot in the pet shop can be taught to quote John 3:16 or portions of the Apostles' Creed if you give him tidbits as a reward. If all we want is to have someone feed truth into us without knowing or understanding why it is like it is, then we are simply Christian parrots saying "I believe! I believe!"

I think we Christians should spend a lot more time thinking about the meaning and implications of our faith, and if we ask God Almighty to help us, we will know why He has dealt with us as He has and why the future holds bright promise for God's children.

So, the scriptures do support our belief that while the body cannot act apart from the spirit, it is possible for the spirit to act apart from the body.

Do you remember what the Apostle wrote in First Peter 3:18? Peter said that "Christ also hath once suffered for sins, the just for the unjust, that he might bring us to God, being put to death in the flesh, but quickened by the Spirit: By which also he went and preached unto the spirits in prison; which sometime were disobedient, when once the longsuffering of God waited in the days of Noah."

Now, that tells us very plainly that Christ Jesus was actively doing something specific and intelligent and creative while His body was resting in Joseph's new tomb. The body could not move, it could do nothing apart from His spirit; but while the body was still in the tomb of Joseph, His spirit was busy and active about His Father's business, preaching to the spirits in prison, which aforetime were disobedient in the days of Noah.

"But, that was Jesus the Christ," you may say. "What about others?"

Let me refer you to the sixth chapter of Revelation, beginning at verse nine:

"When he had opened the fifth seal, I saw under the altar the souls of them that were slain for the word of God, and for the testimony which they held: and they cried with a loud voice, saying, How long, O Lord, holy and true, dost thou not judge and avenge our blood on them that dwell on the earth? And white robes were given unto every one of them, . . . that they should rest yet for a little season, until their fellowservants also and their brethren, that should be killed as they were, should be fulfilled."

We notice that here were some souls, tucked up safely under the altar of God, and they were the souls of the men and women who had been slain. What was slain? The bodies, not the souls. Jesus told His disciples: "Fear not them which kill the body, rather fear him which is able to destroy soul and body in hell."

It is interesting and profitable for us to note what these souls were doing. We find them intelligent, we find they had memory, we find they prayed, we find that they have a sense of justice. Further, we note their knowledge that God is holy and true, that men dwell on the earth and they know that God is a judge who avenges Himself and those whose blood had been shed. All of these things were true of the souls of those whose bodies had been slain.

So, it is fully possible for your spirit to act without your body, but it is not possible for your body to act without your spirit. Further, I would suggest that you do not try to demonstrate the actions of your spirit without your body while in this life. God does not suggest it in this life.

The spiritists, so-called mediums, tappers, peepers and glass-ball gazers try to loose the spirit and talk about it soaring off and freeing man here below. No, no, not that! Ghosts and wizards and spooks—all of that activity is under the stern interdiction of the God Almighty. God expects us to stay inside these bodies now, serving Him until that day when the Lord releases us and our spirits can soar away.

Why can't we take our bodies along in that day? I say it is because of sin. Man's sin has separated us in terms of our spirits and bodies.

At this point in our thinking, the question must occur: "If our bodies are separated at death, why have a heaven at all?" Some have actually taken the position at this point that there is no such thing as heaven—that the earth is to be man's heaven, and that man will receive immortality and the earth will be his sphere of operation.

That may be an interesting thought from the human point of view, but that is not what the Bible teaches!

The Bible has a definite answer for us. It tells us that God made us in His image in giving us His breath, making us living souls. Then, in that indescribable calamity, that moral disaster of the fall, all men lost the blessings of that first estate and have felt the sad results of that fall ever since in spirit, soul, mind and body.

The Bible answer includes God sending His Son to redeem us and to make us whole again. Some people seem to think that Jesus came only to reclaim us or restore us so that we could regain the original image of Adam. Let me remind you that Jesus Christ did infinitely more in His death and resurrection than just undoing the damage of the fall. He came to raise us into the image of Jesus Christ, not merely to the image of the first Adam. The first man Adam was a living soul, the second man Adam was a life-giving Spirit. The first man Adam was made of the earth earthy, but the second man is the Lord from heaven!

Redemption in Christ, then, is not to pay back dollar-for-dollar or to straighten man out and restore him into Adamic grace. The purpose and work of redemption in Christ Jesus is to raise man as much above the level of Adam as Christ Himself is above the level of Adam. We are to gaze upon Christ, not Adam, and in so doing are being transformed by the Spirit of God into Christ's image.

So, we can say that earth may have been good enough for that creature who was created from the dust and clay, but it is not good enough for the living soul who is redeemed by royal blood! Earth was fit and proper to be the eternal dwelling place for that creature who was made by God's hand, but it is not appropriate nor sufficient to be the eternal dwelling place of that redeemed being who is begotten of the Holy Ghost. Every born-again Christian has been lifted up—lifted up from the level of the fallen Adamic race to the heavenly plane of the unfallen and victorious Christ. He belongs up there!

But, in the meantime, sin separates body and soul. That is why the Lord Jesus Christ, as He was about to leave the earth after His resurrection, told His disciples: "In my Father's house are many mansions . . . I go to prepare a place for you. And if I go and prepare a place for you, I will come again, and receive you unto myself; that where I am, there ye may be also."

It is an amazing thing that Jesus Christ claimed that He never left the bosom of the Father. He said the Son of Man, who is in the bosom of the Father, hath declared it. While Jesus was upon earth, walking as a man among men, by the mystery of the ever-present God and the indivisible substance of the Deity, He could remain in the bosom of the Father, and He did.

So, you and I are to be elevated and promoted. Let us not forget that it was the Lord God Almighty

who made man and blew into him the breath of life
so that he became a living soul. That was man—
and then in redemption God raised him infinitely
above that level, so that now we hear the Lord and
Saviour promising, "I have gone to prepare a place
for you." In the time of our departure, the body that
He gave us will disintegrate and drop away like a
cocoon, for the spirit of the man soars away to the
presence of God. The body must await that great
day of resurrection at the last trump, for Paul says,
"The dead shall be raised incorruptible, and we
shall all be changed."

With the promises of God so distinct and beautiful, it is unbecoming that a Christian should make
such a fearful thing of death. The fact that we Christians do display a neurosis about dying indicates
that we are not where we ought to be spiritually.
If we had actually reached a place of such spiritual
commitment that the wonders of heaven were so
close that we longed for the illuminating Presence
of our Lord, we would not go into such a fearful
and frantic performance every time we find something wrong with our physical frame.

I do not think that a genuine, committed Christian ever ought to be afraid to die. We do not have
to be because Jesus promised that He would prepare a proper place for all of those who shall be
born again, raised up out of the agony and stress of
this world through the blood of the everlasting covenant into that bright and gracious world above.

Notice that Jesus said, "In my Father's house are
many mansions." If it is His Father's house, it is also
our Father's house because the Lord Jesus is our
elder brother. Jesus also said, "I go to my Father

and your Father—my God and your God." If the
Father's house is the house of Jesus, it is also the
house of all of His other sons and daughters.

Yes, we Christians are much better off than we
really know—and there are a great many things
here below that we can get along without and not
be too shaken about it if we are honestly committed to the promises concerning the Father's house
and its many dwelling places. It is one of the sad
commentaries on our times that Christians can
actually be foolish enough to get their affections
so centered upon the things of this earth that they
forget how quickly their little time in this body and
upon this earth will flee away.

I am sure that our Lord is looking for heavenly-
minded Christians. His Word encourages us to
trust Him with such a singleness of purpose that
He is able to deliver us from the fear of death and
the uncertainties of tomorrow. I believe He is up
there preparing me a mansion—"He is fixing up
a mansion which shall forever stand; for my stay
shall not be transient in that happy, happy land!"

Read again what John said about his vision of
the future to come.

"I saw a new heaven and a new earth: for the
first heaven and the first earth were passed away;
and there was no more sea. And I John saw the
holy city, the new Jerusalem, coming down from
God out of heaven, prepared as a bride adorned
for her husband."

Brethren, I say that it is just too bad that we have
relegated this passage to be read mostly at funeral
services. The man who was reporting this was not

on his way to a funeral—he was on his way to the New Jerusalem!

He continued: "And I heard a great voice out of heaven saying, Behold, the tabernacle of God is with men, and he will dwell with them, and they shall be his people, and God himself shall be with them, and be their God. And God shall wipe away all tears from their eyes; and there shall be no more death, neither sorrow, nor crying, neither shall there be any more pain: for the former things are passed away."

John then describes that great and beautiful city having the glory of God, with her light like unto a stone that was most precious, even like as jasper, clear as crystal.

"And I saw no temple therein: for the Lord God Almighty and the Lamb are the temple of it. And the city had no need of the sun, neither of the moon, to shine in it: for the glory of God did lighten it, and the Lamb is the light thereof."

Ah, the people of God ought to be the happiest people in all the wide world! People should be coming to us constantly and asking the source of our joy and delight—redeemed by the blood of the Lamb, our yesterdays behind us, our sin under the blood forever and a day, to be remembered against us no more forever. God is our Father, Christ is our Brother, the Holy Ghost our Advocate and Comforter. Our Brother has gone to the Father's house to prepare a place for us, leaving with us the promise that He will come again!

Don't send Moses, Lord, don't send Moses! He broke the tables of stone.

Don't send Elijah for me, Lord! I am afraid of Elijah—he called down fire from heaven.

Don't send Paul, Lord! He is so learned that I feel like a little boy when I read his epistles.

O Lord Jesus, come yourself! I am not afraid of Thee. You took the little children as lambs to your fold. You forgave the woman taken in adultery. You healed the timid woman who reached out in the crowd to touch You. We are not afraid of You!

Even so, come, Lord Jesus!

Come quickly!

CHAPTER
9

Will You Allow God to Reproduce Christ's Likeness in You?

"I am crucified with Christ: nevertheless I live; yet not I, but Christ liveth in me: and the life which I now live in the flesh I live by the faith of the Son of God, who loved me, and gave himself for me." Galatians 2:20

THERE SEEMS TO BE a great throng of professing Christians in our churches today whose total and amazing testimony sounds about like this: "I am thankful for God's plan in sending Christ to the cross to save me from hell."

I am convinced that it is a cheap, low-grade and misleading kind of Christianity that impels people to rise and state: "Because of sin I was deeply in debt—and God sent His Son, who came and paid all my debts."

Of course believing Christian men and women are saved from the judgment of hell and it is a reality that Christ our Redeemer has paid the whole slate of debt and sin that was against us.

But what does God say about His purposes in allowing Jesus to go to the cross and to the grave? What does God say about the meaning of death and resurrection for the Christian believer?

Surely we know the Bible well enough to be able to answer that: God's highest purpose in the redemption of sinful humanity was based in His hope that we would allow Him to reproduce the likeness of Jesus Christ in our once-sinful lives!

This is the reason why we should be concerned with this text—this testimony of the apostle Paul in which he shares his own personal theology with the Galatian Christians who had become known for their backslidings. It is a beautiful miniature, shining forth as an unusual and sparkling gem, an entire commentary on the deeper Christian life and experience. We are not trying to take it out of its context by dealing with it alone; we are simply acknowledging the fact that the context is too broad to be dealt with in any one message.

It is the King James version of the Bible which quotes Paul: "I am crucified with Christ." Nearly every other version quotes Paul as speaking in a different tense: "I have been crucified with Christ," and that really is the meaning of it: "I have been crucified with Christ."

This verse is quoted sometimes by people who have simply memorized it and they would not be able to tell you what Paul was really trying to communicate. This is not a portion of scripture which can be skipped through lightly. You cannot skim through and pass over this verse as many seem to be able to do with the Lord's prayer and the twenty-third Psalm.

This is a verse with such depth of meaning and spiritual potential for the Christian believer that we are obligated to seek its full meaning—so it can become practical and workable and liveable in all of our lives in this present world.

It is plain in this text that Paul was forthright and frank in the matter of his own personal involvement in seeking and finding God's highest desires and provision for Christian experience and victory. He was not bashful about the implications of his own personality becoming involved with the claims of Jesus Christ.

Not only does he plainly testify, "I have been crucified," but within the immediate vicinity of these verses, he uses the words *I, myself* and *me* a total of 14 times.

There certainly is, in the Bible, a good case for humility in the human personality, but it can be overdone.

We have had a dear missionary veteran among us from time to time. He is learned and cultured—and overly modest. With a great wealth of missionary exploits and material to tell, he has always refused to use any first person reference to himself.

When asked to tell about something that happened in his pioneer missionary life, he said: "One remembers when one was in China and one saw ..." That seems to be carrying the idea of modesty a bit too far, so I said to him, in a joking way, that if he had been writing the Twenty-third Psalm, it would likely read: "The Lord is one's shepherd, one shall not want; he maketh one to lie down in green pastures. He leadeth one ..."

I believe Paul knew that there is a legitimate time and place for the use of the word *I*. In spiritual matters, some people seem to want to maintain a kind of anonymity, if possible. As far as they are concerned, someone else should take the first step. This often comes up in the manner of our praying, as well. Some Christians are so general and vague and uninvolved in their requests that God Himself is unable to answer. I refer to the man who will bow his head and pray: "Lord, bless the missionaries and all for whom we should pray. Amen."

It is as though Paul says to us here: "I am not ashamed to use myself as an example. I have been crucified with Christ. I am willing to be pinpointed."

Only Christianity recognizes why the person who is without God and without any spiritual perception gets in such deep trouble with his own ego. When he says *I*, he is talking about the sum of his own individual being, and if he does not really know who he is or what he is doing here, he is beseiged in his personality with all kinds of questions and problems and uncertainties.

Most of the shallow psychology religions of the day try to deal with the problem of the ego by jockeying it around from one position to another, but Christianity deals with the problem of *I* by disposing of it with finality.

The Bible teaches that every unregenerated human being will continue to wrestle with the problems of his own natural ego and selfishness. His human nature dates back to Adam. But the Bible also teaches with joy and blessing that every individual may be born again, thus becoming a "new man" in Christ.

When Paul speaks in this text, "I have been crucified," he is saying that "my natural self has been crucified." That is why he can go on to say, "Yet I live"—for he has become another and a new person—"I live in Christ and Christ lives in me."

It is this first *I*, the natural me, which stands confronted with the just anger of God. God cannot acknowledge and accept me as a natural and selfish man—I am unregenerate and an alien, the complete essence of everything that is anti-God!

I know there are men and women who dismiss the idea of anything being anti-God or anti-Christ. They are not willing to pay any heed to the teachings of scripture relative to prophecy and eschatology.

Nevertheless, it is a biblical fact that whatever does not go through the process of crucifixion and transmutation, passing over into the new creation, is anti-Christ. Jesus said that all of that which is not with Christ is against Christ—those who are not on His side are against Him. We do not quite know what to do with those words of Christ, so we try to evade or work them over to a smooth, new version, but Jesus said, "If you do not gather with me, you scatter abroad."

There is a great hue and cry throughout the world today on behalf of tolerance and much of it comes from a rising spirit of godlessness in the nations. The communist nations, themselves the most intolerant, are preaching and calling for tolerance in order to break down all of the borders of religion and embarrass the American people with our social and racial problems.

This is the situation of the people of God: the most intolerant book in all the wide world is the Bible, the inspired Word of God, and the most intolerant teacher that ever addressed himself to an audience was the Lord Jesus Christ Himself.

On the other hand, Jesus Christ demonstrated the vast difference between being charitable and being tolerant. Jesus Christ was so charitable that in His great heart He took in all the people in the world and was willing to die even for those who hated Him.

But even with that kind of love and charity crowning His being, Jesus was so intolerant that He taught: "If you are not on my side, you are against me. If you do not believe that I am he, you shall die in your sins." He did not leave any middle ground to accommodate the neutral who preach tolerance. There is no "twilight zone" in the teachings of Jesus—no place in between.

Charity is one thing but tolerance is quite another matter.

Tolerance easily becomes a matter of cowardice if spiritual principles are involved, if the teachings of God's Word are ignored and forgotten.

Suppose we take the position of compromise that many want us to take: "Everyone come, and be saved if you want to. But if you do not want to be saved, maybe there is some other way that we can find for you. We want you to believe in the Lord Jesus Christ if you will, but if you do not want to, there may be a possibility that God will find some other way for you because there are those who say that there are many ways to God."

That would not be a spirit of tolerance on our part—it would be downright cowardice. We would be guilty with so many others of a spirit of compromise that so easily becomes an anti-God attitude.

True Christianity deals with the human problem of the self life, with the basic matter of "me, myself and I." The Spirit of God deals with it by an intolerant and final destruction, saying, "This selfish *I* cannot live if God is to be glorified in this human life."

God Himself deals with this aspect of human nature—the sum of all our proud life—and pronounces a stern condemnation upon it, flatly and frankly disapproving of it, fully and completely rejecting it.

And what does God say about it?

"I am God alone, and I will have nothing to do with man's selfish ego, in which I find the essence of rebellion and disobedience and unbelief. Man's nature in its pride of self and egotism is anti-God—and sinful, indeed!"

It is in this matter of how to deal with man's proud and perverse and sinful human nature that we discover two positions within the framework of Christianity.

One position is that which leans heavily upon the practice of psychology and psychiatry. There are so-called Christian leaders who insist that Jesus came into the world to bring about an adjustment of our ego, our selfishness, our pride, our perversity. They declare that we may become completely adjusted to life and to one another by dealing with the complexes and the twisted concepts that we have gotten into because our mothers scolded us when we were babies! So, there are thousands of referrals as the clergymen shift our problems from the church to the psychiatric couch.

On the other hand, thank God, the Bible plainly says that Jesus Christ came to bring an end of *self* —not to educate it or tolerate it or polish it! No one can ever say that Jesus Christ came to tell us how to cultivate our natural ego and pride. Jesus never taught that we could learn to get along with the big, proud *I* in our lives by giving it a love for Bach and Beethoven and Da Vinci.

Paul outlined the full spiritual remedy: "I am crucified with Christ . . . and the life which I now live in the flesh I live by the faith of the Son of God, who loved me, and gave himself for me."

This is a decision and an attitude of faith and commitment called for in the life of every believing Christian.

When we see that Jesus Christ came into the world to deal effectively and finally with our life of self and egotism and pride, we must take a stand.

With God's help, we say to that big *I* in our nature: "This is as far as you go—you are deposed. You are no longer to be in control!" In true repentance and in self-repudiation, we may turn our backs on the old self life. We may refuse to go along with it any longer. We have the right and the power to desert its ranks and cross over to spiritual victory and blessing on Emmanuel's side, walking joyfully under the banner of the cross of Jesus Christ from that hour on.

This is what it means to deal with and finally dispose of the "old man," the old life of self, which is still causing problems in so many Christian lives. We take a place of actual identification with Jesus Christ in His crucifixion, burial, and resurrection.

In the Christian life, that is what baptism is supposed to mean, but sad to say, baptism is nothing but a quick dip to the average person because that one does not know what baptism represents. He does not know that baptism genuinely ought to be an outward and visible testimony of a spiritual and inward transformation that has taken place; a symbol declaring that the old selfish and perverse human nature is repudiated in humility, and put away, crucified, declared dead!

That is what baptism should mean to the believer—death and burial with Christ, then raised with Him in the power of His resurrection! It can happen apart from water baptism of any mode, but that is what water baptism should indicate. It should set forth that identification with the death and resurrection of Jesus Christ just as a wedding ring witnesses and sets forth the fact that you are married.

Now, it is impossible to bring together and synchronize these two positions concerning the old life and nature of self. I do not believe that we are ever obliged to dovetail these two positions. Either the Lord Jesus Christ came to bring an end of self and reveal a new life in spiritual victory, or He came to patch and repair the old self—He certainly did not come to do both!

I expect someone to say, "We are interested in spiritual victory and blessing in our group, but our approach doesn't agree with yours at all!"

In answer I can only say that on the basis of the Word of God, true identification with Jesus Christ in His death, burial and resurrection will lead men and women to Christlikeness. God has never promised to work out His image in us in a variety of ways according to the inclinations of our own group. Forming the likeness to Jesus Christ in human lives and personalities is something that He does alike in all groups and all conferences and all fellowships around the world regardless of what they may be called.

There really is no way to patch up and repair the old life of self. The whole burden of New Testament theology insists that the old human self is ruined completely. It has no basic goodness, it holds to false values and its wisdom is questionable, to say the least. It is the new self in Christ Jesus—the new man in Christ—which alone must live. Onward from the point of this commitment, we must reckon ourselves indeed to have died unto sin, to be alive unto God in Christ Jesus.

But the natural self, the natural "I, myself and me," is continually taking inventory, seeking and hoping to find some human help in trying to forget and escape the guilty past, something that will make it more acceptable in God's sight, something that will enable it to develop to the fullest the potential of its nature.

Part of man's natural frustration is the inner feeling and realization that he is never measuring up and achieving to the full potential given him in creation. Actually, I believe God has created each one of us with a master blueprint representing His highest desires for the use of our many capacities in this life.

With God's blueprint stretching forth in all directions, what usually happens to the human life and personality? Well, we may see a utilitarian little house or shack there in the middle of it, and after a few years of hard work, an addition of some kind, but the outreach of our human personality which we picture in this way never stretches out to the limits of the blueprint.

The human nature in its striving and its groping has never been able to finally roll up the blueprint, put it away on the shelf, and say, "Thank God, my earthly existence is everything God desired it to be! The last wall has been raised, that final arch is complete, the roof is without a flaw—it is a habitation that can be considered to be perfect!"

The potential and the abilities of man's mighty nature are almost limitless—but we have to add, not quite! I am always stirred in my being to consider all that created man can do, the great powers and ability to think, the powers of imagination and creativity. Yet, if men and women do not find a way to properly use all of those powers and talents and gifts in bringing praise and honor and glory to God the Creator and the Redeemer, they are still not what they ought to be.

I believe there is a subconscious desire deep within every human being to realize and utilize his full potential—the desire to live a full and complete life, which often means the hope of escaping the past and the ability to face the future in confidence.

But what do men and women actually find when they look into their own hearts in this quest? They find nothing that measures up to their dreams and hopes. They find that they possess nothing of eternal value. They find that they know nothing with any certainty. They find that they can do nothing which is acceptable in the sight of a holy God.

Human beings continue to lean on a variety of crutches to support the ego, to nourish the pride, to cover the obvious defects in human existence. Many have believed that continuing education would provide that missing link between personality and potential. Many have turned to the pursuits of philosophies; others to cultural achievements. Ancestry and environment and status occupy many more.

But the ability to brag about human ancestors, to point with pride to the nation of our descent or the cultural privileges we have known—these do not transform and change and regenerate the human nature. Regardless of our racial strains, regardless of our cultural and educational advantages, we are all alike as human beings. In my own nature, I am nothing. Of myself, I know nothing. In God's sight, without His help and His enabling, I have nothing and I can do nothing.

But the inventory of the new man in Christ Jesus is so different! If he has found the meaning of commitment, the giving up of self to be identified with Jesus Christ in His crucifixion and death, he discovers in an entirely new measure the very presence of Christ Himself!

This new person has made room for the presence of Christ, so there is a difference in the personal inventory. It is no longer the old do-nothing, know-nothing, be-nothing, have-nothing person! That old assertive self died when the crucified and risen Saviour was given His rightful place of command and control in the personality. The old inventory cried out: "How can I be what I ought to be?" but the inventory of the new man is couched in faith and joy in his recognition that "Christ liveth in me!"

Paul expressed it to the Colossians in this way: "Christ in you, the hope of glory!" and then proceeded to assure them that "You are complete in Him!"

Paul wrote to the Ephesians to remind them that the essence of faith and hope in Christ is the assurance of being "accepted in the Beloved."

To the Corinthian believers, Paul promised full spiritual deliverance and stability in the knowledge that Jesus Christ "is made unto us wisdom, righteousness, sanctification and redemption."

Our great need, then, is simply Jesus Christ. He is what we need. He has what we need. He knows what we need to know. He has the ability to do in us what we cannot do—working in us that which is well-pleasing in God's sight.

This is a difficult point in spiritual doctrine and life for many people.

"What about my ambition? I have always been ambitious so it is a part of my being. Doesn't it matter?"

"I am used to doing my own thing in my own way—and I am still doing it in the church. Do I have to yield that?"

"I have always been able to put my best foot forward to get recognition and publicity. I am used to seeing my name in the paper. What do I get from crucifixion with Christ?"

Brothers and sisters, you get Christ and glory and fruitfulness and future and the world to come, whereof we speak, and the spirits of just men made perfect; you get Jesus, the mediator of a new covenant, and the blood of the everlasting covenant; an innumerable company of angels and the church of the firstborn and the New Jerusalem, the city of the living God!

And before you get all that, you have the privilege and the prospect of loving and joyful service for Christ and for mankind on this earth.

This is a gracious plan and provision for men and women in the kindness and wisdom of God. He loves you too well and too much to let you continue to strut and boast and cultivate your egotism and feed your *I*. He just cannot have that kind of selfish assertion in His children, so Jesus Christ works in us to complete Himself and make Himself anew in us.

So, you see, that is really why Jesus Christ came into this world to tabernacle with us, to die for us. God is never going to be done with us in shaping us and fashioning us as dear children of God until the day that we will see Him face to face, and His name shall be in our foreheads. In that day, we shall genuinely be like Him and we shall see Him as He is.

Truly, in that gracious day, our rejoicing will not be in the personal knowledge that He saved us from hell, but in the joyful knowledge that He was able to renew us, bringing the old self to an end, and creating within us the new man and the new self in which can be reproduced the beauty of the Son of God.

In the light of that provision, I think it is true that no Christian is where he ought to be spiritually until that beauty of the Lord Jesus Christ is being reproduced in daily Christian life.

I admit that there is necessarily a question of degree in this kind of transformation of life and character.

Certainly there has never been a time in our human existence when we could look into our own being, and say: "Well, thank God, I see it is finished now. The Lord has signed the portrait. I see Jesus in myself!"

Nobody will say that—nobody!

Even though a person has become like Christ, he will not know it. He will be charitable and full of love and peace and grace and mercy and kindness and goodness and faithfulness—but he will not really know it because humility and meekness are also a part of the transformation of true godliness.

Even though he is plainly God's man and Christ's witness, he will be pressing on, asking folks to pray for him, reading his Bible with tears, and saying, "Oh, God, I want to be like Thy Son!"

God knows that dear child is coming into the likeness of His Son, and the angels know it, and the observing people around him know it, too. But he is so intent upon the will and desires of God for his life and personality that he does not know it, for true humility never looks in on itself. Emerson wrote that the eye that sees only itself is blind and that the eye is not to see with but to see through. If my eye should suddenly become conscious of itself, I would be a blind man.

Now, there is a practical application of the crucified life and its demands from day to day. John the Baptist realized it long ago when he said, "He must increase but I must decrease!"

There must necessarily be less and less of me—and more and more of Christ! That's where you feel the bite and the bitterness of the cross, brother! Judicially and potentially, I was crucified with Christ, and now God wants to make it actual. In actuality, it is not as simple as that. Your decision and commitment do not then allow you to come down from that cross. Peace and power and fruitfulness can only increase according to our willingness to confess moment by moment, "It is no longer I, but Christ that liveth in me."

God is constantly calling for decisions among those in whom there is such great potential for displaying the life of Jesus Christ.

We must decide: "My way, or Christ's?"

Will I insist upon my own righteousness even while God is saying that it must be the righteousness of His Son?

Can I still live for my own honor and praise? No, it must be for Christ's honor and praise to be well-pleasing to God.

"Do I have any choice? Can I have my own plan?"

No, God can only be honored as we make our choices in Christ and live for the outworking of God's plan.

Modern theology refuses to press down very hard at this point, but we still are confronted often with spiritual choices in our hymnology. We often sing: "Oh, to be dead to myself, dear Lord; Oh, to be lost in Thee."

We sing the words, we soon shut the book, and drift away with friends to relax and have a pleasant soda. The principle does not become operative in most Christians. It does not become practical. That is why I keep saying and teaching and hoping that this principle which is objective truth will become subjective experience in Christian lives. For any professing Christian who dares to say, "Knowing the truth is enough for me; I do not want to mix it up with my day-to-day life and experience," Christianity has become nothing but a farce and a delusion!

It may surprise you that Aldous Huxley, often a critic of orthodox and evangelical Christianity, has been quoted as saying: "My kingdom *go* is the necessary correlary to *Thy* kingdom *come*."

How many Christians are there who pray every Sunday in church, "Thy kingdom come! Thy will be done!" without ever realizing the spiritual implications of such intercession? What are we praying for? Should we edit that prayer so that it becomes a confrontation: "My kingdom go, Lord; let Thy kingdom come!" Certainly His kingdom can never be realized in my life until my own selfish kingdom is deposed. It is when I resign, when I am no longer king of my domain that Jesus Christ will become king of my life.

Now, brethren, in confession, may I assure you that a Christian clergyman cannot follow any other route to spiritual victory and daily blessing than that which is prescribed so plainly in the Word of God. It is one thing for a minister to choose a powerful text, expound it and preach from it—it is quite something else for the minister to honestly and genuinely live forth the meaning of the Word from day to day. A clergyman is a man—and often he has a proud little kingdom of his own, a kingdom of position and often of pride and sometimes with power. Clergymen must wrestle with the spiritual implications of the crucified life just like everyone else, and to be thoroughgoing men of God and spiritual examples to the flock of God, they must die daily to the allurements of their own little kingdoms of position and prestige.

One of the greatest of the pre-reformation preachers in Germany was Johannes Tollar, certainly an evangelical before Luther's time. The story has been told that a devout layman, a farmer whose name was Nicholas, came down from the countryside, and implored Dr. Tollar to preach a sermon in the great church, dealing with the deeper Christian life based on spiritual union with Jesus Christ.

The following Sunday Dr. Tollar preached that sermon. It had 26 points, telling the people how to put away their sins and their selfishness in order to glorify Jesus Christ in their daily lives. It was a good sermon—actually, I have read it and I can underscore every line of it.

When the service was over and the crowd had dispersed, Nicholas came slowly down the aisle.

He said, "Pastor Tollar, that was a great sermon and I want to thank you for the truth which you presented. But I am troubled and I would like to make a comment, with your permission."

"Of course, and I would like to have your comment," the preacher said.

"Pastor, that was great spiritual truth that you brought to the people today, but I discern that you were preaching it to others as truth without having experienced the implications of deep spiritual principles in your own daily life," Nicholas told him. "You are not living in full identification with the death and resurrection of Jesus Christ. I could tell by the way you preached—I could tell!"

The learned and scholarly Dr. Tollar did not reply. But he was soon on his knees, seeking God in repentance and humiliation. For many weeks he did not take the pulpit to preach—earnestly seeking day after day the illumination of the Spirit of God in order that objective truth might become a deep and renewing and warming spiritual experience within.

After the long period of the dark sufferings in his soul, the day came when John Tollar's own kingdom was brought to an end and was replaced by God's kingdom. The great flood of the Spirit came in on his life and he returned to his parish and to his pulpit to become one of the greatest and most fervent and effective preachers of his generation. God's gracious blessings came—but Tollar first had to die. This is what Paul meant when he said, "I have been crucified with Christ."

This must become living reality for all of us who say we are interested in God's will for our lives. You pray for me and I will surely pray for you—because this is a matter in which we must follow our Lord!

We can quote this text from memory, but that is not enough. I can say that I know what Paul meant, but that is not enough. God promises to make it living reality in our lives the instant that we let our little, selfish kingdom go!

Christian, Do You Downgrade Yourself Too Much

"Looking for that blessed hope, and the glorious appearing of the great God and our Saviour Jesus Christ; Who gave himself for us, that he might redeem us from all iniquity, and purify unto himself a peculiar people, zealous of good works." Titus 2:13-14

THE PEOPLE OF GOD, Christians who are living between the two mighty events of Christ's incarnation and His promised second coming, are not living in a vacuum!

It is amazing that segments in the Christian church that deny the possibility of the imminent return of the Lord Jesus accuse those who do believe in His soon coming of sitting around, twiddling their thumbs, looking at the sky, and blankly hoping for the best!

Nothing could be further from the truth. We live in the interim between His two appearances, but we do not live in a vacuum. We have much to do and little time in which to get it done!

Stretch your mind and consider some very apparent facts of our day.

Who are the Christians leaving all to staff the missionary posts around the world? Who are the Christians staying at home and sacrificing in order to support the great evangelical thrust of the Christian gospel everywhere? Those who fervently believe that He is coming.

What kind of churches are busy praying and teaching and giving, preparing their young people for the ministry and for missionary work? Churches that are responding to Christ's appeal to "occupy until I come!"

Well, in this text Titus has given us Christian doctrine that has validity both in the light of the expected return of Jesus Christ as well as in the face of death.

It is in the record of the early Methodists in England, when there was persecution and testing in every direction, that John Wesley was able to say, "Our people die well!"

In more recent years, I have heard a quotation from a denominational bishop who estimated that only about ten per cent of the men and women in the membership of his church body are prepared and spiritually ready to die when their time comes.

I believe you can only die well when you have lived well, from a spiritual point of view. This doctrine of the Christian life and spiritual vitality of the believer as propounded by Titus has full validity in the face of any contingency which awaits us.

Titus quickly identifies Jesus Christ as the Saviour "who gave himself for us," and we can quickly learn the value of any object by the price which people are willing to pay for it. Perhaps I should qualify that—you may not learn the true value, for it is my private opinion that a diamond or other jewelry has no intrinsic value at all.

You may remember the story about the rooster scratching around in the barnyard for kernels of corn. Suddenly he scratched up a beautiful pearl of fabulous price which had been lost years before, but he just pushed it aside and kept on looking for corn. The pearl had no value for the rooster, although it had a great value for those who had set a price upon it.

There are various kinds of markets in the world, and something which has no value for a disinterested person may be considered of great value by the person desiring it and purchasing it.

It is in this sense, then, that we learn how dear and precious we are to Christ by what He was willing to give for us.

I believe many Christians are tempted to downgrade themselves too much. I am not arguing against true humility and my word to you is this: Think as little of yourself as you want to, but always remember that our Lord Jesus Christ thought very highly of you—enough to give Himself for you in death and sacrifice.

If the devil does come to you and whispers that you are no good, don't argue with him. In fact, you may as well admit it, but then remind the devil: "Regardless of what you say about me, I must tell you how the Lord feels about me. He tells me that I am so valuable to Him that He gave Himself for me on the cross!"

So, the value is set by the price paid—and, in our case, the price paid was our Lord Himself!

The end that the Saviour had in view was that He might redeem us from all iniquity, that is, from the power and consequences of iniquity.

We often sing the words of a hymn by Charles Wesley in which the death of our Lord Jesus is described as "the double cure" for sin. I think many people sing the hymn without realizing what Wesley meant by the double cure.

"Be of sin the double cure, Save me from its wrath and power." The wrath of God against sin and then the power of sin in the human life—these both must be cured. Therefore, when He gave Himself for us, He redeemed us with a double cure, delivering us from the consequences of sin and delivering us from the power which sin exercises in human lives.

Now, Titus, in this great nugget of spiritual truth, reminds us that the redemptive Christ performs a purifying work in the people of God.

You will have to agree with me that one of the deep and outbroken diseases of this present world and society is impurity, and it displays itself in dozens of symptoms. We are prone to look upon certain lewd and indecent physical actions as the impurities which plague human life and society—but the actual lusting and scheming and planning and plotting come from a far deeper source of impurity within the very minds and innermost beings of sinful men and women.

If we were people of clean hands and pure hearts, we would be intent upon doing the things that please God. Impurity is not just a wrong action; impurity is the state of mind and heart and soul which is just the opposite of purity and wholeness.

Sexual misconduct is a symptom of the disease of impurity—but so is hatred. Pride and egotism, resentfulness and churlishness come to the surface out of sinful and impure minds and hearts, just as gluttony and slothfulness and self-indulgence do. All of these and countless others come to the surface as outward symptoms of the deep, inward disease of selfishness and sin.

Because this is a fact in life and experience, it is the spiritual work of Jesus Christ to purify His people by His own blood to rid them of this deep-lying disease. That is why He is called the Great Physician—He is able to heal us of this plague of impurity and iniquity, redeeming us from the consequences of our sins and purifying us from the presence of our sins.

Now, brethren, either this is true and realizable in human life and experience or Christianity is the cheap fraud of the day. Either it is true and a dependable spiritual option or we should fold up the Bible and put it away with other classical pieces of literature which have no particular validity in the face of death.

Thank God that there are millions who dare to stand as if in a great chorus and shout with me, "It is true! He did give Himself to redeem us from all iniquity and He does perform this purifying work in our lives day by day!"

The result of Christ's purifying work is the perfecting of God's very own people, referred to in this passage from the King James version as "a peculiar people."

Many of us know all too well that this word *peculiar* has been often used to cloak religious conduct both strange and irrational. People have been known to do rather weird things and then grin a self-conscious grin and say in half-hearted apology: "Well, we are a peculiar people!"

Anyone with a serious and honest concern for scriptural admonition and instruction could quickly learn that this English word *peculiar* in the language of 1611 describing the redeemed people of God had no connotation of queerness, ridiculousness nor foolishness.

The same word was first used in Exodus 19:5 when God said that Israel "shall be unto me a peculiar treasure above all people." It was God's way of emphasizing that His people would be to Him a treasure above all other treasures. In the etymological sense, it means "shut up to me as my special jewel."

Every loving mother and father has a good idea of what God meant. There are babies in houses up and down every street, as you can tell by the baby clothes hanging on the lines on a summer day.

But in the house where you live, there is one little infant in particular, and he is a peculiar treasure unto you above all others. It does not mean neccssarily that he is prettier, but it does mean that he is the treasure above all other treasures and you would not trade him for any other child in the whole world. He is a *peculiar* treasure!

This gives us some idea, at least, of what we are—God's special jewels marked out for Him!

Titus then clearly spelled out one thing that will always characterize the children of God—the fact that they are zealous of good works.

Titus and all of the other writers who had a part in God's revelation through the scriptures agree at this point—our Lord never made provision for any of His followers to be "armchair" Christians. "Ivory tower" Christianity, an abstract kind of believing, composed simply of fine and beautiful thoughts, is not what Jesus taught at all.

The language in this passage is plain: The children of God in Jesus Christ, redeemed by the giving of Himself, purified and made unto Him as special jewels, a peculiar people, are characterized by one thing—their zeal for good works.

Because of the grace of God, we learn, these followers of Jesus Christ are zealous of good works and in their daily experience they live "looking." The Christian should always live in joyous anticipation of the blessed hope and the glorious appearing of the great God and our Saviour Jesus Christ!

Now, there is something in Christian theology that I want to share with you. Some people say they cannot bother with theology because they do not know either Greek or Hebrew. I cannot believe that there is any Christian who is so humble that he would insist that he knows nothing about theology.

Theology is the study of God and we have a very wonderful textbook—actually 66 textbooks rolled into one. We call it the Bible. The point I want to make is this: I have noted in study and in experience that the more vital and important any theological or doctrinal truth may be, the devil will fight it harder and bring greater controversy to bear upon it.

Consider the deity of Jesus, for example.

More and more people are arguing and debating and fighting over this absolutely vital and foundational truth.

The devil is smart enough not to waste his attacks on minor and non-vital aspects of Christian truth and teaching.

The devil will not cause any trouble for a preacher who is scared stiff of his congregation and worried about his job to the extent that he preaches for thirty minutes and the sum of what he says is "Be good and you will feel better!"

You can be as good as you want to and yet go to hell if you have not put your trust in Jesus Christ! The devil is not going to waste his time causing any trouble for the preacher whose only message is "Be good!"

But the believing Christian lives in joyful anticipation of the return of Jesus Christ and that is such an important segment of truth that the devil has always been geared up to fight it and ridicule it. One of his big successes is being able to get people to argue and get mad about the second coming— rather than looking and waiting for it.

Suppose a man has been overseas two or three years, away from his family. Suddenly a cable arrives for the family with the message, "My work completed here; I will be home today."

After some hours he arrives at the front door and finds the members of his family in turmoil. There had been a great argument as to whether he would arrive in the afternoon or evening. There had been arguments about what transportation he would be using. As a result, there were no little noses pushing against the window glass, no one looking to be able to catch the first glimpse of returning Daddy.

You may say, "That is only an illustration."

But what is the situation in the various segments of the Christian community?

They are fighting with one another and glaring at each other. They are debating whether He is coming and how He is coming and they are busy using what they consider to be proof texts about the fall of Rome and the identification of the anti-Christ.

Brethren, that is the work of the devil—to make Christian people argue about the details of His coming so they will forget the most important thing. How many Christians are so confused and bewildered by the arguments that they have forgotten that the Saviour has purified unto Himself a peculiar people, expecting that we will live soberly, righteously and godly, looking for the glorious appearing of the great God and Saviour.

That is the Epiphany, which is an expression in the Christian church, and it is used in reference to Christ's manifestation in the world.

It is used in two senses in 1 Timothy and 2 Timothy.

First, Paul says in 2 Timothy 1:8-10: ". . . God, who hath saved us, and called us with an holy calling, not according to our works, but according to his own purpose and grace, which was given us in Christ Jesus before the world began, but is now made manifest by the appearing of our Saviour Jesus Christ, who hath abolished death, and hath brought life and immortality to light through the gospel."

In that passage we have the record of His first appearing, the shining forth when He came into the world to abolish death by His death and resurrection.

Then, the apostle in one of those moving and wonderful doxologies, said in 1 Timothy 6:13-16: "I give thee charge in the sight of God, who quick-eneth all things, and before Christ Jesus, who before Pontius Pilate witnessed a good confession; that thou keep this commandment without spot, unrebukeable, until the appearing of our Lord Jesus Christ."

Paul speaks of the second appearing, when Christ "shall shew, who is the blessed and only Potentate, the King of kings, and Lord of lords; Who only hath immortality, dwelling in the light which no man can approach unto; whom no man hath seen, nor can see: to whom be honour and power everlasting. Amen."

When I read something like this given us by the apostle Paul, it makes me think of a skylark or a meadowlark mounting a branch and bursting into an unexpected but brilliantly melodious song. Paul often breaks forth with one of his wonderful and uplifting ascriptions of praise to Jesus Christ in the midst of his epistles, and this is one of those!

Paul reminds Christian believers here that when Jesus Christ appears again, He will show forth, and leave no doubts at all, as to the Person of the King of kings and Lord of lords.

Paul was also careful to comfort those in the early church who feared that they might die before this second appearing of Jesus Christ. Actually, there were believers in the Thessalonian church who were worried on two counts, the first of which was their thought that the Lord had already come and they had been passed by. The second was their thought that they would die before He came and that through death, they would miss out on the joys of His appearing.

So, Paul wrote the two epistles to the Thessalonian church to straighten them out on the truth concerning Christ's second appearing.

"If we believe that Jesus died and rose again, even so them also which sleep in Jesus will God bring with him"—that is, if you die and go to be with the Lord, God will bring you along with Jesus at His appearing—"for this we say unto you by the word of the Lord, that we which are alive and remain unto the coming of the Lord shall not (run ahead of those) which are asleep. For the Lord himself shall descend from heaven with a shout, with the voice of the archangel, and with the trump of God: and the dead in Christ shall rise first: Then we which are alive and remain shall be caught up together with them in the clouds, to meet the Lord in the air: and so shall we ever be with the Lord. Wherefore comfort one another with these words."

You see, Paul's inspired explanation instructs us that those who died before the coming of Jesus will not be at a disadvantage. If anything, they will be in a position of advantage, because before the Lord glorifies the waiting saints throughout the earth, He will raise in glorified bodies the great company of believers who have been parted from us by death throughout the centuries.

Brethren, that is very plainly what the apostle Paul tells us in the instructions originally given to the Thessalonian Christians.

Don't we have the right to think that it is very strange that the majority of the Christian pulpits are completely silent concerning this glorious truth of the imminent return of Jesus Christ? It is paradoxical that there should be this great silence in Christian churches at the very time when the danger of suddenly being swept off the face of the earth is greater than it has ever been.

Russia and the United States, the two great nuclear powers, continue to measure their ability to destroy in terms of *overkill*. This is a terrible compound word never before used in the history of the English language. The scientists had to express the almost incredible destructive power of the nuclear bombs in our stockpiles—so the word *overkill* is a new invention of our times.

Both the United States and Russia have made statements about the overkill power of nuclear stockpiles sufficient to kill every man, woman and child in the world—not once, but 20 times over. That is overkill!

Isn't it just like that old enemy, Satan, to persuade the saints in the Body of Christ to engage in bitter arguments about post-tribulation rapture and pretribulation rapture; post-millennialism, a-millennialism and pre-millennialism—right at the very hour when overkill hangs over us like a black, threatening cloud.

Brethren, this is the kind of age and hour when the Lord's people should be so alert to the hope and promise of His coming that they should get up every morning just like a child on Christmas morning— eager and believing that it should be today!

Instead of that kind of expectancy, what do we find throughout His church today? Arguments pro and con about His coming, about the details of the rapture—and some of this to the point of bitterness. Otherwise, we find great segments of Christians who seem to be able to blithely ignore the whole matter of the return of Jesus Christ.

Very few ministers bother to preach from the Book of Revelation any more—and that is true of large areas of evangelicalism and fundamentalism, too! We have been intimidated by the cynicism and sophistication of our day.

There are so many apparent anomalies and contradictions in society and in the ranks of professing Christians that someone will certainly write a book about it.

There is the anomaly of the necessity of getting to know one another better in order to love and understand one another better. Millions are traveling and meeting other millions and getting acquainted, so if the premise is true, we ought all to love each other like one big blessed family.

Instead, we hate each other like the devil. It is true that all over the world the nations are hating each other in startling, record-breaking measure.

I will mention another contradiction that is all too apparent. Our educators and sociologists told us that all we had to do was allow the teaching of sexual education in the schools and all of our vexing sexual problems in society would disappear.

Is it not a strange anomaly that the generation that has been teaching and outlining more about sexual practices than any twenty-five generations combined did in the past is the generation that is the most rotten and perverted in sexual conduct?

And is it not strange, too, that the very generation that might expect to be atomized suddenly by overkill is the generation that is afraid to talk about the coming of the Lord and unwilling to discuss His gracious promises of deliverance and glorification?

You may not expect me to say it, but I will: what a bunch of weirdies we are! What a strange generation we are!

God has said that He would place a great premium on the holy, spiritual consistency of the Christian saints, but how inconsistent we are when we allow the devil and our own carnality to confuse and mix us up so that we will be diverted from patient waiting for His appearing!

So, we live between two mighty events—that of His incarnation, death and resurrection, and that of His ultimate appearing and the glorification of those He died to save. This is the interim time for the saints—but it is not a vacuum. He has given us much to do and He asks for our faithfulness.

In the meantime, we are zealous of good works, living soberly, righteously, godly in this present world, looking unto Him and His promise. In the midst of our lives, and between the two great mountain peaks of God's acts in the world, we look back and remember, and we look forward and hope! As members of His own loving fellowship, we break the bread and drink the wine. We sing His praise and we pray in His Name, remembering and expecting!

Brethren, that moves me more than anything else in this world. It is such a blessed privilege that it is more beautiful and satisfying than friendships or paintings or sunsets or any other beauties of nature. Looking back to His grace and love; looking forward to His coming and glory; meanwhile actively working and joyously hoping—until He comes!

Do You Love Your Lord, Never Having Seen Him?

". . . Jesus Christ, whom having not seen, ye love . . ."
1 Peter 1:8

I THINK IT MAY BE safely said of the human family that it is possible to love someone we have never seen, but that it is totally impossible for us to love one whom we have not "experienced" in some way.

The apostle Peter, who had seen Jesus Christ in the flesh with his own eyes, passed along to every believing Christian the assurance that it is possible for us to love the Saviour and to live a life that will glorify Him even though we have not yet seen Him.

It is as though Peter is urging: "Love Him and work for Him and live for Him. I give you my testimony that it will be worth it all when you look upon His face—for I have seen Him with my own eyes, and I know!"

Once Peter was occupied with the chores of his fishing trade along the shores of Galilee as a quiet Man passed by, a Man with a marvelous magnetism, a glorious wonder about His face. When He flipped His pleasant finger at Peter, the big fisherman jumped up and followed and was in His company for three years.

Peter came to know personally the meaning of bitter tears and strong weeping after his denial of the Lord. I am sure he wept often when his thoughts would sweep him along to the memories of the broken body of the Messiah hanging on a cross. But his eyes had also seen Jesus after He was risen from the grave, for the Lord came forth and put His hand on Peter's head and forgave him!

Peter had also seen Him before that in the glory of the transfiguration—the preview of the glory that awaited the Son of Man. Finally, Peter stood with the other disciples as Jesus bade them farewell and ascended into heaven from the Mount of Olives. All of these were incidents in Peter's life which were actual experiences in his relationship with the person of Jesus Christ, his Lord and Master.

So, Peter had seen Jesus in the flesh, and was moved to write to the strangers scattered abroad—the Christians of the dispersion—to remind them that they should love Jesus Christ even though they had not seen Him in the flesh.

The Lord Jesus Himself had set His own stamp of approval and blessing upon all Christians who would believe, never having seen Him in the time of His own flesh. He told Thomas after the resurrection, "Because thou hast seen me, thou hast believed: blessed are they that have not seen, and yet have believed."

I think it is a mistake for Christians to nurture a kind of plaintive and pensive regret that they did not live 2,000 years ago when Christ was upon the earth. We are reminded of this attitude in a children's hymn that most of us have sung at one time or another:

"I think when I read the sweet story of old,
How Jesus was here among men;
How He called little children as lambs to His fold,
I would like to have been with Him then."

I do not go on record as objecting to that song, but I do not think it has any biblical authority. I truly believe that God has ordained that we may actually know Jesus now, and love Him better never having seen Him, than Peter did when he saw Him!

Now, about this matter of being able to "experience" others.

In our human race, some persons unfortunately are born without the ability to hear and others are born without the great gift of sight.

One who is born without the ability to hear may still know and experience and appreciate relatives and friends through the communication of the eyes.

One who is blind but has the faculty of hearing soon discovers the ability to experience and to come to know those who are around him by hearing their voices and learning all the sweet cadences of affection and love through the ears.

Even those who have had the double handicap of deafness and blindness have come to experience and know and appreciate other human beings—like Helen Keller, for instance, who learned to love people by feeling their faces with her sensitive fingers.

The story has been told that when Helen Keller was a young woman, she was introduced to the great tenor, Caruso. Unable to hear him, of course, she asked for the privilege of putting her fingers on his neck and chest bones while he sang one of his favorite operatic renditions. Her sensitive hands experienced the great range of the vibrations of his voice, and she stood as though transfixed. She could not hear his voice, but she experienced him in a most unusual way through the reading of her fingers.

I am sure it is true that we can love people we have not seen—but that it is impossible to love one whom we have not experienced in any way. It is a total impossibility for me to find any emotional response toward a person who has never come within the circle of my human experience.

For instance, do I love Abraham Lincoln?

Well, Abraham Lincoln is dead. I respect and admire his memory and I honor his great contributions to our nation and society. I believe he was a great man, but I feel no emotional response or personal human affection toward him.

If I had lived in the day of Lincoln and there had been opportunity for some correspondence between us, that opportunity to know and feel his great depth of personality would have certainly given me an emotional sense of affection and attachment. But as it is, I only know about Lincoln. I had no communication with him.

Actually, there have been people who confessed that they had fallen in love with another person through the writing of letters and the use of the mail. It is possible to experience others through the writing of letters—you get the pulse of them through the things they write and your imagination pieces it out and you may well experience love for the person of one whom you have not seen. It has happened.

God has seen fit to give us wonderful and mysterious faculties, and thus we human beings are able to know and experience and love someone we have not seen.

That is why Peter was able to witness to us of Jesus Christ and to tell us that we could and we should love Him, never having laid eyes upon His person in the flesh.

Notice that Peter did not assure us that we could love Jesus Christ without meeting Him in experience, in spirit, in His Word.

I think that one of the most hopeless tasks in the world is that of trying to create some love for Christ our Saviour among those who refuse and deny that there is a need for a definite spiritual experience of Jesus Christ in the human life.

I cannot understand the activities of many churches—their futile exercise of trying to whip up love and concern for Jesus Christ when there is no teaching of the new birth, no teaching of redemption through His blood, no dependence upon spiritual illumination by the Spirit of God!

No one can love the Lord Jesus Christ unless the Spirit of God is given opportunity to reveal Him in the life. No one can say that Jesus is Lord except the Holy Spirit enables him through spiritual life and experience.

Knowing this fact makes me question how any congregation can love and serve and glorify a Saviour whose very saviourhood is denied from the pulpit.

Peter writes that we are dedicated to the glory of the One whom we have not seen, because we love Him. That is the sum of Christianity—to know Him and to love Him!

"This is eternal life, that they might know me," Jesus taught. So, the knowledge of God is eternal

life and the knowledge of setting forth the life of
God in man is the business of the church.

It is a wonderful facet of love that we always take
pleasure and delight in doing those things that are
pleasing to the one we love. I find that the believing Christian who really loves his Lord is never
irked or irritated in the service he is giving to Jesus
Christ. The Lord will give him delight in true service for God—and I say it this way because generally the irksome and boring features of Christian
service are some of the things that people and
organizations have added on. I refer to things that
have no scriptural validity.

It is always pleasant and delightful to set forth
the praises of someone you really love. I think I see
the illustration of that very often among the grand-
parents I meet, for they always whip out a wallet or
a sheaf of pictures of their beautiful and talented
grandchildren—whom they dearly love!

Those who truly love Jesus Christ find it one of
the greatest pleasures in life to be able to simply
describe how we discovered His great love for us,
and how we are trying to return that love and devotion as we follow and serve Him in faith each day.

Now, Peter speaks out of a close relationship
to Jesus, and in all of his writings speaks often of
Jesus Christ, our Lord. He knew Jesus and had
been instructed and taught of the Lord. There is
reverence and dignity in his manner whenever he
uses the name and titles of the Saviour.

Jesus was His name for Mary was told, "Thou
shalt call his name Jesus because he is to be the Saviour of the world." The name Jesus had the same
meaning as Joshua, which is "Jehovah saves."

Then, when Jesus went to the Jordan river and was anointed by the Holy Spirit, the title of Anointed One was His, which we express in the English language as Christ. This is His name and title—Jesus the Christ. Jesus, the Anointed One!

When Jesus Christ arose from the dead He took precedence over all creatures, whether in heaven or earth or hell. His exalted position in relation to all beings everywhere gave Him the title Lord, one who has the right and the power and the wisdom and the ability for sovereignty and dominion.

So, Jesus means Saviour. Christ means the Anointed One. Lord means just what it means in English—one who rightfully holds dominion, and, in this case, our Lord Jesus Christ is the One about whom the entire creation turns.

Now, before considering further the place of Jesus Christ in the creation, I want to remind you that the whole Bible and the complete life of the believing church also are wholly dependent upon God's final revelation of Himself in the person of Jesus Christ, His Son.

Our Lord Jesus Christ was that One who was with the Father and who was God and who is God and who was given the divinely-bestowed commission to set forth the mystery and the majesty and the wonder and the glory of the Godhead throughout the universe. It is more than an accident that both the Old and New Testaments comb heaven and earth for figures of speech or simile to set forth the wonder and glory of God.

The Son of God is described by almost every fair and worthy name in the creation. He is called the Sun of Righteousness with healing in His wings.

He is called the Star that shone on Jacob. He is described as coming forth with His bride, clear as the moon. His Presence is likened unto the rain coming down upon the earth, bringing beauty and fruitfulness. He is pictured as the great sea and as the towering rock. He is likened to the strong cedars. A figure is used of Him as of a great eagle, going literally over the earth, looking down upon the wonders and beauties of lake and river and rock, of the mountains and the plains.

Brethren, you can be perfectly free to go to your Bible with assurance that you will find Jesus Christ everywhere in its pages. I am convinced that it was God's design that you should find the divine Creator, Redeemer and Lord whenever you search the scriptures, and you do not have to "read" anything into the Word that is not already there.

Where the person of Jesus Christ does not stand out tall and beautiful and commanding, as a pine tree against the sky, you will find Him behind the lattice, but stretching forth His hand. If He does not appear as the sun shining in his strength, He may be discerned in the reviving by the promised gentle rains falling from the heavens above.

I do not mind telling you that I have always found Jesus Christ beckoning to me throughout the scriptures. Do not be disturbed by those who say that Old Testament portions cannot be claimed by the Christian church. God has given us the Bible as a unit, and Jesus referred in His teachings to many Old Testament portions which foretold His person and His ministries.

For illustration, I would say that it would be very difficult for a man to live and function in a physical body that existed only from the waist up. He would be without some of the vital organs necessary for the sustenance of life.

Similarly, the Bible contains two parts of one organic revelation and it is divided so that the Old Testament is the Bible from the waist down and the New Testament is the Bible from the waist up. This may give an understanding to my expression that if we have one organic Bible and we cut it in two, we actually bleed it to death and we can, in effect, kill it by cutting it.

Let us read the Bible as the Word of God and never apologize for finding Jesus Christ throughout its pages, for Jesus Christ is what the Bible is all about!

As for the men who seem to be able to preach the Bible without finding Jesus Christ as the necessary way and truth and life, I can only comment that they are more blind than I ever thought it possible for anyone to be. Jesus Christ the Lord is the revelation from the Father—and His being has made God's written record for man both a necessity and a reality.

Now, in our day, the Christian church seems to have a variety of concerns, but in reality it has only one reason for being—and that is to show forth the life and mercy and grace of Jesus Christ. Study the relationship of the Body of Christ to Jesus Christ, its Head, and you soon realize that the life and witness and proclamation of the church is all about Jesus Christ.

You will understand that when I speak of the Christian church I am not speaking of any particular denomination. Christ's church is the church of the firstborn, purchased with His blood. Christ's church includes all twice-born believers who have been inducted into the kingdom of God by the operation of the Holy Spirit.

There is an example of what the church is all about in Acts 13. The believers had met together. They ministered unto the Lord and prayed. That is the chief concern and ministry of the Christian church, and it cancels out any question about the problem of "which denomination?"

Wherever you find the Lord Jesus Christ you will find the church. Our Lord Jesus and the company of His people—in that fellowship you find His church.

Years ago they described the teaching prowess of a certain well-known educator in this way: Put that accomplished teacher-communicator on one end of a log and a boy on the other—and instantly you had a college!

It is even more true that when Jesus Christ by His Spirit meets with two of His believing people, you have a church! You have it without any upkeep and without any overhead and without any elections. But Jesus Christ must be central and His Presence must be known among His people.

Some Christian groups seem to think that doctrine comes first. Doctrine is necessary to the understanding of Christ—but it will be a rather sad Christian group if it has only doctrinal emphasis and fails to recognize first of all the Presence of Jesus Christ. A church pleasing to Jesus Christ must be dedicated to honoring Him who shows forth the wonder and the glory of the Godhead.

Those who are engaged merely in ecclesiastical motions have missed the point—Jesus Christ

Himself wants to be known and honored in the midst of His people, and this is what our life and fellowship is all about. Peter says it will be true above all in the midst of the church that we will honor and love Him, although we have not yet seen Him! In the Christian church, then, our objectives and our activities should only be those which scripturally point to the Lamb of God who takes away the sins of the world and which minister to the eternal welfare of men and women.

Now, let us consider the Person of Jesus Christ and His mandate from the Father in the creation of all things.

In a more relaxed generation, when people did not have to hustle and scurry to keep out of the way of automobile traffic, men would often go out and lie down under the stars, gaze up, and say: "What is man that Thou art mindful of him?" Now, it is hard to see through the smoke and the smog.

Modern man does occasionally halt long enough to think and wonder about the creation of the universe. With the use of one word in this passage, the word *whom*, referring to Jesus Christ, Peter gives the only possible answer—the creation is about *whom*— "Jesus Christ, *whom* having not seen, ye love."

The believing Christian who sees in the creation of all things the setting forth of the wonder and glory of Jesus Christ as Lord and Sovereign will have no more unholy days. He will no longer be inclined to divide existence between secular interests and holy interests. There is a divine sanctification of everything in his life when the believer fully realizes that God has made His creation as a garment to show forth the Lord Jesus Christ. I do not believe that any scientist or educator or anyone else can ever know or fathom the deep mysteries of creation without admitting that there is One *whom*—One who holds all things together in the vast universe, the One in whom all things cohere, as Paul told the Colossians.

Brethren, creation is the setting forth of Jesus Christ as Lord and Sovereign, for Jesus Christ is the purpose of God in creation! Let me urge you to go back and read again the first chapter of Ezekiel in which the man of God said, "I saw heaven opened, and I saw visions of God."

Ezekiel had a remarkable vision in which there were whirlwinds, great clouds, an unusual fire and brightness, and out of which came four living creatures, and the four had the face of a man, the face of a lion, the face of an ox and the face of an eagle.

Now, these living creatures coming out of the mysterious fire, it seems to me, stand for a heavenly and visible representation of the creation, and our Lord Jesus Christ, whom we have not yet seen, is the One that creation is all about.

Those strange creatures out of the fire show forth, in some measure, what our Lord Jesus Christ is like. The prophet saw the fourfold representation of the faces of a man, a lion, an ox and an eagle.

Years ago it was called to my attention that this fourfold division of the character of Jesus corresponds in a remarkable way to the presentation of His ministries recorded in the four Gospels.

This is not new to us by any means, but it is of great significance to students of the Word of God and to all who love our Lord Jesus Christ in truth.

Luke in his record clearly sets forth the emphasis upon the man, Jesus. Matthew sets Him forth as a lion and Mark, as an ox. John's record refers to His heavenly qualities, with the representation of the high-flying eagle.

Jesus was indeed a man and Luke's record seems suited particularly for the Greek culture which had long sought for perfection in manhood.

Matthew's record is intent upon its appeal to the Jewish heart and mind, giving emphasis to the messianic and kingly fulfillment of Jewish hopes in Jesus Christ, and thus the figure of the Lion of Judah.

Mark gives a brief, straight-from-the-shoulder record of Jesus, the man of action and power, a mighty worker. The representation in figure is that of the strength and faithfulness of the ox and the appeal, no doubt, was to the Roman mind and mentality of the day.

Coming to John's Gospel, we note a different emphasis. Luke had traced the genealogy back to Adam. Matthew had traced the ancestors of Jesus back to Abraham. But John goes back to the beginning of all things and appeals to all men and the whole world to consider the necessity for Jesus, the Divine Son of God, to become flesh and dwell among us.

John, in his record, insists that Jesus antedates all biography and all chronology, and he goes back to the beginning to set forth the wonder and the mystery and the glory of Jesus Christ. Let me tell you one of my fancies—something that I cannot actually prove.

I believe that there is a time coming in the plan of God when it will be plainly seen that all of the laws of nature and all of the beings that are in nature—beasts on the earth and fish that swim in the waters and birds that fly in the air, even tiny hoppers and creeping things that lisp their pitifully little note on the night breezes—are all necessary in setting forth even a little of the wonder of Jesus Christ!

You will recall that Jesus sent disciples to bring a little donkey for His use with the words, "Say that the Lord hath need of him." Even the sad-faced, comical, long-eared donkey was necessary to set forth the glory of the Messiah-Saviour on that day when the cries of "Hosannah" came from the admiring multitudes.

Now, I did not intend to say this, but I might as well make the application. I do not infer that there is any relation between the little beast and us, but I want to emphasize that many mem and women have lost all sight of the fact that they are important to God. We are all important to God in setting forth the glory of the Lord Jesus Christ.

In a good sense, I want you to think more of yourself. My appeal is that you should love Christ and then love yourself for Christ's sake, because you are important. It is not an accident of fate that God created you and redeemed you—if you are a Christian. Your Saviour and Lord does have need of you to show forth His glory and praise.

I thank God that the kingdom of God is not divided into areas for big, important people and areas for little, unimportant people. Every one is just as needful in God's sight as any other!

So, I conclude here with this idea: there are two levels on which Christians are living.

It has been revealed that animals have one level while angels live on a completely different level, and we human beings are a cross between angels and beast. We have bodies like the animals and we have souls like the angels above.

God has made us a little lower than the angels, but He has made us a little higher than the animals.

We have a body that came from the earth. But in that precious human body, the like of which our Lord yielded to a cross, we also have a spirit like unto that of the angels above. When God said we were made a little lower than the angels, He did not mean that He made our spiritual part lower than the angels—He did not! He made man's spiritual being higher than the angels, for that was made in the very image of God!

So, it is with these two levels of our human being that we look at Jesus. These human and physical eyes have never seen Him. These eyes that gaze out like the deer gazes out of the thicket—these eyes have not seen Him.

But we do love Him, do we not? Yes—and the reason is that there is another level, another part of us! There is the invisible, the eternal, inward and spiritual being, which has its own sight and its own vision, and with those eyes we have seen Him, known Him and loved Him.

Brethren, Peter encourages every Christian believer to know and serve and love Jesus Christ now, our understanding being enlightened through this inner spiritual sight He has given us! We live to show forth the honor of our God in Jesus Christ, until that gracious day of the Lord when we shall see Him face to face!

CHAPTER 12

Will There Be Any Lazy Folks in Heaven?

". . . and shewed me that great city, the holy Jerusalem, descending out of heaven from God, having the glory of God . . ." Revelation 21:10-11

A RE YOU AMONG THOSE who hold the mistaken idea that there will be nothing to challenge you in the life to come? Are you among those who have read the account of the New Jerusalem, the City of God, and have wondered if it will be just a haven for the lazy and an endless gathering of bored and listless beings?

Let me refer you to the biblical doctrine of the image of God in man. I say this to you, sir, that apart from God Himself, the nearest thing to God is a human soul. And I promise you that in that Great Day you will not be without something to do, for God Himself is the great worker. He is the Creator—He is creative. All that He does is creative.

God did not create the heaven and the earth and all of the universe and then put a period after it, and write, "It is done—finale!" He is always creating. He has made us in His image. God is the great worker without limit, and we are the little workers with limit, or up to our limits, which we haven't found yet. But our creative powers will be in use.

Actually, one of the supreme glories of man is his many-sidedness. He can be and do and engage in a variety of interests and activities. He is not fatally formed to be only one thing. A rock is formed to be a rock and it will be a rock until the heavens melt with fervent heat and the earth passes away. A star is made to shine and a star it ever will be. The mountain that pushes up into the sky has been a mountain since the last geological upheaval pushed it up there. Through all the years it has worn the garment of force on its back but it has always been a mountain—never anything else.

But man can be both cause and effect—he can be servant or master. He can be doer and thinker. He can be poet and philosopher. He can be like the angels to walk with God or like the beasts to walk the earth. Man is a many-faceted diamond to catch and reflect back the glory of the only God.

It is this versatility in the nature of man which has enabled him to enjoy both solitude and togetherness. If a human being is normal, he will need and enjoy both of these extremes.

Jesus said, "Enter into thy closet"—there is solitude.

The Apostle said, "Forsake not the assembling of yourselves together." There is society. These words, of course, were spoken to Christian believers, and it is true that every believing child of God is supposed to be able to enjoy, understand and appreciate both solitude and fellowship with others.

Every normal person must have time to be alone. He must have time and inclination to become acquainted with himself. He must become oriented to the universe in which he lives. He must have the blessing of quietness to send out his thoughts like flocks of obedient birds exploring the wonders of the universe. He must get acquainted with God and himself in the solitude of his own chamber.

But remember that there must always be a reaction for every action. As the moon must always wane after it waxes and the tide must always go out after it comes in, so mankind must have society as well as solitude.

After a time of loneliness and heart-searching and communion with the living God through His Spirit, a person must again seek the face of his fellowmen. God has meant it to be so. God has meant that we should be together in fellowship.

The fact is that God has made us for each other, and it is His will and desire that Christian believers should understand and appreciate one another.

Why, then, we ask, do we have such problems in our togetherness?

You cannot talk for five minutes about mankind without coming to the ugly, hissing word we call *sin*. It is sin, the disease of the human stream, that ruined everything. It is sin that has made us greedy, sin that has made us hate. Sin makes us lust for power, sin creates jealousy and envy and covetousness.

Anything that comes close to being peace in our society will be destroyed by the ravages of sin, and men without God and His grace and His will cannot know or attain to the gracious blessings of true peace.

But in the final state of humanity, in the final state of perfection minus all of the diseases of the mind and of the being, we will dwell in perfect enjoyment of each other's company and that will be the New Jerusalem, the holy city, that descends out of heaven from God.

It will be in that blessed society that we will truly appreciate one another and we will be recognized truly for what we are in Christ. In this present earthly order, it seems the one who gets attention and notice and appreciation is the noisy one or the aggressive one. Many worthy and splendid persons never have the opportunity to enrich the lives and friendship of others because they are quiet, self-effacing persons who will not push themselves to the front. Some others are handicapped by features that may not be considered attractive and others do not have a "winsome" personality. When will we humans learn that we lose the richness of many a rewarding personality because we are not more discerning and wiser?

But in that final consummation, when the City of God descends, we shall be able truly to appreciate each other. If it were not for the deadening and corroding effects of sin, the human soul would catch and reflect the light of God as diamonds catch and reflect the light of the sun, and we would know each other for we would see in each other something of the nature and beauty of God. God is infinite and without limit and through Him we could come to know one another without ever feeling "I am weary of him and bored with him."

We have assurance in the Word of God that in that day when the limitations of the flesh are removed and the negative qualities in our personalities are gone and the minor notes are all taken out of the symphony of personality, we will thank God for one another. We will know God better through one another as we find that we are simply prisms and lenses through which God shines. God shines in many ways throughout His universe, but I do believe that He shines best of all in the lives of men and women He created and then redeemed.

It is only sin that has cracked the lenses and distorted the image. It is only sin that has marred the vision and spoiled the picture, so that when we look at each other we do not see the true depth of potential.

When our Lord looked at us, He saw not only what we were—He was faithful in seeing what we could become! He took away the curse of being and gave us the glorious blessing of becoming. Scoffers say a man can only be what he is, but Jesus Christ said, "No, he is not what he is—but what he can become."

It is the Lord Jesus Christ who gives us the power to "become." John the Apostle sensed this in his words: "It doth not yet appear what we shall be, but we know that, when he shall appear, we shall be like him; for we shall see him as he is." It is the ability to become—to grow, to change, to develop, to move out to the edges of the perfection of human personality—that is the glory of the Christian life!

Therefore, in that day when the holy city descends, there will no longer be the blight of jealousy. No personality in that day will want to ensnare or enslave another. There will be no one with the spirit of war or force to march on another's domain, or make others subject to his greed. We will not suspect one another, there will be no arrests and there will be no courts in which to file a grudging complaint. Violence and murders will be gone and in that society all will fare graciously as one—there will be no slums and no ghettos and there will be no private compounds of the rich marked "No Trespassing."

Many wary humans have said, "The prospect is too good to be true!" But it is written, "I heard a great voice out of heaven saying, Behold, the tabernacle of God is with men, and he will dwell with them and they shall be his people. And God himself shall be with them, and they shall be his people, and God himself shall be with them, and be their God. And God shall wipe away all tears from their eyes; and there shall be no more death, neither sorrow, nor crying, neither shall there be any more pain: for the former things are passed away."

Anyone who has love and concern for the human race will say a quiet but fervent "Amen" to this prospect for the future with God and man dwelling together and with the former things—tears, sorrow, pain and death—having passed away.

We give credit to men in all ages of human history who have dreamed and longed for a perfect human society. They wanted to make the world a better place in which to live, but all have had to settle for a dream. All of their dreams and all of their Utopian ideas have been spoiled and brought to naught by human forces of pride and prejudice, of selfishness and cynicism.

This world system in which we live can never be made perfect by a social regeneration based on man's own hopes and dreams, foibles and failures. We notice that the man who was in the Spirit on the Lord's day did not refer to social regeneration. He clearly and plainly said that this perfect, future world comes down out of heaven from God. Man's hopeless condition cannot be perfected by some slow process of social regeneration—it must be brought about through the miraculous process of individual regeneration.

Actually, there is really no such thing as "society." It is a word that reaches out and rakes in a whole world of ideas, but in truth, I am society, you are society, and the man next door and the boy that sells papers and the milkman and the mayor of the city and the president and the office boy that does the chores—that is society. It is the individual, actually, so when we try to put them together and call it society, we are building a false concept. We are likely to think of society as an organism, which it is not! Society is a name given to a great number of individual organisms.

It was for that reason that Jesus Christ rebuked completely any idea of the regeneration of human society when He came into this world. He said to a man, "You must be born again." He said, "Where two or three are gathered together in my name, there am I in the midst." He spoke of an individual and exclaimed, "One soul is of more value than all the world." Study the New Testament and you will find Jesus continually placed His emphasis upon the value and worth of the individual.

An individualist Himself, Jesus still plainly taught that there would ultimately be a society of the blessed, an assembly of the saints, a happy gathering of the children of God. There would be a New Jerusalem with the spirits of just men made perfect. He promised many mansions in the Father's house where these individuals—regenerated—could come together and form that holy society.

It is impossible to talk to people about blessedness and holiness and heaven without talking about God's provision of spiritual transformation. Everyone knows there are worldwide forces in our day which emphasize nationalism to the point that the individual is completely forgotten—but the only regeneration known in the entire world is individual regeneration. Many church groups seem to have joined forces with the political and social reformers in the dream that the effective way to bring about a perfect society is to reform and redeem society itself—rather than the redemption of the individual human natures which compose society, so-called.

What does the Bible say? It says there will not be one soul, not one member of that heavenly population, that will not have experienced the mystical and mysterious and spiritual regeneration of the new birth in some way, somewhere, during the brief earthly existence. It must be said of him, as Paul said of the new man in Christ, "Old things have passed away; all things have become new."

It is more than coincidence, then, that we find the same thing said about the New Jerusalem: "Old things have passed away; lo, I make all things new!"

How is it that the Holy Ghost said the same thing about the New Jerusalem that He had said about the converted man? Because the New Jerusalem will be the city of the converted man! This New Jerusalem will be filled with those who can say while they are on earth: "Old things have passed away, and all things have become new!" And then they will be able also to say: "He makes all things new, and the former things have passed away!"

God Himself will have a gracious plan for everyone in that great and eternal and holy city—and it will be a city that will satisfy all of man's nature.

I find that many men and women are troubled by the thought that they are too small and inconsequential in the scheme of things. But that is not our real trouble—we are actually too big and too complex, for God made us in His image and we are too big to be satisfied with what the world offers us!

Augustine put it in classical language when he said, "O God, Thou hast made us for Thyself, and our hearts are dissatisfied until they find their rest in Thee." That expression has been echoed and reechoed and written into our hymns, because it is true! Man is bored, because he is too big to be happy with that which sin is giving him. God has made him too great, his potential is too mighty. People do not actually commit suicide because they are too little and insignificant, but because they are big in a little world. God made man to be able to enjoy all of the vast expanses of His heaven and they have been forced through sin to be satisfied with paying their taxes and mowing the lawn and fixing the car and keeping the kids out of jail and paying their debts—yes, and getting older every day! They are sick of it, actually sick of it! Their bodies are breaking down and their tabernacle is too small for the spirit that dwells within.

That is the reason why humans are always trying to explore some new place. That explains the interest in trying to visit the moon. That explains why we want to be able to travel faster than sound. It explains, at least in part, why Charles Lindbergh jumped in an old egg-beater and was the first man to fly alone over the ocean to Paris. It explains why Admiral Byrd went down to the Antarctic and Admundsen explored the North Pole region. It is the reason for men always trying to do the impossible. It explains why we explore the secrets of the universe and come up with the atomic bomb—men are too big for the little world that sin has given them!

But the society that God is promising from above, that great City of God, will truly satisfy man's full nature. The day will be a long golden day without a cloud and without a sundown. Travel where you will in all those wide regions above and you will not find a wrinkle on anyone's face nor a gray hair on anyone's head. You will never hear anyone mutter, "I am discontented." You will never hear a voice raised in criticism. You will never meet a peevish man and you will never see an unkind face. You will never hear a growl from any throat, never a scream of fear or pain. You will never see a tear running down anyone's cheek.

Someone will break in here and say, "Just a minute, Mr. Tozer! That is the old-fashioned idea of heaven, where we are kind of glorified butterflies waving our wings gently in the zephyrs that flow down from the celestial mountains. What about a challenge? What about something to work for? How will the redeemed be occupied?"

Well, I can set you right there, because God promised that in the New Jerusalem He has provided all that is good and blessed and useful and has ruled out and barred only those things that offend.

When God put Adam and Eve in the garden, He did not put them there to sit and look at each other and to hold hands. He said they were to take care of the garden. You remember that—they were given something to do. Some people believe that work is a result of the curse, but that's not true. The idea is abroad that the man who works is a boob, and that work is only for fools—but God made us to work.

You know, the anthropologists say that when God made man with his four fingers and his thumb opposite those four fingers so that he could hold and use every kind of tool and instrument, He guaranteed that man would conquer the world. God made you and me like that, you see. So, some-time when you have a little time alone, look at that hand of yours, that amazing hand of yours!

The plain truth is that in all the machinery and all the gadgets and all the instruments around your house put together there is nothing that can remotely compare with the intricacy, beauty of performance and versatility of that right hand of yours. And God did not give you that hand to hang on to some chandelier in the New Jerusalem—God means that you are to go to work up there.

But it will be a tireless work—it will not be a work of boredom. It will be happy, joyous work. It will be work without fatigue. I do not know what God will have us doing. Maybe He will have you doing something that you can do.

"Our Lord was a worker," says one of our hymns, and our Lord is always looking for work-ers. So we are all going to be workers, and you need not imagine for a second that you will have nothing to do in heaven.

But along with work, heaven is also a place for you to rest.

You say, "How can you make these two statements agree?"

Well, you will work and you will not be tired. Jesus now works but without tiring. He rests always while He works. So the saints of God will work.

What was that which Kipling said?

"When earth's last picture is painted, and the tubes are twisted and dried; the brightest colors have faded and the youngest critic has died; we shall rest and they that need it shall lie down for an aeon or two; and the Master of all good workmen shall put us to work anew."

Kipling goes on to say, "We'll sit in a golden chair and splash on a ten-league canvas with brushes of angel hair."

I do not know whether angels have hair—Kipling thought so. He thought it was a nice thing to do—to use a ten-league canvas instead of a miniature and sit there and work.

I think in that sense Kipling was right—heaven is not going to be a haven for lazy bums. Heaven is going to be a place where men released from tensions and inhibitions, released from prohibitions from the outside, released from sin, and made in the image of God can go to work like the young gods they are. For He said, "Ye are gods"—He didn't mean you are God, but "You are little images of mine, born to do the kind of work I do, creative work."

So, the New Jerusalem will be fresh opportunity for all of the imaginative and the industrious and the busy—who, like God, must find expression.

Ah, the beauty of it all—how can I go on? The beauty of it—not the done-up beauty of a woman's face, not the beauty of a carefully-padded form, not the beauty of the primrose that smiles in the sunshine, but the great, rich, strong beauty of eternity in God. Ah, that city of gold, with all its beauty!

Way back there in the beginning, God made man to live with Him. Sin came and God divorced man like an unfaithful wife from His presence. But through the miracle of redemption, through the cross of Jesus Christ, man is reborn back to his ancient place and raised yet above that.

Now, why was there no mention here of a temple, a church, a synagogue? Why was there no meeting place for worshipers?

Because all of that new City of God was a temple. God Himself was the temple. Like a great expanse of beautiful arches, the Father, Son and Holy Ghost surrounded and settled down and mingled with all of that carefree, busy, joyous throng. There they do not have to wait for an hour in which to pray—all hours are prayer hours there.

You won't have to wait to go to a special place to pray there—all of it is a temple and God and the Lamb are the temples thereof. There's no need for an artificial light to brighten the night, for the Lamb is the light thereof.

We must seriously consider whether we are headed in that direction. Every one of us must seriously consider whether we have—by the blood of the Lamb and the word of our testimony—overcome and escaped from the thralldom of sin, or whether we are still bound by it, cursed with the curse, and about to be destroyed in the destruction.

This is the gracious reality of our look to the future: We are by faith the children of God, given a place in that great society of the ransomed and promised an eternal inheritance in that Great City because our names are written in the Lamb's Book of Life!

Book 7

Twelve Sermons Relating to the Life and Ministry of the Christian Church

Contents

Preface

Dr. A. W. Tozer, during his fruitful preaching ministry, was concerned about the spiritual shortcomings of the visible Christian churches.

His preaching from week to week always displayed love and appreciation and concern for the church, the true Body of Christ on earth. The pattern of his preaching revealed a consistent yearning that every assembly of Christian believers would realize its full potential in producing spiritual fruit for the honor of Jesus Christ.

This seventh volume in the Tozer Pulpit Series is the first to deal exclusively with subjects related to the Christian church and the spiritual basis for its varied and continuing ministries.

As we have done in the past, we point out that Dr. Tozer's sermons are not to be read as textbooks in a doctrinal sense. His appeal chapter by chapter is more likely to be devotional and inspirational.

We are truly thankful for the continuing demand for Dr. Tozer's edited sermons, the only available source for his often-prophetic and incisive material since his death in May 1963.

The Publisher

An Assembly of Saints: Love Unity in the Spirit

*But now hath God set the members every one of them in
the body, as it hath pleased him . . . having given more abundant honour to that part which lacked: That there should be
no schism in the body; . . . Now ye are the body of Christ,
and members in particular. 1 Corinthians 12:18, 24-25, 27*

STATING IT IN JUST about the most simple
terms we know, the Christian church is the assembly of redeemed saints.

And stating it in what is probably the most important teaching in the New Testament concerning
Christ and the church, Paul pointedly relates the life
and service of the Christian church to a true unity
which can only be wrought by the Holy Spirit!

Paul wrote specifically to the first century Corinthian believers to remind them that "as the body
is one, and hath many members, and all the members of that one body, being many, are one body: so
also is Christ."

Then he continued: "For by one Spirit are we
all baptized into one body, whether we be Jews or
Gentiles, whether we be bond or free; and have
been all made to drink into one Spirit. For the body
is not one member, but many" (1 Cor. 12:12-14).

Now, in our local church or assembly, we know that we are not an end in ourselves. We want to see the church, the Body of Christ, as a whole. If we are going to be what we ought to be in the local church, we must come to think of ourselves as a part of something more expansive, something larger that God is doing throughout the entire world.

There is an important sense here in which we find that we "belong"—belonging to something that God has brought into being, something that is worthy and valuable, and something that is going to last forever.

We do not have to be ashamed as redeemed men and women that we desire to belong to the work that God is doing through the church.

You know, sociologists and psychologists talk about the need for belonging. They tell us that a rejected child, one who no longer belongs to anyone, will develop dangerous mental and nervous traits.

They tell us that the wolf packs—the neighborhood clubs of young boys and girls who roam and terrorize the streets—come largely from homes where they have been rejected. Many young children in our day cannot remember ever having been loved by a mother or a father, and so they come together and find some answer to their own need in belonging to a gang.

These young people and many others in every walk of life have found a new sense of human strength in their "belonging" to others. That is the reason there are many popular secret orders and societies. Men who are pushed around by their wives and submerged and humiliated by their superiors at work soon get the feeling that they have no soul to call their own. Because they need some point at which to rally their self-respect they join a lodge or fraternal society—and they "belong" to something.

Perhaps you saw the recent cartoon in which the wife blocked the doorway and said to the husband: "The high exalted potentate can't go out tonight because I won't let him!"

The point is that little men want to belong to something and that is basically not a bad thing because we are gregarious by nature.

We are not wolves, to go alone or travel in narrow packs which break up immediately.

No. Actually, we are sheep. Sheep travel together in flocks and stay together for a lifetime.

We are thinking together here about the whole church, the Body of Christ, and the fact that in our local congregation we have the joyful sense of belonging to an amazing fellowship of the redeemed throughout the world.

This is entirely different from belonging to an order or a society or a group that is man-made.

Most of you know that God made my knees hard to bend, and I am sure you have never imagined me getting on my knees and swearing to follow some order of this or some secret society of that. My American upbringing has made it almost impossible to bend my knees in that regard—unless God bends them!

But I am not ashamed that I want to belong to something good and great and eternal—for no man is ever individually big enough to go it alone.

No man—unless he is sick. The hermit, for instance, is sick. The man who lives alone in his attic, refusing to answer the door, sneaking out in the dark to buy a little food—that man is sick. He is not a normal man.

A normal man, good or bad, sinner or saint, wants to walk out and look around at others of his kind with the inward feeling: "I belong. This is my race. These are my people. This is my language being spoken. That's my flag there on top of the school building. I belong here!"

That is a kind of personality thing that is necessary to our human welfare—necessary to our health, our mental health.

And that is why unwanted children and other persons who feel themselves rejected may develop serious and dangerous behavior trends.

That's why we enjoy singing songs about the church—because we have come to think of ourselves in relationship to the whole church of Christ.

Our hymns repeat with meaning that we are the church, the redeemed, and that Jesus Christ purchased us with His own blood. We are the church, now part in heaven and part on earth, and of "every color and tribe and nation and tongue around the world," as the Bible teaches.

Thankfully, we are a part of that!

I dare to say to you that we did not get our beginning when Dr. A. B. Simpson organized the society for Christian missions in New York City in 1884. If I thought for a second that that was our beginning, I would never finish this sentence. I would just break it off with a semi-colon. I would close the Bible and leave the pulpit and resign.

But I believe that we are a part of that great Christian body that goes back to Pentecost. I believe in a true kind of apostolic succession, not a succession of bishops and men with names and organizations, but a living organism vitally a part of the true church of Christ that began when the Holy Ghost came upon a body of believers and made them one, making them God's people in a way that none ever had been before!

This is an important Biblical concept—that every believing Christian has a part with us and we have a part with every faithful Christian group throughout the world!

This is so true that when I hear of some good thing that has been said or done by a good man or woman anywhere in the world for the sake of Christ's gospel, I have a good feeling in my heart. That has become a part of me—that belongs to me, and I have a part in it. It doesn't matter whether I will ever personally meet that person on earth, for the church of our Lord Jesus Christ is one.

Now, I want to think of you and your relation to God first of all.

A minister got his name in the papers here by starting a campaign to get all the members of his church to vote.

As your pastor, just let me say that I expect you to vote as a good Christian citizen, but that's your own business. If you do not vote, I am not going to needle you about that. I can only remind you that every nation pretty much gets the kind of leaders it deserves.

This is what I mean: I am more deeply concerned about your relationship to God and your continuing spiritual life than I am about a campaign to get you out to the polls. Before there were any Tories or

Whigs or Democrats or Republicans or Socialists or Christian Fronts—there was God! And before men and women ever knew the privilege of the ballot—there was God.

There is no doubt in my mind that your relationship to God is the matter that must come first—absolutely!

Then your relationship to others may be next in importance, followed by such things as your service for our Lord and your habits of life.

What about prayer and its meaning in our Christian fellowship?

It is my belief that it is a high Christian privilege to pray for our own congregation and then to pray for other believers throughout the Christian church.

Speaking as a minister it is my strong feeling that no man has a right to preach to a crowd that he has not prayed for.

Some people want to shy away from the word *duty*, but nevertheless I believe I have a duty and a responsibility to pray for those who are striving to walk with God in the fellowship of the church.

Just this word about duty: a frisky young colt in the pasture knows nothing about anything that could be called duty. But that colt's well-trained, hardworking mother in the harness and pulling a wagon or plow is an example of fulfilling the implications of duty.

The colt only knows freedom, but the work horse knows duty.

I cannot help but wonder if our inordinate desire for freedom and our strange fear of duty have had an effect upon the life of the church. We ought to consider it a privilege as well as a sacred duty to pray for our church and for others who are included in the fellowship of the Christian faith.

I know that there are people who attend churches where there is never any appeal or desire to engage in effectual prayer for others. They can tell you the name of their church and when it was organized and what part it plays in the "religious community."

That's not enough. Strictly speaking, you cannot bring a true segment of the Body of Christ into being by organizing.

Now I do not want to be misquoted. I believe that within our Christian fellowship and in our efforts to evangelize there must of necessity be some proper organization freely exercised. Paul himself must have had this in mind as he wrote to Titus and told him to set things in order and to appoint men to tasks within the fellowship.

But I am saying that you cannot organize a Christian church in the same way that you would organize a baseball club. In baseball you need a captain, so many pitchers and so many catchers, outfielders and infielders and a number of coaches.

You can have an organized ball club with the right number of players and coaches and still not have a ball club, as a certain Chicago team has proven!

No, you cannot organize a true Christian church in that sense. Even after the adoption of a proper church constitution there may not actually be a New Testament church. Perhaps the church is within that organization—it is possible—but that organization is not the church, for the church is the assembly of the saints!

No congregation or church group has the right to feel that it has finally arrived and is fully matured. Every congregation with a true desire for the knowledge of God must continually seek and reach out-determining its own needs and what it should be to be well pleasing to the Lord.

Any assembly of the saints must continue in the study of the Bible to determine what the Holy Spirit wants to do in the life of the church and how the Spirit will provide the power and special abilities to glorify Jesus Christ.

You will know what I mean when I say that to do all this requires in itself a gift of the Spirit!

Let me here refer to words of the prophet Isaiah which I love very much. They are in Isaiah chapter 11:

"And there shall come forth a rod out of the stem of Jesse, and a Branch shall grow out of his roots: and the spirit of the Lord shall rest upon him, the spirit of wisdom and understanding, the spirit of counsel and might, the spirit of knowledge and of the fear of the Lord; and shall make him of quick understanding in the fear of the Lord: and he shall not judge after the sight of his eyes, neither reprove after the hearing of his ears: but with righteousness shall he judge the poor, and reprove with equity for the meek of the earth"(Isaiah 11 vv. 1-4a).

Now as you well know all of that was spoken by the prophet concerning Jesus, the One who was to come to Israel.

But don't you think that description of spiritual life and ministry also should be true of all who are members of the Body of Christ by faith?

Just as in the Old Testament when the oil of anointing was poured out on the high priest's head and ran down to the skirt of his garment and on down to his feet, giving fragrance and sweetness to his whole body, so the mighty power that was poured upon the head of Jesus must flow and trickle down to every member of the body. What was true of Him, our Lord, can just as surely be true of those who minister His grace and truth.

"The spirit of wisdom and understanding, the spirit of counsel and might, the spirit of knowledge and of the fear of [Jehovah]; and shall make him of quick understanding . . . and he shall not judge after the sight of his eyes" (vv. 2-3).

What a powerful message from the prophet to our own day. The curse of modern Christian leadership is the pattern of looking around and taking our spiritual bearing from what we see, rather than from what the Lord has said.

"Neither [shall he] reprove after the hearing of his ears" (v. 3).

But what are we prone to do in church leadership? We are likely to listen carefully to see which way things are moving and then act accordingly. But the Spirit of God will never lead us into that mistake.

"But with righteousness shall he judge the poor, and reprove with equity for the meek of the earth. . . . And righteousness shall be the girdle of his loins, and faithfulness the girdle of his reins" (vv. 4a, 5).

Led by the Spirit of God, the members of the Body of Christ will always be right in their spirit, right in their wisdom, and right in their judgment. They will not be judged nor will they allow themselves to be judged on the basis of what is currently taking place all around them.

I believe God wants to do something new and blessed for every believer who has the inner desire to know Him better. I am aware of the fact that it takes a store of patience and persistence and a lot of courage to find and pursue the will of God in this day. There has been a reviving within the ranks of our own fellowship, and I see no reason why it should not flow out and down and over and up and around until we are all swimming in it.

Brethren, we fellowship here and mingle together and worship the Lord Christ as an assembly of the saints. We confess that all of the privileges and responsibilities rest upon us that once rested upon those believers at Pentecost. The plan and promises of God for His believing children have not diminished one little bit.

Nowhere in the Word of God is there any text or passage or line that can be twisted or tortured into teaching that the organic living church of Jesus Christ just prior to His return will not have every right and every power and every obligation that she knew in that early part of the book of Acts.

I am determined that we are not going to give up to the kind of times in which we live! There is such a thing as just getting tough about this, my brethren. There is such a thing as saying in the power of the Spirit, "I am not yielding and I will not give up to the times!" This is something we can say to our Lord and to ourselves, and betimes, maybe, over our shoulder to the devil!

The faithful Body of Christ is not going to give up to the ways of the world or even to the more common ways of religion that we see all about us.

Faithful believers in Christ are not going to give up to the temptation to judge themselves according to what others are doing.

Neither will they allow their church to be judged and its spiritual life to be affected by the attitudes of others. They will be happy and continue to rejoice in the fact that they have taken the New Testament standard as their standard in their Christian fellowship.

Believing Christians and the groups that trust and obey the Scriptures are now known generally as fundamentalists—and that's not bad. But I think we need a caution and a warning in our midst that it is not enough just to have the label of orthodox belief.

I really think that all of us who love our Lord Jesus Christ are facing such great changes in this period before the return of Christ that we are going to have to recall and have back upon us the kind of spiritual revival that will eventuate in a new moral power, in a new spirit of willing separation and heart purity, and a new bestowing of the enablings of the Spirit of God.

If we do not earnestly seek it and if we do not obtain it, it is my opinion that God will somehow raise up some new segment of the Body of Christ to carry the torch.

This is a prophecy that has little chance of contradiction in the kind of times in which we live. If we do not make a hard swing back to the very roots of Christian faith and Christian teaching and Christian living, beginning again to seek the face of God and His will, God is going to pass us up!

He will pass us up as a farmer deals with *egg* shells that are empty. He carries them out and buries them, as we bury the dead after the spirit has departed.

There was a day when leaders in Israel, believing in the perpetuity of her place in the sun, said to Jesus, "We be not born of fornication. We be the seed of Abraham. And this temple is the temple of God."

And Jesus answered, "They are the children of Abraham who do the works of Abraham. As for this temple, there is coming a day when not one stone will be left upon another."

And that, of course, came to pass later when the Roman emperor sent his plows to raze the foundation and to separate all of the great temple stones. He had never heard those prophetic words of Jesus, but this was the means of fulfilling them in the program of God. It had been a sacred temple to the Jews—but the Roman conquerors knocked down every stone level with the ground.

God makes His moves in dealing with nations and men and with men's favorite religions and temples. There is no religious group or church organization or denominational communion in the world that God will not desert and abandon in the very hour it ceases to fulfill and carry out His divine will.

There is no possible way that ecclesiastical robes are impressive enough nor cross and chains heavy enough nor titles long enough to save the church when once she ceases to fulfill the will of God among sinful men who need the transforming news of Christ's gospel.

The God who raised them up in centuries past will turn away and abandon them unless they continue to fulfill the gracious will of God, following on to know the Lord, humbly and meekly in faith and in love.

I am talking about the crowd, now. Not the individual members. Just because some organization has a great crowd is not the significant issue with God. The Lord will turn His blessing to some small mission, to simple-hearted people somewhere whose greatest possession is the desire to love God and to obey Him.

God never leaves or forsakes His believing children. But I surely believe that God has lifted the cloud and the fire of His presence from groups and assemblies that plainly forsook Him and His eternal Word.

And, dear God, I pray that if it ever lifts from this church, you will tell me 24 hours before the tragedy occurs—for I want to get out of town! I want time to get away where I won't have to stand and look at the despoiling of the church.

Oh, brethren, we may lack everything else, but we must have the cloud and fire of His presence; we must have the enabling and the power of the Holy Spirit and the glow of the Shekinah glory— God with us!

For then, even lacking everything else, you still have a true church!

No Second-Class Christians: The Church Still the Church

For as the body is one, and hath many members, and all the members of that one body, being many, are one body: so also is Christ. For by one Spirit are we all baptized into one body. . . . Now ye are the body of Christ, and members in particular. 1 Corinthians 12:12-13, 27.

THE ETERNAL PROMISES OF Jesus Christ to His believing people are of such inestimable value that those who are truly Christian today are not to be designated as marginal or second-class Christians because of the passing of time and of generations gone before.

We are Christians because God has perpetuated the church and keeps it going by doing the same thing within individual lives generation after generation since Pentecost.

Do we believe as truth and claim it as we should that the true church as it meets in the Name to worship the Presence finds Christ still giving Himself in the life of the fellowship?

It is not the form that makes the church or its service. The Presence and the Name—these make the church.

Wherever people are gathered together in the Name, there also is the Presence. So it is that the Presence and the Name constitute the true assembly of believers and it is recognized by God in heaven.

In my estimation this brings to light a most wonderful truth! In the Body of Christ there are no insignificant congregations. Each has His Name and each is honored by His Presence.

It has been related that a young pastor commented when introduced to a well-known church leader: "Doctor, I am sure you don't know me. I am the pastor of just a little rural church."

I think it was a wise reply that came from that churchman: "Young man, there are no little churches; all churches are the same size in God's sight."

Large or small—it must be an assembly of believers brought together through a Name to worship a Presence. The blessed thing is that God does not ask whether it is a big church or a little church.

But people do insist on asking questions about the size and number of people in a church because they are carnal. I know all about such human judgments: "This is a very little church" or "That is a poor, unknown church."

Meanwhile, God is saying, "They are all My churches and each has every right to all that I bestow!"

I am of the opinion that every local church should be fully aware of its relationship to the church in the New Testament.

We should ask ourselves if we are as truly interested in spiritual attainment as were the New Testament believers. We must confess that the spiritual temperature among us may often be lower than in the early church. But we cannot escape the message that those who truly meet in His Name to honor the Presence of the Saviour are included in this relationship which goes back to the New Testament and to the apostles.

Consider with me some very serious thoughts about the fact that God works to perpetuate by repetition.

First, let us review how God keeps the human race going.

In every human being there is the strange, mysterious and sacred life stream which God created in Adam and Eve. This has been perpetuated throughout the centuries by constant repetition in each generation. It is the same human race with the same human nature. It simply repeats itself in every generation.

It is true that we who inhabit the earth today are not the same persons who inhabited the earth when Columbus discovered America. Not one individual living now was alive then. Nevertheless, it is the same race. God has activated the continuity of the human race by perpetuating each generation and repeating each generation through the mystery of life in procreation.

Israel is an illustration of this concept.

Israelites living at the time of Moses were not the same Israelites who lived in the time of David. It was, however, the same Israel by the mystery of repetition in procreation.

It was the same God, the same covenant, the same relationship, the same revelation, the same fathers, the same intention and purpose. It was the same nation.

That is why God could speak to Israel in Moses' day, in David's day, and in Christ's day, and be speaking to the same Israel. Actually it was the same Israel secured and perpetuated in unbroken continuity by the creative mystery of procreation and repetition.

I believe that it is exactly the same with the church of our Lord Jesus Christ—the true church that is alive today.

In this context I am not referring to lifeless churches and unbelieving churches. I have in mind the true churches, the assemblies of faithful believers.

The personnel is not the same as in the days when Wesley preached. When Wesley preached, there was not one person who was alive when Luther preached. When Luther preached, there was not a man or woman remaining of those who lived when Bernard, the ancient saint, wrote his great hymns.

My point is that each generation has different personnel, but it is the same church which comes down in unbroken lineal descent from that earliest church.

You and I confess that we are not the same as Adam nor are we the same as Adam's grandchildren or great-great-great grandchildren. Nevertheless, we contend that we are truly related to him as were his sons, Cain and Abel—all being related to him by the mystery of procreation and the continuity of life that solidifies and holds together in one the human race.

I think it should be plain that the truth concerning the on-going life of the Christian church is not the same as the continuing historical progression of national life.

There is only a political unity that can be achieved in a nation. The British empire existed through its many generations by means of a political unity. But it is not a political unity that holds the human race together—it is a biological unity, the life stream that makes it one.

Regardless of how you break up the human race into political parties and distinctions it is still one by the mystery of perpetuated life.

So it is with the church of Christ. It has never been the political organization or segments that hold it together. When we talk about our Protestant tradition—the tradition of the fathers—we talk metaphorically and beautifully. But we do not mean the same thing that I mean when I say that a local assembly of faithful believers is in straight biological lineal descent from the apostles!

That is not political nor ideological but biological. It has to do with the mystery of life. It has to do with the life of God in man—the Holy Ghost doing in men of our day what He did in men of long ago.

While I thank God in appreciation for all of the great and godly men in the history of the church, we actually follow none of them. Our charter goes farther back and is from a higher source. They were looked upon as leaders, but they were all servants even as you and I are.

Luther sowed, Wesley watered, Finney reaped, but they were only servants of the living God.

In our local assemblies we are part of the church founded by the Lord Jesus Christ and perpetuated by the mystery of the new birth. Therefore our assembly is that of Christian believers gathered unto a Name to worship and adore that Presence.

If this is true—and everything within me witnesses that it is—all the strain is gone. I mean the strain is gone even about traditional religious forms—the pressures that we must sing certain songs, recite certain prayers and creeds, follow accepted patterns in ministerial leadership and service. All of these begin to pale in importance as we function in faith as the people of God who glorify the Name that is above every name and honor His Presence!

Yes, I contend that He is able to do for us all that He did in the days of the apostles. Oh, the power that is ours—the potential that we possess because He is here. Our franchise still stands! There has been no revocation of our charter!

If a poll should be taken today to name the six greatest men in the world and our names would not be included, we would still have the same privileges in God's world that they would have! We can breathe God's beautiful air, look at His blue sky, gaze into a never-ending array of stars in the night sky. We can stand upon the hard earth and stamp our little feet—and our big feet, too—and know that it will sustain us. We are as much a part of this human race as the greatest men and women.

And spiritually there is no blessing or privilege ever given by God that is withheld from us today—understanding, of course, that we know what the Bible really says.

For instance, we know that we cannot have the new heavens and the new earth right now although we can have the essence of them in our beings now.

We also know that right now we cannot have the new body that God is going to give at the coming of Christ.

But all things that are for us now we can have, and it is easy to find out what they are!

Why is it, then, that believers are not experiencing all that God desires for them? Why is it that our church attendance has become a social thing? Why does it become merely form and ritual?

Well, it is because we are badly instructed. We have been badly taught.

We have been told that we are a different kind of religion now and have been since the passing of the apostles.

"This is a different age in the church. The devil is busy and we cannot have and know and experience what they had then," we are told.

I have a strong reaction to that kind of teaching. I believe that any person who dares to say that is in the same position as a man who refuses to let your children open your own pantry door and refuses to let them sit down at your table.

Any kind of teaching or exposition, so called, that shuts us out from the privileges and promises of the New Testament is wrong, and the man who tries to shut me out is a false teacher!

Who gave any man the right to stand at your dining room table when your wife announces that dinner is ready and not let your children partake of the meal?

Who has the right in the name of bad teaching to keep your children away from your table? They are your children and you are responsible for them. You have an unwritten covenant with them and that table is spread for them. You may reserve the right to tell them how they should behave, but no one has the right to shut them out.

Let me ask the question: what right has any man to tell me, in the name of Bible teaching, that I belong to a different church than that early church?

Who should tell me that the fire has dimmed down in glory and that the mighty arm of God's Christ is now a diminished power?

When I am reading my New Testament, who can say, "But this portion is not for you. That portion is not for you. That promise is not for you"?

Who has been given the right to stand thus at the door to the kingdom of God?

Nobody!

Any kind of teaching or exposition, so called, that shuts me out from the privileges and promises of the New Testament is wrong. The man who tries to do so is a false teacher.

Another very evident reason why we do not receive as much from God as we should is because of the general low level of spiritual enthusiasm and the chilling effect of bad examples.

We would be foolish to try to deny that there are bad examples in our Christian circles.

I hope that we will never go into panic because someone cynical declares: "I repudiate the Christian church because of all the bad things I know about certain congregations!"

There are always pretenders. We have all heard of instances of fleshly extravagances among professing followers of Christ. It cannot be denied that such behavior is always a hindrance to the faith— and discourages faithfulness on the part of others.

Now, bad examples are one thing—but would we repudiate the twelve apostles because there was a Judas? the thousands because there was an Ananias and a Sapphira? Would we repudiate Paul because there was a Demas?

I say certainly not!

I will not repudiate the assembly of the saints because a bad example shows up occasionally.

I doubt that any one of us following the Lord has been so perfect that he could claim he had never been a bad or wrong example.

But this is what our Christian gospel and the victorious life in the Body of Christ is all about!

It is the blood of the everlasting covenant that makes the sinner clean and makes the weak strong, providing forgiveness and justification through God's mercy and grace.

What God has made clean let us never call unclean! There is a fountain filled with blood—and whatever the child of God's past, his present life is revealed by the Spirit of God as a beautiful gift from God shining as a witness for the Saviour in the fellowship of the body.

Christ sealed that eternal covenant of grace with His blood when He gave Himself on the cross. It is a covenant that cannot be broken. It is a covenant that has never been amended or edited or altered. It is an effective truth that the power and the provisions, the promises and gifts that marked that early church can belong to us now.

If we will let Him, Christ will do in us and through us that which He did in and through the committed believers after Pentecost.

The potential is ours. Do we dare believe that the faithful Christian believers may yet experience a great new wave of spiritual power?

It probably will not come across the wide, broad church with its amusements and worldly nonsense, but it will surely come to those who desire the presence and blessing of God more than they want anything else!

It will come to the humble, faithful, and devoted believers whoever and wherever they are!

I confess I want to be in such a spiritual condition that I may share in God's blessings as they come, no matter what the cost may be.

I want you as followers of Christ and in lineal descent from the apostles who meet regularly in His Name to honor His Presence to share in all the revelation of His fullness.

To miss out in any degree of all that God provides for us is tragedy—pure and simple.

No Christian can afford to miss God's best!

God's Eternal Purpose: Christ, the Center of All Things

*And as they thus spake, Jesus himself stood in the midst
of them, and saith unto them, Peace be unto you. Luke 24:36*

CONTRARY TO THE OPINION held by many
would-be religious leaders in the world, Christianity was never intended to be an "ethical system"
with Jesus Christ at the head.

Our Lord did not come into the world 2,000 years
ago to launch Christianity as a new religion or a
new system. He came into this world with eternal
purpose. He came as the center of all things. Actually, He came to be our religion, if you wish to put
it that way.

He came in person, in the flesh, to be God's salvation to the very ends of the earth. He did not come
just to delegate power to others to heal or cure or
bless. He came to *be* the blessing, for all the blessings
and the full glory of God are to be found in His person. Because Jesus Christ is the center of all things,
He offers deliverance for the human soul and mind
by His direct, personal and intimate touch. This is not
my one-man interpretation. It is the basic teaching of

salvation through the Messiah-Saviour, Jesus Christ. It is a teaching that runs throughout the Bible!

I remind you that Jesus Christ came into a world of complex religious observances. Perhaps it can be likened to a kind of religious jungle, with a choking and confusing multiplicity of duties, rituals and observances laid upon the people. It was a jungle grown so thick with man-made ordinances that it brought only a continuing darkness.

Into the midst of all this came the Light that was able to light every man that was to come into the world. He could say and teach, "I am the light of the world," because He shone so brightly, dispelling the darkness.

Jesus Christ came in the fullness of time to be God's salvation. He was to be God's cure for all that was wrong with the human race.

He came to deliver us from our moral and spiritual disorders—but it must also be said He came to deliver us from our own remedies.

Religion as a form is one of the heaviest burdens that has ever been laid upon the human race, and we must observe that it is a self-medicating burden. Men and women who are conscious of their moral and spiritual disorders try to medicate themselves, hoping to get better by their own treatment.

I often wonder if there is any kind of self-cure or human medication that man has not tried in his efforts to restore himself and gain merit.

Millions of pilgrims may still be seen in India, flat on the ground, crawling like inchworms toward the Ganges river, hoping for a release from the burden of guilt in the sacred waters.

History tells of countless persons who have tried to deal with guilt by self-denial and abstaining from food and drink. Many have tried a kind of self-torture by putting on hair shirts or walking on spikes or on hot coals. Men with the hermit complex have shunned society and hidden themselves in caves, hoping to gain some merit that would bring them closer to God and compensate for their own sinful nature.

Mankind is still inventing new ways of self-treatment and medication for failures and weaknesses and wrongdoing, even in our own day, not recognizing that the cure has already come.

Simeon, the old man of God who had waited in hope around the temple, knew that the cure had come! When he saw the baby Jesus, he took Him up in his arms, looked down at Him and said, "Lord, now lettest thou thy servant depart in peace . . . for mine eyes have seen thy salvation" (Luke 2:29-30).

So, I say to those who doubt or to those who are not instructed that it is Jesus Christ Himself that Christianity offers to you. I know that some churches are confused because of the introduction of human ideas, such as the self-medication idea, which has grown and expanded much like the proverbial mustard tree.

But, really, all Christianity offers is Jesus Christ the Lord, and Him alone—for He is enough! Your relation to Jesus Christ is really the all-important matter in this life.

That is both good news and bad news. It is good news for all who have met our Saviour and know Him intimately and personally. It is bad news for those who hope to get into heaven some other way!

Notice in the record that Jesus stood in the midst and said, "Peace be unto you."

Here is a beautiful explanation of the angels' words, "Peace on earth, good will to men." The angels could say that only because it was Jesus who was coming! He is our peace. I once had a wall motto which said, "He is our peace." Because of the coming of Jesus, the angels could announce, "Peace on earth."

This portion of Scripture illustrated Jesus' method of imparting health, directly and personally. It was Christ in the midst—at the center—and He could take that place because He is God, He is spirit, He is: timeless, He is spaceless, He is supreme, He is all in all. Therefore, He could be at the center!

Here I borrow an illustration to stress the point that Christ is the center of all things. He is, as it were, the hub of a wheel around which everything revolves. Centuries ago someone said that Christ is like the hub and everything that has been created is on the rim of the wheel.

One of the old church fathers said, "Everything that exists is equally distant from Jesus and equally near to Him."

There is the hub in the middle of each wheel with spokes going out to the rim. Then, in the perfectly shaped wheel, the rim goes around equal distance at all points from the hub. To us, Jesus Christ is that hub and everything else is on the rim. When Jesus Christ has His place as hub, we are all equally close or equally far from Him.

Jesus is in the midst, and because that is true, He is accessible from anywhere in life. This is good news-wonderful, good news!

This truth makes it possible for us to insist that Jesus Christ is at the center of geography. No one, therefore, can claim an advantage with Christ because of location.

It so happens that I am at the present time reading Neuman's *History of Latin Christianity* and have read again the story of the Crusaders. At the time of the historic crusade, many believed that merit was to be gained by making a pilgrimage to the very place where Jesus was born, and particularly to the sepulcher where His body was laid.

When Peter the Hermit, old and barefooted, whipped all of Europe into a white heat to get the crusades launched, he set the goal of liberating a grave out of which Jesus Christ had stepped more than a thousand years before. The crusaders felt that if that empty tomb could be taken from the Moslems, everything would be all right. Today there is still great interest in being where Jesus had been, but I don't know why we insist upon being spiritually obtuse.

Have we not heard Jesus' words: "I tell you that neither in this mountain nor in Jerusalem do men worship the Father, for the Father seeketh such to worship Him who worship Him in spirit and in truth" (see John 4:21-24). It is not on a certain mountain or in a city!

We wonder why the crusaders did not consider that. Why all the bloody wounds, starvation, suffering and death? Why the long, weary treks to get to the place where Jesus had been born or where He died, or where He had been buried? For there is no geographical advantage anywhere in the world. Not one of us would be a better Christian just by living in Jerusalem. If you lived at some spot in the world actually farther from Jerusalem, you would be at no disadvantage. Jesus Christ is in the very center of geography. It is just as near to Him from anywhere as it is from anywhere else! And it's just as far from Him also! So geography doesn't mean anything in our relationship to Him!

Plenty of money has been spent by preachers who felt that they could preach better if they could just visit Jerusalem. So they go over and look on Jerusalem, and when they come back, they have just a few more stories to tell. Actually, they are no better and their audiences are no better. Let's believe it—Jesus is the hub and geography is all around Him!

Then, we must come to the conclusion that Jesus Christ is the center of time. Many people become sad when they talk about missing the time of Christ on earth. It is good to recall and study the life and ministries of Jesus long ago. We sing a song that says: "I think when I read that sweet story of old, / When Jesus was here among men, / How He called little children as lambs to His fold, / I should like to have been with Him then!" Many a tear has been wiped out of the eyes when people have sung that, but did you know that the people who were with Jesus at the time when He walked among men were not as well off as they were ten days after He left them?

Ten days after He departed, He sent the Holy Spirit, and the disciples who understood only in part suddenly knew the plan of God as in a blaze of light.

But we say, "I would like to have lived in the time of Christ."

Why? There were hypocrites and Pharisees and opposers, murderers and unbelievers in the time of Christ! You would not have found things any better two thousand years ago.

Some of you who look back with nostalgia upon what you consider the good old days ought to be delivered from that!

Consider, too, that Jesus Christ is the center of the human race. With Him there are no favored races. We had better come to the point of believing that Jesus Christ is the Son of Man. He is not the Son of the first century nor the twentieth century. He is the Son of Man—not a Son of the Jewish race only. He is the Son of all races no matter what the color or tongue.

When Jesus Christ was incarnated in mortal flesh, He was not incarnated only in the body of the Jew, but in the body of the whole human race.

Go to Tibet or Afghanistan, to the Indians of South America, the Mohammedans of Arabia, the Englishmen of London, or the Scots of Glasgow and preach Jesus. If there is faith and willingness to follow, He will bring them all into His fellowship. They are all in the rim. They are all as near and all as far. That's the reason for the kind of missionary philosophy we hold. We do not first go into a country to educate the people and then preach Christ to them. We know better than that! We know that Jesus Christ is just as near to an uneducated, uncultured native as He is to a polished gentleman from New York or London.

Christ is at the center of all cultural levels. Preach Christ and show the love of God to the most primitive, most neglected, most illiterate people in the world; be patient and make them understand. Their hearts will awake, the Spirit will illuminate their minds. Those who believe on Jesus will be transformed. This is a beautiful thing that is being demonstrated over and over again in the world today.

In New Guinea and throughout parts of Indonesia, for instance, stone-age men and repulsive cannibals are being born again just as quickly as those with college degrees, because it is just as near to Jesus from the jungle as it is from the halls of ivy.

He is in the midst of all cultures!

Jesus is in the midst of all ages as well. By that I mean our human ages, our birthdays. It is just as near to Jesus at 80 years old as it is from eight; just as near from 70 as it is from seven.

We have been told that as we get older, we are harder to reach for God and the likelihood of our coming to Jesus diminishes. But our ability to come to Jesus—the distance we are from God—is no greater when we are 90 than when we were youngsters.

So, Jesus Christ stands in the middle of the human race, at the center of geography, the central figure in time, and in the midst of all cultures.

Our Lord is at the center of all life's experiences!

Our Lord speaks peace to us throughout life's experiences. An experience is awareness of things taking place around us. A newborn baby does not have experience. So far, he is just a little stranger in our world. But he learns fast, and very soon experience will teach him that when he howls, he will get attention.

The man who lives to be 100 years old has really had some experiences. However, if he lives somewhere in the hills and seldom comes out, he probably will have a narrow field of experience.

If he is a world traveler with a good education and a wide circle of friends, his experience will be so vast that it is a mystery as to how his brain can file away so much for future memory and reference.

I ask, which is nearer to Jesus? Does the child with little experience have an advantage over the man of wide experience? There is no difference! Jesus Christ stands in the middle of life's experiences and anyone can reach Him, no matter who he is!

Jonathan Edwards, that mighty preacher of the earlier days in our country, was converted when he was only five years old. He wrote, "I never backslid. I went right on." What experiences can a five-year-old boy have?

Read the early chapters of First Samuel and consider that the boy Samuel was twelve. He was just a lad. And then there was Eli, 98 years old. Here are the two of them—the boy and the aged man.

What experience had the boy had? Practically none. What experience had the old man had? Practically all. He had run the whole scale, the gamut of human possibilities. Yet it was just as near to God from young Samuel who had no experience as it was to Eli who had found out through the years what life was all about.

Remember that when our Lord hung on the cross, a superscription was written in Hebrew, Greek, and Latin and placed on the cross above His head: "This is Jesus Christ, the King of the Jews." Someone has pointed out that in doing this,

God had taken in the whole world. Hebrew stands for religion; Greek for philosophy, and Latin for Rome's military prowess. All the possibilities of human experience on a world scale were taken in.

It was just as close from the Roman soldiers to the Son of God as from the Hebrew teacher, Nicodemus, who said, "Master, Thou art sent from God!"

So, the world of that day was really divided into three parts, and that is about all we have today, isn't it?

We still have religion, culture and the combination of military and politics. Everything else seems to fall somewhere inside those brackets.

Jesus Christ was crucified in the very center of man's world. So it is just as easy to reach Him from the philosopher's ivory tower as it is from the priest's sanctuary. It is just as easy for the uniformed soldier to reach Him as it is for the thinker with his big books.

Christ Jesus our Lord stands in the midst so no one can claim advantage. Thank God! No one can frighten me, intimidate me or send me away.

No one can put me down and say, "Ah, but you don't know!"

They have tried. They smile when they say it and I smile back and think, "Brother, you are the one who doesn't know—because I do know!"

I know that I can reach Him as quickly from where I am as any other man.

Einstein, with his great mind, could reach out and touch his Messiah if he would. There are many in America who cannot read or write. Einstein and the man who marks an X for his name are in the same category. Both are equal on the rim. No man can actually say that he has been given an advantage over others.

You say, then: "Why doesn't everybody come?"

- Because of inexcusable stubbornness.
- Because of unbelief.
- Because of preoccupation with other things.
- Because we do not believe that we really need Him!

Millions turn their backs on Him because they will not confess their need. If you have found you need Him, you can come to Him in faith, you can touch Him and feel His power flowing out to help you, whoever you are.

Jesus did not come to save learned men only. He came to save the sinner! Not white men only—but all colors that are under the sun. Not young people only—but people of all ages!

Let us believe that and let us honor Jesus in our midst! The most important thing about you and Jesus is that you can reach Him from where you are!

The Failing Believer: God Has a Remedy

My little children, these things write I unto you, that ye sin not. And if any man sin, we have an advocate with the Father, Jesus Christ the righteous; And he is the propitiation for our sins; and not for our's only, but also for the sins of the whole world. 1 John 2:1-2

ALTHOUGH THERE IS PLAIN teaching throughout the Old and New Testaments concerning God's willingness to forgive and forget, there are segments of the Christian church which appear to be poorly taught concerning God's clear remedy through the atonement for the believer who has yielded to temptation and failed his Lord.

How important it is that we know how to encourage and deal with the distressed and guilt-ridden disciple who cries out in utter dejection and misery of soul: "I quit! I quit! It is no use. I am just worse than other people!"

Basically, why does God forgive sin?

Because God knows that sin is the dark shadow standing between Him and His highest creation, man. God is more willing to remove that shadow than we are to have it removed.

He wants to forgive us—and that desire is a part; of His character.

The Word of God gives us the blessed authority to claim that all of God's believing children have a remedy and a sacrifice for the guilt of sin: "Bring your lamb! Bring your offering!"

In the Old Testament pattern of forgiveness, the Jew had to bring a lamb. In this church age, the New Testament Christian surely knows that he can bring no offering other than his trust in the eternal Lamb of God, offered once and forever efficacious!

By no stretch of the imagination can anyone claim that John was "excusing" sin in the writing of this important first epistle. Actually, his paragraphs bristle with condemnation of everything evil and certainly carry the message of a sin-hating God.

But under the inspiration of the Holy Spirit, John takes the position of a realist and indicates what our Lord has done to make it possible for weak and vacillating believers to find forgiveness and assurance in their daily experiences.

The apostle is not suggesting some theoretical posture for believers. He is taking things as he found them and dealing with them on the basis of their reality—and not theorizing on how they should have been.

John was a father in the Christian faith and had wide experience with human beings, particularly with redeemed human beings. With the Holy Spirit's guidance, the old apostle provides us with the truth that Christian believers should be aware of their need to depend upon the Lord moment by moment—for during our lifetime there will never be a time when there will not be at least a possibility of sinning!

John's language cannot be interpreted as encouragement for those in the kingdom of God to sin carelessly and willfully.

Here is an illustration that comes to my mind when I consider this portion of Scripture.

It is a common thing to find clinics and infirmaries within the great manufacturing and industrial complexes in metropolitan areas of our nation. Would you say that providing these services means that the companies involved are encouraging accidents and illnesses?

Recognizing the human situation, the companies build the clinics because the statistics indicate just about how many accidents and sicknesses will occur among the given number of people every year.

No, John's teaching is not an encouragement to sin. It might be considered a kind of spiritual clinic that extends a caution: "Watch out and do not sin. But if any man sin, he does have an advocate with the Father."

That advocate, that representative is Jesus Christ, the Righteous One, John continues, with the assurance that He is the propitiation for our sins, and then adds a beautiful, expansive parenthesis, "Not for ours only, but also for the sins of the whole world" (1 John 2:2).

Now it would be well to note that this "clinic" idea was actually instituted and carried out in Old Testament times.

I want to take you back into the fourth chapter of Leviticus to connect the Old and New Testament plans of forgiveness, to show that the same Holy Spirit provided the inspiration throughout and that it is the same eternal Christ shining through every page and every chapter.

In this passage in Leviticus, there was a spiritual "clinic" provided for the people of Israel and for congregations that had become infected with evil and wrongdoing. Perhaps those who have neglected the Old Testament will be surprised to learn that even in that period of the Law, God promised and offered an immediate and efficacious remedy for those who fell short of His commands.

Notice what they were told to do about sin in Leviticus:

"If a soul shall sin through ignorance against any of the commandments of the Lord concerning things which ought not to be done, and shall do against any of them . . ." (Leviticus 4:2), there is a remedy for that man.

First, think with me about this phrase indicating that some wrongs may be done through ignorance.

I do not think the words *through ignorance* should cause you to picture in your mind a starry-eyed, honest-hearted person who just happened to sin accidentally. I think in realism we must face up to the fact here is a careless soul, one who has perhaps neglected the Scriptures and neglected to hear the Word of the Lord, and following the intent of his own heart has sinned against the commandments of the Lord.

But, thankfully, there is a remedy for him. God cares about him!

Continuing in this section of Leviticus, God's remedy for sin and wrongdoing was provided for several categories of persons within Israel.

We are told of the possibility of sin even among those who were the anointed priests of God.

I wish that did not have to be in the record—but I am glad it is. They were men and they were not perfect.

I have read something of the life of the godly Saint Theresa, who confessed that she felt that she was the least of all Christians, because she read of Christ's great saints before her time who began to live so earnestly for God immediately after they were converted that they no longer caused Him any grief by sinning.

And she said: "I cannot say that. I have to admit that I grieved God after I was converted and that makes me less than they."

That was a humble and very touching way to put it, but I think if the truth were known about any of the saints of God, Theresa's confession would be their confession, too!

Brethren, I wish it were possible to anoint the head of every Christian preacher so that he would never sin again while the world stands. Perhaps some would consider that a happy way to deal with the subject-but if any man can be removed from the possibility of sin, he can only be some kind of robot run by pulleys, wheels and pushbuttons, morally incapable of doing evil and, by the same token, morally incapable of doing good.

This squares with what I have always preached in this pulpit: if man's will is not free to do evil, it is not free to do good!

The freedom of human will is necessary to the concept of morality.

That is why I have not accepted the doctrine that our Lord Jesus Christ could not have sinned. If He could not have sinned, then the temptation in the wilderness was a grand hoax and God was a party to it!

Certainly as a human being He could have sinned, but the fact that He would not sin was what made Him the holy man He was.

On that basis, then, it is not the inability to sin but it is the unwillingness to sin that makes a man holy.

The holy man is not one who cannot sin.

A holy man is one who will not sin.

A truthful man is not a man who cannot talk. He is a man who can talk and he could lie, but he will not.

An honest man is not a man who is in jail where he cannot be dishonest. An honest man is a man who is free to be dishonest, but he will not be dishonest.

But returning to the Old Testament priest—there was a possibility that he would sin and be found standing in need of God's remedy.

He was an anointed priest, set apart to serve his fellowmen and represent them before the Lord. But if there were no possibility that he could sin and he was nothing more than a robot, he would never understand the needs and the guilt of his people.

He never could have known their difficulties and troubles.

A physician who himself had never felt any pain surely could never sympathize with an ailing, suffering patient.

Now, in Leviticus, what was the sinning priest to do? Should he give up to discouragement and gloom and failure?

The answer is no: there is a remedy!

And what about ministers and all of God's servants today? In a time of temptation and weakness and failure, do they just quit? Do they write a resignation and walk out, saying, "I am not an Augustine nor a Wesley nor a Simpson—therefore I will give up."

If they know the Word of God, they seek God's remedy.

The remedy in the Old Testament was clear and plain: "Let him bring for his sin, which he hath sinned, a young bullock without blemish unto the Lord for a sin-offering, and he shall bring the bullock unto the door of the tabernacle of the congregation before the Lord; and shall lay his hand upon the bullock's head, and kill the bullock before the Lord. And the priest that is anointed shall take of the bullock's blood, and bring it to the tabernacle of the congregation: and the priest shall dip his finger in the blood, and sprinkle of the blood seven times before the Lord, before the vail of the sanctuary. And the priest shall put some of the blood upon the horns of the altar of sweet incense before the Lord, which is in the tabernacle of the congregation; and shall pour all the blood of the bullock at the bottom of the altar of the burnt-offering, which is at the door of the tabernacle of the congregation" (Lev. 4:3-7).

Now, there you have atonement for sin in the Old Testament. The Lord our God was providing a day-by-day remedy for spiritual weakness and failure.

The next category of sinners in Leviticus was the entire assembly or congregation of Israel.

"If the whole congregation of Israel sin through ignorance, and the thing be hid from the eyes

of the assembly, and they have done somewhat
against any of the commandments of the Lord concerning things which should not be done, and are
guilty; when the sin, which they have sinned against
it, is known, then the congregation shall offer a
young bullock for the sin" (Leviticus 4:13-14), going
through the same process of sacrifice for atonement.

Then Moses recorded the result of God's remedy: "And the priest shall make an atonement for
them, and it shall be forgiven them" (Leviticus 4:20).

There was another category of men said to be in
need of the remedy—the rulers who have sinned
and done somewhat against the Lord.

The crux of all these instructions in Leviticus
brings us to identification with a needy but blessed
group—the common people!

"If any one of the common people sin through
ignorance, while he doeth somewhat against any of
the commandments of the Lord concerning things
which ought not to be done, and be guilty; or if his
sin, which he hath sinned, comes to his knowledge;
then he shall bring his offering . . ." (4:27-28).

I think the reference to "if his sin comes to his
knowledge" speaks of his conscience awaking to
the fact that he has sinned. We read in the Gospels
of the willful prodigal who left his father and went
into a far country. But at last he came to himself,
and acknowledged his guilt. Prior to that awaken-
ing, he had been just as thoroughly a sinner but
would not confess it or acknowledge it.

I delight in these instructions of the Lord to the
common people, and when I say I love the common people, I do not mean "common" in the sense
of ugliness, ignorance, crudeness or vulgarity. But

when I think of the common people so much loved by our Lord Jesus, I think of people like you and me. We make up that great throng of folks who are entirely without fame; we probably will never have our names in "Who's Who" and we may never win the international peace or science or literature prize awards.

But we are the plain people—just the great multitude of common folks that God made!

When we look at a prize chrysanthemum in a flower show or florist's window, we are astonished at the beauty of the bloom. A lot of professional help goes into the making of a chrysanthemum. But for simple, plain people, I recommend a wide expanse of daisies or a great field of goldenrod nodding in the balmy, autumn sun. They are among the common flowers, plain and simple blooms—and they don't have an artificial price tag.

Also, a goldenrod doesn't require anything but God's spacious heaven above and His bright sunshine and space in which to grow. It will nod there in all its natural beauty, together with the yellow and white daisies and the black-eyed susans. They will all be there. They had their place centuries ago, and they will still be there in centuries to come, if the Lord tarries. They don't require much—they are the common flowers!

I believe there's more joy in discovering a common wild flower in the spring when you are scarcely expecting it than in paying inflated dollars for a bouquet of flowers that have been carefully tended by horticulturists.

Now that is not to speak against nice flowers—I like them all! But sometimes I wonder if they are worth all they cost. The common field flower costs nothing—just the effort to see it, that's all.

In the spiritual life, God has His chrysanthemums, I guess. We read the stories of the great saints, and I am a great admirer of every one of them. Perhaps in the long run I am more at home with God's common daisy varieties than I am with the great, carefully cultivated churchmen who have been His showpieces for centuries past. Wouldn't it be tragic if we had to say, "Now, God, we just have a few that we can call to your attention. We will give you Paul and Chrysostom and Augustine and Francis, and we will add Knox and Luther and Wesley, and that's about all we can muster."

God would smile and say, "No, those are just my prize chrysanthemums. They were some of the great fellows, with more potential, somehow. I am glad for every one of them, but I am not so poverty stricken for spiritual leadership that I need say I have no others."

Behold, gaze, look . . . see an innumerable company that no man can number—nodding, common flowers of field and meadow that just somehow took root and grew in the sunshine and looked heavenward and gathered the rain and the dew and loved God for His own sake.

They were men and women whose hands may have been grimy, and they perhaps did not understand all the learned illusions of the highly-educated preacher. They may have no degrees, but they form a great company, and they have the blessed marks of the family. The family resemblance is upon them. They belong to God. They may have grown up in an atmosphere where they had no opportunity to cultivate themselves: as others did, but they were true to God in their day. These are the plain people with whom many authors have been intrigued—the simple, mute, unknown millions, the plain people willing to share their fragrance even in the desert places. That's my crowd—all the time—that's my crowd!

When I am with men known as "big preachers," I sit down and talk with them when they are willing. If we can talk about God or faith or good books, we hit it off for awhile. But mostly I wander off and hunt up some butcher from Atlanta or a carpenter from Detroit, perhaps a rubber worker from Akron, a machinist from Minneapolis or a small-time farmer from Ottumwa. I feel more at home among them because they are God's plain people, God's common people, and there are so many more of them.

Well, back to Leviticus!

If any one of the common people sin through ignorance, the Lord instructed, while he doeth somewhat against any of the commandments of the Lord concerning things which ought not to be done and be guilty, there is a remedy!

In this gathering of believers, it could be that some of us common people have sinned. I trust that we will let the Holy Spirit bring it to our knowledge and that we will not be careless about it. If it comes to our knowledge, and we know that we have sinned somewhat against any of the commandments of the Lord concerning things that ought not to be done, then what shall we do?

Shall we give in to discouragement and guilt and say, "I cannot be a Christian! It is impossible! The world is too tough! There is too much temptation! I am too weak! I am too busy! I cannot make any progress!"

No! There is a remedy in the atonement. It says, "Let him bring his offering; let him bring his offering . . ."

An offering has already been provided. It does not mean that you should bring your money. No, no man of God will ever trick you like that—God forbid! I would live on rolled oats the rest of my life before I would identify any gift to the church with the offering of the Lamb of God!

But, bring your offering! Your offering has already been made: "Behold the lamb of God who beareth away the sin of the world!" You do not have to search for a lamb. Your sacrifice has been made once and is efficacious forever!

Not all the blood of beasts on Jewish altars slain
Could give the guilty conscience peace, or wash
away the stain.
But Christ, the heavenly Lamb, takes all our sins
away;
A sacrifice of nobler name and richer blood
than they!

Continuing, Isaac Watts, that man of God, confessed,

My faith would lay her hand on that dear head
of Thine;
While like a penitent I stand, and there confess
my sin.
My soul looks back to see the burden Thou
didst bear,
When hanging on the accursed tree, and knows
her guilt was there!

So in the covenant of grace, you need only lay your hand upon the head of the sin offering, the Lamb which was provided!

Oh, what does that mean to us? It means identification.

In the New Testament there is much said about the laying on of hands. It was symbolic of identification and union.

We lay our hands on the head of a young minister being ordained as we identify ourselves with him and with others who laid their hands on our heads, a holy succession through the years.

The one who recognized his guilt was to lay his hands on the head of the offering in the Old Testament plan—thus identifying himself with the offering of sacrifice. That common man who had sinned was saying, "Oh, God, I deserve to die. Through faith in the mystery of atonement, I am going to live and this lamb will die. I lay my hand on his head, confess my sins, and my sins will be laid upon the lamb, as it were."

In the sacrificial death of the lamb, God was telling us that one day a perfect Lamb would come who would not merely symbolically take away sin, but would actually take away sin, because His blood would be richer and His name would be nobler.

He—Jesus—is the propitiation for our sins and for the sins of the whole world.

Sometimes when I am alone with my Bible, I get on my knees and turn to Isaiah 53. For every pronoun there I put all three of my names in. Then I read it aloud.

"Surely he hath borne Aiden Wilson Tozer's griefs, and carried Aiden Wilson Tozer's sorrows: . . . He was wounded for Aiden Wilson Tozer's transgressions, he was bruised for Aiden Wilson Tozer's iniquities."

That is laying your hand on the head of the sacrifice and identifying yourself with the dying lamb.

You can do that today!

CHAPTER
5

The Resurrection of Christ: More Than a Festival

And the angel answered and said unto the women, Fear not ye: for I know that ye seek Jesus, which was crucified. He is not here; for he is risen, as he said. Come, see the place where the Lord lay. And go quickly, and tell his disciples that he is risen from the dead; and, behold, he goeth before you into Galilee; there shall ye see him. Matthew 28:5-7

A NY CHRISTIAN CHURCH THAT looks back to the crucifixion only with sorry tears, and is not pressing forward in the blessed life of the risen Christ, is no more than a "pitying kind of religion."

And I must agree with one of the old writers in the faith who said, "I cannot away with it!"—meaning, "I cannot tolerate this pitying kind of religion."

True spiritual power does not reside in the ancient cross but rather in the victory of the mighty, resurrected Lord of glory who could pronounce after spoiling death: "All power is given unto me in heaven and in earth!" (Matt. 28:18)

Let us be confident, Christian brethren, that our power does not lie in the manger at Bethlehem nor in the relics of the cross.

The power of the believer lies in the triumph of eternal glory!

The Man who died on the cross died in weakness. The Bible is plain in telling us this. But He arose in power. If we forget or deny the truth and glory of His resurrection and the fact that He is seated at the right hand of God, we lose all the significance of the meaning of Christianity!

The resurrection of Jesus Christ brought about a startling change of direction. It is interesting and profitable to look at the direction of the prepositions in Matthew's account of the resurrection morning.

First, the women came *to* the tomb.

They came in love, but they came in sadness and fear, and they came to mourn. That was the direction of their religion before they knew Jesus had been raised from the dead. Their direction was towards the grave—the tomb which held the body of Jesus.

Many who still face in the direction of the tomb, knowing only mourning and grief, uncertainty and the fear of death, are all around us.

But on that historic resurrection day, the faithful women had a dramatic change of direction.

They heard the angelic news and they saw the evidence: "He is not here: for he is risen, as he said!" (Matt. 28:6) The mammoth stone had been rolled away and they themselves could see the stark emptiness of the tomb.

"Go quickly, and tell His disciples!"

So the record tells us they departed immediately *from* the sepulcher.

What an amazing change of direction! What a change wrought by the joyful news!

The preposition is now *from* the grave instead of *to* the grave. The direction is suddenly away from the tomb—because the tomb was empty and stripped of its age-old power.

The direction is suddenly no longer toward the end—for with Jesus alive from the dead and about to be glorified at the right hand of the Father, the direction changed toward endlessness—the eternity of eternal life and victory!

If this is not the message and meaning of Easter, the Christian church is involved in a shallow one-day festival each year, intent upon the brightness of colors and the fragrance of flowers and the sweet sentiments of poetry and spring time.

The Christian church should have its priorities in the right order.

Easter is not just a day in the church calendar, something to be celebrated each year as an end in itself, something that began early on that first day of the week and ended at midnight.

The resurrection morning was only the beginning of a great, grand and vast outreach that has never ended and will not end until our Lord Jesus Christ comes back again.

The reality of Easter and of the resurrection and of the great commission of the risen and ascending Christ is the reality of the great missionary priority of the Christian church throughout today's world.

The resurrection of Christ and the fact of the empty tomb are not a part of the world's complex and continuing mythologies. This is not a Santa Claus tale—it is history and it is reality.

The Christian church is helpless and hopeless if it is stripped of the reality and historicity of the bodily resurrection of Jesus Christ. The true church of Jesus Christ is necessarily founded upon the belief and the truth that it happened. There was a real death, there was a real tomb, there was a real stone. But, thank God, there was a sovereign Father in heaven, an angel sent to roll the stone away, and a living Saviour in a resurrected and glorified body able to proclaim to His disciples, "All power is given unto me in heaven and in earth!"

Since that is our prospect and hope, there is no reason for any of us to be continually asking for pity for the Lord Jesus Christ.

The church has too many radiant, beckoning opportunities to be occupied with this: "Let us kneel down by the cross and let us weep awhile."

It is wrong for us to join those whose concept seems to be that our Lord was a martyr, a victim of His own zeal, a poor pitiable Man with good intentions who found the world too big and life too much for Him, He is still portrayed by too many as sinking down in a helplessness wrought by death.

Why should we in His church walk around in black and continue to grieve at the tomb when the record clearly shows that He came back from death to prove His words: "All power is given unto me in heaven and in earth!"

Brethren, He died for us, but ever since the hour of resurrection, He has been the mighty Jesus, the mighty Christ, the mighty Lord!

Power does not lie with a babe in the manger.

Power does not lie with a man nailed and helpless on a cross.

Power lies with the man on that cross who gave His life, who went into the grave and who arose and came out on the third day, then to ascend to the right hand of the Father.

That is where power lies.

Our business is not to mourn and weep beside the grave.

Our business is to thank God with tearful reverence that He once was willing to go into that grave. Our business is to thank God for the understanding of what the cross meant and for understanding of what the resurrection meant both to God and to men.

Do we rightly understand the resurrection, in the sense that it placed a glorious crown upon all of Christ's sufferings?

Do we realize the full significance of our Lord Jesus Christ being seated today at the Father's right hand, seated in absolute majesty and kingly power, sovereign over every power in heaven and in earth?

There is always someone with a rejoinder: "But, Mr. Tozer, how can you back up that big talk? If Christ is sovereign over all the world, what about the world condition?

"What about Russia and spreading Communism?

"What about atom bombs and hydrogen bombs and impending doom?

"If He is sovereign, why is there a continuing armament race? Why does the Middle East situation continue to plague the entire world?"

There is an answer and it is the answer of the prophetic Scripture.

God has a prophetic plan in His dealing with the world, its nations and its governments.

God's plan will continue on God's schedule. His plan has always called for the return of Israel

to Palestine. The nations of the earth are playing themselves into position all over the world—
almost like a giant checker board—while God
waits for the consummation.

While Israel gathers and while the King of the
North beats himself out, the Christian church prays
and labors to evangelize the world for the Saviour.

Christ waits—even though He has all the power.
He waits to exercise His awesome power.

He is showing His power in many ways in the
life and ministries of His church.

I believe He would exercise His unlimited power
if His church would truly believe that He could and
would do it!

When Jesus announced that "All power is given
unto me in heaven and in earth," what did He
expect His followers to do? What are the implications for all of us who are in the Body of Christ?

The answer is plain; Jesus said, "Go ye, therefore!"

Therefore is the word that connects everything
together. Christ has been given all power; therefore
we are to go and evangelize, discipling all nations.
All of the implications of the resurrection add up
to the fact that the Christian church must be a missionary church if it is to meet the expectations of
the risen Saviour!

Because He is alive forevermore Jesus could
promise, in the same context as His command, that
He would be with us always, even unto the end of
the world, or age.

There have been many little wall plaques and
mottoes on display in Christian homes reading:
"Lo, I am with you alway, even unto the end of the

world." But that is only a partial quotation and it overrides certain implications.

You know how skillfully we take the knife of bad teaching and separate a little passage from the context even as we might take the rind from an orange. We peel the promise off and put it on our mottoes and calendars.

Let's be truthful and let our Lord say to us all exactly what He wants to say.

Is this what He said, "Lo, I am with you alway"?

Not exactly, my brother.

He actually said, "Go ye therefore, and teach all nations, baptizing them in the name of the Father, and of the Son, and of the Holy Ghost: teaching them to observe all things whatsoever I have commanded you:

AND, LO, I AM WITH YOU ALWAY, EVEN UNTO THE END OF THE WORLD" (Matt. 28:19-20).

That little word *and* is not there by accident. Jesus literally was saying that His presence was promised and assured in the Christian church if the church continued faithful in its missionary responsibilities.

That's why I say that the resurrection of Jesus Christ is something more than making us the happiest fellows in the Easter parade.

Am I to listen to a cantata and join in singing "Up from the grave He arose," smell the flowers and go home and forget it?

No, certainly not!

It is truth and a promise with a specific moral application. The resurrection certainty lays hold on us with all the authority of sovereign obligation.

It says that the Christian church is to go—to go into all the world, reaching and teaching all nations, or as the margin has it, "Make disciples among all nations."

So, the moral obligation of the resurrection of Christ is the missionary obligation, the responsibility and the privilege of carrying the message and telling the story, of praying and interceding, and of being involved personally and financially in the cause of this great commission.

I have asked myself many times why professing Christian believers can relegate the great missionary imperative of our Lord Jesus Christ to the sidelines of our Christian cause.

I cannot follow the reasoning of those who teach that the missionary commission given by Jesus Christ does not belong to the church but will be carried out during the great tribulation days emphasized in Bible prophecy.

I cannot give in to the devil's principal, deceitful tactic which makes so many Christians satisfied with an Easter celebration instead of experiencing the power of His resurrection. The enemy of our souls is quite happy about the situation when Christians make a big deal of Easter Sunday, put the emphasis on flowers and cantatas, and preachers use their soft-voiced and dewy-eyed technique in referring to Jesus as the greatest of all earth's heroes.

The devil is willing to settle for all of that kind of display as long as the churches stop short of telling the whole truth about the resurrection of Christ.

"It's fine with me if they just make a big hero of Jesus, but I don't ever want them to remember for a minute that He is now seated in the place of power and I am actually a poor, frightened fugitive"—that's the reasoning of the devil.

And it is his business to keep Christians mourning awhile and weeping with pity beside the tree instead of demonstrating that Jesus Christ is risen indeed, is at the right hand of the Father in glory, and has the right and authority to put the devil in hell when the time comes, chaining him and hurling him down according to God's revealed prophetic plan.

The devil will do almost anything to keep us from actually believing and trusting that death has no more dominion and that Jesus Christ has been given all authority in heaven and in earth and hell, holding the keys thereof.

When will the Christian church rise up and get on the offensive for the risen and ascended Saviour?

When we come to know the full meaning of the cross and experience the meaning and the power of the resurrection in our own lives—that is the answer. Through the power of His resurrection we will take the spiritual offensive; we become the aggressors and our witness and testimony become the positive force in reaching the ends of the earth with the gospel.

We can just sum it all up by noting that Jesus Christ asks us only to surrender to His Lordship and obey His commands. He will supply the power if we will believe His promise and demonstrate the reality of His resurrection.

These promises of Christ have taken all the strain and pressure from our missionary responsibility.

When the Spirit of God speaks and deals with our young people about their own missionary responsibility, Christ assures them of His presence and power as they prepare to go.

"All power is given unto Me. I am no longer in the grave. With all authority and power I can protect you, I can support you, I can go ahead of you, I can give you effectiveness in your witness and ministry. Go, therefore, and make disciples of all nations, and I will go with you. I will never leave you nor forsake you!"

Men without God suffer alone and die alone in time of war and in other circumstances of life. All alone!

But it can never be said that any true soldier of the cross of Jesus Christ, no man or woman as missionary or messenger of the truth has ever gone out to a ministry alone!

There have been many Christian martyrs—but not one of them was on that mission field all alone. No missionary that ever laid down his life in the jungle was actually alone—for Jesus Christ keeps His promise of taking him by the hand and leading him triumphantly through to the world beyond.

Do you see it, my friend? Resurrection is not a day of celebration—it is an obligation understood and accepted!

Because Jesus Christ is alive, there is something for us to do for Him every day. We cannot just sit down, settling back in religious apathy.

We can dare to fully trust the Risen One who said, "All power is given unto me in heaven and in earth . . . go ye therefore . . . and, lo, I am with you alway, even unto the end of the world."

God's Eternal Work: Only by the Holy Spirit

And gave gifts unto men . . . he gave some, apostles; and some, prophets; and some, evangelists; and some, pastors and teachers; for the perfecting of the saints, for the work of the ministry, for the edifying of the body of Christ. Ephesians 4:8, 11-12

T HE SCRIPTURAL TEACHING THAT the work of God through the church can be accomplished only by the energizing of the Holy Spirit is very hard for humans to accept, for it is a concept that frustrates our own carnal desire for honor and praise, for glory and recognition.

Basically, God has been very kind and tender with us—but there is no way in which He can compromise with our human pride and carnality. That is why His Word bears down so hard on "proud flesh," insisting that we understand and confess that no human gifts, no human talents can accomplish the ultimate and eternal work of God.

Even though God has faithfully reminded us that it is a ministry of the Holy Spirit to submerge and hide the Christian worker in the work, the true humility He seeks among us is still too often the exception and not the rule.

I think we ought to be mature enough to confess that many have been converted to Christ and have come into the church without wrestling with that human desire for honor and praise. As a result, some have actually spent a lifetime in religious work doing little more than getting glory for themselves!

Brethren, the glory can belong only to God! If we take the glory, God is being frustrated in the church.

With this background, let us consider the Apostle's account of what Jesus Christ actually did:

He gave special gifts "for the perfecting of the saints for the work of the ministry for the edifying of the body of Christ" (Eph. 4:12).

Did you notice that we have purposely eliminated the commas? God did not put the commas in this passage—the translators did!

The commas make the passage read as though there are three separate results of these gifts in the Body of Christ.

The work of the ministry which the saints are to do will bring about the edifying of the Body of Christ—and this is not just in reference to the ordained ministry as we know it. It is the ministry of all Christians to have some share in the building up of the Body of Christ until we all come into the unity of the faith and of the knowledge of the Son of God unto a perfect man, with a measure of the stature of the fullness of Christ.

It is rather common for visitors in our church to ask me frankly about some of the things they do not find in our fellowship. They want to know why we frown on some customs found in other contemporary groups.

I try very hard to keep from drawing uncomplimentary comparisons with other churches and other groups. If there are failures in meeting high spiritual and scriptural standards, God will have to deal with us, no matter who we are.

But we are responsible to our Lord for the conduct of the work which He has given us and we have prayerfully studied the Scriptures to determine how we can fit into those methods through which God accomplishes His eternal work.

I think that there are three basic methods whereby God uses the Body of Christ to do His final work—His eternal work.

First, Christian believers and Christian congregations must be thoroughly consecrated to Christ's glory alone. This means absolutely turning our backs on the modern insistence for human glory and recognition.

I have done everything I can to keep "performers" out of my pulpit. We do not think we are called to recognize "performers." We are confident that our Lord never meant for the Christian church to provide a kind of religious stage where performers proudly take their bows, seeking human recognition for themselves.

We do not believe that is God's way to an eternal work. He has never indicated that proclamation of the gospel is to become dependent upon human performances.

Instead, it is important to note how much the Bible has to say about the common people, the plain people—like you and me.

The Word of God speaks with such appreciation of the common people that I am inclined to believe it is a term dear to God.

Jesus was always surrounded by the common people. He had a few "stars," but largely His helpers were from the common people, the good people—and surely, not always the most brilliant.

Jesus looked first for consecration and in our own day it is surely true that His Spirit uses those who are no longer interested in their own promotion, but are consecrated to one thought—getting glory for Jesus Christ, who is Saviour and Lord!

To please God, a person must be just an instrument for God to use.

For a few seconds, picture in your mind the variety of wonderful and useful appliances we have in our homes. They have been engineered and built to perform tasks of all kinds.

But without the inflow of electrical power they are just lumps of metal and plastic, unable to function and serve. They cannot do their work until power is applied from a dynamic outside source.

So it is in the work of God in the church.

Many persons preach and teach. Many take part in the music. Certain ones try to administer God's work—but if the power of God's Spirit does not have freedom to energize all they do, these workers might just; as well have stayed home.

Natural gifts are not enough in God's work. The mighty Spirit of God must have freedom to animate and quicken with His overtones of creativity and blessing.

There have been great preachers in the past who were in demand all over the world. I think of one of the greatest, a recognized divine in New England. We still may think of him as an evangelical, but he was not known primarily as a Bible preacher. He expounded on such subjects as nature and science, literature and philosophy. His books had instant sales and his pulpit oratory attracted great crowds.

But when that preacher died, the bottom just dropped out of all the work which had kept him so busy. The work of the Spirit of God had been given no place in directing all of that natural talent and energy. God's eternal work had not been furthered.

We may recall, however, that when Spurgeon and G. Campbell Morgan passed away, their work and outreach went right on. Both of these well-known preachers had built their lifetime ministries on the Word of God and the power of the Spirit.

You can write it down as a fact: no matter what a man does, no matter how successful he seems to be in any field, if the Holy Spirit is not the chief energizer of his activity, it will all fall apart when he dies.

Perhaps the saddest part about that is that the man may be honored at his death for his talents and abilities, but he will learn the truth in that great day when our Lord judges the work of every man. That which is solely his own work and is wrought by his own talent will be recognized as nothing but wood, hay and stubble.

A second important element in God's use of the believing church is His response to our prayers raised to Him in true faith.

This matter of prayer really bears in on the great privileges of the common people, the children of God. No matter what our stature or status, we have the authority in the family of God to pray the prayer of faith, that prayer that can engage the heart of God and that can meet God's conditions of spiritual life and victory.

Our consideration of the power and efficacy of prayer enters into the question of why we are a Christian congregation and what we are striving to be and do.

We have to consider whether we are just going around and around—like a religious merry-go-round. Are we just holding on to the painted mane of the painted horse, repeating a trip of very insignificant circles to a pleasing musical accompaniment?

Some may think the path of the religious carousel is a kind of progress, but the family of God knows better than that. We are among those who believe in something more than holding religious services in the same old weekly groove. We believe that in an assembly of redeemed believers there should be marvelous answers to prayer.

We believe that God hears and actually answers our praying in the Spirit. Let it be said that one miraculous answer to prayer within a congregation will do more to lift and encourage and solidify the people of God than almost any other thing.

Answers to our prayers will lift up the hands that hang down in discouragement and strengthen the feeble spiritual knees.

I do believe that all of the advertising we can do in a variety of ways will never equal the interest and participation in the things of God resulting from the gracious answers to the prayers of faith generated by the Holy Spirit.

Actually, it will be such prayer and the meeting of God's conditions which will turn loose the third method of God's ordained accomplishments through the church. I speak of the Christian's dependence on the Holy Spirit and the willingness to exercise the Spirit's gifts.

This is an overflowing subject, one not easily exhausted, leading us into consideration of the presence and power and blessings of God available only through the ministries of His Spirit.

There are very few perceptive Christians who will argue with the fact that the gentle presence of the divine Spirit is always necessary if we are to see revival wonders.

I still have in my files an old sermon outline on revival in the church. I preached on revival when I was young; I soon found out it was easy to preach revival sermons but very difficult to make them come to life in the churches.

What do I mean by "revival wonders"?

Well, you will find such wonders among the people of God when someone in the congregation steps out into a new and wonderful spiritual experience. Just let that happen to one young person and it will do more to cause the youth work to lift and move and get off the sandbar than a host of scheduled meetings and special conferences.

The same is certainly true of older Christians. Just let one person step out in faith, claiming the fullness of the Spirit, crowning Jesus Christ as Lord, and the spiritual fallout will be felt and enjoyed by the entire group of believers.

I think we have to accept this and believe it as a spiritual principle, according to God's promises concerning the Holy Spirit.

We do not believe such spiritual blessings can be bought.

We do not believe that a true spirit and work of revival can be brought in by airplane or by freight. We do not believe that God's presence and blessings in the souls of men can be humanly induced.

We believe such revival wonders can take place only as the Holy Spirit energizes the Word of God as it is preached. Genuine blessings cannot come unless the Holy Spirit energizes and convinces and stirs the people of God.

Now, what does this all add up to? If we are intent upon God's glory alone, if we are using the resources of prayer and if we are obedient to the Spirit of God, there will assuredly be an attitude of true joyfulness in Christ's church.

Now, you who know me probably do not think of me as an overwhelmingly cheerful man. But, thank God, I know about the true joy of the Lord and I believe we should be a joyful people.

Each member of the Body of Christ must face up to the question of whether or not we actually fit the description of "a joyful people."

How many of you bring family and domestic problems right along with you, in thought and mind, when you come to worship?

How many businessmen bring their weekday troubles home on Friday night and carry them along to church on Sunday?

When income tax time rolls around, how many of you react by getting down in the dumps?

And what about the family's health? the worries about the children? How many of God's people continue to lug these worries and problems around on a fulltime basis?

We ought not to do it and we cannot be a joyful people if we do!

Why should the children of the King go mourning all the day? Why should the children of the King hang their heads and tote their own burdens?

Brethren, we are missing the mark about Christian victory and the life of joy in our Saviour. We ought to be standing straight and praising our God!

I must agree with the psalmist that the joy of the Lord is still the strength of His people. I do believe that the sad world is attracted to spiritual sunshine—the genuine thing, that is.

Some churches train their greeters and ushers to smile, showing as many teeth as possible. But I can sense that kind of display—and when I am greeted by a man who is smiling because he has been trained to smile, I know I am shaking the flipper of a trained seal.

But when the warmth and delight and joy of the Holy Spirit are in a congregation and the folks are just spontaneously joyful and unable to hide their happy grin, the result is a wonderful influence and effect upon others.

I am sure I have said a hundred times that the reason we have to search for so many things to cheer us up is the fact that we are not really joyful and contentedly happy within.

I admit that we live in a gloomy world and that international affairs, nuclear rumors and threats, earthquakes and riots cause people to shake their heads in despair and say, "What's the use?"

But we are Christians, and Christians have every right to be the happiest people in the world. We do not have to look to other sources—for we look to the Word of God and discover how we can know the faithful God above and draw from His resources!

Another promise of God is that the Holy Spirit with His gifts and graces will also give us genuine love for one another.

I will tell you this: I am determined that I am going to love everybody, even if it kills me! I have set my heart on it. I am going to do it.

Some people are just naturally winsome and love-able—but then there are others of whom some have said that only their mothers could love them. But I am determined that I am going to love them for Christ's sake!

Some people don't like me—and they have said so. But I am going to love them and they are not going to be able to stop me.

Brethren, love is not just feeling—love is willing. You can will to love people. The Lord says to me, "Love people!" I know very well that He does not mean just to feel love for them. He means that I should will to love them!

I think it would be wrong to mention the blessed things the Holy Spirit wants to do in our midst and not add sympathy and compassion to the list.

I dare to trust that we are a sympathetic body of believers. I hope that none of us can ever hear of a fellow Christian being in trouble or experiencing trials without feeling concern, suffering over it and taking the matter to God in prayer.

This kind of concern for one another comes out of love and understanding. If we have this grace by

God's Spirit, we will take no superior attitudes; we will not be censorious of others.

Every one of us should be keenly aware of the fact that if the Lord should take His hand from under us, we would all plunge down and be gone forever. We thank God for His goodness, which He continues to reveal to us in spite of our many weaknesses and faults.

It is in this context that I recall a conversation with a devoted English brother, Noel Palmer, a tall, expressive Salvation Army fellow with a great voice.

I said to him, "Brother Palmer, what about sanctification in the heart? What does it mean to you?"

He quickly responded.

"I believe that if the heart loves God and wants to do right, God will overlook a lot of flaws—and He will give us light as we walk with Him!"

I say with him, thank God you don't have to be flawless to be blessed!

You need to have a big heart that desires and wants the will of God more than anything else in the world. You need also to have an eye single to His glory.

These are the things that matter—exercising the gifts of God's Spirit by the energy of the Spirit.

These are the things that must be important to us in our congregational fellowship, all adding up to the fact that the Holy Spirit is making Jesus Christ our chief joy and delight!

Gifts of the Spirit; Necessity in the Church

So we, being many, are one body in Christ, and every one members one of another. Having then gifts differing according to the grace that is given to us . . . Romans 12:5-6

Now there are diversities of gifts, but the same Spirit. And there are differences of administrations, but the same Lord. And there are diversities of operations, but it is the same God which worketh all in all. But the manifestation of the Spirit is given to every man to profit withal. 1 Corinthians 12:4-7

T HE BIBLE TEACHES US that the genuine gifts of the Holy Spirit are a necessity in the spiritual life and ministries of every Christian congregation serious about glorifying Jesus Christ as Saviour and Lord.

Having said that, I also must add that I do not know of any group or denomination or communion anywhere in the world that has come into full and perfect realization of the Pauline doctrine and goal of spiritual life in the believing Body of Christ.

Now that is a conclusion that may not give much encouragement to the critical and restless ones who seem to be found in nearly every Christian fellowship—apparently just perched and ready to fly away to more spiritual pastures as soon as they can locate a perfect congregation made up of perfect people and led by a perfect minister!

It seems to me that Paul was trying to make it as plain as he could in his epistles that any segment of the Body of Christ, anywhere in the world, should recapitulate—gather up and sum up within itself—all of the offices and gifts and workings of the entire church of Christ.

A careful study of the Apostle's teachings concerning Jesus Christ and His church should persuade us that any local assembly ought to demonstrate all of the functions of the whole body. Paul clearly teaches that each Christian believer ought to demonstrate a proper gift or gifts, bestowed by God the Holy Spirit, and that together the believers would accomplish the work of God as a team.

Let us review something here that all of us probably know—the doctrine of the life and operation of Christian believers on earth—starting with the fact that the Christian church is the Body of Christ, with Christ Himself the head of the body.

Every true Christian, no matter where he lives, is a part of that body, and the Holy Spirit is to the church what our own soul is to our physical body. Through the operation of the Holy Spirit, Christ becomes the life, the unity and the consciousness of the body which is the church. Let the soul leave the physical body and all the parts of the body cease to function.

Every human body is thus an apt illustration of the spiritual life and functions of the church. Paul uses the illustration in three of his epistles in the New Testament, indicating really that it is more than an illustration for it is something carefully planned—members designed and created for distinct functions under the control of the head, Jesus Christ.

Illustrations are never perfect and parallels will generally break down at some point, particularly when we come to the sacred and infinite things of God.

For instance, for a man's physical body to function, the members have to be in one place. If you separate the man and scatter him around, he is dead.

But the Body of Christ, the church, does not have to be in one place because it has a unity, the unity of the Spirit. All of the members do not have to be in one place, for many of them are already in heaven, and those on earth are scattered in widely diverse areas.

And yet the true church, the Body of Christ, is not torn nor divided, for it is held together by the Holy Spirit, who maintains the life of the body and controls the functions of the members.

In the illustration of the physical body, the members are all designed for specific functions. The eye is designed for seeing. The ear is designed for hearing. The hand is designed in a most special way to perform distinct functions. The lungs are designed for breathing, the heart for the circulation of the blood.

These are all designed to cooperate and act and serve in concert with each other.

So it is to be in the Body of Christ—and we are members. According to Paul, the whole body exists for its members and the members exist for the whole body. And that of course is the reason God gives gifts, that the body may profit spiritually and maintain spiritual health and prosperity in its service for Jesus Christ in an unfriendly world.

Now, what about the control of the members? This is the point that many people seem to forget: that all of the effective and cooperating members of the body take their direction from the head.

When a man's head is separated from the rest of his body there can be no more control or direction of those members which had functioned together so well during his lifetime. This is plain physiology— that the physical body must get its control and direction from the head.

It is just as plain in Bible teaching that the church, the Body of Christ, must get its life and control and direction from its living head, Jesus Christ our Lord!

Every Christian, then, should be vitally concerned and personally interested in what the Bible tells us about the functions of the members.

These functions—called gifts in the Bible—are special abilities; they are gifts from God out of the store of His grace.

Paul wrote to the Roman church this reminder: "For I say, through the grace given unto me, to every man that is among you, not to think of himself more highly than he ought to think; but to think soberly, according as God hath dealt to every man the measure of faith" (Romans 12:3).

Paul then makes it plain that all believers in the church had been given "gifts differing according to the grace that is given to us" (v. 6).

Some teachers seem to think that they know exactly how many gifts of the Spirit are mentioned in the New Testament letters, but I say it is difficult to be dogmatic about the total number. It is certainly possible that some of the designations are synonymous with one another, such as gifts of ruling and gifts of government, and no doubt there is some overlapping in the varied gift functions.

In the twelfth chapter of First Corinthians, where Paul writes about the diversities of gifts, nine are mentioned specifically. Later in the same chapter he speaks of God setting apostles, prophets and teachers in the church and mentions such other gifts as helps and governments.

In the twelfth chapter of Romans, Paul makes reference to the gifts of exhortation, of giving, of ruling and of showing mercy.

In chapter four of Ephesians, mention is made of the gift functions of evangelists and pastors.

Concerning the apostles, it is generally agreed among Christians everywhere that the apostles chosen by Jesus had a particular office which has not been perpetuated. They were personal witnesses of the life and ministry of Christ Himself.

The New Testament gift of prophecy was not to predict—but to tell forth what God has to say and to proclaim God's truth for the present age.

We cannot deny that Christian teachers should have a special gift. Let us not be afraid to admit that not everyone can teach. Even those with natural capabilities must have a special anointing from the Spirit of God to impart truth. This is undoubtedly true also of the special gifts of wisdom and knowledge.

The basic spiritual life within the Body of Christ has always humbly acknowledged the sovereignty of the Spirit of God in gifts of miracles and healing.

Paul concludes his references to the gifts in writing to the Corinthians by reference to diversities of tongues, and then asks the rhetorical question:

"Are all apostles? are all prophets? are all teachers? are all workers of miracles? Have all the gifts of healing? do all speak with tongues? do all interpret?" (1 Cor. 12:29-30).

The answer to these questions, of course, is no, for Paul then instructs:

"But covet earnestly the best gifts: and yet shew I unto you a more excellent way" (v. 31).

It has been suggested to me that all Christian groups that believe in the authenticity and necessity of the gifts of the Spirit in the church in our time should be able to stand together in a great unity of fellowship.

I can only say here what I have often said to many of my friends in the groups associated with what is called "the tongues movement." I do not believe it is proper to magnify one gift above all others, particularly when that gift is one that Paul described as of least value.

I cannot believe that the unscriptural exhibition of that gift in public, like a child with a new toy, can be pleasing to God.

I believe that in any setting, the tendency to place personal feeling above the Scriptures is always an insult to God.

Where the wise and gentle Spirit of God is in control, believers ought to exhibit genuine discernment. In some "gifted" circles today, there is an almost total lack of spiritual discernment and a credulity beyond belief, revealed in many splits and divisions, acceptance of immature child preachers, and the use of a kind of gospel "rock and roll" music long before Elvis Presley.

With this review I am certainly not condemning individuals or churches or groups on a blanket basis. But there are some who say, "We have the gifts of the Spirit—come and join us!"

Before I join a movement, a school of thought, a theological persuasion, or a church group or denomination, I must make the proper tests.

What have been the characteristics and the earmarks of that group over a long period of years? Is there an exercise of sharp spiritual discernment that knows the flesh from the spirit? Is there an emphasis on spiritual cohesion and unity? Is there a scriptural emphasis on purity of life or is there a careless attitude concerning moral living?

For our fundamentalist Christian circles in general, I fear that there is an alarming lack of spiritual discernment. Because we have shut out the Holy Spirit in so many ways, we are stumbling along as though we are spiritually blindfolded. Ruling out the discernment and leadership of the Holy Spirit is the only possible explanation for the manner in which Christian churches have yielded to the temptation to entertain, entertain!

There is no other explanation for the wave of rationalism that now marks the life of many congregations. And what about the increasing compromise with all of the deadening forces of worldliness? The true, humble and uncompromising church of Christ is harder and harder to find.

It is not because leaders and men and women in the church are bad—it is only because the Holy Spirit of God has been so forcefully shut out and the needful gift of discernment about spiritual things is no longer present.

I believe we definitely need the gift of faith, and I do not mean that faith that we all must exercise to be saved. I believe we need men and women with a special and peculiar gift of faith, which often links with the gift of discernment by the Spirit.

There is a simple gift function of helps. I do not know all that it means, but I know many Christians who are just to be helpers in the work of Christ.

Related to that is the gift of showing mercy; going about doing good and encouraging the discouraged, as Jesus did so often.

There is a gift of government in the church, and it may be the same as the gift of ruling.

Some may not know that there is a true gift of giving. All believers are taught to give—but there is such a thing as a special gift of giving.

The Bible also speaks of the gift function of the evangelist and the pastor in the church.

God has given us in His Holy Spirit every gift and power and help that we need to serve Him. We do not have to look around for some other way.

The most solemn aspect of this is our individual responsibility. The Bible teaches that a day is coming when we must all appear before the judgment seat of Christ; that everyone faces a review of the things done in his body, whether good or bad.

In that day we will be fully exposed and the things that we have done in our own strength and for our own glory will be quickly blown away like worthless straw and stubble, forever separated from the kind of deeds and ministries which were wrought by the Spirit and which are described as eternal treasures in the sight of God, gold and silver and precious stones that the fire cannot harm.

In that day, all that is related to the work of the flesh will perish and pass away, and only that which has been wrought by the Spirit of God will remain and stand.

Do you dare to accept the fact that the sovereign God had designed to do all of His work through spiritually-gifted men and women? Therefore, He does all of His work on earth through humble and faithful believers who are given spiritual gifts and abilities beyond their own capacities.

Let me shock you at this point: A naturally bright person can carry on religious activity without a special gift from God. Filling church pulpits every week are some who are using only natural abilities and special training. Some are known as Bible expositors, for it is possible to read and study commentaries and then repeat what has been learned about the Scriptures.

Yes, it may shock you, but it is true that anyone able to talk fluently can learn to use religious phrases and can become recognized as a preacher.

But if any man is determined to preach so that his work and ministry will abide in the day of the judgment fire, then he must preach, teach and exhort with the kind of love and concern that comes only through a true and genuine gift of the Holy Spirit— something beyond his own capabilities!

We need to remember that even our Lord Jesus Christ ministering in the time of His humanity among us, depended upon the anointing of the Spirit. He applied the words of the prophet to Himself when He said, "The Spirit of the Lord is upon me, because he hath anointed me to preach the gospel to the poor; . . . and recovering of sight to the blind, to set at liberty them that are bruised" (Luke 4:18).

Do we realize that when leaders and members of a church do not have the genuine gifts of the Spirit—the true anointing of the Spirit—they are thrown back to depend upon human and natural capabilities?

In that case, natural talents must come to the fore.

We hear that some fellow can whistle through his teeth. Someone else has marvelous talent for impromptu composition of poetry. Some musicians are talented composers and singers. Others are talented talkers-let's admit it!

So in this realm of religious activity, talent runs the church. The gifts of the Spirit are not recognized and used as God intended.

Also, much of church activity and fellowship falls back upon the practice of psychology. Many leaders in church groups are skilled and masterful psychologists. They know how to handle people and get the crowds to come, and the operation qualifies as an amazingly "successful" church.

Part of the successful operation of that church depends upon men with business talents and part of it depends upon men with natural gifts as salesmen and politicians.

I say that a Christian congregation can survives and often appear to prosper in the community by the exercise of human talent and without any touch from the Holy Spirit! All that religious activity and the dear people will not know anything better until the *great* and terrible day when our self-employed talents are burned with fire and only that which was wrought by the Holy Ghost will stand forever!

Through His Spirit, God is waiting and willing to do for us or for any church what He waits to do for the entire Body of Christ!

It was the promise of Christ that "you shall receive power" through the ministry of the Holy Spirit, and the disciples were taught that the Holy Spirit would also bestow sweet graces and pleasant fruits of godliness when He could gain control of our persons.

Let me share my earnest hope and expectation with you—I believe the Holy Spirit of God wants to do some gracious new thing in our midst!

With the dignity and self-control that is basic to the Christian faith, the calmness and sweetness that belonged to Jesus Christ, and the abandonment that marked the spiritual life of the apostles in the early church, let us throw ourselves out on the great fullness of God with expectation!

Wouldn't it be a wonderful thing if that outpouring of the Spirit of God which came to the Moravians centuries ago would come upon us again? They could only explain, "It was a sense of the loving nearness of the Saviour instantaneously bestowed."

Oh, what that would do for us—a sense of the loving nearness of the Saviour instantaneously bestowed! With it comes a love for God's Word, loving cohesion, dignity, usefulness, high moral living and purity of life—because that's the only kind of nearness the Holy Spirit ever brings!

CHAPTER
8

Tragedy in the Church: The Missing Gifts

But the manifestation of the Spirit is given to every man to profit withal. 1 Corinthians 12:7

THE CHRISTIAN CHURCH CANNOT rise to its true stature in accomplishing the purposes of God when its members operate largely through the gifts of nature, neglecting the true gifts and graces of the Spirit of God.

Much of the religious activity we see in the churches is not the eternal working of the Eternal Spirit, but the mortal working of man's mortal mind—and that is raw tragedy!

From what I see and sense in evangelical circles, I would have to say that about ninety per cent of the religious work carried on in the churches is being done by ungifted members.

I am speaking in this context of men and women who know how to do many things but fail to display the spiritual gifts promised through the Holy Spirit.

This is one of the very evident ways in which we have slowed down the true working of God in His church and in the hearts of unbelieving men all around us—acknowledging and allowing ungifted members of the body to do religious work without possessing the genuine gifts of the Spirit.

I expect I will hear a reply to this assessment. Someone will say, "Well, that's just Tozer's private view!"

But in recent conferences, such as the International Fellowship of Evangelical Students, the counter-part of Inter-Varsity in Canada, it has been gratifying to fellowship with internationally-known ministers who are preaching about the great need for the Spirit's operation among the people of God. This conviction is being echoed and reechoed throughout the world as our Lord is confirming the same need to many thousands in denominations everywhere.

Now, someone else will ask, "Why this emphasis? Doesn't every Christian have the Holy Spirit?"

Yes—there is plenty of Biblical authority that every regenerated believer does have a measure of the Spirit!

Paul wrote to the Corinthian church and reminded the believers that they were all baptized into one body by the Spirit. Paul also wrote to the church at Rome insisting that "if any man have not the Spirit of Christ, he is none of his" (Romans 8:9).

But in the same letter in which he explained to the Corinthian Christians the operation of the Spirit of God in their regeneration, he also told them: "I do not want you to be ignorant about spiritual gifts," and then, "Covet earnestly the best gifts."

I think it is plain that if Paul only wanted them to know that they have a measure of the Spirit upon conversion, he would have said that and stopped right there.

But he went on at great length to explain the necessity for the functioning of the gifts of the Spirit in the church—and I believe he was explaining that these spiritual functions and capabilities are the birthright of every Christian.

Paul did not say we must be important and well-known Christians to be useful to the Spirit of God in the functioning of Christ's Body, the church. This is not something reserved for the great. It is the birthright of the most humble saint.

Paul reminded the Corinthian Christians that God was actually seeking the simple people because they were willing to respond to the outworking of God's plan through the Holy Spirit and His functions.

"Where is the wise?" Paul asked them. "Where is the scribe? where is the disputer of this world? ...

"But God hath chosen the foolish things of the world to confound the wise; and God hath chosen the weak things of the world to confound the things which are mighty" (1 Cor. 1:20, 27).

So, brethren, the Spirit of God, His presence and His gifts are not only desirable in our Christian congregations, but absolutely imperative!

Now here is another aspect of truth often overlooked:

The regenerated, converted men and women who joyfully have found their place in the Body of Christ by faith are still humans—even though redeemed through faith in the death and resurrection of Jesus Christ. Having found divine forgiveness through God's mercy and grace, they delight in the complete lifting of the sense of guilt and in the fellowship they find in varied segments of the visible church of Jesus Christ here on earth—here and now.

My point is this—they still are human and they are living in bodies as yet unredeemed! If they are to continue in the blessing of the fellowship of the spiritually redeemed, if they are to successfully engage in the Christian witness God expects of them, they must consciously know and experience the indwelling illumination of the Holy Spirit of God. They must depend upon His gifts and His enduement and His anointing if they hope to cope with the universal blight which is upon mankind.

Believers are yet in their unredeemed bodies. This is true of every believer, every member of the Body—whether the oldest and sweetest saint of God that has followed on to know the Lord or the newest convert that has just found forgiveness of sins and the joy of salvation!

Yes, brethren, this is orthodox Christian theology, and this is how the apostle Paul revealed it to us:

"For the creature was made subject to vanity; not willingly, but by reason of him who hath subjected the same in hope, because the creature itself also shall be delivered from the bondage of corruption into the glorious liberty of the children of God. For we know that the whole creation groaneth and travaileth in pain together until now.

"And not only they, but ourselves also, which have the firstfruits of the Spirit, even we ourselves groan within ourselves, waiting for the adoption, to wit, the redemption of our body" (Rom. 8:20-23).

There is no other way we can have it—the saints of God in this age do live in an unredeemed temple. The body is potentially redeemed for that is the promise of God. But in this life it is not yet actually redeemed.

That is why we take the theme for this message—it is impossible for God to use men and women who yet must die to bring about His eternal purpose. The Eternal Spirit alone can do that kind of an eternal work.

Perhaps we need an illustration here.

The accomplished artist gives his hands and eyes credit for his paintings.

The musician gives his hands and fingers credit for the harmonies produced from keys and the strings of instruments.

Talented people everywhere think that their feet or their hands, their ears or their vocal chords are the means of their productions.

There never was a greater mistake than to believe that!

The credit all has to go to the marvelous brain that God has given every man. The hands have never really done anything except at the bidding and control of the brain.

If the brain should suddenly be cut off and die, the hands will lie limp and helpless. It is the brain of a man that paints a picture, smells a rose, hears the sound of music.

This is all a matter of common physiology. All of us learned this fact in school and doctors know it well in an advanced way. Your hand does not originate anything. If you crochet or paint, cut or trim, operate a machine—the origination and control rests with the brain and the hands function only as the instrument and organ through which the brain works.

The Holy Spirit must be to the members of the Body of Christ what the brain is to eyes and ears and mouth and hands and fingers and feet and toes. The Bible does say "it is God which worketh in you to will and to do . . ." (Phil. 2:13).

Someone may give me credit for something they think I have done for God—but in actuality, God is doing it and using me as an instrument, for there is a sense in which we are unable to do any spiritual work of any kind.

The important thing is that the Holy Spirit desires to take men and women and control them and use them as instruments and organs through which He can express Himself in the Body of Christ.

Perhaps I can use my hands as a further illustration of this truth.

My hands are about average, I suppose. Perhaps a little large for the size of my body. Probably because I had to do a lot of farm work when I was a boy.

But there is something I must tell you about these hands. I cannot play a violin. I have ungifted hands. I cannot paint a picture. I have ungifted hands.

I cannot play the organ or the piano. I can barely hold a screwdriver to do a small repair job to keep things from falling apart at home.

I am perfectly willing to paint a picture, but my hands are ungifted. My brain can give some direction to the members of my body, but there is no response from my brain in the matter of color and form and outline and perspective.

If my brain should say, "Tozer, play something for us on the organ," I could only respond, "Brain, I would love to do it, but my hands know nothing of that gift!"

You will agree that it would be foolish for me to try to bring forth any delightful and satisfying music using such ungifted members as my own hands.

Is it not appalling, then, to think that we allow this very thing to happen in the Body of Christ? We enlist people and tell them to get busy doing God's work-failing to realize the necessity for the Spirit's anointing and control and functioning if a spiritual result is to be produced.

Work that is only religious work and religious activity can be done by ungifted men and women and it can be done within the framework of the Christian church. But it will wind up with the judgment upon it that it is only a product of a human mind.

Let's bring it down to our level.

Religious "activists" have many things of which they can boast. They build churches. They write hymns and books. Musically, they sing and play. Some of them will take time to engage in prayer. Others will organize movements and crusades and campaigns.

No matter how early in the morning they begin and no matter how late at night they stay with their project, if it is an exercise in human talent for religious purposes, it can only wind up as a mortal brain doing a mortal job.

And across it God will write a superscription: "It came to die and it came to go!"

I have taken the pains to say all of this as a reminder that mortality and temporality are written all across the church of Christ in the world today because so many persons are trying to do with human genius and power of the flesh what only God can do through the Holy Spirit.

None of us ought to be fooled by the loose and careless use of the word *immortal*. Art galleries claim that the paintings of Michaelangelo are immortal. In truth, there are no immortal paintings, no immortal sonnets, no immortal musical compositions, for immortality is unending existence.

For myself, I would rather be among those who are unknown, unsung and unheralded doing something through the Spirit of God that will count even a tiny little bit in the kingdom of God, than to be involved in some highly-recognized expression of religious activity across which God will ultimately write the judgment: "This too shall pass!"

It is true that much church work and activity is thrown back upon a shaky foundation of psychology and natural talents.

It is sad but true that many a mother-in-law is actually praying that her handsome son-in-law may be called to preach because he would have such a marvelous "pulpit presence."

We live in a day when charm is supposed to cover almost the entire multitude of sins. Charm has taken a great place in religious expression. Brethren, I am convinced that our Lord expects us to be tough enough and cynical enough to recognize all of this that pleases the unthinking in our churches—the charm stuff, the stage presence in the pulpit, the golden qualities of voice.

We had better not forget what the apostle Paul said about "presence" and "speech."

We accept the fact that Paul was one of the greatest men that ever lived and that he became available as a human channel for a great work by God Almighty.

Do you know what they said about him in his day? The cosmopolitan Corinthians commented that "his letters . . . are weighty and powerful; but his bodily presence is weak, and his speech contemptible" (2 Cor. 10:10).

When they had read his first epistle, they said, "He writes tremendous letters. This is hot stuff!"

But later when they heard him in person, they were disappointed that he seemed to have so few natural talents!

Let us not miss the significance of that assessment. Here is one of the world's greatest minds—but apparently he would have flunked out in any test given radio announcers. He had no charming pulpit presence. He had no golden qualities of voice or manner. But wherever he went he was led by the Holy Spirit. Whatever he did was at the prompting of the Holy Spirit. His great missionary work brought no glory to himself but advanced the cause of Christ throughout the known world of his day.

I feel sorry for the church that decides to call a man to the pulpit because "his personality simply sparkles!"

I have watched quite a few of these sparklers through the years. In reality, as every kid knows at Fourth of July time, sparklers can be an excitement in the neighborhood, but only for about one minute! Then you are left holding a hot stick in your hand—and suddenly it cools off.

Many with the sparkling personalities have come into our churches—but most of them have done their sparkling and are gone.

The Holy Spirit, my brethren, rules out all of this sparkle and charm and pulpit presence and personal magnetism. Instead, He whispers to us: "God wants to humble you and fill you with Himself and

control you so that you can become part of the
eternal work that God wants to do in the earth in
your day!"

Now, brethren, a word of encouragement. Just
because the true gifts of the Spirit are so rare among
us does not mean that they are missing entirely.

There has never been a time in the history of the
Christian church that some of the gifts were not
present and effective. Sometimes they have functioned even among those who did not understand
or perhaps did not believe in the same way that we
think Christians should believe. But the churches
have prevailed and the faithful have been true to
Christ. Link upon link, a chain of spiritual Christianity in consecutive linkage has been fashioned by
the Holy Spirit!

What we do for God must be done in the power
of the Holy Spirit and we know that we may have
little praise from men. But what we do accomplish
for Him as true spiritual work done with eternity
in view will have His praise written across it: "This
came to live and to last!"

Most of us have never heard—or do not remember—the name of the humble 16-year-old girl whose
singing ministry brought such spiritual results in
the Welsh revivals with Evan Roberts.

This quiet, humble girl would sing the gospel
songs even though the singing of solos was not
regularly a part of their services. They sang in cho-
ral groups and they used the metric psalter which
did not particularly lend itself to solo expression.

Much has been said about the young woman's
spiritual gift—the Spirit-given ability to glorify the
Saviour when she would rise to sing. Not too much

has been said about her voice. I do not know how much lyrical beauty or quality was in her voice, but the record is clear that she was a gifted soul—that the Holy Spirit seemed to be singing and moving through her yielded expression.

When she sang about the Lord Jesus Christ and the plan of salvation, the goodness and mercy of God and the need of all for the Saviour, the hearts of men and women in the audience melted and the Spirit brought His conviction.

Evan Roberts would rise to preach and there was little left for him to do. He said that he would quote from the Scriptures and add an exhortation, and the people were ready to come to Christ. She had melted them with the warmth and power of the Spirit—she humbly exercised the unusual gift which God had bestowed.

It was not just a local incident. Wherever she went to sing for the Lord, the results were the same.

Oh, what we would be tempted to do with her ministry in this day! We would put her on the radio and show off her talent—and spoil her. Thank God that they knew better than to start writing her life history. Thank God she was not pressed into writing a tract: "My Life—from Nursery to Pulpit!"

She was a beautiful example of what we have been pleading for—the humble use of our spiritual gifts for the glory of Jesus Christ. She was a simple Welsh girl—willingly controlled by the Holy Spirit of God. As far as I know, there was never a music critic anywhere that ever said she had a good voice—but she had something far better!

The Holy Spirit is the gentle dove of God and His coming to us in blessing and power is without pain or strain. The painful part is the necessity of our own preparation—for the Holy Spirit will search us out completely and deal with us solemnly.

He will guide us in necessary confessions that we must make. He will guide us in the necessity of pouring out all of that which is selfish and unlike Jesus in our lives. He will guide us in getting straightened out with people with whom we have had differences. He will guide us in seeking forgiveness where it is necessary and He will show us the necessity of old-fashioned restitution and restoration in our willingness to be a clean vessel.

Plainly I can say that some folks who carry their big Bibles to impress others will never be filled with the Holy Spirit until they drop their sleek, smooth exterior of being "well taught" and earnestly desire God's humble plan for their lives.

After the desire must come a determination to go through with God on His terms—and even then, they will not be filled and owned and controlled by the Spirit of God until in desperation they throw themselves into the arms of God!

In the desire of our faith, we have to close our eyes and make a leap into the arms of Jesus! After all the help, after all the instructions, after all the study, after all the Bible verses you can remember have not done the work, after every trick and everything you know to move toward God have failed, your heart in desperation cries, "Fill me now! Oh, fill me now!"

Then you move into that zone of obscurity where the human reason has to be suspended for a moment and the human heart leaps across into the arms of God. It is then, I say, that man's talents, man's glory, man's duty and even man's favor all flow out into the darkness of yesterday. Suddenly, everything is God's glory and God's honor and God's beauty and God's Spirit in your heart! You have been broken and melted and finally filled with His mighty Spirit to such a degree that no man can change your mind!

I was nineteen years old, earnestly in prayer, kneeling in the front room of my mother-in-law's home, when I was baptized with a mighty infusion of the Holy Ghost. I had been eager for God's will and I had been up against almost all of the groups and "isms" with their formulas and theories and teachings.

They had all tried to beat me down. Some said I went too far and others said I had not gone far enough. But let me assure you, brethren, that I know with assurance what God did for me and within me and that nothing on the outside now held any important meaning. In desperation, and in faith, I took that leap away from everything that was unimportant to that which was most important—to be possessed by the Spirit of the Living God!

Any tiny work that God has ever done through me and through my ministry for Him dates back to that hour when I was filled with the Spirit. That is why I plead for the spiritual life of the Body of Christ and the eternal ministries of the Eternal Spirit through God's children—His instruments!

Christian Uniformity: An Evangelical Answer

Finally, be ye all of one mind, having compassion one of another, love as brethren . . . 2 Peter 3:8

WITHIN THE FRAMEWORK OF evangelical Christianity, we do not pay a great deal of attention to current religious trends and fads. One of these in our day is the growing emphasis toward uniformity in the churches.

I think it is only fair, however, to reserve the right to put in our own word about the achievement of Christian unity, particularly in the face of continuing insistence that everyone in the church ought to be just like everyone else!

The Christian uniformity taught in the Bible can only come through genuine love and sincere compassion in the Christian fellowship. It can only come through the work of God in the soul of man— and then there can be unity even where there is a blessed and free diversity!

There is in Christian literature a statement by an old bishop that the uniformity we desire in the Christian church is not just a matter of achieving "solidarity"— for he reminds us that anyone can achieve a solid unity out of variety just by the freezing process!

We can distinguish this kind of frozen unity in the conduct of those churches where no one ever disagrees with anyone else because they all started out by agreeing that they would hold no basic tenet or positive belief "because nothing really matters that much anyhow."

But the apostle Peter writes to Christian brethren about the reality of "being of one mind" in their Christian fellowship.

Leading commentators tell us that the expression "being of one mind" literally means "unanimous."

So, let me tell you first what being unanimous is not, in order that we may discover what unanimity really is.

Being unanimous—spiritual unanimity—does not involve a regulated uniformity.

I cannot comprehend how the churches have fallen into the error of believing that unanimity means uniformity. Some actually hold that to be like-minded means the imposing of a similarity from the outside.

This has been a great error—the belief that harmony within religious bodies can be secured by imposing uniformity.

Look at the word *uniform*. In one use it is a word describing a situation, but it is also a noun referring to identifying garments worn by members of certain groups. We have such uniforms in the armed services—various military uniforms.

Such garments provide a uniformity for military personnel—a uniformity imposed from the outside. But anyone who has ever served in the armed forces knows there is a world of disagreement and grousing among those who wear the uniforms.

Merely putting on the uniform does not in any sense bring about a basic unity and harmony in any group of men and women.

Imposed uniformity is a great error because it assumes that uniformity is an external thing and that it can be achieved by imposition, failing to acknowledge that the only valid unity is unity of the heart.

Actually, it is variety—and not uniformity—that is the hallmark of God. Wherever you see God's hand, you see variety rather than uniformity or similarity.

Paul tells us that one star differs from every other star in glory and when the "ceiling" lifts occasionally—ceiling being the word we use for all the smoke and grime and smog that lies over the city—we can all see the starry city of God and realize that no star is exactly like another. They differ from each other in glory for God made them.

If God had made all the stars in heaven according to a uniform pattern of size and distance from the earth, it would be like gazing at a glaring theater marquee rather than at the mysterious, wonderful heaven of God that we see when the skies are clear.

Anyone inclined to check can find out in five minutes that no two leaves on any tree are exactly alike. They all differ. They are somewhat alike—they may even be alike basically, but God allows them a certain freedom of variety in formation.

Visit the shore of any ocean and you will notice that even when the winds are high and the waves are running, there are no two waves exactly alike. If you look carelessly you may say they look alike, as there is a monotony and a uniformity as they roll in over the sand. But look more closely and you will agree that no two of them are alike.

The artist who paints the ocean waves all alike has imposed something of his own mind upon the Creator-God's work for the ocean is never guilty of repeating the same size and shape and formation even though the billows reach into numbers that man is unable to count.

As many of you know, the same rule is applied to birds. We may hear a bird song and say, "That bird is a cardinal—or a warbler," as the case may be.

We may say, "The one I hear singing is a robin."

But those who have been trained to listen and to listen closely tell us that no two robins sing exactly alike. It is a fact that is too well known to need any explanation.

Consider the Bible saints and the same rule. We make a great deal of similarities between Bible personalities when actually the variety is still more marked and apparent than the similarity.

Who can conceive of two men any more opposite than Isaiah and Elijah? If they had been sitting together in the same congregation, they would hardly have been recognized as belonging to the same race, let alone the same faith! Their similarities were within. They belonged together inside, but they certainly were different on the outside.

Or, take men like Peter and Moses and stand them up together. Or, just stay within the little circle of Peter's own group, the disciples. Look at Philip, look at John, then on to the strong, Elijah-like Peter. Altogether unlike each other in variety of character and traits, yet their likeness was genuine and valid because it was a likeness within.

When God gave His church to the world, He gave a church that was to be unanimous within. But He also gave the church as much variety as an attractive flower garden.

I knew a dear man of God—a black man by the name of Collett—who used to preach. I have heard him say that "God makes His bouquets from the flowers which contain all His created colors. If they were all your color, there would be no variety, so God put me here in your midst to provide His variety."

He was perfectly right! God has His own variety throughout all the church, everywhere—not only in looks but in personality, in taste, in gifts and in ministries.

And yet Peter encourages us to be like-minded—to be unanimous!

What does he mean?

He means that the Spirit of God making Christ real within our beings will make us alike in certain qualities and disposition.

True Christian compassion is one of those qualities. Peter leaves us little doubt about the fruits of genuine Christian unanimity within. "Be alike compassionate. Be alike loving. Be alike pitiful. Be alike courteous . . . and be alike forgiving!"

Then he sums it all up: "Finally, be ye all of one mind."

This is the path to a blessed Christian unity and unanimity. This is the way to have one mind. Having compassion one for another, loving as brethren, having pity where it is needed, the willingness to be courteous, the ability that God gives to be forgiving in spirit, and not rendering evil for evil.

There you have the blessed uniformity of the children of God, the unanimity Peter was looking for among the followers of Christ. Every earnest believer must know the unanimity of compassion, the ability to love others, the uniformity of a spirit that can reach out in pity, the tenderness of heart that finds a true expression of God's grace in reaching out in a delightful courtesy and a willing forgiveness of others.

Are you willing to measure the compassion in your own spirit?

Compassion literally means a sympathetic understanding and wherever one life touches another there must be compassion if we are to please our Lord. This is what our true Christian unity demands—a likeness, a sympathetic understanding wherever our hearts touch, at every point of contact. We must be in agreement wherever our hearts touch.

This is the example we find in the Word of God-earnest men and women who touched God and where they touched Him they were alike. In other things they were different and not like each other at all. So it is to be in the Body of Jesus Christ, His church here on earth—that wherever we touch each other there is to be unity, but in all other things there can be diversity and variety. The variety among God's believing children is in itself an artistic scheme that God introduced to bring beauty to the church and its fellowship.

As an illustration, consider the variety of strings within a piano. They can all be combined to produce a beautiful oneness in harmony. All of the strings are different but they are alike in this—they all bow to a certain pitch. So, the believing people of God are alike in that they bow in recognition of the one holy, divine pitch to which they are to be set and keyed! After that, they can be just as unlike and as free to be themselves as they may be led.

I suppose there never was a body of Christians that succeeded in being freer than the Quakers even though they themselves did the best they could to choke it and kill it. They imposed a uniform and a certain dress, they imposed a certain use of language—but in spite of these they had so much of that inner flame that they succeeded in presenting to the world a wonderful flower-garden variety.

So, we must have the compassion of Christ within us, operating as a sympathetic understanding wherever we touch, with the agreement that it is possible for us to disagree in those areas where we do not touch.

Then Peter calls to mind the reality of loving one another. We are to love the brethren and love is oneness where hearts touch. This is a true and blessed unity—the feeling and the knowledge that the two have become one through the bonds of God's love. This is God's way, the genuine way, of bringing people together in a unity that is living and which will abide.

Now, without any desire to be on the side of disruptive elements in society, I must ask a question about the many insistent demands for getting everybody into some worldwide yoke of unity and uniformity:

"Why is it that the generation that is talking the most and making the most of unity is also the generation that has the greatest amount of hate and suspicion, the biggest bombs and the largest armies?"

They can't kid me! I refuse to be taken in by all of the smooth talk and gentle assurances that "all men are brethren and we must all forget our differences because of the Fatherhood of God and the Brotherhood of Man."

They don't fool me because I know that there is no unity in the world—there is division and hatred and hostility and plenty of open strife which we don't call war if we can keep it localized. When they say, "Let's forget all the differences," I just want to have opportunity to feel and see if that lump is still on their hip-that lump that means a gun is still there!

God's love shed abroad in our hearts—compassion and love which can only be found in Jesus Christ, our Lord—these are the only elements of true unity among men and women today. All other emphasis on unity is a sadly strange and ironic joke that must have had its origin in the seventh hell below!

Is it possible to be a believing child of God and not be tenderhearted? Let me remind you that when Peter advises that Christian brethren are to be "full of pity" for one another, he is actually teaching us that our hearts are to be tender towards one another.

With this in mind, I must point out to you that religion will either make us very tender of heart, considerate and kind, or it will make us very hard.

Anyone who has studied history does not have to be informed that men and women can be very severe, engaging even in the worst of cruelties, explaining it all in the name of religion and "the principle" which is supposed to be involved.

I have a rule for myself here:

"Whose side am I on—principle or people?"

Within the history of our own American government, we bow in respect to one of our great presi-
dents who was a man first and president second.
They called him Honest Abe. He had a gift for
sensing the humorous in life and a heart that cried
easily over other people's sorrows.

During the Civil War, Lincoln had to deal with
the military leaders who stood on ceremony and
acted on principle in their treatment of young lads
taken out of the hills and away from the farms, con-
scripted and sent with little training to the front
lines of battle.

When the terror of gunfire and the screaming
of the dying became overpowering, some of the
boys turned away and fled in fear. When they were
caught they were sentenced to die.

Along with his many other duties, Abraham Lincoln was busy doing everything he could to save
these young men. One day his associates found him
sadly turning over papers from a file and writing
something at the bottom of each, one after another.

Someone asked, "What are you doing, Mr.
President?"

"Tomorrow is 'butcher day' in the Army," he
replied. "They are going to shoot my boys so I have
been going over their papers once more to see if I
can't get some of them off."

We love and honor the memory of Abe Lincoln
for that kind of spirit. He was a man who loved people and was not ashamed of being tender in heart
and full of pity for those in need. I do not mention
Lincoln here to imply that he was a great Christian,
for I am not a judge of that, but he was a great man
and he had much that we Christians could borrow.

I am convinced that he was a tender hearted, pitiful man who put people ahead of principle!

I don't have to tell you that principle has been a hard, rough cross upon which human beings have been nailed throughout the centuries.

"There's a principle involved," zealous men have always cried as they nailed the man on the scaffold. His blood and tears and sweat never affected them at all because their pride assured them, "He is dying for a principle!"

Brethren, let people argue as they will; it is not principle that holds the moral world together, but rather the presence of a holy God and love for God and mankind!

Sure, moral laws exist in the world—and no one preaches that with any greater emphasis than I do. But to extract the principle from the holy and loving heart of God and then nail men on it is a far cry from the teaching and example of our Lord Jesus Christ.

Do you realize that Jesus never spent His time talking about principles? He always talked about people.

Even in His illustrative stories—the parables—He was not citing principles. He was talking about people—someone in trouble, someone gone astray or lost, someone sent out to bring other folks in. Always there were people.

Make of this what you will, but I don't think I would offer to give my life for a principle. I trust I would die for those I love. I trust that I would die for the church of Jesus Christ. I trust that I would give my everything for the love of God and the love of mankind. If I did not, I would surely be ashamed.

Now, that is one thing, but it is quite another thing to extract a stiff, iron principle and then nail a man on it, for God's Word tells us to be full of pity, tender of heart, loving and kind.

Jesus Christ did not come down from His place in glory riding on a steel beam of divine principle—hard and stiff and cold.

Full of pity and love, tender hearted and submissive to the will of His Father on behalf of mankind, He went from the womb of the Virgin to the cross on Golgotha.

Of course He died for the moral government of Almighty God—but it was people He cared for and served. He achieved His end not by hardness and harshness and legal principle but by love and care and compassion for people. Back of it all, certainly, was the unchanging, divine principle—the moral righteousness of God, for the holiness of the deity must be sustained even if the world falls.

But being our divine Saviour and Lord, He walked in and out of His experiences with men and women with all sweetness and tenderness, never leaving an irritation or a scratch. We could well say that love lubricated His spirit as He loved the people—men and women and children, the low as well as the high.

There isn't anything that will make us more tender at heart and more compassionate in spirit than true religion—the true reception of the mercies of God. The Word of God plainly teaches that God our Father wants us to know the trusting spiritual life which makes us tender hearted and sensitive to His will. We see the contrast in the New Testament record of the proud and unbending religious life of the Pharisees—and how it gave them hardness of heart. Religion will do the one thing or the other!

CHAPTER
10

The Presence of Christ: Meaning of the Communion

For I have received of the Lord that which also I delivered unto you, That the Lord Jesus the same night in which he was betrayed took bread: And when he had given thanks, he brake it, and said, Take, eat: this is my body, which is broken for you: this do in remembrance of me. After the same manner also he took the cup, when he had supped, saying, This cup is the new testament in my blood: this do ye, as oft as ye drink it, in remembrance of me. For as often as ye eat this bread, and drink this cup, ye do shew the Lord's death till he come. . . . He that eateth and drinketh unworthily, eateth and drinketh damnation to himself, not discerning the Lord's body. 1 Corinthians 11:23-26, 29

It is amazing that many people seem to believe that the Christian church is just another institution and that the observance of communion is just one of its periodic rituals.

The Bible makes it plain that any church that is a genuine New Testament church is actually a communion and not an institution.

The dictionary says that a communion is a body of Christians having a common faith. Sharing and

467

participation are other terms used in the definition of communion.

Regardless of traditions and terms and definition, the basic question in our coming to the Lord's table is this: "Have we come together to recognize the Presence of our divine Lord and risen Saviour?"

Brethren, how wonderful if we have found the spiritual maturity and understanding that allows us to confess: "Our congregation is so keenly aware of the presence of Jesus in our midst that our entire fellowship is an unceasing communion!"

What a joyful experience for us in this church age—to be part of a congregation drawn together with the magnetic fascination of the desire to know the presence of God and to sense His nearness.

The communion will not have ultimate meaning for us if we do not believe that our Lord Jesus Christ is literally present in the Body of Christ on earth.

There is a distinction here: Christ is literally present with us—but not physically present.

Some people approach the communion table with an awe that is almost fear because they think they are approaching the physical presence of God. It is a mistake to imagine that He is physically present.

Remember that God was not physically present in the burning bush of the Old Testament. Neither was He physically present between the wings of the cherubim in the tabernacle, nor in the cloud by day and fire by night.

In all these instances, He was literally present.

And so today, God who became Man—the Man who is God—this Man who is the focal point of divine manifestation, is here!

When we come to the Lord's table, we do not have to try to bring His presence. He is here!

He does ask, however, that we bring the kind of faith that will know and discern His presence; the kind of faith that will enable us to "forgive one another even as God for Christ's sake hath forgiven" us (Eph. 4:32).

Out of our worship and from the communion, God wants us to be able to sense the loving nearness of the Saviour—instantaneously bestowed!

There is nothing else like this in the world—the Spirit of God standing ready with a baptism of the sense of the presence of the God who made heaven and earth and holds the world in His hands. Knowing the sense of His presence will completely change our everyday life. It will elevate us, purify us, and deliver us from the domination of carnal flesh to the point where our lives will be a continuing, radiant fascination!

Here I want to refer back to Paul's message to the Corinthian church. We read and understand that there was trouble in that early church because the members came together for reasons other than recognizing the divine Presence.

Paul said they met without "discerning the Lord's body."

I have checked many sources of Christian scholarship, and I agree with Ellicott and other commentaries who believe this means that they met "without recognizing the Presence."

They were not required to believe that the bread and wine were God, but they were required to believe that God was present where Christians met to serve the bread and wine. Because they refused to recognize His presence, they were in great spiritual trouble.

Actually, they were meeting together for purposes other than that of finding God at the focal point of manifestation in the person of His Son!

There was a judgment upon them because they were too carnal, too worldly, too socially minded, too unspiritual to recognize that when Christians meet they should at least have the reverence that a Greek had when he led a heifer to the sacred grove. They should at least have the reverence that a Greek poet had when he quietly composed sonnets to his deity. When they came together they ought to have at least the reverence of a Jewish high priest of the Old Testament when he approached the sacred holy place and put blood upon the mercy seat.

But they came with another attitude. They did. not come to commune in the Presence, and so the purpose and meaning of communion became vague.

It was true in other churches as well as set forth in Revelation 2 and 3.

Today, I say, we ought to be a company of believers drawn together to see and hear and feel God appearing in man. That man is not a preacher, or elder, or deacon, but the Son of Man, Jesus Christ— back from the dead and eternally alive!

It is impossible to separate the communion table from the centrality of Jesus Christ in the revealed Word of God.

Some think of communion as a celebration—and in the very best sense it is our Lord Jesus Christ whom we celebrate when we come to this table.

In order for us to grasp the spirit of this commemoration, notice the relationship of Christ, the

Son of Man, in five words with their prepositions attached.

First, we celebrate Christ's "devotion to"—noting, for instance, His devotion to the Father's will.

Our Lord Jesus Christ had no secondary aims. His one passion in life was the fulfillment of His Father's will. Probably He was the only human being after the fall about whom this could be said in perfect terms. With any other person, it can be only an approximation. Realism requires that we say we suppose there never has been anyone who has not mourned the introduction, however brief, of some distraction.

But Jesus never had any distraction or deviation. His Father's will was always before Him, and it was to this one thing that He was devoted.

As part of that, He was devoted to the rescue of fallen mankind—completely devoted to it. He did not do a dozen other things as avocations. He did that one thing! He was devoted to the altar of sacrifice—to the rescue of mankind.

It may be helpful if I remind you about a famous symbol of one of the old Baptist missionary societies. It showed an ox quietly standing between an altar and a plow. Underneath was the legend, "Ready for either or for both!" Plow awhile, and then die on the altar. Or, only die on the altar or only plow awhile.

The meaning of the symbol was readiness—"ready for either or ready for both." I think it is one of the most perfect symbols that I have ever known picturing submission to God's will, and it certainly describes our Lord Jesus Christ.

He was ready first for His labors on earth, the work with the plow; to be followed by the altar of sacrifice. With no side interest, He moved with steady purpose—almost with precision—toward the cross. He would not be distracted nor turned aside. He was (completely devoted to the cross, completely devoted to the rescue of mankind, because He was completely devoted to His Father's will!

Even "if we remain not faithful," as the Bible says, that does not change His faithful devotion. He has; not changed. He is devoted as He was devoted! He came a devoted One, and the word *devoted* is actually a religious word referring to a sacrifice, usually a lamb that was selected and marked out. It was fed, it was cared for, but everyone considered it already dead on the altar of sacrifice.

It was the lamb that had been selected, and even though it waited in its place a few days, everyone knew of the coming sacrifice. They knew it was devoted. It was an expendable lamb. So, our Lord Jesus Christ was devoted—completely devoted as a lamb to the sacrifice!

Then, the second word is *separation* and the preposition is *from*. Devotion *to* and separation *from*.

There are many ways in which our Lord deliberately separated Himself. He separated Himself from men for men.

There are those who have separated themselves for other reasons. Tymen of Athens, you will remember, turned sour on the human race and went up into the hills, separating himself from mankind because he hated the human race. His separation was the result of hatred. But the separation of Jesus Christ from men was the result of love.

He separated Himself from them for them. It was for them He came—and died. It was for them that He arose and ascended and for them appeared at the right hand of God.

This separation from men was not because He was weary of them, nor that He disliked them. Rather, it was because He loved them. It was a separation in order that He might do for them that which they could not do for themselves. He was the only one who could rescue them. So Jesus was a separated man from the affairs of man.

Separation from is the phrase that marks Him. He was separated from the net of trivialities. There are so many things that are done in the world by Christians that are not really bad—they are just trivial. They are unworthy, much as if we found Albert Einstein busy cutting out paper dolls. Though deeply disappointed, no one would go to him and say, "Einstein, that's a great sin you are committing." But we would go away shaking our heads and saying, "With a mind like that? One of the six great minds of the ages-cutting paper dolls!"

There are so many trivialities in which great minds seem to engage. Yes, your mind, I mean! Great minds.

You smile and say, "Me?"

Yes, I do mean you!

I mean your mind with its endless capabilities. I mean your spirit with its potential for angelic fellowship and divine communion. Yet we engage in trivialities.

Jesus was never so engaged—He escaped the net of trivialities!

He was separated from sinners, it says in the Bible. He was separated not only from their sins, but separated from their vanities. Vanities. Separated from!

Do I need to remind you in this context that if these words characterized Jesus, they must also characterize each of us who claims to be a follower of Jesus?

Devotion to! Yes, devotion to the Father's will; devotion to the rescue of mankind by the preaching of the gospel; devotion to any necessary sacrifice, having no interests aside, but moving with steady purpose to do the will of God!

Separation from! But not in sourness nor contempt, but like the runner, separated from his regular clothing in order that he might strip himself for the race—or like a soldier separated from his civilian garb in order to wear only that which is prescribed to free his arms and legs for combat. It is this separation we must know as His loving disciples.

The third word is *rejection* and this is the phrase of *rejection by.*

Plainly, Jesus suffered rejection by mankind because of His holiness. Then He suffered rejection by God because of His sinfulness. But someone will say, "Wait a minute! Would you say our Lord was sinful?"

Yes, vicariously sinful.

He Himself never sinned, but He that knew no sin became sin for us, that we sinners might become the righteousness of God in Him.

In that sense, He suffered a twofold rejection. He was too good to be received by sinful men and in that awful moment of His sacrifice He was too sinful to be received by a holy God. So He hung between heaven and earth rejected by both until He cried, "It is finished. Father, into Thy hand I commend my spirit." Then He was received by the Father.

But while He was bearing my sins and yours, He was rejected by the Father. While He moved among men He was rejected by them because He was so holy that His life was a constant rebuke to them.

Identification with should also be noted. Surely He was identified with us. Everything He did was for us. He acted in our stead. He took our guilt. He gave us His righteousness. In all of these acts on earth, it was for us because by His incarnation, He identified Himself with the human race. In His death and resurrection He was identified with the redeemed human race.

The blessed result is that whatever He is we are; and where He is, potentially, His people are, and what He is, potentially, His people are—only His deity being excepted!

Finally, consider His *acceptance at.*

Jesus Christ, our Lord, has acceptance at the throne of God. Although once rejected, He is now accepted at—and that bitter rejection is now turning into joyous acceptance. The same is true for His people. Through Him, we died! Identified with Him, we live, and in our identification with Him we are accepted at the right hand of God, the Father.

This is the meaning of our celebration. Surely I do not need a picture of the holy family to remind me. Surely I do not need to wear beads around my neck to remind me.

If my love for Him does not remind me 24 hours a day, then I simply need to confess and repent and ask for the restoring of the grace and mercy of God that will keep me always in remembrance!

One of the great Scottish dissenters who lived in the last century was Horatius Bonar. He belonged to the Free Church of Scotland which came into being through a break with the state church. A critic of his once said:

"Bonar was a wonderfully good man and a wonderfully gifted man, but his imagination led him astray. His imagination led him to believe that Jesus Christ was coming back to raise the dead and change the living, and that He was going to restore Israel to the Holy Land, and transform the church and bless mankind, destroy the anti-Christ with the brightness of His coming."

The critic went on to say it was too bad that Bonar went so far astray.

In reply, we say that if he went so far "astray" as to believe that, perhaps that is why he could write hymns that said, "I heard the voice of Jesus say, (Dome unto me and rest" and "I lay my sins on Jesus, the spotless Lamb of God."

He wrote this about the Lord's Supper:

Here, O my Lord, I see Thee face to face;
    Here would I touch and handle things unseen,
Here grasp with firmer hand th' eternal grace,
    And all my weariness upon Thee lean.

Here would I feed upon the bread of God,
    Here drink with Thee the royal wine of heaven;
Here would I lay aside each earthly load,
    Here taste afresh the calm of sins forgiven.

This is the hour of banquet and of song;
    This is the heavenly table spread for me;
Here let me feast, and feasting, still prolong
    The brief bright hour of fellowship with Thee.

Too soon we rise; the symbols disappear;
    The feast, though not the love, is past and gone;
The bread and wine removed, but Thou art here,
    Nearer than ever; still my Shield and Sun.

Mine is the sin, but Thine the righteousness;
    Mine is the guilt, but Thine the cleansing blood;
Here is my robe, my refuge, and my peace,
    Thy blood, Thy righteousness, O Lord my God.

Feast after feast thus comes and passes by,
    Yet passing, points to the glad feast above,
Giving sweet foretaste of the festal joy,
    The Lamb's great bridal feast of bliss and love.

So, my brethren, the Lord's table, the communion, is not as a picture hung on the wall or a chain around the neck reminding us of Him.

It is a celebration of His person—a celebration in which we gladly join because we remember Him, testifying to each other and to the world of His conquering and sacrificial death—until He comes!

CHAPTER
11

Don't Ever Lose Hope: You Can Be Changed

As obedient children, not fashioning yourselves according to the former lusts in your ignorance: but as he which hath called you is holy, so be ye holy in all manner of conversation. 1 Peter 1:14-15

THE CHRISTIAN CHURCH CANNOT effectively be Christ's church if it fails to firmly believe and boldly proclaim to every person in the human race: "You can be changed! You do not have to remain as you are!"

Brethren, this is not just a hope held out to the desperate dope addict and the helpless drunkard—it is the hope of every average sinner no matter where he may be found in the world.

Shall we heed what the Holy Spirit is trying to say to us about human nature and God's grace in this apostolic injunction?

"Not fashioning yourselves according to the former lusts"—here is a truth negatively stated but carrying with it a positive assertion. We all know from our studies how every concept carries its opposite along with it in its understanding.

For instance, if you say "short," the opposite, "long," is conjured up in the back of your mind. Otherwise, there would be no reason to call something short.

Notice that the Apostle did not say, "Do not fashion yourselves . . ."—that would be contrary to Scripture and contrary to human nature.

His injunction is: Fashion not yourself after the old pattern, the pattern of your former lusts in your ignorance.

So, it is the positive element that we consider. Certainly and positively you will fashion yourselves, but do not fashion yourselves after the old pattern, we are cautioned.

This is at the insistence of the Holy Spirit, and the Scriptures give no room for argument here. We are given no excuse whatsoever to read this, or sit in a church service and find fault with what the Holy Spirit says. You may have reason to disagree with an interpretation given by the preacher, but that is another matter. Once we know what the Holy Spirit has said, as believers we are committed to carry out that injunction without one word of objection. What else should we do with the Word of God but obey?

So, our English word, *fashion*, expresses the Apostle's admonition that Christian believers ought to shape themselves according to proper pattern.

"Fashion yourselves—conform yourselves to the right pattern" is what Peter was actually saying.

In essence, Peter was also stressing a most important fact, that human nature is fluid. Human nature is not fixed and unchangeable as many people seem to believe.

Perhaps clay is the very best illustration to give us a simple understanding of this biblical principle.

Clay is not fixed. It is malleable. In a figurative sense it is "fluid" so it can be shaped.

After clay has been fashioned and shaped by the potter, after he has given it the form that he wants, he puts it into the oven. He bakes it and burns it and then, perhaps, he glazes it.

That clay is now permanently fixed. It is no longer fluid, no longer subject to any changes. The only way it can be changed now is by being destroyed. It can be crushed and ruined, but it can never be changed into something more beautiful and useful because it can never regain its fluid and malleable state.

I believe, then, that the very fact that the Holy Spirit would indicate through the Apostle, "Fashion and shape yourselves after the right pattern," makes it plain that the burning and baking and glazing have not yet happened to human nature. Thankfully we are in a state of fluidity regarding moral character.

Now, there are two things that can be said about any person, whether it is a youngster or the man sitting in the death cell of the state prison awaiting his fate for kidnapping and murder.

The first thing that can be said is: "You can be changed!" The second thing is like unto it: "You are not finished yet!"

We hear a lot about men being hardened, but we should always remember that we need modifiers if we are going to get at the truth.

When we say that a man is hardened and that he is beyond help, we are saying that insofar as any power and influence that we may have, the man is probably in a state beyond our changing.

But actually and in truth, no one is beyond changing as long as he is alive and conscious!

The hope may be dim in many cases, but the hope of change does exist for every man. It may be a dim hope for the drunkard who allows himself only a few sober moments for serious thought, but he may be saved from complete despair by the knowledge that he can be changed.

It is still a hope even for the drug addict who is in frightful misery and who would sell his own soul to get the shot for the fix to carry him through one more day. The only reason he does not commit suicide is that faint flicker of hope that he can still be changed. He knows that he has not yet been cast or glazed in a final, unchangeable state—there is still a fluidity.

Let us thank God that there is that kind of hope, and the possibility of great change even for those who would likely be written off by our own human judgment. History has truly and completely confirmed this possibility.

The blessed aspect of this truth is that there is no sinner anywhere in the world who is compelled to remain as he is today.

He may be floundering in his sin, so deeply enmeshed that he is ashamed of himself. But the very fact that he is ashamed indicates that there is a model and a pattern to which he may still attain. It is this hope of change that keeps men alive on the earth.

The second part of this ray of hope for any man is the prospect that he is not yet "finished."

I dare to say that whoever you are and wherever you may be, old or young or in-between, you are not yet a finished product. You are only in process.

I admit that it is our human tendency to fix certain terminal points and to say, "Beyond these we do not go."

Take human birth for instance.

Looking at birth in one way, we recognize that the obstetrician, after examining the new baby and finding it healthy, may say: "Now this is fixed. As far as I am concerned, a child is born into the world, and my part is complete." He fixes a terminal point there and goes about his other concerns.

During the months just preceding he was very anxious and concerned. For him, the terminal point has now been reached—a healthy, normal child has been born into the world.

But the mother of the child does not join in any terminal point at this juncture. She knows there is a tiny life involved and she knows the long continuing process which lies ahead. She knows of the childhood problems and troubles. She knows the educational process ahead from the time she teaches him to play patty-cake until he walks out of the college hall with his degree. The child is not "fixed"—there is the long process of shaping and fashioning.

Then when he has gotten his college degree, the parents are likely to rejoice and fix their own terminal point: "Well, we have succeeded in getting him through college!" Parents have a tendency to put a period there and say, "Now he is finished. He is complete."

But beyond all of that we know the truth—he is not done. He is not finished. There are still many changes to come and he is still being shaped and fashioned.

There will soon be another terminal point—his marriage. Many a mother breathes a sigh of relief when the child suddenly becomes serious, settles down, gets married, establishes a home.

Her sigh is really her way of saying within: "Now my worries are over!"

But not everything and everyone that is settled down is finished either. Parents are gratified when success comes and their boy becomes vice president of his company, drawing a big check and driving an expensive car.

The parents smile at each other and say, "Now he is fixed. He has arrived. He is a big American businessman!" It is not easy for parents to look beyond this pleasant terminal point.

But their child is still moving along. He will come to middle age when, as the poet said, "Gray hairs are here and there upon him." The parents comment that his gray hairs really give him a distinguished look and they cannot conceive that things will ever really change for him.

"He has really arrived," is their consolation. "He is a portly, well-proportioned businessman, an executive. He hunts in the fall and fishes in the spring and goes to baseball games in the summer—all the things that professional businessmen do. Don't worry about him. He is fixed!"

But he is a human being, and he is not fixed. He will never be finished until the soul leaves the body. Even the old man in his dotage is still changing in some ways. The rapidity and scope of change may not be as great, but there is change nevertheless.

It is at this point that someone will want to establish a dialogue. Someone will say, "Oh, yes, Mr. Tozer, but I do know a terminal point. You have been talking in terms of humanity, unregenerate humanity. The fixed point, the terminal point is the time of our conversion to Christ."

Yes, there is a point there when we can say, "Now rest my long-divided heart, fixed on this blissful center, rest!"

But does our conversion to Christ and our assurance of forgiveness mean that the fluidity in our nature is gone and that we are finally "fixed"?

My friend, the answer is "No!" You are still fluid. You are still subject to being fashioned and changed and shaped. God expects that you will still grow and develop and change and be fashioned as a Christian in maturity and Christlikeness.

Peter was recognizing that Christian believers are still in process when he wrote, "Do not fashion yourselves after the old pattern but after a new and holy pattern!"

I think there are many followers of Christ who have never been brought into this realization and understanding. Perhaps Christian workers are at fault at this point, when we work so hard to get people converted and then put a period after their conversion and speak the comfortable words: "Now rest your long-divided heart!"

There is a sense in which that old hymn is beautifully, brilliantly true and I love it and sing it often. But I am sure that the writer was not intending to imply a terminal point. I am sure he was not suggesting that the believer is no longer fluid, malleable. The fact is that he was assuring us that our being fixed in Christ is settled by an act of faith—and that's what we mean. But when it comes to the shaping and developing and growth and enlargement—these must go on after we are converted!

I expect some objections here from the people who would insist that Christians cannot fashion themselves.

"God must fashion us. God is our heavenly Father and He must do the fashioning and changing," they point out.

Let me agree this far: that is the ideal and that is the way it *should* be.

If every believer could be completely and wholly surrendered from the moment he is saved until the time he dies, knowing nothing but the influences of God and the heavenly powers working in him, then that would be true.

But there are powers that shape men even in the kingdom of God, that are not divine powers.

Let me use an illustration here of the person interested in getting a sun tan, exposing himself to the sun at the beach or in his own back yard.

Now, who is tanning his hide? Where is the tan coming from? What does the person himself have to do with it?

There is a sense in which he is doing it, for if he had kept his shirt on, his shoulders and body would never be tanned.

But there is a sense in which the sun is doing it. The sun is tanning him, but he had to take the necessary step to cooperate with the rays of the sun in order for the sunlight to do its work.

Now, that is exactly what we mean when we say that we fashion ourselves. A Christian believer fashions himself by exposing himself to the divine powers which shape him. Just as a man may wear his jacket and never get the sun tan, even though the sun is up there brightly in view, so a Christian may keep himself wrapped in a cloak of his own stubbornness and never receive any of the beneficial graces which filter down from the throne of God where Jesus sits as mediator.

Yes, it is possible for a Christian to go through life without very much change taking place. Converted? Yes. A believer in Christ? Yes. Having the root of the matter in him? Yes. The seed of God in him? Yes.

But such a believer is infantile and the growth and development and beautifying and enlarging and shaping have not taken place because he refuses to cooperate and expose himself to the divine powers that would shape him.

The reverse side of this proposition must also be considered. It is entirely possible for the Christian believer to shape himself by exposing himself to the wrong kind of influences. I think this is happening to an extent that must indeed be a grievance to God.

Now, what about these powers that can fashion us?

We know full well what the old powers were. Those old powers were the "former lusts."

The Apostle soberly reminds us of those powers in the second chapter of Ephesians:

"Wherein in time past ye walked according to the course of this world, according to the prince of the power of the air, the spirit that now worketh in the children of disobedience; among whom also we all had our conversation in times past in the lusts of our flesh, fulfilling the desires of the flesh and of the mind; and were by nature the children of wrath, even as others" (2:2-3).

Those were the forces which had a part in shaping us in our past. But now, even though weary, worn and sad, we have come to the Saviour and found in Him a resting place. And He has made us glad!

Therefore, we are encouraged to put away those old forces. We are not to expose ourselves to them any more.

But the question is often raised: "How can I hold myself from being shaped? I am thrown daily among the people of this world. I work in a situation where men are wicked and vulgar and obscene."

Here's my answer: You must engage your own will in the direction of God's will for your life. You can keep yourself from being shaped by your situation just as a man on the beach can keep himself from being tanned by the sun. You can draw your being tightly up in faith by an act of your will and take a positive stand: "Stay out, you devilish influences, in the name of my Saviour! Let my soul alone—it belongs to God!"

Many of our students can tell of the dirty talk and irreverence in their schools. Some of our Christian young people have even found a way to turn those things to personal spiritual blessing. Hearing an obscenity, they have an instant reaction and a compensation within: "Oh, God, I hate that so much that I want you to make my own mind and speech cleaner than it ever was before!"

Seeing an injurious, wicked habit in others, they look within at once and breathe a silent prayer: "Oh, God, you are able to keep me and shield me from this thing!"

It is possible, even in this sensuous world with its emphasis on violence and filth, that we can use those very things and react or compensate in the direction of God's promised victory. We are assured in the Word of God that we do not have to yield in weakness to the pull that would drag us down.

When we see something that we know is wrong and displeasing to Him, we can react to it with a positive assurance as we say: "God helping me, I will be different from that!" In that sense, the very sight of evil can drive us farther into the kingdom of God.

Now, what can we put into practice from this approach?

I share with you a few very simple thoughts about basic things in our own day that have powers to shape us, whether or not we are Christians. These are everyday things, and they have influence upon our lives, whether we know it or not, whether we believe it or not, or whether we like it or not.

What can you say about the kinds of books and magazines you read? The things you read will fashion you by slowly conditioning your mind. Little by little, even though you think you are resisting, you will take on the shape of the mind of the author of that book you are reading. You will begin to put your emphasis where he puts his. You will begin to put your values where he places his. You will find yourself liking what he likes and thinking as he thinks.

The same thing is certainly true of the power of modern films on the minds and morals of those who give themselves over to their influences.

Then, what about the kind of music you enjoy?

It seems almost too late in these times to try to give a warning that many in our society seem to revel in—the vile and vicious and obscene words of gutter songs. But there are other accepted types of music just as dangerous and just as damaging to the human spirit, just as harmful to the soul.

It is not overstating the case to insist that the kinds of music you enjoy will demonstrate pretty much what you are like inside.

If you give yourself to the contemporary fare of music that touches the baser emotions, it will shape your mind and emotions and desires, whether you admit it or not.

You can drink poison if you want to, but I am still friend enough to warn you that if you do, you will be carried out in a box. I cannot stop you but I can warn you. Nor do I have authority to tell you what you should listen to, but I have a divine commission to tell you that if you love and listen to the wrong kinds of music your inner life will wither and die.

Think with me also about the kind of pleasures in which you indulge.

If we should start to catalog some of your pastimes, you would probably break in and ask: "What's wrong with this?" and "What's wrong with that?"

There probably is no answer that will completely satisfy you if you are asking the question, but this is the best answer: "Give a person ten years in the wrong kind of indulgence and questionable atmosphere and see what happens to the inward spiritual life."

The pleasures in which we indulge selfishly will shape us and fashion us over the years, for whatever gives us pleasure has the subtle power to change us and enslave us.

What are the fond ambitions you entertain for your life?

The dream of whatever you would like to be will surely influence and shape you. It will also lead to choices of the places where you spend your time. I realize that we are not going to be very successful in advising people where they should go and should not go. Just the same, those who are on their way to heaven through faith in God's Son and God's plan should be careful of the kind of places they frequent, because these will shape and leave their imprint on man's spirit and soul.

We would do well to consider also the kind of words we speak.

Of all the people in the world I have read about, I think American people must be the most careless with language and expression.

For instance, any typical American joke must be an exaggeration. Mark Twain used the device of exaggeration, and it has become an accepted form not only of comedy but of communication among Americans. Are you watching your own language and are you careful of your own expressions in view of what it could mean to the effectiveness of your own Christian testimony?

Next, consider how important it is to make and cherish the right kind of friends in this life.

I value friendship very highly. I know we can appreciate and honor one another in friendship, even in this wicked world.

Because it is possible that friendships can be beautiful and helpful, I have always felt something like a churlish heel to stand before an audience and insist: "You must break off certain friendships if you want to truly serve God."

But our Lord Jesus said it more plainly and more bluntly than I could ever say it. He told us that in being His disciples we must take up our cross and follow Him and there would be instances when we must turn our backs on those who would hold us back—even our own relatives and close friends. Jesus Christ must be first in our hearts and minds and it is He who reminds us that the salvation of our souls is of prime importance.

Better to have no friends and be an Elijah, alone, than to be like Lot in Sodom, surrounded by friends who all but damned him. If you give your cherished friendship to the ungodly counsellor and the scorner, you have given the enemy the key to your heart. You have opened the gate and the city of your soul will be overwhelmed and taken!

Finally, what kind of thoughts do we spend our time brooding over?

It is quite evident that for every murder or robbery, an embezzlement or other evil deeds, someone has spent long hours brooding over the idea, the plans, the chance of gain or the hope of revenge. In our great increasing wave of crime and violence, every deed is conditioned or preceded by some brooding thoughts.

Whatever thoughts you are willing to brood over in the night seasons will shape you and form you. The thoughts you entertain can change you from what you are into something else, and it will not be for the better unless your thoughts are good thoughts.

In the light of all these influences, Paul appeals to us all: "Be not conformed . . . but be transformed!" You do have a soul and you have influences that will shape you. God gives the clay to the potter and says, "Now, shape it!" God gives the material to the builder and says, "Now, build it into a worthy temple!"

Then, God says at last, "How did you shape it? How did you fashion it? What do you have to bring me from the material that I gave you? What did you do with those forces and influences that came to you daily?"

I trust that in that last great day none of us will have to stand before the judgment seat of Christ and confess with shame that we allowed unworthy things to have a place in shaping our lives.

Rather, it is time now to be transformed by the renewing of our minds that we may know what is the perfect and acceptable will of God!

CHAPTER
12

The Second Coming: Doctrine on the Blessed Hope

And when he had spoken these things, while they beheld, he was taken up; and a cloud received him out of their sight. And while they looked stedfastly toward heaven as he went up, behold, two men stood by them in white apparel; which also said, Ye men of Galilee, why stand ye gazing up into heaven? this same Jesus, which is taken up from you into heaven, shall so come in like manner as ye have seen him go into heaven. Acts 1:9-11

O NLY THE CHRISTIAN CHURCH in the midst of all the world religions is able to proclaim the Bible's good news that God, the Creator and Redeemer, will bring a new order into being!

Indeed, it is the only good news available to a fallen race today—the news that God has promised a new order that is to be of eternal duration and infused with eternal life.

How amazing!

It is a promise from God of a new order to be based upon the qualities which are the exact opposite of man's universal blight—temporality and mortality!

God promises the qualities of perfection and eternity which cannot now be found in mankind anywhere on this earth.

What a prospect!

We are instructed that this new order, at God's bidding, will finally show itself in the new heaven and the new earth. It will show itself in the city that is to come down as a bride adorned for her husband.

The Word of God tells us that all of this provision for the redeemed has the quality of eternal duration.

It is not going to come just to go again. It is not to be temporal.

It is a new order that will come to stay.

It is not going to come subject to death. It is not to be mortal.

It is a new order that will come to live and remain forever!

God in His revelation to man makes it very plain that the risen Christ Jesus is the Head of this new creation and that His church is the Body. It is a simple picture, instructing us that individual believers in the risen Christ are the Body's members.

It seems to me that this is revealed so clearly in the Bible that anyone can see it and comprehend it.

The whole picture is there for us to consider.

The first Adam—the old Adam—was the head of everything in that old order, so when he fell, he pulled everything down with him.

I know that there are some bright human beings who argue against the historicity of the fall of human kind in Adam and Eve. But no man, however brilliant, wise, and well-schooled, has been able to escape two brief sentences written across all of his prospects by the great God Almighty.

Those sentences are: "Man, you cannot stay—you must go!" and "Man, you cannot live—you must die!"

No human being, regardless of talents and possessions and status, has yet won a final victory over his sentence of temporality and mortality.

Temporality says, "You must go!"

Mortality says, "You must die!"

Because this is true, then all of the works that men do actually partake of what man is. The same blight that rests upon sinful, fallen man—namely, temporality and mortality—rests upon every work that man does.

Mankind has many areas of life and culture of which he is proud. Man has long used such words as beauty, nobility, creativity and genius. But all the work of a man's hand, however noble it may be, however inspired by genius, however beautiful and useful-still has these two sentences written across it: "You cannot stay!" and "You cannot live!"

It is still only the work and hope and dream of fallen man and God continually reminds him, "You came only to go and you came surely to die!"

Everything and anything, whether a sonnet or an oratorio, a modern bridge or a great canal, a famous painting or the world's greatest novel—every one has God's mark of judgment upon it. Temporality and mortality!

Not one can remain—it is in the process of going.

Not one is eternal—it is only the work of fallen man who must die. And all of the work that man does cannot escape the sentence of partaking of what man is.

But a second man, the new and last Adam, came into this world to bring the promise of a new and eternal order for God's creation. The Son of Man, Christ Jesus the Lord, came and died, but rising from the grave, lives forever that He might be the Head of the new creation.

God's revelation says that Jesus Christ is the eternal Victor, triumphant over sin and death! That is why He is the Head of the new creation which has upon it the banner of perfectivity rather than temporality and the mark of life forevermore rather than the mark of death.

When we think of the ebb and flow of man's history and the inability of men to thwart the reality of death and judgment, it seems incredible that proud men and women—both in the church and outside the church—refuse to give heed to the victorious eternal plan and program of Jesus Christ!

Most of the reasons for the neglect of Christ's promises are all too evident among us today.

For one thing, modern man is too impatient to wait for the promises of God. He takes the short-range view of things.

He is surrounded by gadgets that get things done in a hurry. He has been brought up on quick oats; he likes instant coffee, he wears drip-dry shirts and takes 30-second Polaroid snapshots of his children.

His wife shops for her spring hat before the leaves fall to the ground in autumn. His new car, if he buys it after July 1, is already an old model when he brings it home.

He is almost always in a hurry and can't bear to wait for anything.

This breathless way of living naturally makes for a mentality impatient of delay, so when this man enters the kingdom of God he brings his short-range psychology with him. He finds prophecy too slow for him. His first radiant expectations soon lose their luster.

He is likely, then, to inquire: "Lord, wilt thou at this time restore again the kingdom to Israel?"

When there is no immediate response, he may conclude, "My Lord delayeth his coming!"

Actually, it has taken some people a long time to discover that the faith of Christ offers no buttons to push for quick service. The new order must wait for the Lord's own time—and that is too much for the man in a hurry.

He just decides to give up and becomes interested in something else.

Also, there is little question that the prevailing affluence of our society has much to do with the general disregard of Christ's promises that He would come to earth again to intervene in human history.

If the rich man enters the kingdom of God with difficulty, then it is logical to conclude that a society having the highest percentage of well-to-do persons in it will have the lowest percentage of Christians, all things else being equal.

If the "deceitfulness of riches" chokes the Word and makes it unfruitful, then this would be the day of near-fruitless preaching, at least in the opulent West.

And if surfeiting and drunkenness and worldly cares tend to unfit the Christian for the coming of

Christ, then this generation of Christians should be the least prepared for that event.

On the North American continent, Christianity has become the religion of the prosperous middle and upper middle classes almost entirely; the very rich or the very poor rarely become practicing Christians.

The touching picture of the poorly dressed, hungry saint, clutching his Bible under his arm and with the light of God shining in his face, hobbling painfully toward the church, is chiefly imaginary.

One of the most irritating problems of even an ardent Christian these days is to find a parking place for the shiny chariot that transports him effortlessly to the house of God where he hopes to prepare his soul for the world to come.

In the United States and Canada the middle class today possesses more earthly goods and lives in greater luxury than emperors and Maharajas did only a century ago.

There surely can be little argument with the assumption that since the bulk of Christians comes from this class, it is not difficult to see why the genuine expectation of Christ's return has all but disappeared from among us.

It is hard indeed to focus attention upon a better world to come when a more comfortable one than this can hardly be imagined. As long as science can make us so cozy in this present world it is admittedly hard to work up much pleasurable anticipation of a new world order even if it is God who has promised it.

Beyond these conditions in society, however, is the theological problem—too many persons holding an inadequate view of Jesus Christ Himself.

Ours is the age in which Christ has been explained, humanized, demoted. Many professing Christians no longer expect Him to usher in a new order. They are not at all sure that He is able to do so; or if He does, it will be with the help of art, education, science and technology—that is, with the help of man.

This revised expectation amounts to disillusionment for many. And, of course, no one can become too radiantly happy over a King of kings who has been stripped of His crown or a Lord of lords who has lost His sovereignty.

Another facet of the problem is the continuing confusion among teachers of prophecy, some of whom seem to profess to know more than the prophets they claim to teach.

This may be in the realm of history, but it was only a little more than a short generation ago, around the time of the first World War, that there was a feeling among gospel Christians that the end of the age was near and there was anticipation and hope of a new world order about to emerge.

In the general outline of the scriptural hope, this new order was to be preceded by a silent return of Christ to earth, not to remain, but to raise the righteous dead to immortality and to glorify the living saints in the twinkling of an eye. These He would catch away to the marriage supper of the Lamb, while the earth meanwhile plunged into its baptism of fire and blood in the Great Tribulation. This would be relatively brief, ending dramatically with the battle of Armageddon and the triumphant return of Christ with His Bride to reign a thousand years.

Let me assure you that those expectant Christians had something very wonderful which is largely lacking today. They had a unifying hope. Their activities were concentrated. They fully expected to win.

Today, our Christian hope has been subjected to so much examination, analysis and revision that we are embarrassed to admit that we believe there is genuine substance to the hope we espouse.

Today, professing Christians are on the defensive, trying to prove things that a previous generation never doubted. We have allowed unbelievers to get us in a corner and have given them the advantage by permitting them to choose the time and place of encounter.

We smart under the attack of the quasi-Christian unbeliever, and the nervous, self-conscious defense we make is called "the religious dialogue."

Under the scornful attack of the religious critic, real Christians, who ought to know better, are now "rethinking" their faith.

Worst of all, adoration has given way to celebration in the holy place, if indeed any holy place remains to this generation of confused Christians.

In summary, I think that we must note that there is a vast difference between the doctrine of Christ's coming and the hope of His coming.

It surely is possible to hold the doctrine without feeling a trace of the blessed hope. Indeed there are multitudes of Christians today who hold the doctrine—but what I have tried to deal with here is that overwhelming sense of anticipation that lifts the life upward to a new plane and fills the heart with rapturous optimism. It is my opinion that this is largely lacking among us now.

Frankly, I do not know whether or not it is possible to recapture the spirit of anticipation that animated the *early* Christian church and cheered the hearts of gospel Christians only a few decades ago.

Certainly scolding will not bring it back, nor arguing over minor points of prophecy, nor condemning those who do not agree with us. We may do all or any of these things without arousing the desired spirit of joyous expectation. That unifying, healing, purifying hope is for the childlike, the innocent-hearted, the unsophisticated.

Brethren, let me tell you finally that all those expectant believers in the past have not been wholly wrong. They were only wrong about the time. They saw Christ's triumph as being nearer than it was, and for that reason their timing was off; but their hope itself was valid.

Many of us have had the experience of misjudging the distance of a mountain toward which we were traveling. The huge bulk that loomed against the sky seemed very near, and it was hard to persuade ourselves that it was not receding as we approached.

So the City of God appears so large to the minds of the world-weary pilgrim that he is sometimes the innocent victim of an optical illusion; and he may be more than a little disappointed when the glory seems to move farther away as he approaches.

But the mountain is really there—the traveler need only press on to reach it. And the Christian's hope is substance, too; his judgment is not always too sharp, but he is not mistaken in the long view— he will see the glory in God's own time!

Book 8

*Ten Sermons
on the Voices of
God Calling Man*

Contents

Preface

The ministry of Dr. A. W. Tozer is frequently identified by his gift that urges believers to press into all the possibilities of the grace of God. In his zeal to bring Christians to maturity Tozer never neglected the basic themes of the gospel. An unbeliever could not hear his sermons or read his writings without learning something about the way back to God. Dr. Tozer's gift as an evangelist is often overlooked. In this series of sermons he explored the mercy of God in calling sinners to repentance and salvation.

Beginning in the garden of Eden, the voice of the Creator sounded out to Adam a clear invitation to return from the path of disobedience. That loving call has been echoing and reechoing ever since. God has spoken and He is now speaking to men through the voice of love, the voice of the Holy Spirit, the voice of conscience, the voice of the soul, the voice of reason, the voice of Jesus' blood, the voice of accountability, and the voice of judgment.

The theology of the calling of God has seldom been better stated than in these messages. Such a lucid treatment of this great truth is needed by the church in our day. At a time when Madison Avenue methodology and doctrinal fuzziness have taken over so much of contemporary evangelism it is essential to restate in biblical terms the divine calling of man by his Creator and Savior. Anyone concerned about true evangelism will find these studies sharpening his understanding of the basic issues the soul-winner must confront.

A Sick Planet without Meaning: A Fallen Race without God

And the Lord God called unto Adam, and said unto him, Where art thou? Genesis 3:9

ALTHOUGH THE HUMAN MIND stubbornly resists and resents the suggestion that it is a sick, fallen planet upon which we ride, everything within our consciousness, our innermost spirit, confirms that the voice of God is sounding in this world—the voice of God calling, seeking, beckoning to lost men and women!

At first thought, the human being wonders why it should be necessary for the divine voice of entreaty to be heard at all in the earth.

There is only one possible answer: it can only be because we are out of the way, lost and alienated from God. Even the very world we inhabit is a lost world.

There are many reasons to believe that the earth upon which we ride is a lost planet. Hints of this are found throughout the entire Bible and I believe that through the anointed intellect such evidences may be found also in nature.

In the Book of Genesis, after the great failure of our first parents, God said this about our planet as He spoke to Adam and Eve:

"Cursed is the ground for thy sake; . . . Thorns also and thistles shall it bring forth to thee; . . . till thou return unto the ground; for out of it wast thou taken: for dust thou art, and unto dust shalt thou return" (Gen. 3:17b-19).

Now, why were those words ever spoken?

I believe they were spoken to describe the planet which is our habitation. We have our clue here that it is a lost planet.

I would quote here also from the writings of a man of profound intellect, the Apostle Paul. I believe that it would be generally conceded in most circles that Paul possessed one of the most brilliant and profound minds that ever set a pen to paper.

This is the passage from the eighth chapter of the Book of Romans, the quotation taken from the British Williams translation:

This world of nature was condemned to be without meaning, not by its own will but by the will of him who condemned it, in the hope that not only mankind but this world of nature also might be set free from bondage to decay, to enter the glorious liberty of the sons of God. For to this day, as you know, the whole world of nature cries out in pain like a woman in childbirth.

So, long before our time, this world of nature was condemned to exist without meaning, that is, vanity.' Perhaps it is not strange that the very words that the philosophers like to use are used here by the sacred writer—that nature is without meaning!

And yet there is a glorious promise here as well—giving hope that not only mankind but this world of nature is to be set free from bondage to decay.

But there is something worse than the fact that this is a sick, fallen planet and that is the truth that the inhabitants of this planet are also lost.

We believe that God created us living souls and gave us bodies through which we can experience the world around us and communicate with one another. When man fell through sin, he began to think of himself as having a soul instead of being one. It makes a lot of difference whether a man believes that he is a body having a soul or a soul having a body!

For the moral 'unlikeness' between man and God the Bible has a word—alienation. The Holy Spirit presents a frightful picture of this alienation as it works itself out in human character. Fallen human nature is precisely opposite to the nature of God as revealed in Jesus Christ. Because there is no moral likeness there is no communion; hence the feeling that God is far away in space.

Yet when we speak of men being far from God we speak truly. The Lord said of Israel, "Their heart is far from me," and there we have the definition of 'far' and 'near' in our relation to God. The words refer not to physical distance, but to likeness.

Actually, men are lost but not abandoned. That is what the Holy Scriptures teach and that is what the Christian church is commissioned to declare.

For any who may doubt it, let me ask, just in the name of reason: does it seem reasonable to you that unique human beings, made in God's image, should each be given just one little turn at bat?

I ask this, knowing what God says about the potential of a human being.

I know also, of course, that there is a theology, or a color or complexion of theology, that squirms uneasily as soon as you say something good about mankind. Many are prepared to say that you are a liberal or a modernist, or a borderline liberal at the least, if you say something good about mankind.

It is my studied opinion that except for sin, it would be very difficult to overpraise human beings. Consider what we are and what we know and what we can do: our memories, imaginations, artistic abilities, our sensibilities and potentialities.

When you thoughtfully consider it, you cannot justly and properly sell mankind short! Sin, God knows, is like a cancer in the heart of a man's being. It ruins the man and damns him at last!

But the man is not all sin, for man was made in the image of God. It is true that sin has ruined him and condemned him to death forever unless he is redeemed through the blood of Jesus. Yet man as a being is only one degree removed from the angels and in some ways is superior indeed to the angels.

Again I ask: does it seem reasonable to you that if this were not a lost world that such a being as man—a Shakespeare or a Churchill or an Edison or any of the great thinkers and writers, artists or engineers—does it seem reasonable that each one of them should, like a little kid, be given his one little turn at bat and then be told to sit down while the ages roll on?

Does it seem reasonable to you that a being so Godlike as man should take all of this marvelous comprehension and ability only toward the grave? Should he carry his memory gifts, his brilliant imagination, his artistic creative powers and all those gifted traits that make him a man only to the grave?

Would the Creator God waste His time on such a being as He has made man to be, only to say, "I was just fooling around with man. I just made this marvelous creature for a short day. I am just having some fun!"

That does not seem reasonable to me.

Why does man as we know him consistently live beneath his own ideals? Why is he everlastingly far below what he knows he ought to be? Why is a man doomed to go to the grave frustrated and disappointed at last, never having attained his highest ideals?

You cannot tell me that mankind does not continue to dream of a shining world beyond him. Every man secretly believes that shining world is somewhere there before him—yet nevertheless it is always lost to that man or he is lost to it.

Even those followers of Jesus in His day on earth confessed: "Lord, we know not whither Thou goeth and how can we know the way?"

No truer words were ever uttered by any man on this earth!

Sacred revelation declares plainly that the inhabitants of the earth are lost. They are lost by a mighty calamitous visitation of woe which came upon them somewhere in that distant past and is still upon them.

But it also reveals a glorious fact—that this lost race has not been given up!

There is a divine voice that continues to call. It is the voice of the Creator, God, and it is entreating them.

Just as the shepherd went everywhere searching for his sheep, just as the woman in the parable went everywhere searching for her coins, so there is a divine search with many variations of the voice that entreats us, calling us back.

If we were not lost, there would be no voices reminding us: "This is the way; walk ye in it."

If we were not far from home, there would be no Father's voice calling us to return, calling us back.

So, I say again that we have not been given up.

Think with me now of the Genesis account: Adam fleeing from the face of God, hiding among the trees of the garden. It was then that the sound of God's gentle voice was heard, saying "Adam, where art thou?"

I would remind you that His seeking voice has never died out. The echo of that voice is sounding throughout the widening years. It has never ceased to echo and reecho from peak to peak, from generation to generation, from race to race, and continent to continent, and off to islands and back to the continent again.

Throughout all of man's years, "Adam, where art thou?" has been the faithful call.

There are many voices, but it is really only one voice.

When a child is lost in the swamp or in the woods, searching parties are organized immediately.

Who is back of that organized search?

Is it not the throbbing, anguished heart concern of the mother and father? They have encouraged the officers and the volunteers to hover overhead with helicopters, to send out sound trucks, to organize soldiers, and Boy Scouts, and friendly neighbors—always calling, calling, calling.

There will be many voices calling. It may be the voice of a soldier, a deputy, a volunteer, a neighbor—but always it is in a true sense the father's voice. All of the voices are simply overtones of the same loving father's voice that organized the search and whose distraught heart is calling for his lost child.

So it is with the voice of God!

Actually, many voices call us.

But it is all one voice.

Man may hear the voice of God's love or the voice of Jesus' blood or the voice of conscience; it may be the voice of the dead or the voice of the living or the voice of the lost or the voice of the saved. Whatever the voice, it is only another inflection of the voice of the One who calls.

It is the distraught heart of God seeking His lost race; calling men and women in any way that He can call them.

He may call from above or from below; He will likely call from around the bend or from down the road or beside the river or on the plateau.

Yes, it is the voice of God entreating us, searching us out and always calling us to return home!

One of Our Greatest Mistakes: Measuring God's Love by Our Own

The Lord hath appeared of old unto me, saying, Yea, I have loved thee with an everlasting love; therefore with lovingkindness have I drawn thee. Jeremiah 31:3

PERHAPS THE GREATEST MISTAKE we humans make is in our insistence upon trying to measure the love of God by our own human standards of love.

As men and women, is it not true that we are most likely to love people for what they are—often for their good behavior?

Let me describe for you what is likely to happen when you tell a sinner that "God really loves you!"

That person will say, "I don't believe that."

You see, he can only measure the love of God by his own kind of love.

"I know better than to believe that," he will say. "I know what I am on the inside. I have lied. I have cheated. I have stolen. There probably is not a sin that I have not committed, either overtly or in my heart.

"I am worse than anyone knows, so if God is the moral God the Bible says He is, He cannot love me!"

At this point, we must say that he is right, and also that he is wrong.

He is right if he believes that God cannot love him for his sin's sake. But he is wrong because he fails to see that he is loved of God and for God's own sake.

He is wrong if he fails to believe that God can love anyone, no matter how sinful, for His own sake and for His Son's sake.

Now, I would tell you a few things about the love of God that you are not hearing very often in these days.

God being the divine Person that He is, must love Himself first, because His love is a pure and blameless and perfect love.

Please do not say: "Mr. Tozer, you do not really mean that!"

That is exactly what I mean: that God, being Himself God, an uncreated being, deriving from no one, owing nothing to anybody, must necessarily be the fountain of all the love there is!

That is why I say that as our God, He must love Himself forever with pure and perfect love.

This kind of love, God's love, holy and blameless—this is the love which the three Persons of the Godhead feel and hold for one another.

The Father to the Son; the Son to the Father; the Father and Son to the Spirit; the Spirit to the Father and Son—the divine Trinity in perfect and blameless and proper love; loving one another with a holy, poured-out devotion!

The Trinity: three fountains, eternal, infinite, pouring without measure into each other from the bottomless, boundless, shoreless sea of perfect love and bliss.

This, I say, is the love of God for His own holy self. God being who and what He is, is Himself the only being that He can love directly. Everything else and everyone else that God loves, He loves for His own sake.

That is why we can believe and say that God loves Himself—and that when it comes to His creatures, His divine or perfect love cannot fall directly upon any man.

God must find something of Himself there in order that He may love it. God can only love Himself and that which is like Himself.

If God should love and cherish anything unlike Himself, it would be equivalent in our knowledge to a pure and holy woman loving and cherishing an evil man, perhaps a murderous gangster.

God must love that which is equal to Himself and like Himself.

So, when God looks at the mute creation that the translator calls the world of nature, He loves it because it reveals to Him something of the glory and power of His own Godhead. It shows something of His own wisdom.

When God looks on His sun and His moon and all the stars that He has made, His lakes and His rivers, His mountains and His seas, God loves them because they remind Him of His own wisdom and power that gave them being.

But when God looks at the seraphim and the cherubim and the holy angels before the throne, He loves them because they remind Him of His own holiness. They are holy angels and their holiness is derived from God.

God loves in them that which came from Himself. God can properly and with moral propriety love the holy angels because they are holy beings.

Now, when God considers men and women, He loves in them the fallen relic of His own image!

It is at this point that I seem to be in trouble with a lot of people who write to me and abuse me and insist that I am a liberal.

But I do not have education enough to be a modernist and I am not a liberal. I believe that the Bible says what God wanted it to say, and it is plain in the Scriptures that the living and eternal God made man in His own image.

Therefore, when Jesus Christ was incarnated He came to us in the body of a man—without embarrassment and without change.

"How can that be?" we ask.

Because man was an image of the God who created him; the image of that God who said, "Let us make man in our image."

Yet, that man is fallen—and that brings in another element here, a foreign element that has crept in.

It is the element of man's sin!

It is the deadly sting of the serpent, going back to the scene of failure in the garden. That is why man, made in the image of God is now a dying man; sick unto death because of sin which like the poison of an adder has gotten into his moral veins.

But extract that sin and take it out and you have the image of God again, and Jesus Christ was the true image of God because He was a man without sin.

That is Bible truth—no modernism there; no liberalism there!

I say that those who deny that fallen man bears upon him something of the original potential of what he once was are not true friends of the Bible. They themselves are guilty of taking liberties with the Holy Scriptures.

It is still true that when God looks on a sinner and loves the sinner, never while the stars burn in their silence can it be said that God loves the sin in the sinner.

Never can it be said that a holy God loves an unholy thing.

And yet God loves sinners—bringing the often-repeated question, "Why?"

God loves them for that which He sees in them of His lost and fallen image, for God can never love anything but Himself directly!

God loves everything else for His own sake.

You are loved of God, but you are loved of God for the sake of the holy Son, Jesus, who is the Godhead incarnate, who is the second Person of the Godhead, the Word who became flesh and dwelt among us.

God sees in Jesus Christ what you would have been: that is, He sees that in His perfect humanity, not His deity. You and I could never be divine in that sense.

But this is why God loves lost men. He loves them not by the excusing of their sin; not by taking an attitude of carelessness; not by any willingness on His part to become morally lax—but He loves them because He once stood and said, "Let us make man in our image."

Here is an illustration that could fall within our own human experience.

A man and a woman meet. After falling in love, they marry and have one child, a son.

They have a great deal of pleasure as they consider the boy's features. Each says that he looks like the other. Then they change it around and insist that he looks like this one—then again, that one.

But the child is their son, and they try to see each other in that boy!

The years pass and the boy grows up and aproaches manhood. The hour comes when he breaks with society. He chooses to go outside the law. He drinks, gambles, lies, steals, cheats—and then he murders. He becomes a fugitive from justice, known to be vicious and cruel.

The father of that lad dies before the outlaw is caught and thrown into prison. But the grieving mother goes to see him.

She knows he is finished. Evidence of every kind is against him, fingerprints everywhere, a thousand witnesses. He will pay for his crimes.

The mother looks through the bars. It is her son standing there, now a full-grown man.

Can she love his cruel deeds as an outlaw?

Can she love those heartless acts of gangsterism?

Does she love his cold-eyed cruelty?

No! She hates them with everything in her good heart.

But as he stands there, cornered and silent, she sees beyond him in her memory the man who is no longer with her, and she thinks, "If only he had been a good boy—he would have just been the image of his father."

She pours out her heart in tears, doesn't she?

She loves the boy—but she does not love one thing in him that made him an outlaw!

She loves the image of the man she loved and to whom she gave herself with the promise to follow until the separation by death.

We know that God looks down at the human race and sees us in our awful sin. The Apostle Paul has recorded seventeen deeds which he describes as the works of the flesh—but they are only the beginning.

It would take many sheets of paper to write down the long and dreadful list of sins that man has been capable of committing and is still doing.

God is still looking and He hates jealousy, deception, lying, gluttony, uncleanness, impurity, outlawries, cruelty.

We cannot ever think that God loves sinners carelessly, loosely, foolishly, with the thought: "I don't care—I love them anyway!"

No, I think it is plain that He loves them because He sees in them the image of what Adam was and what Christ is and loves them redemptively now for Jesus' sake.

In the light of God's love and grace, no man ought to strut down the street, proudly professing, "God loves me—I am a fundamentalist!"

Careful, careful!

Your sins have violated and lost to you every right you ever had to be loved by God. But God sees that you are of the loins of the man who once stood up on the earth and looked about for a help-meet. He was made in the image of God and God was not ashamed of him.

And now God sees an image of the man who went to the tree and died between heaven and earth—His only begotten Son.

So, God loves you for other reasons than who you are and what you are. Therefore, humble yourself—it will pay!

How we ought to thank God for the love that comes to us mediated through the Man, Christ Jesus. That everlasting love that is not only everlasting in its object but everlasting in its own quality!

God must love and will love man until hell has erased the last trace of the remaining image. Men are lost now—that we dare not forget. But they are still loved of God, and the man with the worst record is still dear to God for Jesus' sake, because Jesus died on that tree for lost men everywhere.

We cannot get away from God's words of old: "I have loved you with an everlasting love."

That love is everlasting because it is the eternal God who loves.

Now, consider the fact that God no longer loves the devil.

There was a day when God loved the devil as He now loves the angels and archangels, because He saw in that created being traces and proofs of His own wisdom.

Although not an image of Himself in the sense that man is, the devil was called the covering cherub, of whom God said, "My wisdom and beauty were created in thee in the day thou wast created."

Before his utter rebellion against his Creator, the devil was loved because he was a reflection of what

God could do and an evidence of His moral artistry and His omniscient skills.

But the devil sinned—and he sinned in some way that erased forever everything within him of which God could be proud.

It is for that reason that God can no longer love the devil. He sent no redeemer for him, for there is not anything in Satan that can remind God of Himself. The last trace of that which might have reminded God of Himself has been washed out in the filthy bilge water of iniquity as century has been added to centuries.

Believing that, I have long thought upon the continuing love of God for lost men and women for whom Christ died.

I share with you a speculation about the future, and because it is speculation you do not have to agree with me.

I believe the time will come when God will no longer love lost human beings!

I believe that God now loves all lost men. There are lost men in jails and prisons and insane asylums. They are in saloons and houses of ill fame and in all circumstances and environments, and God loves them all because the last trace of response has not been erased. He still remembers them and remembers His Son or. the tree, suffering in a body like theirs.

He still remembers that the second person of the divine Being was incarnated in the Man who has a body like that man, yet without sin.

The Bible says the day is coming when "he that is holy will be getting holier still, but he that is filthy will be getting filthier still."

Therefore, the day will come when lost man will no longer be loved by God Almighty; for God must love everything for His own sake if He is to continue to be God.

We must face the fact that when a human has sold himself out to sin and the mutilating power of iniquity has wrought to make him to be a devil and not a man, God will no longer love the lost man.

Further, it must be said that we ought not to imagine for a second that God will be pining over hell and grieving in His heart over lost men in hell. That cannot be true!

God grieves over lost men now because man can still pray and believe and hope and dream and aspire, so there is still something that reminds Him of the Man who died on the tree.

But when that is all gone, there will be nothing left upon which God can pour out His love. There will no longer be any image, no response and no reception of that love.

Therefore, the love of God though everlasting in its source, will no longer light upon fallen man.

Let me point out another fact to you: that wherever there is love there has to be good will, as well. As a rule, people will never do anything really bad to those they genuinely love. Love is always accompanied by good will and I think it is true to say that God is inflamed with good will.

We have read in the newspapers once in a while about the kind of man who will kill a woman because she looked at another man and his excuse to the court is: "I loved her so much that I killed her!"

True love never killed anyone! Love never willed ill or evil to anyone. Love must always have with it good will—and God is inflamed with good will. This means that whatever we think of Him, God is always thinking about us. When the angels sang their song or uttered their marvelous chant it was the message of "Good will to men."

But you try to tell the sinner that God loves him and that God is inflamed with good will towards him and he will express his doubts about it because he measures love only by his own human experience.

It takes quite a grasp of theology to make people see and understand that God does not love them because they are trying to be good. Many seem to believe that God must love them because they try to cultivate good habits; they have always pleased Mama and Papa; they have had good marks in school. Their attitude seems to be: "I can sort of understand how God can love me."

The truth is that God does love you—but for another reason altogether. He loves you because He sees even in you some trace of that glory that once walked in the garden. Though lost and ruined by the Fall and on your way to hell, God loves you for His own sake and not for your sake!

God's love is unique in this universe, for He loves us for His own sake.

Where there is this kind of love, there is good will, and there is also yearning!

Who but our God could tell us, "Therefore with lovingkindness have I drawn thee"?

He draws us toward Himself. To a lost race and a lost world there is a clear call from God. There is nothing that can stand in the way: not character, reputation, the past—nothing can stand in the way except our own sin.

God calls you to turn around. He calls you to make a moral "about face." He calls you to throw yourself on His mercy. Do not come expecting to bring a lot of character witnesses to tell God how good you are. Come just as the prodigal son came home, willing to confess: "Father, I have sinned!"

Would you ask God sincerely to draw your heart from earth away; would you ask Him to speak to your inmost soul and tell you once more: "I am your love. I am your God. I am your all"?

The voice of God's love continues to entreat you—that mighty love that is equal to God Himself, calling you back to the cross and back to the forgiveness in the Father's house.

The Presence of the Holy Spirit: A Silent, Holy, Eloquent Witness

And when he is come, he will reprove the world of sin, and of righteousness, and of judgment. John 16:8

THE HOLY SPIRIT, WHOM Jesus also called the Spirit of Truth, has not come into this world to fool around; He will be found wherever the Lord's people meet, and in confirming the Word and the Person of Jesus Christ, He will demand moral action!

It is for that reason that when a man goes to a gospel meeting he never knows when the last shred of excuse will be stripped from his naked, trembling conscience forever. Men may joke and play—even about sacred and spiritual matters—but the Spirit of God is in dead earnest!

God is still speaking in this lost world and one of His voices is the presence of the Holy Spirit, convicting a lost human race of such weighty matters as sin, righteousness, and judgment. While the Holy Spirit continues in His ministries, we know that this lost world is not yet a forsaken world.

We have said that God is speaking to mankind with more than one voice but it must be said that the clearest, most distinct and most easily distinguished voice is that of the Holy Spirit. The call and reproof and conviction by the Holy Spirit give grave and serious meaning to all other voices calling men home.

If it were not for the presence of the Holy Spirit speaking through the consciences of men and women, no other voice would have any significance.

For the Holy Spirit, the divine Comforter, came to confirm Christ's words and Christ's work and Christ's person.

Now the words of the Lord Jesus Christ were words so lofty and so astounding and so filled with authority that no other religious teacher in history could ever match His teachings. Other teachers have established their religious systems, some major and many of them minor, but the words and teachings of Jesus are in a class by themselves.

Frankly, the claims that He made brand Him immediately as being God—or an idiot! The authoritative claims He made outstrip the claims of all other religious teachers in the world.

Of His own body He said, "Destroy this temple and in three days I will raise it up!"

He told His hearers, "I saw Satan as lightning fall from heaven."

He declared with authority, "Before Abraham was, I Am."

He predicted that "then shall they see the Son of Man coming in the clouds of heaven and before him shall be gathered all nations. And he shall separate them as sheep from the goats."

No one else has ever been able to say, "Marvel, not at this, for the day will come when they that are in the grave shall hear my voice and shall come forth."

No one else has ever talked like that!

So, the Holy Spirit has come as a silent, penetrating, immediate witness of the words of Christ, and the penetrating stillness of the divine Spirit is more terrible than the loudest shout from the housetop.

Yes, the Holy Spirit is here confirming the words of Jesus, and that is why the critics are all in confusion. That is why God immediately makes a fool of the man who becomes a doubter and begins to try to pull the Word of God apart. God withdraws the inner life from such a man so that when he speaks, he speaks as a fool, because the penetrating voice of the Holy Spirit is not heard in his words.

The Holy Spirit is also among us to confirm to the consciences of men the works of Jesus.

There was no denying that in His earthly ministry, Jesus was a mighty worker of miracles. He did raise the dead. He did cleanse the leper. He did turn the water into wine. He did feed the multitude with a few pieces of bread.

The Pharisees did not try to deny the miracles He wrought. They could not deny them—for the man who was blind only moments before was now walking among them, with full vision. You cannot deny a fact that stands and stares you in the face: a fact that you can touch and feel and push around and investigate!

The Pharisees simply said: "He does his work in the power of the devil."

The Holy Spirit came that He might confirm and verify the divine quality of those mighty works of Jesus and prove Him indeed to be the very God who had made the world and who could make it do what He pleased for it to do.

Then there is the confirmation of the person of Christ, the most significant, the most telling force that ever lived in the world, standing head and shoulders above all the great in history.

The Holy Spirit came to do a confirmatory work and He raised Him from the dead and since this mysterious witness is come, Jesus Christ is no longer on trial. It is no longer a question of "Was Jesus the Son of God?"

The Holy Spirit has taken that out of the realm of polemics and has put it in the realm of morals. The silent, immediate witness, this penetrating voice in the conscience of men tells us that this person was indeed the very Son of God.

As soon as Peter was filled with the Holy Ghost he immediately stood and preached what he had never preached before; namely, that this man whom they had crucified is the Christ of God, raised from the dead to be Lord and Christ.

Then, too, as soon as Paul was filled with the Spirit, he immediately reasoned and proved from the Scriptures that Jesus was the Son of God, that the looked-for-Messiah was to be the Son of God, and that that man was Jesus.

Yes, the Holy Spirit's witness is a witness to the lordship and deity of the Son of God. Jesus Christ needs no more books written to prove that He was God. He needs no advocate pleading His cause before the unfriendly court of this world. He needs no witness to rise and say, "I know He was the Son of God."

The proof of the Sonship of Jesus has been removed from the realm of the intellect and placed where it has always belonged—in the realm of morals.

And it is the Holy Spirit who has put it there. He came, as Jesus had promised, and He is here. He may be grieved and He may have to withdraw from some places, but He is here and He is a silent, holy, eloquent witness.

So, Jesus Christ is no longer on trial before men: but men are now on trial before Him!

Strange and wonderful as it may be, He who once stood before Pilate now makes Pilate stand before Him. He who pleaded His cause before the unfriendly world now sits and judges the same world.

He has transferred the religious question to the heart. On the throne He sits, in the form of a Man so we would recognize Him instantly, and He is there invested with full authority and full power and with full right of judgment.

And in our world there is still the holy witness of the Spirit, who in all things speaks for this Man who sits on the throne.

Now, with all my heart I believe in the historicity of the Christian gospel, but that does not mean that the eternal fate of the individual man depends upon historic evidence. The Holy Spirit is here now to convince the world, and however we treat the warnings of the Holy Spirit is exactly how we treat Jesus Christ Himself.

If faith must depend upon a man knowing enough of the historical evidences to arrive at a scholarly belief in the deity of Jesus, then there could only be a relatively few people saved. But I do not have to be a scholar, a logician, and a lawyer to arrive at belief in the deity of the Lord Jesus Christ, for the Holy Spirit has taken the deity of Christ out of the hands of the scholars and put it in the consciences of men. The Spirit of God came to lift it out of the history books and write it on the fleshy tablets of the human heart.

I am sure you know that the missionaries go to the jungles where the most primitive men and women cannot read and write. When they proclaim the story of Jesus, when they preach the good news of Jesus Christ as the final answer to sin, the Holy Spirit is faithful in His witness of sin and righteousness and judgment. Those primitive people have never heard of Rome or Greece. They have no idea where Jerusalem is. They never heard of Abraham or David. But when the missionary tells the story of Jesus and the cross and forgiveness of sin, they will begin to tremble and sweat with conviction for they know they are sinners.

When those savage jungle people put their faith in Jesus Christ as Savior, they are transformed, turned inside out, made honest and good and clean and humble and right. They will learn to read and they will begin to sing songs about the Lord Jesus. They will form themselves into a church. Those great, brawny fellows born in the jungle will become deacons and elders and preachers in that church.

Remember now—they had no knowledge of history, no scholarship, no ability to weigh evidences. They know nothing of relevance or irrelevance; they had never heard of the laws of evidence.

God is able to do His mighty work in His own way and the Holy Spirit has come into this world to take polemics away from the scholar and give it back to the human heart. The believer's faith in the deity and person of Jesus does not rest upon his ability to comb through history and arrive at logical conclusions concerning historic facts. The Holy Ghost will blaze in on him like a lightning flash, blinding him with the wonder of it!

That is what Jesus meant when He said, "My doctrine is not mine, but his that sent me. If any man will do his will, he shall know of the doctrine, whether it be of God, or whether I speak of myself."

That is why the Holy Ghost has come and that is why He is here, and I think that this is one of the most important truths that can be taught in the world today. I find myself wondering about the great majority of preachers and teachers in Christian circles who seem so intent upon making the deity of Christ rest upon historical evidences. I think they must not discern that the Holy Spirit has taken that matter completely out of the realm of evidences and has put it as a burning point in the human conscience. It is no longer an intellectual problem—it is a moral problem!

I have another word for you at this point: let's not be too humble and admit that we are a bunch of dumbbells who barely know our letters. Augustine had a brilliant mind. Luther was adept in languages, both in Latin and German.

No, no! You do not have to pump out your head so that it is a vacuum in order to be a Christian. We have many ways in which to make use of the minds God has given us. So keep yours!

However, I repeat: that the use for it will not be in the realm of divine evidences. The Holy Ghost takes care of that.

When our Lord Jesus was here upon the earth all of His ministries to men and women were in dead earnest. When He went into the heavens He sat down in utter and solemn sincerity at the right hand of the Majesty on high. Then the Holy Spirit was sent to us, that wave of silvery light containing in Himself all of the essence of the Father and of the Son. Then as fire He sat upon each of those believers and they had no further question—they knew that Jesus was the Son of God, the Messiah and the Savior. They knew it instantly. They had sensed it before but they did not know for sure. But now they knew!

These are the important things—confirmation by the Spirit of God concerning sin, righteousness, and judgment.

Let me assure you that the Holy Ghost has not come among us to become involved in a lot of our minor concerns, the trivial things that take up much of our attention.

The Holy Spirit is not here to back you up in your little private quirks and quibbles in prophetic interpretations. The Holy Spirit cannot be used for your arguments about a certain mode of baptism. I have refused to become involved in arguments and controversy over the matter of eternal security, because I want the Holy Spirit to help me and guide me and He will not help me if I insist on fooling around in those areas that are not the most important in Christian truth and proclamation.

Now, a lot of people think they are escaping the conviction of the Spirit by pretending. Many pretend by saying, "I am a seeker after light."

More often than not, the problem is not a lack of light. The problem generally turns out to be a moral problem—but that is how men and women try to hide and escape—by pretending.

Actually, unbelief is the sign and proof of sin.

On the other hand, saving faith is not a conclusion drawn from facts presented; saving faith is a gift of God to a penitent man or woman.

There are some frank things that need to be expressed about saving faith in our day, for even in our evangelical Christian circles there is a basic misunderstanding of faith.

It is a simple matter to get people to come forward when the invitation is given. It is a simple matter to get them on their knees.

Then what happens?

Someone rushes in with a marked New Testament, sticks a text under their nose, and demands, "Now, who said that?"

The kneeling person says, "God?"

"Do you believe God?"

"Yes."

"Well, then, do you believe the text?"

"Yes. I must believe it because I believe God."

"Well, then, get right up and testify."

In so many cases, he gets up with an intellectual faith that has no saving quality.

I continue to oppose that kind of instruction and teaching—the kind that would pick little chickens out of their shells and let them die. I continue to oppose that kind of practice that would take over the work of the Holy Ghost and crowd Him out and retire Him.

This is the age of a superannuated Holy Ghost. We have retired Him and said, "Thanks, we have our Bibles, good King James translation, and we really will not need You until the millennium!"

Others are insisting that it is not the "sin" problem but the "Son" problem that is troubling mankind.

This statement has been credited to a preacher in our day: "Sin has no more meaning to God. On Calvary sin beat itself to death and perished. And now sin has no meaning to God, since Calvary."

He may have been a good man but he was talking like a blooming idiot when he said that.

The problem between God and man has always been the sin problem, since that evil hour in the garden. It is true that when the sin question is settled, the Son question comes leaping in—and happily so!

The Holy Spirit deals with us in those three vital areas—sin, righteousness, and judgment.

The Holy Spirit confirms the fact that there has been only one truly holy and righteous Man in the world—and He had to leave. They hounded Him out of the world. They said, "This man is not going to make moral fools out of us!"

They nailed Him to a cross—and He died for their sins.

Now the Holy Spirit is here to convince the world concerning that unpardoned act, that act of crucifying the world's only truly holy man. For He was holy without being made holy.

There may be holy men now and there may be righteous men now. A man may be righteous now because he has been made righteous by saving faith in the One who never had to be made righteous.

The fact of a coming judgment is ridiculed and ignored by millions who try to shut out the voice of the Spirit.

"It is ridiculous to think of God as a bookkeeper or as a file clerk, making little entries and the date of every sin," men have scoffed.

The omniscient God of the universe sees everything perfectly. He knows every person's heartbeat; He knows every thought; He knows every act and every deed. Judgment will not be a difficult thing for the living God. He already knows—and the Holy Spirit is here to convince and confirm.

The Holy Spirit is still among us with transforming power for that one who hears the gospel message and really believes it.

The Spirit still raises the consciences of men out of the deep mud of their past. He still converts. He still regenerates. He still transforms. He still makes Christians out of dead clods.

It is tragic that we try to hide from Him in the caves and dens of the earth, among the trees of the garden. It is tragic that men and women keep their hearts so hard that they cannot feel, and so deaf that they cannot hear.

There are many who are hearing the Voice of God, but they insist that the "way" should be made easier for them.

Oh, listen! If hell is what God says it is, if sin is what God says it is, if Jesus Christ had to die to save the sinner—is it asking too much for you to rise, and let the congregation know that you are turning from sin?

No, Jesus Christ never taught that His people would sneak in the easy way. He did not say we could come into the Kingdom of God crawling unobtrusively through the cracks. Never!

If Jesus Christ is your Savior, He has a right to your bold and fearless witness, for He said, "He that will come after me let him deny himself and take up his cross daily and follow me."

If you are not willing to do that, you are too big a coward to go to heaven!

The Word of the Lord is not easy but it is safe; humble yourself and the Lord will draw near to you!

The Blood of Jesus Calls for Mercy and Forgiveness

And he said, What hast thou done? the voice of thy brother's blood crieth unto me from the ground. Genesis 4:10

And to Jesus the mediator of the new covenant, and to the blood of sprinkling, that speaketh better things than that of Abel. Hebrews 12:24

GOD'S REVELATION TO MAN is very plain, declaring that life is of God and the blood is the symbol of that life. Therefore, our human life is sacred because it is in fact a loan from God Himself.

For that reason, the violent crime of shedding another's blood and taking the life is one of the gravest and most destructive sins dealt with in the Scriptures.

The theme of bloodguiltiness is a recurring theme in the Bible and here we have two concepts. The Old Testament picture is that of the blood of murdered Abel crying out for justice; the New Testament picture is that of the blood of Jesus Christ the Savior and mediator crying from the throne of God for mercy!

We cannot properly consider the voice of Jesus' blood without starting with God Himself, where all true theology begins and where all sermons should begin.

Now, I know that some have said about me: "That man is always talking about God!" I can only say in reply that if that is the only charge that anyone can properly bring against me, I will be quite a happy man.

I know that I talk a lot about God—about the triune God, because I still believe in God. I believe in Him as God Almighty, the Father, and Jesus Christ, His Son and our Lord, and the Holy Ghost, the Comforter.

We do begin with God here, where all truth begins, for God is the one true and absolute reality. Back of all, and underneath and supporting all things, He girds the universe and holds it up and guides it.

God does that. That is the only explanation for the universe and the only explanation of human life, for as Creator He gives to human life its meaning and significance.

He is the sacred meaning that gives validity to all meaning. Exclude God from your thinking and you will find yourself with no sense of moral values—you will have no standard of right or wrong.

Exclude God from your thinking and good becomes the same as evil and evil is the same as good. Your lie will become truth and truth will be as a lie. Exclude God and it becomes impossible to prove that love is any better than hate.

Exclude God from your thinking and you will not know whether life is any better than death, or whether anything is anything!

So, we begin with God for God is life. All life that exists is God's life. He has given life to all living things and the amazing fact is that God lends life without giving it up!

As humans, we are aware that if we give something away, we give it up for the time it is away from us.

But God lends without giving anything up. God gives you life but He is still the life He gives you so He loses nothing by giving it to you.

So with everything else. God is power but when He gives you power He does not give His power away. He gives wisdom but He does not lose it when He gives it. He gives grace but He does not part with His grace. He keeps it while He gives it because it is Himself that He gives.

So it is with everything—wisdom, being, power, holiness and every quality God bestows upon men. God is constantly giving of Himself to us, because God is life!

Life is sacred indeed but we do not fully realize it if we do not believe and confess that it is a gift from God. There is a great truth involved here for human beings—for eternal life can best be described as having God in the soul!

One of the old Puritan fathers gave us that expression: "The life of God in the soul of a man—that is Christianity!" When God gives His life to us He does not give it in the sense of cutting it off from Himself—He knows no diminution of His life or being because He gives us of Himself.

Now, we know the Bible account of how Cain turned on his brother Abel and killed him in a bloody way. We know, too, that Cain's action was not overlooked nor forgotten—for the Lord confronted him with the words, "The voice of thy brother's blood crieth unto me from the ground."

In a later time, when David the king was guilty of a number of grievous sins, he had to lay them before his God in confession and prayer. As a man, he was guilty of deception, deceit, and disloyalty; he was guilty of adultery and finally of murder.

When David threw himself down to confess and repent, all of these were summed up in his earnest prayer: "Deliver me from bloodguiltiness, O God!"

The compulsion laid upon David, the remorse that brought him to his knees was his own awareness that he was guilty of violating the sacred precincts of life and turning that life out—bloodguiltiness!

Wherever there is bloodguiltiness anywhere in the world you may be sure that society is in trouble.

At this point, some of you may be expecting me to enter into the great modern controversy concerning capital punishment in our society.

I do not get involved in the heat of that question.

I can only say that I believe the Bible. In the Old Testament it was plain that the only way to deal with bloodguiltiness was to avenge it. The blood of Abel cried from the ground against the man who had shed that blood.

God wrote into the law of the old patriarchs, even before the law of Moses, that if a man shed the blood and took the life of another, he would die for that shedding. The murderer is a presumptuous intruder into the sacred precincts of life. God being life, the murderer in a sense sneaks into the very presence of God and takes that which no man has the right to take except at the hand of God.

Bloodguiltiness lays a great and ruinous burden upon human society, for the voice of blood is the voice of life and the voice of shed blood is the voice of violated life.

I have only the voice and opinion of one man—but I do fear for the future of our great nations on this continent where our laws are taking little account of sin and authorities are letting crime on crime pile up with soft sentiment taking over in so many areas.

There are gangsters and killers who boast about their many crimes, and authorities arrest one of the offenders and tell him: "You are a bad boy—you did not pay your income tax!"

Meanwhile, the eloquent voice of shed blood cries out to God Almighty!

Shedding of blood has always been a grave sin, because life is in the blood and God gave life to the world, and the nearest thing to life is blood. It follows, then, that the nearest thing to killing God is the killing of the man who was made in the image of God!

I have little fear that any nation or combination of nations could bring down the United States and Canada by military action from without. But this I do fear—we sin and sin and do nothing about it. There is so little sense of the need of repentance—so little burden for the will of God to be wrought in our national life. I fear that the voice of blood will become so eloquent that God Almighty will have no choice but to speak the word that will bring us down.

I do pray often: "Oh God, send a revival of repentance and the fear of God that will sweep through the continent that we may be spared and that we may honor Thee!"

God does hear the eloquence of blood, the eloquence of violated life, and remember that God will always act like Himself—no other way!

God became flesh and dwelt among us.

He had said, "What will I do with these blood-stained people? What will I do with the blood-stained world? What shall I do with those who have entered into the holy place and shed the blood of men whom I have made in my image?"

God said, "I know—I will go myself and become one of them. I will take upon myself the form of a man and I will have blood running in my veins. It will not be the tainted blood of Adam but the pure blood of a second Adam."

So, our Lord came, born of the virgin Mary. There is not a day of my life goes by without my thanks to God for sending His Son, Jesus, made flesh to dwell among us and to die for us.

He came unto His own and His own received Him not.

But He was here and in His veins, I say, there ran that thrice-holy blood of the sinless, untainted Son of Man. Yet, for our sakes, all of the moral corruption of the world, all of the moral pollution of the world was laid on that holy body and charged against that holy soul, for "He made His soul a sacrifice for sin," the Scripture says.

The Savior offered not only His body but His soul as well, for the redemption of mankind. All of the offenses of the human race against God and against each other He bore on that cross—the offenses of Cain against Abel; the offenses of Esau against Jacob; the offenses of David against Uriah; the offenses of Judas in his betrayal of his Lord; the offenses of all of those who killed the martyrs through the centuries; the sins and the offenses of us all!

Oh, I cannot think that we even half believe this!

I think if we even half believed this it would transform us. It would get into us and possess us so that we could no longer talk about ordinary things. Our minds would run to this wonder so that we could no longer be intent upon everyday matters. We would constantly thank Him and honor Him because in that holy soul and body He bore all of the offenses and pollutions of mankind.

We all reveal the remaining traces of our own Pharisaism when we point to the Cains and the Neros and the Hitlers and their worst offenses which were laid upon our Lord Jesus Christ, but we were involved at His cross, no matter how quiet and how harmless we seem to be.

One of the great German poets of 200 years ago, von Goethe, summed it up for us all, when he wrote: "I have never heard of a sin being committed without knowing full well that I had the seed of it within myself."

We are on the most blessed ground with our forgiving Savior when we dare to be honest, telling Him, "O dear Lord, I have the potential of all those sins within me! I did not get them done but I have had the seed within me. Forgive me and cleanse me and keep me, for Thy glory!"

Yes, the voice of Jesus and the voice of His blood is pleading for us, and remember this: the voice of Jesus is not the voice of a murdered man.

The Holy Spirit through the Apostle Peter charged that generation of Jesus' day with these words: "You men of Israel have taken Him, a man approved of God among you, and by wicked hands have crucified and slain Him."

It was not a murder they committed, although they meant it to be so. It was a Sacrifice offered, God turning a cross into an altar and the condemned one into a Lamb. It was a Man offering himself on an altar of sacrifice, not a man dying on the cross for his sin. He was the only Man who had no sins for which to die. He died and shed His blood for violated blood.

I have said I fear for human society today, piling up blood on violated blood, but I also find this hope coming to my heart.

I remember that in the blood of Christ the blood of the world was shed. Sometimes we sing

"Bread of the world in mercy broken;
  wine of the soul in mercy shed;
By whom the words of life were spoken,
  and in whose death our sins are dead."

Paul was speaking for us when he said, "For the love of Christ constraineth us, because we thus believe, that if one died for all then are all dead: And that he died for all, that they which live should live no longer unto themselves, but unto him which died for them, and rose again."

So, Christ's blood was our blood—and this is the theology of New Testament victory for the believer. This is the theology that I experienced as a young man in the Alliance.

This is the theology that tells me that Christ and I are united, so that when He died I died, and when He arose I arose! This is the doctrine of spiritual victory and there is no other way that consistent victory can be found.

Spiritual victory comes only by the knowledge that we died.

I must die! I must die!

It is not true, as some seem to think, that God can make a transfer and say: "Well, I will let this Man die in your stead and you will just go free and all out of it!"

That is not quite the way God has done it.

What He did was to join me to that Man, Jesus Christ, by the wonder and mystery of incarnation on His part, and regeneration in us.

He joined us to that Man so that when He died, we died. It was not only a transfer, it was not only a vicarious act—it was an actuality!

The Scriptures say that every Christian believer may consider himself to have died in Christ. Give yourselves over for a time to the study of chapters 5 through 8 in the Book of Romans. You will see for yourself that this is the doctrine of the Bible: that when Christ became humanity, He made it possible for us to get up into deity—not to become deity but to be united with deity.

God counts Christ's death to be my death and He counts the sacrifice Christ laid down to be mine.

I repeat: "for the love of Christ constraineth us; for we thus judge that if one died for all, then were all dead—that they which live should no longer live unto themselves."

No man has any right to sin again now—the voice of Jesus' blood is eloquent now, one of the most eloquent sounds in the human mind.

Wherever you find Christ's church, wherever her songs are raised, wherever the prayers of her saints rise we hear the voice of Jesus' blood pleading eloquently, and witnessing that "in the blood of Christ the sins of the world died."

Oh, if men and women will only believe it!

When will we realize and confess that every sin is now a moral incongruity?

As believers, we are supposed to have died with Jesus Christ our Lord. When we were joined to Him in the new birth we were joined to His death. When we were joined to His rising again, it should have been plain to us that sin is now a moral incongruity in the life of a Christian.

The sinner sins because he is out there in the world—and he has never died. He is waiting to die and he will die once and later he will die the second death.

But a Christian dies once and that is all the dying he does. The Christian dies with Christ and dies in Christ and dies along with Christ, so that when he lays his body down at last the Bible says he will not see death.

God will cover the eyes of all Christians when the time comes—they never see death. The Christian stops breathing and there is a burial but he does not see death—for he already died in Christ when Christ died, and he arose with Christ when Christ arose.

That is why sin is a moral incongruity in the life and deportment of the Christian believer. It is a doctrine and theology completely unknown to those whose Christianity is like a button or flower stuck on the lapel—completely external.

I believe the gospel of Jesus Christ saved me completely—therefore He asks me for total commitment. He expects me to be a disciple totally dedicated.

Joined to Jesus Christ, how can we be other than what He is? What He does, we do. Where He leads, we go. This is genuine Christianity!

Sin is now an outrage against holy blood. To sin now is to crucify the Son of God afresh. To sin now is to belittle the blood of atonement. For a Christian to sin now is to insult the holy life laid down. I cannot believe that any Christian wants to sin.

All offenses against God will either be forgiven or avenged—we can take our choice. All offenses against God, against ourselves, against humanity, against human life—all offenses will be either forgiven or avenged. There are two voices—one pleading for vengeance, the other pleading for mercy.

What a terrible thing for men and women to get old and have no prospect, no gracious promise for the long eternity before them.

But how beautiful to come up like a ripe shock of corn and know that the Father's house is open, the doors are wide open, and the Father waits to receive His children one after another!

Some years ago one of our national Christian brothers from the land of Thailand gave his testimony in my hearing. He told what it had meant in his life and for his future when the missionaries came with the good news of the gospel of Christ.

He described the godly life of one of the early missionaries and then said: "He is in the Father's house now."

He told of one of the missionary ladies and the love of Christ she had displayed, and then said: "She is in the Father's house now."

What a vision for a humble Christian who only a generation before had been a pagan, worshipping idols and spirits—and now because of grace and mercy he talks about the Father's house as though it was just a step away, across the street.

This is the gospel of Christ—the kind of Christianity I believe in. What joy to discover that God is not mad at us and that we are His children—because Jesus died for us, because the blood of Jesus speaketh better things than the blood of Abel. What a blessing to find out that the mercy of God speaks louder than the voice of justice. What a hope that makes it possible for the Lord's people to lie down quietly when the time comes and whisper, "Father, I am coming home!"

Oh, we ought to make more of the blood of the Lamb, because it is by the blood that we are saved; by the blood atonement is made.

You know I encourage you to sing some of the old camp meeting songs with plain theology and clear message. This is one of those:

"The cross, the cross, the bloodstained cross,
The hallowed cross I see;
Reminding me of precious blood
That once was shed for me.

"A thousand, thousand fountains spring
Up from the throne of God;
But none to me such blessings bring
As Jesus' precious blood.

"That priceless blood my ransom paid
When I in bondage stood;
On Jesus all my sins were laid,
He saved me with His blood.

"By faith that blood now sweeps away
My sins, as like a flood;
Nor lets one guilty blemish stay:
All praise to Jesus' blood!

"This wondrous theme will best employ
My heart before my God;
And make all heaven resound with joy
For Jesus' cleansing blood."

The blood of Jesus Christ continues to plead eloquently. At the right hand of God the Father I do not believe that Jesus, our great high priest, has to talk and talk. I am sure His intercession for us lies in His two wounded hands.

When children of God violate the covenant, God hears the voice of the wounded Son of God and forgives, but is that reason for us to be careless? Never! Never while the world stands!

We Christians ought to be the cleanest, purest, most righteous, holiest people in all the world—for the blood of Jesus Christ can sweep away our sins "as like a flood, nor let one guilty blemish stay—all praise to Jesus' blood!"

The Ground of Human Conscience: Christ's Presence in the World

So when they continued asking him, he lifted up himself, and said unto them, He that is without sin among you, let him first cast a stone at her.

And again he stooped down, and wrote on the ground.

And they which heard it, being convicted by their own conscience, went out one by one, beginning at the eldest, even unto the last . . . . John 8:7-9

THE ENEMY OF OUR souls has long been using a subtle, pseudo-learned type of propaganda to bring derision and disrepute to many of life's verities—and among these is conscience.

When human conscience is mentioned in learned circles in our day, it is mentioned only with a smirk.

If it is to be considered seriously, it is necessary that we must defend the whole concept of human conscience. That seems almost unbelievable—but it is true!

Personally, I cannot ignore that which the universal wisdom of the human race in all ages has approved—the idea of a moral conscience within the being of every man.

Neither do I feel that I must defend that which the Christian Scriptures take for granted and consistently teach throughout. If you will trace it through your concordance you will find that conscience is mentioned in many, many places. Beyond that, the idea which the word conscience embodies appears throughout the Bible, as though woven into its very fabric.

We should first explore what we mean by conscience; then point to this Bible example to see it in operation, and finally, show that it is a voice still calling to mankind.

I think it must be said of conscience that it is a moral awareness; that it always deals with right and wrong and the relationship of the individual to right and wrong. Conscience never deals with theories about anything.

You will also note a strange thing in the Bible record: conscience always deals in the singular, never in the plural, as in this instance: "they . . . being convicted by their own conscience, went out."

It is always true in the Bible that conscience refers to right and wrong, and is individual and personal and singular.

Conscience never lets you lean on someone else. Conscience singles you out of the crowd as though no one else exists.

John does not record that the scribes and Pharisees departed in a group when Jesus said, "Let him that is without sin cast the first stone." They went out one by one. Each went out driven by his own conscience.

In this sense, the word conscience means a moral sight It means to see completely. It means a secret, inward awareness, and I think we would call that the psychological definition of conscience.

But that is not our concern in this lesson. We want to study and learn something more about the ground of human conscience—and I believe that the ground of human conscience is the secret presence of Christ in the world.

That explains why conscience is a moral awareness!

This brings me to a verse that is very basic in my theology, John 1:9: "That was the true Light, which lighteth every man that cometh into the world."

Jesus is that light that is in the world, and His secret presence lights every man that comes into the world.

That is the ground of moral conscience. However it operates, that is the ground. That is how men and women in this world have a secret awareness of moral values.

There are some Bible teachers who insist that when the Bible says that we are dead in trespasses and sins it means we are dead in a very literal sense of the word. Their teaching is this: the sinner, being dead, has no moral awareness at all.

I think that kind of exegesis is so bad and so confused that it has no place at all in considering the Scriptures. I do not think you can make the Bible say that a man who is dead in sin is a completely dead man—one who can neither be persuaded nor convinced, pleaded with nor appealed to, convicted nor frightened.

Who can say that the person who has not yet come to Christ is just a dead lump?

Being dead in our sin means that we are cut off from the life of God—and that is so bad that it is impossible to think of anything worse.

But that man who is dead in sin, cut off from the life of God, does have a moral awareness. He does hear a secret inner voice. The light that lighteth every man that comes into the world—that is the singular voice in the bosom of every human being, accusing or else excusing him, as the Apostle Paul said.

That is what I mean by conscience.

In the eighth chapter of John, we have a striking Bible example of the conscience in operation.

The scribes and Pharisees insisted that they were strict moralists, and they appeared to be when anyone was watching. They wanted to silence Jesus and to discredit His teachings, so they dragged a miserable woman into His presence and said, "She is a harlot, taken in the very act of adultery. The Law of Moses says we are to stone her to death. What do you say?"

Jesus looked at the accusing men and He knew everything that was in their hearts. He knew they had no concern at all for the wretched woman. He knew that their concern was not at all for the broken law. He knew they had no thought for the religion nor for the society of Israel.

He knew they only had one thing in mind—discrediting Him forever. He knew the woman was only a pawn in their plan. They had no love for her and they really had no hatred for her sin. But they hated Jesus and they would do anything to get at Him.

They thought they had an open-and-shut case. If Jesus said, "Stone her to death," and they did, the Roman rulers would immediately throw Jesus into prison and that would be the end of Him.

If Jesus said, "Let her go," they could make their case against Him: "We always knew you were against the Law of Moses!" If they could discredit His teachings concerning the Law of Moses that would be the end of Him in Israel.

Jesus was well aware of their hatred, of their hypocrisy and of the kind of frame-up they had rigged. He had no regard for their outward pretensions of praying in public to be seen and heard, for their sanctimonious appearance, and for their pious nasal breathing.

But they were anxious for Jesus to speak. They believed the trap was all set.

I think Jesus looked every one of them directly in the eye during that moment—and I have to believe that there was a twinkle in the heart, if not in the eye of Jesus.

First he stooped down and with His finger wrote something in the dust of the ground.

John records that they were anxious and impatient, for they continued pressing Him, asking Him to answer.

Jesus said simply, "Fellows, let the one of you who has never sinned cast the first stone at her."

In his record, John says, "being convicted by their own conscience, they went out one by one."

Each of those accusing men slipped out quietly by himself—each ashamed to say anything to the others. Each one alone—because it is in the power of conscience to isolate the human soul and take away all of its hopes and helps and encouragements.

Some of those seemingly pious religionists had thought that because they were old and had forgotten their early sins, that God had forgotten them, also. But as soon as the voice of Jesus roused them within, they remembered and they sneaked out, afraid to look up for fear God would start throwing stones at them.

Actually, the Mosaic law of stoning never was intended to mean that a wicked man could stone a wicked woman. It never had the intent that one sinner could put another sinner to death—and Jesus knew that.

Pardon me if my language is plain but it occurs to me that when those old hypocrites ran up against Jesus, it was like a cat running into a mowing machine. When they came away, each one was licking his wounds of conviction and conscience.

So, that is how this business of conscience works. It smites the inner life. It touches the heart. It isolates the individual. It sets us off all by ourselves.

That is the terror of the conscience and I think it will be the cosmic loneliness of the lost soul before an angry God that will put the hell in judgment.

Now, I am wondering what has happened that Christians no longer really believe in the human conscience.

The fact of conscience has been laughed out of court, pushed aside by the propaganda of hell, so that even the churches are afraid to admit to conscience.

But the Bible stands firm—it is not afraid to admit the truth of conscience.

The Bible says bluntly: "Being convicted by their own conscience, they went out one by one."

Those men were conscience-stricken, smitten inside, struck as if by a stroke from heaven. They had to get out of there in order to sneak away.

Conscience is that inner voice that keeps speaking within our beings—and it deserves something better from us than wisecracks and humor.

We should all be aware by this time that one way the devil has of getting rid of something is to make jokes about it. Every one of us needs to be warned often about the corruption of our minds by the papers and magazines and entertainment.

There is a legitimate humor, and we all admit that. I think a sense of humor is in us by the gift of God.

But whenever that humor takes a holy thing as its object, that humor is devilish at once. One of the slick jokes you have heard insists that conscience is that part of you that makes you sorry when you get caught. That is supposed to be funny but it is not. It is tragic that so many have yielded so far to the propaganda of hell as to joke about that which is no joke.

I respect the integrity of Emerson, that old New Englander, who would never allow anyone to joke about love or death in his presence. We ought to agree with him that there are some things that are not proper objects of humor.

One of these is conscience, the power that God has set in the human breast, able to isolate a soul and to hang it between heaven and hell, as lonely as if God had never created another soul. The light that lighteth every man that cometh into the world is not a joking matter.

The eternal, universal light-giving presence of Christ is not a joking matter. These things are all too serious to be dealt with lightly.

There is plenty to laugh at in the world, including politics—which is usually funny anyway. But be sure that you do not laugh at something that God Himself takes very seriously.

Remember that conscience is always on God's side—always on God's side. It judges conduct in the light of the moral law, and as the Scriptures say, it either excuses or accuses.

It is not too much to say that every one of us, every one who has come into the world, has heard a voice from God in our own time equal to the voice of Jesus when He was here on earth.

I say that because many people seem to think they are cheated: "Oh, if only I could have heard A. B. Simpson or Dwight Moody."

Brother and sister in the Lord, you have heard the first voice and the last voice. You have heard the voice of the inner conscience. You have known a moral illumination because of the One who by His presence lighteth every man. Do you know that there were tens of thousands who heard Jesus when He was on earth and had no idea what He was talking about?

Do you know that some of His own disciples had to wait for the Holy Spirit at Pentecost to know and understand what Jesus had been telling them?

Jesus had to assure His own disciples, "It is expedient for you that I go away."

Returning to that long-past day is not the answer to the need of the believers in the Christian church today. God is certainly dealing with many who need to give heed and listen to the inner voice, and then do something about it!

The Bible tells us several things that men may do to their consciences.

Timothy wrote that "Now the end of the commandment is charity [love] out of a pure heart, and of a good conscience, and of faith unfeigned: From which some having swerved have turned aside unto vain jangling" (1 Tim. 1:5, 6).

Some people have turned away from a good conscience. They will be found among the Christians who live carelessly. All the sermons in the world will be wasted if there is not a good, clean conscience to receive the truth.

Timothy also wrote by the Spirit about those "who speak lies and hypocrisy having their conscience seared with a hot iron."

We often see that those men and women with a seared conscience will be led into false doctrines.

We wonder how it is possible for a man who has been in the fellowship of the Word of truth to turn away suddenly into some false religion.

Perhaps his friends will say that his mind was confused but we should be honest about this—for false doctrines can have no power upon a good conscience.

But when a conscience has become seared, when a man has played with the fire and burned his conscience and calloused it until he can handle the hot iron of sin without shrinking, there is no longer any safety for him.

Titus wrote in his epistle about those to whom nothing is pure any longer, "but even their mind and conscience is defiled."

Here Titus speaks of an inward corruption, revealed in impure thoughts and soiled language. I am just as afraid of people with soiled tongues as I am of those with a communicable disease.

Actually, a foul tongue is an evidence of a deeper spiritual disease and Titus goes on to tell us that those with defiled consciences become reprobates, something just washed up on the shore, a moral shipwreck.

What a relief to find the writer to the Hebrews encouraging us to "draw near with a true heart in full assurance of faith, having our hearts sprinkled from an evil conscience."

A "sprinkled conscience"—surely this is a gracious thing for men and women in this world to know!

One of the most relieving, enriching, wholesome, wondrous things we can know is that sudden sense of the lifting of the burden as the conscience goes free—God giving freedom to that conscience which has been evil, diseased, and protesting.

Peter wrote about this and called it "the answer of a good conscience toward God, by the resurrection of Jesus Christ."

This is the kind of conversion I believe in—when your sins are cleansed and forgiven through the blood of the Lamb you will know it, my brother!

You can take your sin and your evil conscience to a priest and he will give you absolution. But he is only able to bury your conscience under a little religious rag and if ever you get right with God, it will come right back at you.

Oh, there is an inner voice either accusing or excusing, and when you have had the answer of a good conscience, you can get up and know it is all right. A transaction has taken place within the human spirit. The heart suddenly knows itself clean and the burden lifts from the mind and there is a true sense that heaven is pleased and God is smiling and the sins are gone.

A transaction within the human spirit—that is the kind of forgiveness I believe in!

I once slipped into a noonday service in New York City and I heard something I will never be able to forget.

A minister speaking that day said: "We assume that if a man has heard the Christian gospel he has been enlightened. But that is a false assumption. Just to have heard a man preach truth from the Bible does not necessarily mean that you have been enlightened."

God's voice must speak from within to bring enlightenment. It must be the Spirit of God speaking soundlessly within—that is what brings him in and makes him accountable to God. Just the words of a text falling upon a human ear may not mean anything.

Many years ago, the godly Horatius Bonar wrote: "A seared conscience is the sinner's heritage. It is upon this that the Holy Spirit first lays his hand when he awakens the soul from its sleep of death. He touches the conscience, and then the struggles of conviction come. He then pacifies it by the sprinkling of the blood, showing it Jesus and His cross. Then giving it the taste of forgiveness, it rests from all its tumults and fears."

I believe that God has related these somehow: the voice of conviction in the conscience and the Holy Spirit, the point of contact, witnessing within man's being. A person has not been illuminated until that voice begins to sound within him.

Men and women need to be told that it may be fatal to silence the inner voice. It is always perilous to resist the conscience within; but it may be fatal to silence that voice, to continue to ignore that speaking voice within!

The Christian Is a Realist: He Sees Things as They Are

Wash you, make you clean; put away the evil of your doings before my eyes; cease to do evil; Learn to do well; seek judgment, relieve the oppressed, judge the fatherless, plead for the widow.

Come now, and let us reason together, saith the Lord: though your sins be as scarlet, they shall be as white as snow; though they be red like crimson, they shall be as wool. If ye be willing and obedient, ye shall eat the good of the land. Isaiah 1:16-19

PEOPLE WITH MANY DIFFERENT insights have given us a variety of definitions for the word 'reason'.

The dictionary says reason has to do with comprehension and inference; with a sound mind; with motive and judgment; and with the ground of reality which makes a fact intelligible.

I have thought a good deal about reason and I have come up with a brief sentence which I think may express it well for us: "Reason is a wise recognition of things as they really are."

If this is true, then Christian believers are the most reasonable of all persons—and the true realists.

If this is true, then Christians are not the dreamers, after all! They are truly realists because they insist on stripping things down to their hard core of reality.

Scientists boast that they are realistic; that they test everything and pull it down to its reality. But the genuine Christian is a sounder, truer realist than a scientist can ever be for the Christian insists upon knowing what really is true.

The Christian wants to know what is true about life—the scientist wants to know what is true about life, but by logic.

The Christian wants to know what is true about; life in its broad and everlasting relationships. The Christian wants to know about his sins—where they are and what happened to them. He wants to know about God and judgment and his own relationship to God and to immortality and eternal life.

His insistence upon knowing is according to reason, for reason is a wise recognition of things as they really are—not as they seem to be.

I must charge it back upon the worldling, the unsaved man, that he is really the unrealistic person because he must spend his whole life pretending. If I were to invent a title to cover the *genus homo,*the human being, unsaved and out of Christ, I would have to call him "the great pretender."

For instance, he must pretend all of his lifetime that he is not going to die. He must put on that act day after day, month after month. That is not realism—it is the fuzziest kind of fantasy in which humans can indulge.

What is it with us?—humans continually acting in a pretense that we are never going to die yet knowing all the time that we must and that we will!

But the Christian has become a realist.

He is already prepared for that next chapter. He has packed his suitcase and he is ready to go. In fact, you may see him somewhere sitting on his suitcase, with the pair of steel rails close by. He knows for a certainty that the train is on the way and that it is not going to pass him by.

He is the realist and it is the other fellow who is the dreamer of deadly and fateful dreams.

Throughout his lifetime, the sinner is forced to close his eyes and pretend not to see. He is forced to cover up and hide and dodge and twist and put on another face. When he hears that his friend has dropped dead on the golf course, he swallows his Adam's apple and takes refuge in his masculine vocal chords and says: "Too bad."

He was scared stiff when he heard it because he thought that he might be next.

That man is not a realist. He is a hypocrite and a pretender and a liar—and he is forced to go through life in that way.

It is the Christian believer who deals with things as they are. The Christian is not on the defensive. It is actually the worldling, the unbeliever, who is on the defensive during his entire lifetime.

I believe it is entirely proper and fitting for the Christian church to be on the offensive. I believe that we should be reminding the world that the Christian man and the Christian woman are the true realists— that we have gone through and settled some everlasting facts.

Brethren, the Christian message is according to reason: "come now and let us reason together."

The Christian message takes into account God and man and man's relation to God. It takes into account sin and man's relation to sin and responsibility for sin and accountability to God under that responsibility. It takes into account judgment and death, the shortness of life, and the deceitfulness of appearances.

The genuine Christian is one whose house is always in order. He does not have to stampede and implore heaven in panic when he finds he is going to die. He has only a few legal matters to settle, for as far as his everlasting relationships are concerned he has already realistically taken care of them. To him, the Christian message is according to reason.

Now, God being who He is and what He is, there is in the Godhead and in man's relation to God a transcendency that outstrips reason. But also, it must be said, there is never anything in that relationship that outrages reason.

It is from this position that we ought to be on the offensive for our Christian faith!

We ought to confront the sinner, with all of his learning, and insist that while our faith and assurance transcend reason they never outrage it. We are not unreasonable in our belief—we are just men and women who live according to the highest reason there is. The Christian message is reasonable and altogether according to the facts, and according to the sound judgment and recognition of things as they really are!

Now, if you have done any serious reading you have no doubt discovered the charge made by some critics that reason says one thing and religion says something else.

I dare to say that whoever says that is still wet behind his intellectual ears, for religion is on the side of reason, always.

Whatever is irreligious and unbelieving is on the side of unreason and not on the side of reason.

Consider the fact that when our Lord Jesus Christ calls to men His entreaty is based upon reasonable considerations. One of these is certainly our lost condition. That is a reasonable consideration.

The devil has had a lot of success with his propaganda so that many people no longer accept the Bible doctrine that men are lost.

The argument seems to be: "We are not lost. We are on our way upward. We are still struggling upward!"

No one can fool me with this "struggling upward" business. Man has been struggling for a long, long time and he is no nearer to being "up" than he ever was.

When we are realistic we confess that we are a lost people. We are still quite young when we begin to notice that our physical frame is susceptible to many ills—because we belong to a lost and dying race.

Why do we have wars and rumors of wars? Why do we have political corruption and dictatorships and slavery and bondage of many kinds? Why do we have police on every corner and why do we have jails and prisons and insane asylums?

Because we humans are a lost people—and it is a lost world in which we live. Anyone who refuses to consider the symptoms is completely unrealistic.

It is the Christian message that takes man's lost condition frankly into account and refuses to listen to the propaganda of unreason that says we are not lost.

Actually, the lostness of man is not a dogma—it is a fact. We are not dealing in the realm of fancy. We are dealing with facts as hard and realistic as a brick that goes into the solid construction of a building.

So, the Christian says, "Men are lost and we know they are lost."

The Christian message is based upon reason. It is based on the redeeming work of Christ which is made necessary by the lost condition of mankind.

It is based upon the love of God in Christ Jesus and it is based upon the power of the gospel.

It is based upon the fact that humanity is perishing. It is based upon the abiding permanence of the will of God, and it is based upon the importance of immediate action!

The Christian message is based upon all of these sound, realistic facts, so it is the unbeliever who is put on the defensive. He is the one who must be able to give a reason for what lies within his being. The Christian knows—and he has confessed his need and confessed his Savior and is ready for the next chapter.

Notice that in the text there is the stern voice of exhortation as well as the gracious voice of promise.

These are joined, as a poet has said, "in reason's ear."

We do listen to the stern voice of God's exhortation: "Wash you. Make you clean. Put away the evil of your doings from before mine eyes. Cease to do evil; learn to do well. Seek judgment and relieve the oppressed. Judge the fatherless. Plead for the widow."

"Come now and let us reason together," the Lord is saying to us. "Though your sins be as scarlet they Shall be as white as snow. Though they be red like crimson they shall be as wool."

Surely that is the gracious voice of promise.

Will you believe me when I say that we do a great injury to mankind when we divide these two voices—exhortation and promise?

We have no excuse for insisting that we make a solo out of that which God meant to be a duet.

God meant this message to be two sides of the same coin—but we split the coin edgewise and in a sense ruin both sides.

The illustration holds for it takes both sides of a half dollar coin to be worth fifty cents. Get a fine saw and split it edgewise and neither side will buy you a one-cent stamp.

Many get into the Bible and become adept in the art of splitting texts edgewise and destroying both.

I go to my Bible and I read: "Wash you. Make you clean. Put away the evil of your doings. Cease to do evil. Learn to do well." If I stop there I am splitting the coin edgewise and it is of no value.

If I go to my Bible and I skip the first part and only read: "Come, let us reason together. Though your sins be as scarlet they shall be as white as snow," and read nothing before or nothing after, I have split the coin edgewise and it has no value either. Yet we have whole schools of Christian theology based upon such splitting, texts ripped apart and divided asunder.

In this portion, the voices are here as a duet. God is sovereign and reason is singing her two songs— the stern voice of exhortation and the gracious voice of promise!

I believe we can do great soul injury to men and women by trying to indicate that we can have our sins forgiven, washed and cleansed, without first turning from evil and putting it away from before God's eyes; ceasing to do evil, learning to do good.

The teaching of forgiveness without any turning from sin is a great error and it has filled the churches with deceived members and helped to fill hell with deceived souls.

It cannot be denied that many people have come into the church on a half-text. "Though your sins be as scarlet, they shall be as white as snow"—they forget that that is only half of the text.

Neither can it be denied that there are some who are driven away from the churches because of the preaching of only the first half of the text—"Wash you, make you clean!"

They stand back and say, "Dear God, how can I? How can a man as vile as I am ever wash me? Even if I had all the acids in the world I could not cleanse my soul!" Such as these go away discouraged—because they hear the emphasis on only half of the text.

This matter is a grave error, because the teaching and the hope of being forgiven while persisting in sin is a great moral impossibility. It does violence to the Scriptures and it also violates moral reason.

The voice of moral reason insists that all pardon is conditioned upon intention to reform, and I realize here that some people will not allow the use of the word 'reform'.

I have heard people condemn this word reform. They stand straight and brack their heels together and declare: "I do not believe in reformation; I believe only in regeneration."

I could very well say to them: "I do not believe in the 'In God We Trust' side of the coin—only the '*E Pluribus Unum*' side."

Both sides are there. They are necessary to give any value to the coin and let me tell you that reformation and regeneration are not enemies! They are friends. I could say they are Siamese twins, for forgiveness is based upon the intention to reform.

Actually, reform is another word for repent. Do your first works. Clean up. Get right. Straighten out.

A story has been told about a governor of one of the states. He was concerned about the plight of many in the prison system, and he visited one of the prisons, going incognito. The prisoners did not know who he was.

Having opportunity to talk to a young man, he asked why he was there and for how long.

"I suppose you would like to get outside again," the governor said in conversation.

"I would sure like to be out," was the reply. "But I doubt it. They threw the book at me."

Then the governor asked: "Tell me, if you were free again, what would be the first thing you would do?"

The face of the inmate changed to a grim scowl and he almost growled as he said: "The first thing I would do would be to cut the throat of that blankety-blank judge that sent me here!"

The governor, the man with the power of pardon and release, had not expected to hear that kind of snarl. He was hoping for an indication of remorse and repentance and reform. He was hoping he might hear a prisoner's desire to be a good man again, desiring to try and straighten out the wrongs that had put him in that place.

He stayed in there, you see, because pardons are conditioned upon intention to reform. You cannot save a man who insists upon continuing in the thing that caused him to be unsaved.

A lifeguard can pluck a drowning man out of the water but what can he do if the man turns right back and throws himself into the water again?

A fireman can carry a person out of a flaming, settling building but what can he do if the person runs right back into the fire?

In the spiritual and moral realm, then, it is a glaring inconsistency to try to teach forgiveness where there is no intention to reform. To teach pardon and cleansing where there is no intention to change the life would upset heaven and turn it into a moral insane asylum, and in a hundred years you would not know heaven from hell!

Another thing to mention here is that intention can be proved only by the changed and transformed life. That is the only way of knowing.

Notice that in the text we have taken there are nine active verbs. Wash, make, put, cease, learn, seek, relieve, judge, plead: nine active verbs.

Perhaps you recall your English class and the difference between the passive voice and the active voice.

When the passive voice is used the subject receives the action. I just stand here and someone does something to me. I passively receive the act.

But, if I do something, that is the active voice.

If I say, "I am loved," that is passive. Someone loves me. I receive the action. I do not have to do a thing but stand here and look pretty.

But, if I say, "Love someone," that is active voice. That is positive.

This brings me right to the point that the curse of religion today is that we are completely in the passive voice. We are on the receiving end of everything. We want everything coming our way.

God has said, "Though your sins be as scarlet they shall be as snow." But God saw fit to put nine active verbs ahead of that word.

We say, "I am washed." That is the passive voice.

The Lord says, "Wash you. Put away the evil!"

Our danger in spiritual matters is that everything is done for us and everything is done to us. We are spectators instead of being participants.

The Lord has spoken to us all and said, "If you are willing and obedient you shall eat of the good of the land."

Willing and obedient Christians—where are they? Why do we have so many spineless and shrinking Christians, apparently without any strength o f character?

Why should we find a Christian man praying, "Oh Lord, help me to be honest." He knows well enough that if he is not honest he will go to jail.

I have heard people pray, "Oh Father, help me to quit lying." God never taught them to lie—He just says "Quit your lying."

Many Christians seem to go through life unable to resist temptation, unable to wage the warfare of prayer, unwilling to suffer for Jesus' sake.

Our Lord Jesus Christ asked us to be His witnesses and to stand firm in the faith. Instead, many of us settle for being a kind of religious jellyfish.

It is time that we Christians wake up and assume our spiritual responsibilities. Let us ask God to wind up our backbones; let us ask Him to give us the courage to pray, "Now, God, show me what to do!" and get out there and get active.

If we are willing and obedient we shall eat the good of the land—that is the promise of God. But if we refuse and rebel, nothing but judgment lies before us.

God is calling us and we have every sound reason why we should follow Him faithfully. There is every sound reason why we should be committed, out-and-out Christians; and not one lonely reasonable argument for staying unsaved or staying half-saved.

Every voice of reason cries out for us not only to consider God's gracious plan of salvation but for us to totally yield and obey—"for then will I cleanse you whiter than snow and make you as white as wool."

CHAPTER
7

The Eternal Worth of the Soul: God Calls— "Be Ye Reconciled."

But God said unto him, Thou fool, this night thy soul shall be required of thee . . . . Luke 12:20

It IS DECLARED IN the Bible, as well as being often assumed, that man has a conscious and living soul.

Our Lord Jesus Christ in His teachings took it for granted that men and women know they have souls. You cannot find a passage anywhere in the New Testament where Jesus said, in so many words: "Verily, I say unto you, man has a soul."

He did not need to say it.

The fact that man is a being with a living soul was then, and is now, a common coin of knowledge. It is taken for granted in the Bible just as we take the dollar for granted in our monetary system. A department store does not have to put up big signs on every floor saying: "Remember the dollar is worth ten dimes, four quarters, twenty nickels."

We all take that for granted—it is a common coin, the common unit of value.

So, the Bible takes the fact of the soul of man for granted. It does not have to everlastingly assert it.

Now, consider this fact. If the government should devaluate the dollar to zero, we would have no monetary system remaining in the United States.

Likewise, if you take away the truth that a man has a soul, you devaluate the man. You reduce him to something less than a man, for God in creation breathed the breath of life into man, and he became a living soul.

Now, to some, it might seem like putting up a straw lion to slay to make the insistence that man has a soul. I have long claimed that much in fundamental circles is the solemn repetition of an undisputed thing, and I do not want to fall into that snare.

But on the other hand, I know the age in which I live. I am sure that this is the hour when the soul of man is getting less attention than it has since the beginning and rise of revealed religion.

The eternal worth of the soul needs again to be declared as having worth over against all other human values and that there is nothing else that can be compared with the human soul.

Actually, the Bible not only weaves the truth of man's soul in and out throughout the fabric of theology as a golden thread but it also declares it as a hard tenet of truth.

The truth of reality of the soul has been accepted and believed by all people and all races and all religions since time began. There are differences in the concepts but most people throughout the ages have accepted the fact that there is an essential something that lives within the inner nature of man and that the outward, physical body is only the tabernacle in which the living soul dwells.

One may almost say that the belief in the fact of the human soul is a test of our humanity.

Every once in a while we hear of some rare pig-headed individual who insists that man does not have a soul. It is interesting to me that such individuals generally turn out to be strange and extreme persons. They become suspect and are usually looked upon as something of a monster in society.

Actually, what has he done?

He has dehumanized himself and sold out the value of himself as a human being. He has insisted on being something less than a man.

If such a man leads his dog down the street and stops and talks to a friend, saying, "I do not believe in the soul," he not only dehumanizes himself but he makes himself less than the dog by his side.

If the man does not have a soul, then his dog is better off than he is. The dog can survive under worse conditions. The dog can get along with less food than the man. The dog does not live under the weight of many human responsibilities. The dog pays no taxes and does not worry at all about the future and death and the judgment.

We read in the Scriptures about the souls of the righteous being in the hands of God. The psalmist in the Old Testament admonishes us to be still and talk to our own soul as he did while lying on his bed.

When Jesus spoke of the soul in His time, He was speaking about that part of man's being which is endless, which lives on and on. He certainly was not speaking of the physical body in which man lives.

The body is mere matter, and as the Bible says, fades as a leaf. When we are about sixteen, we are prone to think that our strong, healthy bodies will last forever. When we are about twice sixteen, we begin to worry a little about the body. When we are about four times sixteen we are willing to admit the truth—the physical body has no continuing life of its own.

For that reason I can never get mad at the human body as some people do, blaming the body for everything. Read the Bible and you will find it never blames the human body for anything: it is only the tabernacle in which the human being lives.

The body is completely amoral—it is neither good nor bad. It has no moral quality attached to it. It is simply a dwelling place.

A man buys an automobile and gets behind the wheel and with purpose drives over someone he does not like and kills him. Do we blame the automobile and hold it responsible?

Of course we do not. The automobile as an object is completely amoral. It is the man who gets behind the wheel and guides it who for the moment gives some moral quality to it.

The fact that a good man drives an automobile and guides it so that it takes him to church to worship is a good thing. The same automobile might be driven by an evil man taking him to his companions in a gambling den—but the car itself is neither good nor bad. It is the man who is driving the car who makes it what he wants it to be for the moment.

So with the human body. It is the humble and helpless servant of the man who lives within it.

You live in that body of yours, sir, and you cannot properly blame your body for anything. Your body is what you make it to be. Your body is not a responsible being. It is guiltless and without blame.

Now, when a man is converted by the grace of God, regenerated, he does not get a new body; so he may look exactly the same to his neighbors, but they will recognize that a new man is living inside, and that the direction of the life has been taken over by a new driver.

A neighbor is sure to say: "Isn't that Mr. Jones who lives across the street? He was always on the way to the saloon and took up the whole sidewalk when he came back. Now he goes the other way towards the church and he has a Bible under his arm. I am sure it is the same old Jones. I recognize him."

The soul is the essential part of the man. It is the endless part of man. When the soul is converted to God, the old body begins to live a better life but it is still the same body which will dissolve and go back to dust as soon as the soul withdraws.

Let's use the illustration of what happens to a house when the residents move out and leave it unoccupied. Did you ever go out into the country and see an old, shabby house in which no one has lived for a long time?

Such an untended dwelling always goes to rot and ruin. We maintain our houses from day to day because we live in them. That is a poor illustration of a glorious fact—that as long as the soul is the tenant the body remains alive. It is when the soul withdraws that the doctors must come and pronounce that the body is dead.

With the understanding that God has given us, we have to agree that the physical body is the least essential part of the man. Some scientist has called the body "a concatenation of atoms," just a group of atoms and molecules that have gotten together for a while.

A man is more than likely to put a hat on the top of his body and walk down the street with a little strut, and say, "What a big boy am I!"

But the truth is that he is just a walking concatenation of atoms and that is all.

The truth is that the soul of man is the essential part. Just as soon as the soul decides to wing away there will not be anything there for you to put your hat on. The body will decay and depart.

It is in the soul that our memory lodges and memory can either be a treasure or a terror to a man. To be suddenly called upon to remember the deeds done in the body would be a pleasure to some men but a terror to others.

Likewise with intelligence and moral perception, moral responsibility and everlastingness, hope of heaven and endless peace—all of these repose in the human soul.

My friend, you do have a soul and it is the essential part of you. It is that which speaks when you say "I."

It is that which prays when you say, "Oh God, come to me!"

It is that of which Jesus spoke when He said, "Into Thy hand I commit my spirit." It is the essential part of man.

Theologically there may be a distinction between soul and spirit but for all proper human purposes, I believe they are the same. In the Bible, it is plain that the word soul and the word spirit have sometimes been used synonymously as being the interior part of man, that part of man which is endless.

You do have a soul and the New Testament teaches that man's soul must be saved. It teaches that as a man saves his soul, all of his being is saved. It teaches, too, that if a man loses his own soul, everything else goes down in ruin. That is why Jesus, our Lord, gave us the caution: "What is a man profited if he gains the whole world and loses his soul?"

Jesus taught that a man must be interested in the saving of his own soul and that he has a real part in the saving of his soul.

The Apostle Peter wrote: "Save yourself from this untoward generation." Save is the verb. Yourself is the object. You is the implied subject, right?

"You save yourself," Peter was saying.

Now, do not make me a liberal over this. Peter was not so foolish as to think that a man has any antidote for his grief or that he has any kind of panacea for his ills. Peter was not so foolish as to think that a man can forgive his own soul or wash his own spirit or cleanse his own inward being—he knew better.

What Peter is pointing out is this: "I preach unto you Jesus the Redeemer. You must now take advantage of the opportunity. Go to Jesus as you are and save yourself."

That is what he meant and that is what I mean. The Bible teaches that man has a responsibility in the saving of himself, that he must take advantage of the fountain that was opened in the house of David. It is the fountain for sin and uncleanness that flowed from Emmanuel's veins.

We should realize that a man can cause his own soul to perish through negligence. Man is prone to neglect and to procrastination and they are among the enemies of the soul. It would be wonderful indeed if everything in our world could be geared to the salvation of men's souls, but everything is geared in just the opposite direction.

Fallen nature is no friend of God's. Fallen nature is no friend of God's grace. The winds that blow through the corridors of this world do not blow heavenward; they blow hellward. The man with no place of stability or anchorage goes the way the wind blows.

Nevertheless, you have a soul to save and a God to glorify.

I find some of the theologians are no longer happy to sing Wesley's confession:

"A charge to keep I have,
A God to glorify;
A never-dying soul to save,
And fit it for the sky."

These words bother their consciences and confuse their theology so they run the blue pencil through Wesley's concept of the saving of the soul and our human responsibility, as in his words: "Assured, if I my trust betray, I shall forever die."

In the old marine traditions of the world, the owner of a noble ship loaded with fabulous cargo entrusted the vessel and cargo and crew to the captain with the charge: "Bring her in. Bring her in and get your proper receipts. I want to know that you have taken her through."

In a similar sense, God has given us a serious charge: "I have given you a soul. I have given you that which is the essential part of you. You are in command of a fabulous treasure house stored with memories, imagination, rich treasure—all of these and more belong to you. I charge you that you see to it that you make that shore at last."

An old camp meeting song has these words of assurance: "I'll be present when the roll is called; I'll answer to my name."

It is through the grace and the merit of our Lord Jesus Christ that we will be appearing and answering to our name in that great day, but it will not be an appearance in this old body. The Bible does not teach us that we are going to take this particular body to heaven. The new body that God gives us is going to be somewhat like this one—only it will be a glorified body, perfect in every way.

We will all be good-looking up there because when we see Him as He is, we shall be like Him! We shall be like Him who is the Lily of the Valley and the Rose of Sharon.

When our Lord came to live among men on this earth, His deity was disguised. He wore the common garment of the peasant of Palestine, and the prophet said there was no beauty in Him that we should desire Him. Then when the cruel men plucked out His beard and slapped His holy face and bruised His cheeks, He was marred more than any man in visage. They watched Him die and he was not beautiful then.

It is a different scene now. Resurrected, ascended, glorified again with the Father, He is Lord of Lords and King of Kings. All the shining stars in their splendor shine like the glory and radiance of His face. The beauty of Jesus will be upon all of His people—the redeemed, the cleansed, the forgiven who have walked in faithfulness in the light—and His name shall be on their foreheads. There will be no need of the sun for the Lamb is the light thereof.

We look at one another now and some of us are not too happy about these bodies in which we live. But faith and trust and hope and anticipation belong to the believer—we look confidently over into that heavenly scene with the redeemed of all ages. The brilliance and the radiance and the glory in the scene around the heavenly throne beckon to us even now—and all of this light and radiance is equivalent to and commensurate with the glory in the souls of the redeemed!

Many years ago I was in a youth service in a large church in the city of Akron and something happened that has been vivid in my memory since that day.

This was a church where there were many signs of worldliness as well as great professionalism in the choir and among the musicians. The pastor would come into the pulpit and give his well-known essays, such as "The Harp of a Thousand Strings." It did not seem that there was enough religion around there to save a mosquito even granted that he was salvageable.

But in this service I attended, they had asked a young girl to sing, and she was a hunchback, terribly deformed and twisted.

There she stood, about as high as the desk, and with her face set almost down on her breast.

Sweetly she began to sing and you knew she was singing her testimony of faith and love.

"My soul is so happy in Jesus—for He is so pre-
   cious to me,
Tis Heaven below, my Redeemer to know,
For He is so precious to me."

Then when she came into the last verse she
sounded the personal word of her experience and
hope in the faith:

"Where, some day, through faith in His wonderful grace,
I know I'll be like Him, and look on His face."

A little hunchback girl—not much to look at,
sickly and pale. Deformed in physical body, but
radiant in soul and spirit because she had grasped
the promise that one day she will be like Him, laying her cross and her burden down!

I dare you to show me anything better than that,
brother! Take a fine-tooth comb and search through
the cultures and the treasures of the world and you
will still not come up with any kind of a jewel that
will shine like that simple testimony of faith and
hope in the beauty of the soul!

It makes no difference who we are or where we
live or the status we may have in life—if we have
placed our faith and trust in our glorified Savior we
shall receive an eternal tabernacle worthy of our
soul for it will be a body like unto His glorified body.

What have you ever heard in this life that can
compare with that promise?

Don't let the devil rob you of the glory that God
has promised and prepared. All around you fallen
human nature is determined that your soul shall

not be saved and fallen society is determined that it is not going to let you live a happy, faithful Christian life.

Brethren, in these days we must stand fast in witnessing and living forth the evangelical gospel. We believe in the purifying power of the blood of Jesus. We believe in the grace and mercy of God. We believe in the power of Christ's gospel to make a bad man good and a dirty man clean; to make the evil man righteous and the sinful man pure.

Yes, man has a soul to save and amid all the creature noises around us, there is the still, small voice within man, saying, "Be reconciled to God!" That is the real 'you' under the camouflage—it is that 'you' that will take you to heaven or hell!

What can we do but look to Him as Savior, and say, "Jesus, lover of my soul, let me to Thy bosom fly."

CHAPTER
8

The Fate of the Moral Fool: He Goes Where He Belongs

And he said unto him, If they heard not Moses and the prophets, neither will they be persuaded, though one rose from the dead. Luke 16:31

MAN IS A MORAL wanderer in this present world—but he becomes a moral fool when he has shut out the voice of God and flippantly consoles himself with the excuse: "Well, if I go to hell, I will have plenty of company!"

The moral fool who goes to hell will be surprised indeed to find that hell has its own ways of singling out a man, isolating him from everything that would be a comfort. I am convinced that the lost man who spurns the call of God in this life will suffer all alone in his lostness in hell—completely alone and unsupported and uncomforted!

Now, in this world, people try to take their comfort in strange ways.

It seems to be comforting to many that even if they are bad and they know it, they can always insist that everyone else is bad, too!

Some people actually find comfort in hiding behind verses from the Bible that teach that men are lost. One of the favorite proof texts is Romans 3:23: "For all have sinned and come short of the glory of God."

That is the prime text for the Bible school student who is studying how to win souls in ten easy lessons, and we quote it often in the attempt to bring conviction to the lost soul.

But in many cases it turns out to be a comforting verse to the sinner. Because of the treachery of the human soul, it is possible to hide behind the fact that all have sinned. There is a kind of universal reaction which becomes an acceptable philosophy; that "if this is what is wrong with everybody, then nobody need worry about it."

Therefore, when I say that man is a moral wanderer, away from God and still hiding, I do not want you to hide behind that and take comfort in it.

I want you to know that it is a very personal thing and that the Holy Spirit never meant to give anyone a sense of comfort in universal depravity.

Actually, the Holy Spirit is saying throughout the Scriptures: "Thou art the man!"

God is calling us with many, many voices, but there is no doubt that He entreats mankind most perfectly in the revealed Word of God.

In the sixteenth chapter of Luke's gospel, we have recorded the words of our Lord Jesus Christ concerning the pleading of the rich man who died and was suffering in hell. There must have been many who were in hell but you will notice that when the rich man went there he could not find any comfort. He was alone. As far as he was concerned, there was no one else there.

The only people he knew and remembered were those who were still alive.

Let me remind you again that it is Jesus the Christ, Jesus the Lord of all the worlds and of life and of death and of eternity, who gave us this vivid picture of the pleading from hell. He drew aside the opaque curtain to let us see and hear what had never before been communicated to living men and women.

He let us hear the actual words of a condemned man. This is the only place in the Bible where we meet an eternally condemned man and hear him speak, almost as if we are looking into his face.

Strangely and wonderfully, this lost man becomes an evangelist whose voice still remains a powerful entreaty—the sovereign God showing that hell itself as well as the spirits in heaven will ultimately bow and own God's right and own the righteousness of His ways.

There is more in this account than the suffering of the rich man—there is also the blessedness of the beggar who at his death was carried by the angels to Abraham's bosom.

There was a contrast between the two in their lifetime. The beggar was a poor fellow, with sores and diseases, and he had to beg crumbs from the rich man's table.

You will notice in the account that Jesus said nothing bad about the rich man. I do not see how you can make a rascal out of this rich man. He had plenty of material goods, but the Bible does not charge him with stealing. He might have gotten it with all honesty. He just had it, that's all.

He did live sumptuously—but you and I do, too. If we have it, we spend it—and if we do not have it, we grumble. Our society is guilty of throwing money right and left, millions upon millions; actually we do not use the word millions very often because we are up into the billions.

These are the things I want you to notice: the beggar was not saved because of his poverty and certainly the rich man did not go to hell because he was a rich man!

No one in this world has ever been saved and gone to heaven because he was poor. You can be as poor as a church mouse and still be as bad as a church rat. God has never said anywhere that human poverty is a means of salvation. Poverty never redeemed any man. Wearing rags in this life never has gotten anybody into heaven. That claim is only poetic, religious nonsense!

The poor beggar did not go to heaven because he was poor and a beggar. If that had been true, then salvation would depend upon poverty and rags and you would be able to tell how near a man is to heaven by the size of his bank account or by the lack of it.

That would make religion a completely human thing, which it is not.

Would a beggar lie? Would a poor man cheat? God says that every liar shall have his part in hell. God talks about human hearts that are unclean and deceitful and treacherous. So, you can have rags and sores and be hungry and still be on the road to hell.

Neither did the rich man go to hell because he happened to have plenty of material things in this life. That would be to equate eternity with time and to judge that God is going to take all of the rich people who have enjoyed themselves down here and send them to hell for eternity.

God has made it plain enough that that is not the way He does things.

We will never know the number of wealthy men and women whom God has honored for their faith, for their Christian testimony, for their unselfishness in their stewardship.

You study the Bible and the plan of salvation and the lives of God's great souls among men and you will reject the thesis that men and women go to hell because they are rich and that others go to heaven because they are poor.

Oh, that would be the simplest thing in the world!

"Throw everything of this world's goods away, strip down to bare necessities and flap your wings—you will soon be in the celestial city; for God is going to punish eternally all those who have money in this life!"

Oh, no! No! That is too simple and it destroys moral and spiritual values and ignores completely man's spiritual nature.

Let me tell you why this beggar went to heaven and why this certain rich man went to hell.

This beggar went to heaven because he had a nature that belonged there. This rich man went to hell because he had a nature that belonged there.

That is it—and there is no other answer!

The beggar was carried by the angels into Abraham's bosom and I ask, "What were those angels doing down there?"

Those angels had all the vast universe in which to roam, but some of them turned up at the curbstone when that poor beggar rolled over and groaned, closed his eyes, and said, "Father, here I come."

Angels, messengers of God, full of wisdom and strength, were drawn there by the magnetic attraction of a heavenly nature, and that nature was about to escape the sore, diseased body.

Now, God cannot have a disembodied soul that He has redeemed and that carries His nature in it, roaming like a ghost through the universe. The angels do the will of God and when that body died, the angels escorted his soul, winging away with it to Abraham's bosom.

Why? Because it belonged there!

Remember this: everything must be put in its place in God's universe at last. A man can be living with another man's wife now, but there will be a day when God will put every man where he belongs. Some official may have the widow's property now, but the day will come when God will put everything where it belongs.

That is the picture that God gave Ezekiel of the valley of dry bones. The bones were all out of place—the jackals and buzzards had worked them over for years. But when the Word of the Lord came unto them there was a great rattling and God put everything in order.

God carries out His own plans and He has promised that everything will be put in order.

Right now we live in a confused and mixed-up world.

Some people get the headlines who, if the truth were known, should be getting a striped suit in a prison somewhere.

There are other worthy persons who are completely ignored in this world and, if the truth were known, they would be on the front covers of the news magazines next week.

God is not mixed up, though. God is not confused!

God continues to watch the human scene and He has His own process for sorting things out. Many a person receiving the praise and plaudits of the world today will be sorted out when God's time comes. He does not sort them out down here in our time and He did not even sort them out when His twelve disciples were with Him. Peter was a coward and Judas was a lover of money and a betrayer, but not until the last minute did He even mention it. But when Judas died he was sorted out. He died and went to his own place.

Death sorts us out and if we go to heaven it is because we have a nature that belongs there. It is not hard for the sovereign God to sort out all the natures that belong in heaven and take them there.

In essence, that is the story of Lazarus the beggar and the rich man.

What kind of nature do you have? That is where the decision is made.

The rich man had been intent upon the things of this life. He felt no need of seeking God with his inner nature and that was his sin. That is what stamped him as a lost man.

On the other hand, do not imagine for a moment that all of those old boys down on Skid Row, down and out, will all go to heaven when they die, like a flock of birds at sunset. God will know where they belong by their inner natures, by decisions they have made either to know and love God or to ignore and reject Him.

Now, a fool is someone who acts without regard to consequences; a moral fool is one who never hears any of the voices that are calling to him. He has ears to hear but he hears not.

In His time of ministry on the earth, Jesus told many of those who listened to His teachings that they were fulfilling the prophecy of Isaiah that "this people's heart is waxed gross, and their ears are dull of hearing, and their eyes they have closed; lest at any time they should see with their eyes, and hear with their ears, and should understand with their heart, and should be converted, and I should heal them."

Then with a tender look to His few beloved disciples around Him, He said: "But blessed are your eyes, for they see; and blessed are your ears, for they hear."

The moral fool never hears anything from God. To him, there is no tongue in any tree, no book in any running brook, no sermon in any stone, and no voice in anything.

He is satisfied just to go his own way in this world. He compares one nice automobile with another. He is figuring out how much he can make on his next deal. He is figuring close and cutting corners on his income tax. He has to spend a little time every day with the baseball standings or the football statistics.

He is just spending his time—he is not a bad man.

He is just a moral fool—he never hears the important voices in life.

Oh, if he gets sick, he hears something within that says, "Get to a doctor as quick as you can."

Or, if he gets into financial trouble, he hears the voices of friends who say, "I know a good broker" or "I know a good banker."

But he hears no voice from God. He is living for this world and for this world alone. If he can keep reasonably healthy, keep his hair on his head, drive a car with 'good rubber,' he is satisfied.

He is a moral fool!

What a great contrast in this world between the moral fool and those who are morally wise.

Someone who was supposed to be smart once said that the Christian gospel is all right—but that no one has ever really tried it.

We thank God that that statement is not really true—we are not going to apologize and fall for that.

No one should think for even a split second that the gospel of Jesus Christ is not having its effect or that God does not have His redeemed people all over the world.

We will never admit that the ark was not effective because only eight people got into it and were saved.

We do not apologize for the ark—it worked. Those who tried it found that it worked and they made fools of the millions who rejected and ignored what God said about it.

So, those who are morally wise do hear the entreating voice of God. They always have and they always will—they are hearing that voice now.

God Almighty does not bellow to the wide universe and have it come back as an empty echo through His holy ears. He has told us that His word going forth from His mouth does not ever return void and without results. God's word is always powerful and it needs no one to run around apologizing for it and thinking up clever ways to defend it.

The gospel ship, the ark of God, is not a ghost ship floating idly on the sea. Thank God, she has a full crew and she has her passengers. There are not as many as God wants and there is still room for more. Snap to attention when you see the sails of this mighty ship on the horizon. Fully manned with a faithful crew, the winds of the Holy Ghost in her sails, passengers who are no longer slaves but free men and women, bound for a free port in a holy land!

Throughout this troubled old world, God has His saints and He knows them. They are washed in His blood, born of His Spirit. They are begotten of the Word of Truth, saved by the miracle of redemption. He will call them all home when the time comes.

Now, a final word from Luke 16 about the rich man in hell.

I think we would have to say that he was a better man after he was dead than he was while he lived.

While he lived, he did not care or show concern for anyone around him. He did not have much sympathy for other people.

But in the region of the lost he began to be concerned for his brothers, "lest they come to this place of torment."

He was an evangelist making an altar call from hell—only he did not get through.

Note also that he had had religious connections when he was alive. He called Abraham "Father" and Abraham did not disallow it. Abraham was able to say, "Son, remember." He was a son of

Abraham's flesh, from a Jewish environment, the most religious nation in the world.

But Abraham had to tell him that those still living "have Moses and the prophets; let them hear them."

God knows the human conscience. He knows that the most effective voice throughout the world is the voice of the Word and that if men will not hear the Word of God, they will not hear anything else.

A religious environment, a religious connection—these are not enough. If we could hear them, if they could get through to us now, I have no doubt that there would be voices and the warnings of many who are departed from us. It is not enough to belong to the church board, to be an elder, a deacon, an usher.

How many, how many, if they could tell us now, would say: "I was a moral fool while I lived. I refused to take God's call seriously. Send someone to my brothers and sisters, to my children, to warn them!"

The wise voice of God and Abraham said, "No, it is no use. A church officer who can receive communion and handle funds and lead in prayer and hear the Word of God preached and still resists Me—even if I sent a dead man back he would not listen!"

Yes, the morally wise will hear this, for "the wonder of life is the moral law within and the starry heavens above."

The moral life within, that is our moral constitution, provides always an eloquent, accusing, pleading, and entreating voice. The message is always from the heart of God, "Oh, return ye, unto Me!"

Our Accountability to God: Justified, Saved— But on Trial

For the time is come that judgment must begin at the house of God: and if it first begin at us, what shall the end be of them that obey not the gospel of God? 1 Peter 4:17

THROUGHOUT THE CHRISTIAN CHURCH as we know it today, all sense of accountability to God seems to have been lost.

This must be blamed on preaching and teaching which has overemphasized the "automatic" quality of faith, with the insistence that "acceptance of Christ" passes all responsibility and all accountability from the believer to the Savior—for all time to come!

Christians no longer sing with very much feeling that hymn of Charles Wesley's that asks our Lord to

> "Arm me with jealous care
>   As in Thy sight to live;
> And Oh, Thy servant, Lord, prepare
>   A strict account to give."

Someone has been quoted recently as saying: "If I believed that I had to give an accounting of my service as seen in the eyes of God, I could never be happy!"

A lot of people will not know what we are talking about, but let me tell you about Charles Wesley, who breathed that sincere and holy prayer that he would be able to give a strict account to God.

He was a Christian believer who was only one jump short of being hysterically happy in the Lord. Dr. Samuel Johnson, the great English philologist and critic, said of John and Charles Wesley in their day: "They are the loftiest examples of complete moral happiness that I have ever seen."

I read the hymns of Charles Wesley and I admit that I find myself chuckling with delight. I believe he was so spiritually happy that he must have danced for joy—happy in God and in Christ!

Yet, he believed he was still on spiritual probation. He could write and sing,

"Arise, my soul, arise!
    Shake off thy guilty fears;
The bleeding Sacrifice
    In my behalf appears.
Before the throne my Surety stands:
    My name is written on His hands."

The modern church can join in that expression of faith but finds it very difficult to sing with Wesley,

"Arm me with jealous care
    As in Thy sight to live;
And Oh, Thy servant, Lord, prepare
    A strict account to give."

Now, I do not know how men and women can excuse themselves completely as though one of the voices of God sounding throughout the earth is not the voice of judgment. I have searched the Word again for this message, and I have not been able to get away from the fact of judgment as it pertains to the house of God, to Christians rather than to sinners.

It is well for us to consider here that church history shows plainly that religious people are prone to select a favorite Bible doctrine or truth and to hold to that one truth at the expense of other basic tenets. We may overemphasize that one truth so as to obscure other important truths which may actually disappear as a result.

This is what I mean by a truth disappearing—it falls into disuse and therefore is easily forgotten.

I would illustrate that.

Suppose there is one key on the piano that is not properly attached and it gives forth no sound when it is struck. The pianist is sure to be wincing when he strikes that key and nothing happens. If you would photograph the keyboard, that key would be in its proper place in the picture, but it will not produce any sound no matter how hard you touch it.

That is an illustration of what I mean by a basic doctrine of the Christian faith that has fallen into disuse, so that it is no longer talked about or thought about or preached about. If you go to the book of discipline, the statement of doctrine, you will find it still in place because it will say that we do firmly hold this truth.

But it no longer plays—it is no longer heard. It has no emphasis and no power because it is slurred over and forgotten.

That is how a basic Bible truth may fall into disuse because certain doctrines have been overemphasized to the obscuring of others.

Then, finally, some prophet of God has to come and reassert the forgotten truths and reemphasize and trumpet them forth. That person may be considered a heretic because that segment of Bible truth has been obscured for a generation or two.

But in the midst of the grumbling, the prophet of God keeps persisting until the church awakes, readopts that truth, so that a new sense of life comes as if it were raised from the dead.

Think of Martin Luther. Did he invent a new doctrine?

No, he did not.

Luther dug out a doctrine that had fallen into a dismal tomb and was not being heard. By sounding the trumpet blast of justification by faith, Luther brought about the great Reformation.

What did John Wesley do?

He did not invent any new doctrine but by sounding forth a forgotten doctrine that it is possible to have and to know purity of heart, he aroused the church!

Men who have been used of God in any generation from Calvary down to this hour have not invented and preached new truths. They have simply had the anointed vision to discover truths that had been obscured by the overemphasis of certain other truths.

Now, that is introductory to say this: that justification by faith has become such a doctrine in our time. It has been emphasized to a point where it has obscured certain other closely related truths; so we have lost the cutting power of those truths.

I know it would be difficult for any man to be eloquent enough to overstate the vital importance of justification by faith in the Christian church—that man shall live by his faith and not by works of righteousness which he has done. Therefore, being justified by faith we have peace with God!

Justification by faith delivers us from the fruitless struggle to be good. It delivers us from the bondage of the Pharisees and the pride of the ritualist and the snare of the legalist—all of whom attempt in many human ways to make themselves presentable to God.

But those are just old Adam decking himself out in his best religious garments for the sake of impressing God Almighty, hoping to be ushered in at last as a man who served God faithfully all the days of his life.

That is the bondage some of our fathers fell into because the doctrine of justification by faith was obscured. It was dropped out of the teaching of the church. So, the people had to have holy water and holy beads and holy everything. They had sacred hearts of this and sacred hearts of that. They had days to eat and days to abstain from eating and they tried to make themselves acceptable to God by gifts of money and doing penance for their sins.

Then along came a thoughtful scholar in the Scriptures. He presented no new truth or doctrine, but insisted on the reexamination of an old Bible truth, long buried and forgotten, proclaiming that it is not by our works of righteousness, but it is by faith through grace, that we can be pleasing to God.

Immediately, the Reformation was born!

The Church of Christ got up out of a long sleep and like the dry bones in Ezekiel's vision, she stood up and walked, as a great army. Then, with the passing of the years, that doctrine of justification by faith has been emphasized until it has been thrown out of focus as badly as was the opposite before Luther's time.

As a result, justification as it is now understood and preached and emphasized and hammered on up and down the country, is causing believers to throw all responsibility over on God, and we conceive ourselves to be happy, satisfied Christians without a responsibility in the world except to give out a tract once in a while.

It becomes just an automatic thing—you simply get in the Pullman sleeper, pull down the bed out of the wall, and wake up in the depot in heaven. All judgment has been bypassed, for Christians are not thinking of judgment any more.

I discover that the average Christian now seems to have only one worry—he is concerned that he might lose what we call "fellowship."

In that case, he might not be as happy tomorrow as he was today or as happy day after tomorrow as he was yesterday. He wants to be a happy little moron, with the result that he says, "I must learn to keep up my fellowship so I will be happy."

The idea that a believer is accountable to God for the deeds done in the body has completely passed out of the theological thinking of the modern fundamentalist church. Faith has become a kind of magic having beneficial properties which accrue to the man who believes—and they accrue to him no matter what his state in life may be. He believes—therefore they accrue. There is no longer any consideration of the moral condition of the man, whether or not he is obedient, whether or not he is faithful to God or what kind of Christian he is.

He believes or he has believed—therefore the automatic benefits of this magic faith accrue to him now and in the world to come.

Now, this kind of teaching has obscured other truth, so it is a true doctrine pushed out of focus. It is a doctrine of grace and justification by faith alone pushed by uncorrected logic to a ridiculous and grotesque conclusion.

The Bible truth that has been obscured and buried and forgotten as a result, is the doctrine of probation. We seldom hear anything about it any more and a man who wants to consider it and talk about it and turn back to the Bible teaching is made to feel very much like a heretic.

Let us consider what we mean by our Christian lives here being a probationary period.

We mean that this life is a preparation for the next and that preparation is not concluded when we come to the Lord Jesus Christ for our salvation.

We read in the Gospels that the thief on the cross believed and the dying Savior told him that he would be in paradise the same day. We make that to be the criterion by which we judge the entire transaction of believing faith. We believe in Christ and thus we are prepared for heaven, and there is no such thing as probation or a testing or any judgment to come—nothing like that now in modern theology!

That is why I have said that it is possible to emphasize a good doctrine to the point that it may overshadow and cause another truth to disappear. In this case, it has gone so far that leading teachers now take the position that the doctrine of probation and spiritual preparation is not biblical. They insist that everything is cared for by one act of faith and there is no such thing as an expectation of judgment to come.

Certainly we are all agreed that faith in Jesus Christ has settled many important things forever.

Our faith in Christ has settled forever our past sin—it is forgiven. Our faith in Christ has settled forever our justification before the Father in heaven. It has settled forever that our names are written in the Lamb's book of life. It has settled forever that we are regenerated men and women and the seed of God is in us.

These are things that are settled and made sure by an abiding faith in Christ.

But the great mistake in our day is the total disregard for the fact that believing Christians are on probation from day to day, proving the character of our faith and testing and preparing us for the world to come.

Certainly our Father in heaven has a great interest in what we will do with this gracious spiritual life and new nature we have been given. Certainly He will be testing our obedience to the Word; our faithfulness to Him who has died for us; what we will be doing with our time and gifts, our opportunities and our possessions.

The Apostle Paul plainly taught the believers in Rome that "every one of us shall give account of himself to God."

He wrote to the Corinthian believers that "every man's work shall be made manifest: for the day shall declare it, because it shall be revealed by fire; and the fire shall try every man's work."

The quality of our Christian life is sure to be affected if we do not feel that we are going to give an account to God of how we have used time and abilities and money and possessions He has entrusted to us.

The response of some Christians is: "Just stay out of my business—I will do what I please with my time and with my money."

I know that—and yet I also know that God is testing them and He is going to find out if they have enough moral sense to know what to do with time. Time is a treasured gift which God has given us but He has not given it to use foolishly.

The results of this time of testing will be seen in that great and coming day before the judgment seat of Christ. Someone has written that the Apostle Paul surely lived with one eye on the judgment seat of Christ and the other on the perishing world.

Every Christian is saved—but many have forgotten that they are still on trial. They have forgotten that the Bible has much to say about that "great day" when every man's work shall be made manifest. They are so happy that they are saved that they have forgotten that God is testing moral wisdom and moral courage, testing faithfulness and vision and stewardship for the kind of times in which we live.

We could spend hours describing the dark side of the times in which we live—but I would remind you that they are God's gift to us. We know that crime and corruption are found throughout the nation. We know that many conditions make our country a top-heavy country, and that we could come crashing down as other nations and empires have in the past.

But I do not wish myself in any other period of the world's history. These times are God Almighty's gift to me as a Christian and I consider myself on probation, sensing that God is really interested in what one of the least of His servants is going to do about the times in which he lives.

Justified and saved—but on trial: that is where the Christian should hold himself. But we are so eager to get out from under all responsibility we kick up our irresponsible heels like an unbroken colt and snort our defiance of all judgment.

We are not living in a period of God's expressed judgment at this time, and that is why man thinks he can get away with almost everything now. If this was a period of divine judgment, you would sin and the Lord would punish you immediately. He would prove to you immediately that you were not worthy of His kingdom.

But this is a period of probation and the Holy Ghost says, "Therefore judge nothing before the time until the Lord comes when he will both bring to light the hidden things of darkness and will make manifest the counsels of the heart. Then shall every man have praise of God."

This period in which we live is not the trial—it is the preparation for the trial. This is not the last examination—this is getting ready for the examination.

I remind you that this whole doctrine has been long obscured, but our Lord Jesus set it forth fully in Matthew 25.

Jesus tells the story there of the man who went into a far country and before leaving, called in his three servants. He gave them talents to be held in trust during his absence. He gave one man five talents, another two and another one, each according to his ability. They could not complain for each was given what he deserved.

Then he said, "I will be coming back—remember that I have delivered unto you my goods."

The servants who had received five and two talents began to use that which had been entrusted to them. The third servant buried his talent in the ground.

Then, when the master returned, he called his servants in for an accounting. He wanted their reports.

Consider that while he was gone they could have done just as they pleased. They could have done what they pleased with the responsibility. But two of them realized that they were actually on probation while the third did not.

Two of them said, "We have used your money wisely; here it is with interest."

The third said, "I was afraid so I hid the money in the ground."

The master said to the first two, "You have been faithful over a few things, I will make you ruler over many."

The third servant, who did not realize that he would actually be on trial during the master's absence, was cast out as an unprofitable servant.

What are you going to do with that passage?

I know the ultra-dispensationalist just gets rid of it by saying, "Matthew does not belong to us in the church." Well, I would just as soon believe the modernist when he says Isaiah does not belong to us as to believe the dispensationalist who tells us that Matthew does not belong to us.

As God's sheep, many of us have discovered that the green pastures of His provision are spiritually satisfying wherever we find them in His book. I like one of the standing rules at the Moody Bible Institute: "The Word of God may not be all about me, but it is all for me!"

I consider this an eloquent argument to me about the rest of my Christian life down here. How can we argue that our day-by-day service to God and to our fellow men is not being sharply scrutinized and that it will not be severely judged before the feet of Jesus Christ in that great day?

The believer is justified and saved from that awful appearance before the great white throne judgment, where the lost of all the ages will be judged.

But the hour will come when our kindly faced but serious Savior will call the redeemed and justified to His feet, saying: "I must have an account of the deeds done in the body since you were saved. You have had more abilities entrusted to you than many. You have had many opportunities to shine as a star in the darkness of the times. You have had months and years entrusted to you for faithful and obedient service and witness."

Brethren, there will be no place to hide then. You tried to settle everything in the spiritual life by one act of believing but there are some things that are never settled until death cuts us off or until the Lord comes.

Now what is it that God expects of us, morally and spiritually?

He advises the way of self-judgment: "If we should judge ourselves we should not be judged."

He expects us to be obedient children of God, knowing that it takes a moral determination to obey Him in day-by-day faithfulness.

But that is where our spiritual happiness lies. I trust many more of us are becoming willing to breathe sincerely that prayer with Charles Wesley:

"Arm me with jealous care
    As in Thy sight to live;
And Oh, Thy servant, Lord, prepare
    A strict account to give."

Jesus Is More Than Savior: Finally, He Will Be the Judge

For as the Father hath life in himself; so hath he given to the Son to have life in himself; And hath given him authority to execute judgment also, because he is the Son of man. John 5:26, 27

SOMEONE COULD WRITE A very important book for our day on great Bible doctrines that are either forgotten or neglected.

One of these themes neglected and overlooked is the fact that Jesus Christ Himself is the judge of all mankind.

Jesus plainly told the generation of His own day that the Father in heaven will not judge anyone but "hath committed all judgment unto the Son."

It is a tragedy that so many men and women live among us and die in their time without ever coming to the knowledge that our Lord Jesus Christ is both the Savior and the judge of all mankind.

When we discover all of the implications of this vital truth we discover as well that we both love Him and fear Him. We love Him because He is our Savior and we fear and reverence Him because He knows all about us and knows all that is in us and to Him has been committed all judgment.

I find myself indignant concerning much preaching and teaching which portrays the Christ as a soft and pliant friend of everybody, a painted, plastic figure without any spine and involved in no way with justice.

If that is the only Christ there is, we might as well close our books and shut our doors and let them make a garage or shop of the church building.

But that Christ that is being so preached is not the Christ of God, nor the Christ of the Bible, nor the Christ who will actually deal with mankind, for that Christ has eyes as a flaming fire; His feet are like burnished brass and from His mouth comes a sharp, two-edged sword. He will be the judge of mankind.

The blessed part of that is that Christian believers may leave their loved ones who have died in His hands, knowing that He Himself has suffered; knowing that He knows all and that no mistakes can be made in that day of revelation and judgment.

Now, this has been introductory to our consideration of basic concepts of judgment as found in the Word of God, to some of the human and inadequate points of judgment, and to the qualifications of Jesus Christ for the final judgment of mankind.

There is a basic concept of judgment, a simple concept, held by practically all of the religious people that have ever lived anywhere, with variations in the details. This is the belief that human beings are morally accountable because they are not self-created beings, nor self-sustaining. Their life is derived from another and not from themselves.

God, the Father in heaven, does have life in Himself; so, no one can judge the Father. He is not a derived being—He is the original being.

Jesus infuriated His critics in His time when He taught that the heavenly Father had also given to the Son this quality of having life in Himself. Jesus Christ is not a derived being but is of the Father alone. No one can judge the Son.

It is not inconsistent for us to believe that men are free to decide their own moral choices while believing at the same time that they are also under the necessity to account to God for those choices. That makes them both free and also bound; for they are bound to come to judgment and give an account for the deeds done in the body.

Let us look at some of the inadequate concepts of judgment which are often taught among us.

Probably the first is this: the operation of the law of compensation.

Ralph Waldo Emerson in his essays espoused the teaching that there is no such thing as a judgment to come; that everything is judged and sentenced and rewarded or punished in the present.

The basis of this position is that if you take something from your left pocket, you compensate by putting it in your right pocket, and that everything that you do in one direction is counterbalanced by something done in the opposite direction.

Using this premise, Emerson said that the thief steals from himself, and his punishment is the knowledge that he is a thief.

There is a portion of truth in that but it is not enough. It is an inadequate concept of judgment and it is not taught anywhere in the Bible.

Another inadequate concept is that we are judged only by public opinion.

Of course, we are all responsible to public opinion in some ways but it is rather silly for men and women to argue that there is no other judgment than that which public opinion may impose.

You live beside your neighbor and certainly he is going to judge you as to whether or not you have been a good neighbor. You drive your car on the highway and others will conclude either that you are a good driver or that you are a miserable road hog.

But to argue that final judgment rests with public opinion is to argue like a backward child—for something more is yet to come.

Others have taken the position that judgment rests completely with human law. Every nation teaches that citizens are accountable to human law. Every nation makes its laws—and that is true of the most primitive tribes of New Guinea to the most civilized nations of the world. They have their own laws and all are made responsible to those laws.

"But," you say, "what about the outlaw?"

Generally, he is an outlaw in only a few things. An outlaw may rob a bank in order to get money to pay his legal taxes. He is breaking one law while he is keeping another. Nevertheless, he is an outlaw and is accountable to the law even while he is breaking it. The law has no way of equitably punishing all of those who have broken the bounds of various human restrictions.

You have also probably heard someone say that "man is accountable to society." There is a measure of truth here, as well, but the problem is that society cannot reach us in that sphere of our being where we are most vitally accountable—namely, to God and to ourselves.

I live in an American city. I am accountable to public opinion. I am accountable to the laws of the land. But I am also accountable to myself and to my God.

Thus, in the relationships which are the most vital to me, human society cannot touch me at all.

The man who says, "I will commit suicide," and then turns the gun to his head and kills himself, is no longer accountable to society and will not answer to the law—but he is still accountable to some higher authority.

A man stands up and proclaims that he is an atheist and turns his back on God. There is not a country anywhere in the world that will punish a man for that—not a country in the world that will punish a man for hating God.

Some countries have punished men for not going to church and for not paying the assessed ecclesiastical tax, but men can hate God in their hearts and never be punished because human society cannot reach them in that vital and important realm.

Now, there have always been those who insist that man's accountability is to himself alone—that every man stands before the bar of his own reason and of his own conscience. This belief insists that man's own reason and man's conscience are both jury and judge—that each man is a law unto himself.

This gets directly into the infamous relativity of morals now being taught so widely in our educational processes. It says that a thing is good if it brings social approval and that it is evil if it brings social disapproval.

If this concept were true, then we would have as many moral codes as there are human beings. Each of us would be our own witness, our own prosecutor, our own judge, our own jury, and our own jailer.

In the framework of our own humanity, that concept is so silly and so inadequate that we do not find it worthy of any consideration.

To some humans it may sound very learned and very mystical but it is ridiculous—what man could ever be that honest and that hard on himself?

I know that if I were to be my own prosecutor and judge and executioner I would find some way to lose my axe. I know I would not cut my own head off.

Well, that is not the way it is going to be!

Every one of us is going to be finally accountable to the One who gave us being. We are accountable to the One from whose heart we came and who laid His laws upon us. We are accountable to God!

This is the concept of accountability and morality and transformation that makes men right, that makes character, and that makes nations that can endure.

On the other hand, it is the absence of this belief that makes Christian profession soft and spineless and produces churches without any meaning in them.

A young man in our Sunday school told of visiting a church in another state where the discussions are about books, about dreams—and on the Sunday he visited, about peptic ulcers! I would get an ulcer if I stayed around a church like that.

My brethren, when we backslide from the truth and run away from the Word of God we will build up our own notions out of our own heads—and there is no telling what fools we will become.

I believe it can be quickly and simply seen that when we refuse and get farther and farther away from the concept of God's judgment that the judgment of God actually begins to fall.

It was the belief in the accountability of man to his maker that made America a great nation. Among those earlier leaders was Daniel Webster whose blazing eyes and fiery oratory often held the Senate spellbound. In those days the Congress was composed of strong, noble statesmen who carried the weight of the nation in their hearts and minds.

Someone asked: "Mr. Webster, what do you consider the most serious thought that has ever entered your mind?"

"The most solemn thought that has ever entered my mind is my accountability to my maker," he replied.

Men like that cannot be corrupted and bought. They do not have to worry if someone listens to their telephone calls. What they were in character and in deportment resulted from their belief that they would finally be accountable to God.

I know I do not need to remind you that the judge of all mankind must have certain qualifications, notably, the authority to execute judgment.

The simple meaning of this is that those who are to be judged must be accountable to the judge.

According to the Scriptures, to be a judge in the kingdom of God requires a kind of righteousness which goes beyond the legal structures of man. The judge of all mankind does not pronounce a verdict based upon laws enacted and imposed by someone else, as in this tentative and provisionary world in which we live. Here, one group of men will make the law and the judge, born a hundred or two hundred years later, may enforce the law and not be even remotely acquainted with the person who is being judged.

In order to be a righteous judge of mankind, the judge must himself have all knowledge so that there can be no error and no mistake.

In our earthly systems, many an innocent man has been hanged and many a person has died behind prison walls paying a debt he had never contracted, while the rascal who committed the crime died in his bed surrounded by his friends.

Human justice tries to do its best, but because there is no judge who is all-wise, such mistakes are made.

But God Almighty is never going to judge the race of mankind and allow a single soul to plead that an error has been made.

The judge must be one who has all wisdom—therefore I appeal away from St. Paul, I appeal away from Moses, and Elijah. I appeal away from all men because no man knows me well enough to judge me finally.

We humans may pass brief judgments on one another in simple matters here but when it comes to facing my eternal and everlasting future I do not want any possibility of human mistake.

The judge of mankind must necessarily be someone who will never need the testimony of a third party; he will not depend upon the testimony of another to make his judgment.

Listen to what Jesus said: "I can of mine own self do nothing: as I hear, I judge: and my judgment is just; because I seek not mine own will, but the will of the Father which sent me."

There is another point involved here: the judge has to be disinterested. He must have no personal interest or bias. The motives and actions of some judges in this life may be brought into question, but the Son of God is able to say: "I judge as one who seeks not his own glory but the glory of God alone."

Therefore, He can be the judge. He is personally related and yet He is disinterested—He has nothing to gain or lose by His judgment and all the glory belongs to God.

Jesus Christ, therefore, qualifies to become the judge of all mankind.

Beyond that, there is the matter of the judge having a sympathetic understanding.

I do not want to be judged by an archangel that never shed a tear. I do not want to be judged by a seraphim that never felt a pain. I do not want to be judged by a cherub that never knew human grief or disappointment or woe.

It is plain in the record that the Father in heaven has given the Son power and authority to execute judgment because He is the Son of man. Because He is the Son of man, He can be the advocate, the Savior, by the throne of love, but He can also be the judge to sit upon the throne.

In that great day still to come, there will be no dodging, no whimpering, no whining. No one will be able to charge Him, saying, "But Lord, you did not understand!"

He does understand because He became one of us and walked among us. There was never a tear that He did not shed; never a bit of disappointment that He did not feel; never a temptation that did not come to Him; never a critical situation over which He was not victor. Christ qualifies on every count to be the judge of mankind. The tears He shed and the pains He suffered and the griefs He bore made Him not only a just but a sympathetic judge of mankind.

More than once Jesus said, "For judgment I am come into this world," and He added: "For judgment am I come into this world that they which see not might see, and they which see might remain blind." His presence in the human race is our present judgment on sin. When our Lord, the Son of man, shall come in clouds of glory then shall be gathered unto him the nations. He shall separate them for it is He who is to be the judge. He will have the shoulders of a man and the face of a man and He will be a man—the man, Christ Jesus.

People shrug Him off now and drive away in a cloud of fumes—but one day they will have to come back and deal with Him finally. We may be sure of one thing—He will either be our Savior now or our judge then.

Think with me about the implications of sin and judgment and repentance and forgiveness in these well-known words of Isaac Watts:

"Not all the blood of beasts
On Jewish altars slain,
Could give the guilty conscience peace
Or wash away the stain."

Where is the authority for that? Read the eighth and tenth chapters of the Book of Hebrews.

"But Christ, the heavenly Lamb,
Takes all our sins away;
A sacrifice of nobler name
And richer blood than they."

It is fundamental in our Christian belief and theology that the precious blood of Jesus Christ takes away all sin.

"My faith would lay her hand
On that dear head of Thine,
While like a penitent I stand,
And there confess my sin."

Surely we recognize this picture? In the Old Testament scene, the sinner would come to the priest and he would say, "I have sinned and I bring a lamb," or some other animal. The priest would accept that creature and the sinner would lay his hand on the head of the beast as the priest killed it and sprinkled the blood. Thus, in that day, the sin which had been committed was forgiven.

"My soul looks back to see
The burden Thou did'st bear,
When hanging on th' accursed tree,
And knows her guilt was there."

Do we really believe that, brothers and sisters? That it was our guilt there on that accursed tree? Yes, it was true that "He who knew no sin became sin for us that we might become the righteousness of God in Him."

"Believing, we rejoice
To see the curse removed;
We bless the Lamb with cheerful voice,
And sing His bleeding love."

What curse?

The curse of the broken law; the curse of sin. Oh, what can be more wonderful than this: "We bless the Lamb with cheerful voice and sing His bleeding love!"

If you do not know that you are forgiven, close your eyes and by faith lay your hands upon that dear head of the Lamb of God, and like the penitent, confess your sin. Putting your faith in Him the curse will be removed from your heart and you will know your sin is forgiven because of the cleansing blood.

Which is He going to be for you—Savior or judge?

If He is not the Savior, He must be your judge.

The Bible does speak of certain ones who have sent their sins on before to judgment. By faith you can do that—send your sins on before. Have them judged and settled and dispelled now while you are still on this earth.

Jesus Christ, the Savior, will cover your sins—for by His death He forever put our sins where they cannot be found. Hear His voice of consolation and comfort and forgiveness today!

Other Titles by A.W. Tozer

The following titles are also available as audio CDs, unabridged editions: